vitamin green

Contributors and Nominators

Johanna Agerman Ross
Writer and editor, London

Allison Arieff
Writer and editor, San Francisco

Daniel Ayat
Writer, London

Helen Babbs
Writer, London

Haig Beck & Jackie Cooper
Editors of UME, Melbourne

Yves Béhar
Designer, San Francisco

Beth Blostein
Architect and Associate Professor
at Ohio State University

Joshua Bolchover
Architect and Professor
at Hong Kong University

Jonathan W. Bulkley
Architect, Peter M. Wege Chair
of Sustainable Systems and Professor
at Michigan State University

Lucy Bullivant
Architectural curator, critic and writer, London

Richard Burdett
Director of the Urban Age Programme
and Centennial Professor in Architecture
and Urbanism at the London School
of Economics and Political Science

Nicole Caruth
Writer and curator, Brooklyn

Valerie Casey
Designer and founder of Designers Accord

Eric Chan
Partner, ECCO Design, Inc.

Samuel Cochran
Designer, Brooklyn

Régine Debatty
Writer, blogger, curator and critic

Melanie Dowler
Writer, Toronto

William Drenttel
Graphic designer, editor, President Emeritus
of the American Institute of Graphic Arts and
partner of Winterhouse Studios, New York City

Pete Dungey
Artist, London

Helena Durst
Vice President of The Durst Organization,
New York City

Lukas Feireiss
Curator, writer and artist, Berlin

Rob Fiehn
Writer and editor, London

Jennifer Gabrys
Senior Lecturer in Design at Goldsmiths,
University of London

Mitch Gelber
Director of Sustainability at T.R. Hamzah
& Yeang Sdn. Bhd.

Lori Gibbs
Writer and editor, London

David Gissen
Curator, writer, historian, theorist and
Associate Professor at the California College
of the Arts, Oakland, California

Jaime Gross
Writer, New York City

Ultan Guilfoyle
Documentary film producer
(*Sketches of Frank Gehry*, 2005)
and Guggenheim adviser, New York City

Fritz Haeg
Architect and artist, Los Angeles

Mia Hägg
Architect and founder
of Habiter Autrement, Paris

Alanna Heiss
Director of Art International Radio,
founder and director of P.S.1 Contemporary
Art Cente, New York City

Matthew Hickman
Writer, New York City

Steven Holl
Architect, New York City

Amara Holstein
Writer and editor, Portland

Nicola Homer
Writer, London

Sarah Ichioka
Director of the Architecture Foundation, London

Carlos Jimenez
Architect and Tenured Professor at Rice
University School of Architecture, Houston

Mitchell Joachim
TED Senior Fellow, co-founder of
Terreform ONE, Associate Professor at NYU
and Professor of Architecture at the
European Graduate School, New York City

Will Jones
Writer, Ontario, Canada

Paul Kephart
President, Rana Creek, Monterey

Bareket Kezwer
Writer, New York City

Monica Khemsurov
Co-editor of *Sight Unseen*, New York City

Marc Kristal
Writer, New York City

Stefanie Kubanek
Associate Partner at Pentagram,
New York City

Kengo Kuma
Architect, Tokyo

Andres Lepik
Curator of Contemporary Architecture
at the Museum of Modern Art (MoMA),
New York City

Precious Makwe and Pierre Swanepoel
Directors of studioMAS, Johannesburg

Adam Marcus
Architect and Adjunct Assistant Professor
at Barnard and Columbia University, Brooklyn

Deborah Marton
Director of the Design Trust for Public Space,
New York City

Justin McGuirk
Journalist and critic, London

Jenna McKnight
News editor for *Architectural Record*,
New York City

Stephen Melamed
Industrial designer and Clinical Associate
Professor at UIC School of Art and Design,
Chicago

Matthew Moore
Artist and founder of Urban Plough, Phoenix

Ravi Naidoo
Founder and managing director
of Interactive Africa, Cape Town

Andy Pearson
Writer, London

Laurence Scarpa
Architect and principle of Brooks + Scarpa,
Los Angeles

Matthias Schuler
Managing Director of Transsolar
Energietechnik and lecturer at Harvard
University Graduate School of Design

Mark Shepard
Artist, architect, researcher and Assistant
Professor at University of Buffalo, New York

Jill Singer
Writer and co-editor of *Sight Unseen*,
New York City

Sylvia Smith
Architect at FXFOWLE, New York City

Cynthia E. Smith
Curator at Cooper-Hewitt National
Design Museum, New York City

Bruce Sterling
Writer, journalist, editor and critic, Turin

Maya Suess
Writer and faculty staff at Emily Carr
University of Art and Design,
New York and Vancouver

Troy Conrad Therrien
Writer, New York City

Sophie Thomas
Founding Director of thomas.matthews,
London

Lisa Tilder
Writer and Associate Professor at the
Austin E. Knowlton School of Architecture,
Ohio State University

Ramón Úbeda
Journalist, designer and curator, Spain

Erwin Viray
Architect and Assistant Professor
at the School of Design and Environment,
National University of Singapore

Andrew Wagner
Writer and editor-in-chief of *ReadyMade*, Iowa

Stuart Walker
Co-director of of ImaginationLancaster,
Lancaster Institute for the Contemporary Arts,
Lancaster University

James Wines
Artist, architect, Professor at Penn State
University and author of *Green Architecture*,
Taschen, 2000

Ken Yeang
Writer and principal architect at T.R. Hamzah
& Yeang Sdn. Bhd.

Liam Young
Professor at the Architectural Association,
London

Mimi Zeiger
Writer, Brooklyn

Phaidon Press Limited
Regent's Wharf
All Saints Street
London N1 9PA

Phaidon Press Inc.
180 Varick Street
New York, NY 10014

www.phaidon.com

First published 2012
© 2012 Phaidon Press Limited

ISBN 978 0 7148 6229 3

A CIP catalogue record for this book
is available from the British Library.

Commissioning Editor: Sara Goldsmith

Production Controller: Gary Hayes

Designed by Julie Kim

Printed in China

The publishers would like to give special thanks to the designers, nominators and authors who contributed to *Vitamin Green*. All images are credited to the designers except where noted below:
(t: top; b: bottom; l: left; r: right)

111 Navy Chair Mikio Sekita (14); Emeco (15 l); Magnus Breitling (15 r) / **9707 Bamboo Chair** Craig Sugimoto / **A Forest for a Moon Dazzler** Andres Garcia Lachner / **Adrère Amellal Desert Eco Lodge** Khaled Nagy (24); Nina Wessel (25) / **Andrea Air Purifier** © Véronique Huyghe / **Ann Demeulemeester Shop** © Yong-Kwan Kim (29; 30 tl; 31 tl, bl, br) **Biomega RIO Bicycle** Kenny Viese / **California Academy of Sciences** Tom Fox, SWA Group (38); © Renzo Piano Building Workshop, ph. Jon McNeal (39); Tim Griffith (40, 41) / **Cellophane House™** © Peter Aaron/ Esto (45, 47 tr, br); © KieranTimberlake (46, 47 l) / **Center for Global Conservation** David Sundberg/Esto (48, 49, 50 tl) / **Citigroup Data Centre** Christian Richters (53, 54 t, 55) / **DESI School** © B.K.S. Inan (60, 62); © Construction Team (61); © Katharina Doblinger (63 b) / **DiGi Technology Operation Centre** Robert Such (69, 71) / **Ecopolis Plaza** Emilio P. Doiztua (74, 76 b, 77b); Javier de Paz (75); Ecosistema Urbano (76 t, 77t) / **Edible Estates** Jane Sebire (79, 80 tr); Heiko Prigge (80 tl); Leslie Furlong (81 tl, tr) / **Elm Park Urban Quarter** Michael Moran Photography, Inc. (83, 85) / **Federal Environmental Agency** Jan Bitter (88, 89, 91) / **Floating Community Lifeboats** © Abir Abdullah / **Ford Point** Billy Hustace / **FREITAG** Roland Tännler / **G Park Blue Planet** McLaren Construction/Gazeley UK Ltd. / **Glenburn House** Earl Carter (110, 111, 113) / **Green Lighthouse** Adam Mørk (114, 116, 117) / **Green School** Rio Helmi (119, 121) / **GreenPix Zero Energy Media Wall** Simone Giostra Arup Ruogu (125); Simone Giostra Arup Palmer (126 t, 127 tr, br); Simone Giostra & Partners/Arup (126 b, 127 l) / **Guludo Eco Resort** Amy Carter-James (128, 129 tr) / **Habana Outpost** Jamel Toppin / **Halley VI British Scientific Research Station** BAS (British Antarctic Survey) (132, 135); Andy Cheatle (133); 7-t Ltd. (134) / **Harmonia 57** Leonardo Finotti (136, 137, 138, 139 b) / **Hawaii Preparatory Academy Energy Lab** Flansburgh Architects/Matthew Millman Photography / **High Line** © Iwan Baan 2009 / **Horizontal Skyscraper** © Steven Holl Architects / **Impossible Wood Chair** Alessandro Paderni / **Improved Clay Stove** Ian Capewell (158) / **Infiniski Manifesto**

House Antonio Corcuera (160, 162 t, 163 t) / **Integral House** Jim Dow and Ed Burtynsky / **Kroon Hall** Morley von Sternberg (177, 179 t, 179 br); Nathaniel Moore/Hopkins Architects (178 r) / **Landscape Park Duisburg Nord** © Michael Latz (180, 181, 182); Christa Panick (183 t) / **Lapin Kulta Solar Restaurant** Imagekontainer/Knölke / **Lean + Green Lightweight Wine Bottles** © O-I Europe / **Living Wall at the Musée du Quai Branly** Philippe Guignard (192); Philippe Ruault (193 b); Ateliers Jean Nouvel (193 t) / **Lucy/Carpet House** Tim Hursley (194, 197 b); Auburn University Rural Studio (195, 196, 197 t) / **Lunar Resonant Streetlights** Christina Seely (199) / **Manitoba Hydro Place** Bryan Christie Design (202, 203 b); Gerry Kopelew (201, 203 t) / **Mapungubwe Interpretation Centre** P. Rich (210 r) / **Masdar City** Transsolar (210 r) / **Media-TIC** José Miguel Hernandéz Hernandéz (212, 213, 214 r, 215) / **Mission One** fuseproject / **Open-Air Library** Fest von Oben (222, 223 l) / **Oru Kayak** Kate Lydon (226, 227); Anton Willis (228 t); Erin Kunkel (228 b, 229) / **Plastiki Boat** Luca Babini (231, 233); Michael Pawlyn (232) / **Plumen 001** © Ian Nolan (234); Andrew Penketh (235) / **Public Farm 1** Elizabeth Felicella (245, 247 tr, bl, br) / **PUMA's Clever Little Bag** fuseproject / **Recyclable Loofah Panel Houses** Base ECTA / **Rolling Huts** Tim Bies (256, 257); Chad Kirkpatrick (259) / **SAYL Chair** fuseproject / **SMA Solar Academy** Constantin Meyer Photographie, Köln, Germany (262); Thomas Eicken, Mühltal, Germany (263); HHS Planer + Architekten AG (264); Stefan Daub Fotografie, Darmstadt, Germany (265) / **SOFT Rockers** Phil Seaton, Living Photo / **Solar Handbag** Lisbeth Holten / **Solar Ivy** SMIT: Samuel Cochran, Benjamin Howes, Teresita Cochran / **Solar Umbrella House** Marvin Rand (274, 275, 277) / **Southport Broadwater Parklands** Richard Pearse (285) / **Stockholm Energy Systems** Robota (290, 292 b), Manis Mezulis (293 bl, br) / **Traverwood Branch Library** Jame Haefner Photography (298, 299, 301 b) / **Unilever Headquarters** Adam Mørk (304, 305, 307) / **Victor Civita Plaza** Nelson Kohn (308, 309, 310 b, 311) / **Viet Village Urban Farm** Visual Logic (312, 315 t); Spackman Mossop Michaels (313, 314, 315 b) / **W+W** © Roca / **WASARA** WASARA Co., Ltd. / **Water + Life Museums** Benny Chan/Fotoworks (328, 329, 331 b) / **Zollverein School** Thomas Mayer (336, 337, 339 t); Anja Thierfelder, Stuttgart (339 b); Transsolar (338)

Preface

What is sustainable design? It's a notion that is everywhere, but no one seems to know exactly what it means. To some extent, this is a result of a recent change for the better: the need to take into account problems like pollution and resource scarcity has become so integrated into design thinking that labeling those efforts as a separate enterprise is almost meaningless. At the same time, the lack of a specific definition means that a green label can be stuck on almost anything, leading to skepticism about sustainability in general.

With this thought in mind, we decided to follow in the footsteps of Phaidon's successful surveys of emerging artists within a single medium: *Vitamin P* on painting, *Vitamin D* on drawing, *Vitamin Ph* on photography and *Vitamin 3D* on sculpture and installation. We invited leading architects, designers, curators, critics, writers and thinkers to nominate superlative projects – objects, buildings and landscapes that are technically or conceptually the best of their kind – in order to create a visual definition of sustainability in design. From the nominations, a rigorous selection process yielded over 100 projects, located on every continent, which contain a huge variety of techniques, materials and approaches to problems including climate change, resource consumption and waste. Noting that good ideas tend to jump between scales and disciplines, we have included projects from the fields of product design, architecture, landscape architecture and urban planning. The result is a rich variety of projects with surprising sympathies: a handbag and a neighbourhood that share a power source, a bicycle and a school that share a building material, a boat and a plate that share a life cycle. Each project is explained in detail, with an emphasis on how it works and what makes it unique.

There is no question that, in the twenty-first century, sustainability must be a fundamental concern for every field of design. The only question is, as Amara Holstein asks in her introduction, how will we respond to the problems that we face? Filled with innovative, everyday projects, *Vitamin Green* is a preview of what we hope and expect to come: designers working to create sustainably at every scale, from a pen to a city.

Design is a Necessary Good

Amara Holstein

Design is on the cusp of a green revolution. From the most miniscule changes, like screwing out an incandescent bulb in favor of a compact fluorescent light (CFL), to the design of completely new, energy-efficient cities, there is plenty of creativity in a sustainable approach to the built environment. Yet at the same time, those of us in the top tiers of the world's economies (Americans, Japanese, Australians, Europeans) are living in a period of monumental consumption. As human demands have begun to damage our environment, it becomes ever more imperative to address the question of what we need versus what we want. For design professionals of all types, this is the time to choose between conspicuous consumption and a careful attention to the natural world, and to focus on making objects, buildings and landscapes that are both desirable and useful in the most fundamental sense.

A Culture of Overabundance

We live in a society full of stuff, and full of choices. Particularly in a tough economic climate, it's difficult for products to stand out in a crowded marketplace. Manufacturers have responded to this pressure in different ways. Some have simply cut corners to produce more and cheaper objects; others have focused on high-quality, high-price items, ignoring mass markets in general. But many others have tried to maintain the production of well-designed items at low prices, and so we see Todd Boontje's light shades at Habitat and vases by Hella Jongerius at IKEA. It is undeniable that design – and the designer – has become a selling point like never before, as retailers seek to bestow the commercial power of celebrity on the humble mass-produced good. 'As manufacturers swallow each other up, design becomes the differentiator',[1] says Grant Kirkpatrick of KAA Design, an architecture interior and landscape design firm that recently paired with Design Within Reach for a line of outdoor furniture. There is no question that accomplished designers making thoughtful everyday products can produce great results, but one consequence of the emphasis on name-brand designers is confusion between a *good design* that focuses on aesthetics and a *good design* that truly adds value to the world. For the everyday consumer, the result can be a frantic cycle of consumption fueled by the best of intentions: buying a branded 'I'm Not a Plastic Bag' but always forgetting to bring it along to the supermarket, or purchasing a bicycle only to leave it in the garage, frustrated by the lack of bike lanes or safe parking spaces. The fact that this overconsumption is making us nervous is evident from the number of reality television shows dedicated to helping people glean their belongings, magazines that focus on cutting clutter, and stores that promise to whip your stuff into well-organized, manageable shape. Unfortunately, most of them offer to help us do this by selling us even more stuff.

Our anxious relationship to things and to consumption doesn't end at the checkout counter. All the stuff we buy has to be stored somewhere, and our built environment is getting larger to accommodate the need for more places to put ourselves and our things. This is particularly true in the United States, where homes have become bloated megastructures; according to the 2010 US Census, the average home size for a new, single-family residence was just over 220 m² (just under 2,400 sq ft), up from 158 m² (1,700 sq ft) in the 1970s.[2] And if a house isn't enough to contain all your goods, there are over 2 million m² (20 million sq ft) of self-storage space in the United States – which equals a land mass more than three times the size of Manhattan.[3]

Draining Our Resources

The problems we face are clear and they are well-documented. Carbon levels and global temperatures are both on the rise. Ocean levels are too, while fresh water resources are quickly becoming depleted. As we search for more and different energy resources to fuel the needs of our growing population, every month seems to bring a elevated level of crisis: oil-tanker spills are forgotten when deep-water drilling catastrophes occur and reports of fracking-related earthquakes overtake the devastation of strip-mining as the most terrifying evidence of our energy requirements. With an influx of information on environmental issues, delivered through popular culture in ways that speak clearly – from Al Gore's film *An Inconvenient Truth* to books such as Mike Berners-Lee's *How Bad Are Bananas? The Carbon Footprint of Everything* – alarming information confronts us all the time. As Bill McKibben writes in his book, *Eaarth: Making Life on a Tough New Planet*, 'Global warming is no longer a philosophical threat, no longer a future threat, *no longer a threat at all*. It's our reality. We've changed the planet, changed it in large and fundamental ways.'[4]

The built environment is one of the central players in this environmental crisis. Forty per cent of all energy consumed in the EU is by buildings.[5] In the United States, it's even more: the building sector is responsible for just under half of all energy consumed – including almost 80 per cent of produced electricity – as well as nearly half of the CO_2 emissions in 2009.[6] It's not just the US and the EU who are the culprits; based on indicators from the World Bank, the wealthiest 20 per cent of people consume over 75 per cent of the planet's resources[7]. There are real and positive changes occurring in the way we construct our built environment, but at the moment it can be difficult to understand how to evaluate claims of sustainable building. In 2010, a proposed 'green' home in Berkeley, CA, was 930 m² (10,000 sq ft), including a ten-car garage. One of the neighbours clearly explained the root of the problem in a complaint to the local zoning board: 'Green building begins with using "just enough" and preserving what already exists. Clearly the idea of "just enough"' is not part of the design concept.'[8] Similarly overscaled projects can easily be found in the rest of the United States and beyond – including a 575 m² (6,200 sq ft) 'EcoManor' in Atlanta, GA, designed to become a model home for green builders to emulate.

This confusion extends to products: North American environmental marketing company TerraChoice says that there were 73 per cent more green products on the market throughout the United States and Canada in 2010 than in 2009, from detergent to baby bottles to building materials – which should be good. But in their review of the offerings, TerraChoice found that 95 per cent of the products were guilty of some form of greenwashing – everything from making up facts about recycled content to calling something 'all-natural' (not a useful term when considering human health; arsenic and mercury are also 'all-natural').[9]

A sharp visualization of this phenomenon is an exhibition called O'Mighty Green. Created by Dutch design firm

and architectural rabble-rousers STAR, it consists of photoshopped images of monumental and often infamous places – from Villa Palladio to a nuclear power plant – that become 'green' as soon as a living wall is laid over the exterior. Clever and often provocative, the images are the ultimate poke in the eye at greenwashing, and a reminder to look carefully below the appealing surface of any self-labeled 'green' project.

Moving Towards Solutions
With all this doom and gloom, it would be easy to throw up one's hands in despair and feel there's nothing to be done – or that the best thing to do is nothing at all. In other words, to stop designing, producing, and consuming. That seems at once both defeatist and rather uncourageous. Designers are trained to think towards innovation and discover solutions to issues, be it a comfortable, beautiful chair, or a complete community system that can help mitigate global warming. And right now seems like the perfect time for designers to push boundaries, step beyond simple aesthetics, and help solve many of the problems that the profession has had a hand in creating. Thirty years ago, industrial designer Victor Papanek wrote in his incendiary book, *Design for the Real World*, that 'the best and simplest thing that architects, industrial designers, planners, etc. could do for humanity would be to stop working entirely. In all pollution, designers are implicated at least partially. But in this book, I take a more affirmative view: it seems to me that we can go beyond not working at all, and work positively. Design can and must become a way in which young people participate in changing society.'[10] These words couldn't ring more true today.

The design world has a long tradition of creative green thinkers, well before such thinking became mainstream. A loose line could be traced from John Ruskin's statement of moral imperative to preserve and maintain the earth in his 1849 book *The Seven Lamps of Architecture*[11], through Frank Lloyd Wright's prescient creation of modestly-sized Usonian homes in the 1930s, to Renzo Piano's current-day dedication to using organic technologies in environmentally considered buildings, such as the undulating green hills on the roof of the new California Academy of Sciences building, profiled in this book (pp. 38–43). There are many examples of architects working sustainably throughout the twentieth century: Buckminster Fuller, Alvar Aalto, Richard Neutra and Shigeru Ban, just to name a few. Yet all of these architects worked within a larger social framework in which function and form have regularly been privileged over sustainability. That is starting to change and the past decade in particular has started to mark a slow shift in the industry as a whole towards earth-friendly practices.

Organizational change, often at the government level, is perhaps the most notable transformation in green design. In the United Kingdom, the best known of these changes is the establishment of the Building Research Establishment Environmental Assessment Method (BREEAM), which was created in 1990. In 2000, a similar system was created by the US Green Building Council, called Leadership in Energy and Environmental Design (LEED). Comparable initiatives include Greenstar in Australia and the Comprehensive Assessment System for Built Environment Efficiency (CASBEE) in Japan. All of these essentially provide checklists and a point system. Go down the checklist, tick off everything from water efficiency to eco-friendly materials and passive solar power, and if you accrue enough points, the building will get a green rating. The systems are useful, but the ratings can be laborious and expensive to achieve, and there are definitely shortcomings, such as the way in which the point system forgives trespasses in some areas (say, allowing a 'green' house to be 1,400 m² (15,000 sq ft)) if other aspects overcompensate.

Other systems have since emerged that seek to compensate for these weaknesses and to widen the sustainable playing field. Architecture 2030 is a building challenge, originally issued by architect Edward Mazria in 2006, which argues that all new buildings should be carbon-neutral by 2030. It has since been adopted by the national American Institute of Architects and by states including California, Washington, and Minnesota and it has been incorporated into federal building code as part of the Energy Independence and Security Act of 2007. For landscape architecture, the Sustainable Sites Initiative applies similar standards to outdoor planning as LEED does to structures. The Living Building Challenge, launched in 2006, takes green one step farther, providing advocacy and certification to projects

throughout the United States, Canada, and Ireland (with plans in the works to expand to other countries) to encourage everything from net zero water, waste, and energy to carless living and urban agriculture; over a hundred project teams are currently seeking certification. And then there are evaluation programmes to determine actual levels of compliance, from the United States Environmental Protection Agency's Life Cycle Assessment to Canadian-based Sustainability Scorecard International.

It is in compliance that Europe is ahead of the United States. Most low-energy programmes in the US are either voluntary or implemented on a state-by-state basis, whereas most countries in Europe have nationally mandated minimum building efficiency standards.[12] As a result, everyday green architecture is more common in European countries than it is in the United States – the average building in the US consumes more than a third more energy than a similar German structure[13] – a trend that is likely to continue with the 2009 implementation of the EU directive on the energy performance of buildings, which mandates that by 2020 all new buildings in member states must be nearly zero-energy.

However, non-governmental programmes can also bring real change to our built environment. The Passivhaus initiative started in Germany in the mid-1990s. It encourages the use of passive building components, including high levels of thermal insulation, well-insulated window frames with triple low-emissivity glazing, thermal-bridge-free construction and airtight building envelopes; the result are buildings that require very little energy and which can dispense with conventional heating systems. As of 2010, over 25,000 such structures have been built throughout Europe, with just over a dozen in the US and a single Japanese version, the Kamakura Passive House (pp. 168–171). Similar programmes exist in France (Effinergie) and Switzerland (Minergie).

There are also inventive programmes in place for products. The Designers Accord, created in 2007, is a sort of Kyoto Treaty for designers, bringing designers together in a mutual goal of promoting

Design is a Necessary Good

and promulgating sustainable design. The Sustainable Packaging Coalition promotes more responsible packaging systems and has released both design guidelines and a code system called Comparative Packaging Assessment (COMPASS), which functions much like LEED or BREEAM. But the best-known and most influential idea in the industry is cradle-to-cradle, a term first coined in the 1970s but brought fully to life in 2002 with William McDonough and Michael Braungart's book of the same name. A certification process, a philosophy, and an ideal, cradle-to-cradle is now part of the common lexicon, appearing on the label of products that use a holistic approach by returning to the earth or becoming neutral after their use (or re-use) and therefore creating a waste-free cycle based on nature. Perhaps the largest-scale implementation to date is Venlo, Netherlands – an entire town that's currently trying to go completely cradle-to-cradle as a community.

Global organizations have started to unite all these disparate standards. The World Green Building Council brings together all national green building councils. While localized councils make sense – many issues of sustainability are closely tied to local climate conditions – many changes can be implemented globally, and coordinating some practices will inevitably help clarify the sometimes-confusing array of national organizations and codes.

An Evolving Technological Landscape
Like building codes, technology has been an important driver of sustainable design in the twenty-first century. Technology is becoming smarter and better integrated within overall eco-friendly systems as designers adapt the remarkable innovations of the last decade to the needs of the building or product they are creating. Some new technology is based on nature itself: Solar Ivy (pp. 270–273) climbs up walls, mimicking tree foliage or climbing vines. Elegant, easy to maintain and energy efficient, it's a complete redesign of the traditionally clunky, ugly solar panel. Other products unite contemporary technological advances with historical ones in a complex manner. The Ecooler (pp. 72–73) reinvents air conditioning as zero-energy, hollow ceramic cells; inspired by the traditional Israeli Jara jug,

the technology borrows from the past, but the form of the ceramic cells was shaped by digital modelling and created with the use of a 3D-printed mould – as contemporary a form-making technique as there is.

Building systems have also been developed that take technology beyond high-tech wizardry, integrating sustainable solutions within the architecture itself. There are fanciful options that give new forms to buildings, such as Cloud 9's Media-TIC building in Barcelona (pp. 212–215), where puffs of solar-powered pillows expand and deflate to cool and heat the building, effectively reducing its carbon footprint by some 20 per cent. There are also hidden technological solutions, like the 23 geothermal wells that heat and cool the Integral House in Toronto (pp. 164–167).

Imagining future technologies has also been a useful tool for architects in the twenty-first century. More and more frequently this includes thoughtful appropriations from nature, such as HOK / Venderweil's winning proposal for *Metropolis* magazine's 2011 Next Generation Competition, which called for ideas to renovate a 1960s federal building in Los Angeles. Called Process Zero, the project proposes cladding the building in tubes of algae. Funneled through a bioreactor, the algae would be converted to biofuel, producing pure oxygen and consuming waste water and CO_2 in the process. Then there are the advances in green technology that may be less Promethean, but which can also help realize more efficient buildings. Perhaps the most ubiquitous of these is Building Information Modeling software, in which digital models can account for environmental considerations such as wind shear, heat gain, and energy use. It is now easy for a designer to see exactly how an unbuilt building will perform under every kind of climatic condition – calculations that were previously impossibly complex – and design optimal forms to take advantage of those conditions. This process can have a relatively straightforward influence on the form of buildings – as in Ecosistema Urbano's Ecopolis Plaza (pp. 74–77), where a decision was made to bury half the mass of the building after an energy simulation study – but it can also give designers the tools they need to make seemingly outlandish concepts a reality, as in the Zollverein School (pp. 336–339), where hot water from a nearby coal mine runs in pipes through the walls of the building, replacing insulation. It also continues to assist in a designer's learning process even after the building is complete, as in the Cellophane House™, (pp. 44–47) where the architects were able to track the performance of the high-tech skin from one structure and install a more advanced version on the next.

Last but not least, designers are extending sustainability to landscaping. Lush grassy lawns that devour scarce water resources are on the way out, as are concrete jungles with scant vegetation within city centers. Green is taking over buildings in tremendously resourceful ways. Planted roofs are becoming increasingly popular, with an almost 30 per cent increase in numbers built in the U.S. in 2010 over the previous year.[14] Projects from the large (a 2.75 hectare (6.75 acre) green roof under construction for the Jacob Javits Convention Center in New York City) to the small (green roofed bus stop shelters in Philadelphia) are popping up all over. Yet the overall number of green-roofed buildings in the US is quite small (around 1 per cent of all buildings in the country) and lags behind Europe; over 10 per cent of all flat-roofed structures in Germany are topped with green,[15] and other notable buildings throughout the continent are incorporating planted roofs into high-profile projects, such as Herzog + de Meuron's lushly vegetated roof of the Plaza de España or the massive green roof of the Adnams Distribution Centre (pp. 22–23).

Some restless designers, not content with green roofs, are creating living walls where foliage can cascade down the sides of buildings. Perhaps the most prominent are Patrick Blanc's massive vertical gardens, such as his first large-scale installation in 2006 at the Musée du Quai Branly in Paris (pp. 190–193) or his more recent garden at the CaixaForum in Madrid that stretches up over four floors. French designers R&Sie(n) have combined a rooftop with wall garden, completely engulfing a 130 m² (1,400 sq ft) home in Paris with 1,200 ferns in their Lost in Paris project, and the total area of the greenery on the facade of the Ann Demeulemeester shop in Seoul (pp. 28–31) surpasses the site area of the project. Other designers want to wrest more practical and nutritional use out of their landscape by planting urban gardens, from Fritz Haeg's global transformation of lawns into havens of produce and herbs through Edible Estates (pp. 78–81) to the movable, pop-up gardens of Prinzessinnengärten in Berlin (pp. 240–243). Other projects marry high-tech and plantings: in Ecosistema Urbano's Ecoboulevard of Vallecas in Madrid, a series of three massive 'air trees' comprised of plants and solar cells act together to disperse a fine vapor mist on passersby and lower ambient temperatures up to 10°C (50°F) during the city's hot summers.

With all of this green design innovation and idealism, is there hope after all for the planet? That depends.

Shaping a Sustainable Future

It's time to start thinking not in terms of what we want, but rather, in terms of what the world needs. Every year at Milan Design Week (and at furniture fairs in New York, Stockholm, Tokyo, and Cologne), hundreds of new items are introduced. Chairs, vases, tables, textiles: rows upon rows of new products line the aisles, all eagerly awaiting buyers in the global consumer market. There are beautiful chairs, there are comfortable chairs, there are chairs that look like they'll break if you sit in them. But most fundamentally, should designers put their energy into another sexy chair, or should they rethink what kind of projects they are taking on? 'In industrial circles today, most major research concerns itself not with producing for actual needs, but rather propagandizes people to only desire what has been produced', writes Papanek. 'If industry in all countries were to produce only what is needed, the future would look bright indeed.'[16] If we have less, we will use less. We must learn to use what we have more responsibly, and what we use should be better designed, with sustainability always in mind.

So what form should this sustainability take? 'There is no single, exclusive route to sustainability', Peter Buchanan says in *Ten Shades of Green*.[17] Yet as he points out, buildings (and by extension, products) are where and how we live, play, and work. They shape the lifestyles and values of our cultures, and they impact the environment and transform our surroundings. It's time to create a design ethos that pushes forward the ideals of environmentalism into our products and places, takes people and the earth into account, and attempts to radicalize the notion of need. Ultimately, the built environment shapes the way we live – so it can shape the way we approach sustainability.

First of all, we must redefine need. When considering a purported green design object, it's important to look beyond its recycled material content and ask if it's actually a useful item. In her introduction to *Design Revolution*, Emily Pilloton writes, 'Most sustainable design efforts to date have focused on what things are made of, how they are made, what their lifecycles are, and how we as designers bring them to life – in other words, HOW we design. But few of these efforts go back to square one to consider if what we're producing is even valuable to society in the first place – the WHAT of it … Above all, let us step back to consider whether the objects we as designers are giving life to are worth adding to our physical worlds in the first place.'[18]

There are designers – many featured in this book – who are starting to focus on the creation of objects that are supremely useful or simply essential to everyday life. Some products are smart solutions to existing needs, such as the DBA 98 Pen (pp. 58-59). Made of potato-based bioplastic and intended to biodegrade after 180 days, it's a writing implement that both comes from and returns to the earth – a true interpretation of cradle-to-cradle design – hopefully one day obviating the type of non-degradable disposable pens that are currently dumped into landfills at the rate of 1.6 billion a year. Other everyday products inspire people to go green by making them more attractive than their toxic counterparts. The Plumen 001 light bulb (pp. 234-235) is a sleek and sculptural CFL that overcomes the typical shopper's resistance to ugly CFL styling, while also saving 80 percent less energy than incandescent lights. The biodegradable Wabi shoe by Camper (pp. 324-325) is another good example: after all, everyone needs to be shod, and shoes will wear out, so we could all use a sustainable option.

Then there are the carefully considered objects that benefit billions of people around the world. These are the products with which, to paraphrase Pilloton,

design can achieve social benefit and, indeed, make life better. These items, such as the BioLite Stove (pp. 32-33) and the Improved Clay Stove (pp. 158-159), are products with which people can cook and which reduce pollution in their homes from coal and petroleum, allowing some of the poorest people on earth to be effortlessly more green, and creating a healthier environment for us all. There are purifying water systems for populations without access to clean drinking water, such as the low-tech clay water filters by Australian designer Tony Flynn, which people can make themselves using terra cotta, cow dung, and organic materials such as coffee grounds, and which effectively remove E. Coli and other pathogens from drinking water, or designer Vestergaard Frandsen's LifeStraw Personal, a straw and bucket system that purifies water to 99.9 per cent and costs only £12.50 ($20). There's even the Embrace Infant Warmer (pp. 86-87), an amazing invention that seeks to efficiently combat neonatal hypothermia, and potentially save the lives of more than 100,000 babies by 2013. A sleek chair, or saving children's lives? The latter kind of design might not be as financially profitable in the short term, but it's infinitely more useful. What's notable about these designs is that they aim for more sustainable practices overall: less waste, better water, less pollution, healthier communities. They also aim to integrate within the communities they serve, becoming part of the common lexicon and practice, rather than just one-off pretty trends. But perhaps most importantly, the uses of the products are positive. In other words, a green stove is a wonderful example of overall sustainability. But an 'environmentally-friendly' lead-free bullet, such as those recently introduced by the US Army, simply uses the idea of 'green' as a shield to cover an inherently anti-sustainable practice.

Once we know which needs to meet, we have to consider the entire lifespan of our products – not just how we buy and use them, but whether they will be useful for the long term, or whether they will end up in storage on in a landfill. Products can become technologically obsolete, but they can also become aesthetically obsolete – a problem that classic designs like the 111 Navy Chair (pp. 14-15) and Green Toys™ (pp. 122-123) can help prevent. And even after an object has already been discarded, clever designers can find ways to bring it back to life, as in Cordula Keher's Bow Bins (pp. 36–37) or Domingos Tórora's Kraft and Solo Benches (pp. 172–175).

Building a Greener World

Green products can't exist in isolation from other elements and the same is true for buildings. Architecture should fit within a whole system of sustainability, and it should take into account its surroundings, its users, and ultimately, its purpose for being. In particular, sustainable structures should be firmly rooted in place. 'Touch the earth lightly' is Australian architect Glenn Murcutt's approach to building, and his projects are masterpieces of localism. As Jim Lewis wrote after spending time with Murcutt, 'What he does do is design buildings that are uncommonly responsive to the environment in which they sit, to the indigenous physiognomy of the landscape, the angle of the sun, the path of the wind, the shapes of the leaves on the trees.'[19] This kind of design looks different everywhere: from the southern orientation and round shape of the Green Lighthouse in Denmark (pp. 114–117) to the thin rectangle of the Glenburn House (pp. 110–113).

Even more importantly, locally attentive design can go beyond spatial planning, using local labor and materials to further lighten their footprint on the land and rooting buildings within communities and social networks. In the US, buildings and transportation together account for over three-quarters of all carbon emissions;[20] transportation of building materials – be it by air, land, or sea – accounts for as much as 8 per cent of the total greenhouse gas emissions for any building project.[21] That's a large carbon footprint, and one of which more architects are beginning to take heed. Projects like the DESI School in Bangladesh (pp. 60–63) incorporate readily available local bamboo and mud in innovative ways, pairing building materials abundant to the area with eco-forward technologies such as solar energy and heating. Other projects like the Mapungubwe Interpretation Centre (pp. 204–207), the Quinmo Village Project (pp. 250–253), and the Sra Pou Vocational School (pp. 286–289) not only use local materials and labor but also educate and help create long-term economic viability plans within struggling communities.

Within existing cities, brownfields and abandoned buildings are ripe for redevelopment, and architects should be at the forefront of helping to heal the land through their designs. Some smart examples include the Landscape Park Duisburg Nord (pp. 180–183) in Germany and Victor Civita Plaza (pp. 308–311) in Brazil, both of which have taken polluted industrial sites and turned them into blossoming city parks where railroad tracks have become bicycle tracks, water tanks are turned into lily ponds and careful selections of plants including eucalyptus, ficus, and fruit trees are helping remediate contaminated soil. Gardens Under Glass in Cleveland, Ohio, is taking empty retail shopping centers and malls and turning them into urban farms where cucumbers, tomatoes, and lettuce are grown and indoor farmer's markets and garden supply stores replace empty chain store spaces. And projects like the Hawaii Preparatory Academy Energy Lab (pp. 140–143), set on a former dump for construction waste, churn out more energy than they consume, while educating students and future designers about the innovative green processes that make this possible.

On a larger scale, architects are also creating their own sense of place by constructing whole neighbourhoods, or even cities, modeled around sustainable ideals. A 2011 study commissioned by the Environmental Protection Agency in the US[22] found that living in dense, urban areas that are walkable with plenty of public transit options cuts energy use far more than green homes in the suburbs with hybrid cars in the driveway. Architects have started to respond to this type of urban planning, remaking derelict parts of cities into thriving sustainable centers. Examples of green projects writ large on urban landscapes include Elm Park Urban Quarter (pp. 82–85) in Dublin, Ireland, Tec Architecture's green development plans for Hamburg, Germany and SOM's winning proposal for an independent green tech city in Hanoi, Vietnam.

And of course we can't forget nature itself. Designers are looking to environmental examples of how to create better, stronger, more resilient products and spaces in the new field of biomimicry. Some of these ideas are high-tech: a carbon-neutral building material developed by researchers at the University of Greenwich is based on coral formations, researchers at Purdue University in Indiana have created self-healing solar cells based on the regenerative power of plants and academics at Cal Tech are working on more efficient solar and wind power based on the propulsion methods of jellyfish. There are also decidedly down-to-earth solutions, such as the Eastgate Centre in Zimbabwe by architect Mick Pearce, with passive cooling systems modeled after termite mounds, and skate shelters by Patkau Architects that provide ice skaters with respite from frigid Winnipeg winters by positioning plywood forms in groupings based on the way buffaloes keep warm by huddling together. Then there's Ensamble Studio's Truffle (pp. 302–303), which used soil, hay, and concrete – and the help of a calf named Paulina – to create a home based on the precious fungus. With a vast view over the Atlantic Ocean as its backdrop, the project uses only what is needed to create a rough-hewn, rustic cabin that merges easily with the surrounding land. Creative, clever, and lovely, it solves the essential human need for shelter – which is really what good sustainable design should be all about.

From the macro to the micro, projects are fomenting and coming together as designers begin seriously to reinvent and reimagine sustainability in the built environment. With need as the impetus, and nature as our inspiration, we might actually stand a chance of learning to live in harmony with our planet. We're at a tipping point of design. It's time to decide which way the profession will go.

1   'Designer home décor, retailers mix it up', *Los Angeles Times*, 22 April 2011.
2   US Census Bureau, *Characteristics of New Housing, 2010*, 1 June 2011.
3   Self-storage association, '2011 fact sheet', <www.self-storage.org>, 30 June 2011.
4   McGibben, Bill, *Eaarth: Making Life on a Tough New Planet*. New York: Times Books, 2010. Preface: xiii.
5   Directive 2010/31/EU of the European Parliament and of the Council of 19 May 2010 on the energy performance of buildings, clause (3), OJ L 153, 18.6.2010, p.13–35.
6   Architecture 2030, 'Problem: The Building Sector: Why?', <www.architecture2030.org>. Data taken from the US Energy Information Administration.
7   World Bank, *World Development Indicators 2008*. Washington, DC: International Bank for Reconstruction and Development, 2008.
8   Bernstein, Fred A., 'How Green Is My Mansion?', *New York Times*, 10 March 2010, D4.
9   TerraChoice, 'TerraChoice 2010 Sins of Greenwashing Study Finds Misleading Green Claims on 95 Per Cent of Home and Family Products', Press Release, <www.terrachoice.org>, 26 Oct 2010.
10 Papanek, Victor, *Design for the Real World: Human Ecology and Social Change*. Chicago: Academy Chicago Publishers, 1984. Preface to the first edition.
11 Buchanan, Peter, *Ten Shades of Green*. New York: The Architectural League of New York / WW Norton & Company, 2005, p.14. Buchanan writes, 'John Ruskin, who has been called the father of ecology … saw the necessity of pursuing what we now call sustainability more than a century and a half ago. Thus, in the "Lamp of Memory" (from *The Seven Lamps of Architecture*, 1849) he stated its moral imperative in terms that, except in language, are strikingly contemporary: 'God has lent us this earth for our life; it is a great entail. It belongs as much to those who are to come after us, and whose names are already written in the book of creation, as to us; and we have no right by anything we do or neglect, to involve them in unnecessary penalties, or deprive them of benefits that it was in our power to bequeath.'
12 Ries, Charles P., Joseph Jenkins and Oliver Wise, *Improving the Energy Performance of Buildings, Learning from the European Union and Australia*. Santa Monica, CA: Rand Corporation, 2009.
13 Ouroussoff, Nicolai, 'Why Are They Greener Than We Are?', *New York Times Magazine*, 20 May 2007.
14 Green Roofs for Healthy Cities, 'Annual Green Roof Industry Survey', <www.greenroofs.org>, April 2011.
15 Zuckerman, Laura. 'Green Roofs Sprouting in Rocky Mountains', *Reuters*, 19 November 2010.
16 Papanek, *ibid*.
17 Buchanan, *ibid*.
18 Pilloton, Emily. *Design Revolution: 100 Products That Empower People*. New York: Metropolis Books, 2009.
19 Lewis, Jim, 'The Native Builder', *The New York Times*, 20 May 2007.
20 Architecture 2030, 'Problem: The Building Sector: Why?', <www.architecture2030.org>. Data taken from the US Energy Information Administration.
21 Yan, Hui, Qiping Shen, Linda C H Fan, Yaowu Wang, and Lei Zhang. 'Greenhouse gas emissions in building construction: A case study of One Peking in Hong Kong', *Building and Environment* 45, no. 4 (2010): 949–955.
22 Jonathan Rose Companies for the Environmental Protection Agency, 'Location Efficiency and Housing Type – Boiling it Down to BTUs', <www.epa.gov>, 2011.

The **111 Navy Chair** recycles 111 used plastic Coca-Cola bottles into a long-lived piece of furniture – and a design classic to boot.

Emeco and Coca-Cola

—

Hannover, PA USA

—

2010

The 111 Navy Chair has the same
form as the original Emeco Navy
Chair (opposite), but is cast
in a mould (this page) using plastic
made from recycled plastic
Coca-Cola bottles.

Since its humble beginnings in 1944, Emeco has sold more than one million of its original 1006 (ten-o-six) Navy Chair. Originally designed for the US Navy, it has a cult following including designers as varied as Philippe Starck and Norman Foster. Emeco founder Witton C. Dinges invented the laborious manufacturing process that is still used today for the 1006 Chair, in which a large sheet of lightweight, 80 per cent recycled aluminium, is made into 12 separate pieces that are then welded back together. The chair has to be ground many times in order to smooth out the welds and each one takes a total of 12 hours. To strengthen the construction, the chair is heat-treated, cooled off and heated again in a process that realigns the chair's molecules in a stronger formation – Dinges wanted the 1006 Navy Chair to withstand even torpedo blasts. The iconic object has now been appropriated by Coca-Cola in a collaboration that takes 111 Coca-Cola bottles, reinforced with glass fibre to add rigidity, and recycles them into a chair with the same form as the 1006: a valuable, beautiful object with a long life.

The real star in this collaboration isn't the 1006 Navy Chair or Coca-Cola, but the United Resource Recovery Corporation recycling plant in Spartanburg, South Carolina: the world's largest plastic bottle recycling unit. Every weekday, 20,000 plastic bottles arrive here by truck to be processed into plastic flakes; they are washed, depolymerized and roasted to remove any volatile organic content. Approximately 45 million kg (100 million lbs) of Polyethylene Terephthalate (PET) bales go through this process annually and three million PET bottles are required for the yearly production of the 111 Navy Chair. Before it arrives at the chair factory in North Carolina, the flakes selected for chair production are turned into plastic pellets, mixed with glass fibre and colour pigment at a BASF factory in Tennessee.

Each chair starts out as 6 kg (13 lbs) of plastic pellets that are melted down and then injection-moulded into the shape of a 1006 Navy Chair. When the mould is completed it is tempered in a heat-treatment process that toughens the material, then cooled. The process is quick, lasting only around three minutes, resulting in a much higher production speed for the 111 than the 1006 chairs. The 111 Navy Chair still enjoys some finishing touches by hand, such as the addition of the H-brace, to make the base sturdier, and the smoothing out of any imperfections as a result of the injection moulding. The finishing touch is a stamp on the chair's underside, reading: 'Help your bottle become something extraordinary again'.

When Coca-Cola approached Emeco chairman Gregg Buchbinde in 2006, about the potential collaboration, the firm had already started on other Coca-Cola merchandising projects, making use of recycled plastic bottles and cans. The recycled PET merchandise includes T-shirts, bags, caps and notebooks, but the 111 Navy Chair is the most high-profile project to date and also the most interesting. By highlighting the potential for recycled plastic, it reminds everyone to contribute to the recycling process. The 111 Navy Chair also makes an iconic design accessible to a larger audience. As a result of a faster production process and less manual labour, the chair sells at a much lower price than the original: £140 ($230) in comparison to £250 ($415) for the 1006 Navy Chair.

The three million bottles earmarked for the annual 111 Navy Chair production are a drop in the ocean in comparison to all the plastic that goes to waste across the world. But the visibility of the 111 Navy Chair shows the environmental benefits of a manufacturing process that could be applied to the production of other goods. This marks the beginning rather than the end for this recycling process. *Johanna Agerman Ross*

Each slat of the **9707 Bamboo Chair** is made from a single reed, utilizing the inherent strength and flexibility of bamboo and reducing the need for glue.

Eric Chan
—
Hong Kong, China
—
2007

Celebrating its Chinese heritage, the frame of the 9707 Bamboo Chair was loosely modelled on the shape of a Ming chair. The reeds are finished with a traditional Chinese organic lacquer in a colour that varies from red to brown.

The use of bamboo is integral to Chinese culture; it is used to make everything from kitchen utensils to building scaffolding. So when the Hong Kong Design Centre commissioned designer Eric Chan to produce a chair marking the 10-year anniversary of the city's return to China, bamboo was a natural choice of material to celebrate Hong Kong's Chinese heritage. Founder of the New York-based industrial design firm ECCO Design, Chan worked with furniture manufacturer Herman Miller, with whom he has a well-established relationship, on the concept for the 9707 Bamboo Chair. He used the natural strengths of bamboo to work in concert with technological advances in order to create a durable and comfortable chair.

Bamboo is the ideal solution for sustainable furniture. A naturally renewable material, it grows up to a metre a day and has a low carbon footprint. This seeming sustainbility can be misleading, however: bamboo is frequently sliced into thin stips and laminated together with glue to imitate timber, greatly increasing the material's impact on the environment. This process also mitigates the natural strength and flexibility of the giant woody grass – properties that make it an excellent choice for an innovative ergonomic design. Chan wanted instead to emphasize those properties in his design, and he began the research and development process by returning to his roots in China. He visited Anji County in Zhejiang province, an area well-known for its bamboo production. Chan worked with growers and manufacturers there, eventually working with a local factory in a collaborative effort to improve the quality of the chair.

The seat and back of the 9707 Bamboo Chair are made from individual slats of bamboo. This reduces the need for glue, and the flexibility and resilience of the reed allows the seat to adjust to the weight and shape of each user. The optimum shape was calculated with the help of 3D software. This process created a profile that was ergonomic, but which wasn't stable enough; the bamboo moved too freely under the weight of the sitter. The solution was found in Chan's 'super seat' technology: thin polymer strips running under the seat and behind the back of the chair that lock the individual slats in place. Chan first developed the technique for his high-end Geiger Foray office chair for Herman Miller. In the 9707 Bamboo Chair, the polymer strips improve suspension, controlling movement and maintaining consistent support in order to achieve a natural sense of equilibrium. Both the glue that holds the chair together and the lacquer that finishes it are natural, reducing chemical usage. The result is a comfortable, flexible and stable chair that leverages the natural strengths of bamboo. *Nicola Homer*

9707 Bamboo Chair

Eric Chan

A Forest for a Moon Dazzler is built with timber cleared from its site and more than 4,000 pieces of threaded bamboo naturally ventilate and shade the building.

Benjamin Garcia Saxe

—

Guanacaste, Costa Rica

—

2010

The bamboo used for the walls was cut into pieces and finished so that it could be pieced together to form the facade, allowing in air and light.

The house designed and built by architect Benjamin Garcia Saxe, A Forest for a Moon Dazzler, was made for his mother, Helen Saxe Fernandez. After many years of urban life, Saxe Fernandez wanted to return to the rural lifestyle of her youth. She bought a piece of forested land and lived there, initially in a shack she built for herself from scrap wood, corrugated tin and plastic bags.

The elegant and simple house Garcia Saxe built to replace the shack is set on a rectangular concrete pad foundation. It includes two identical living modules positioned either side of a central courtyard, which is open to the sky. The structural frame for each living module is galvanized steel columns and beams with thin steel wire stretched horizontally between them. More than 4,000 pieces of bamboo, each 15 cm (6 in) long, have been threaded on this wire, creating a cage that provides a secure compound for Mrs Saxe Fernandez's belongings without resorting to solid walls. The bamboo provides a degree of privacy while allowing the warm Costa Rican coastal breezes to percolate through the space.

Materials for the project were all sourced locally. The bamboo was cut from a nearby farm, submerged in diesel to cure and then dried on the site of the house. Once cut to size, the bamboo was finished with a maritime varnish. Corrugated steel sheets, a common building material in the area, were painted in non-corrosive white paint and used as the roof covering. The timber used for the walls, window shutters, floors and terrace was all cut from trees that were cleared from the site, which was once a teak tree plantation.

The house has only rudimentary fixtures and fittings, as is the want of its owner, whose main concerns were to be able to relax in tranquil solitude, watching the shadows that her bamboo walls play across the floor during the day and gazing at the moon and stars at night. The bathroom is also simple: a rainwater collection tank installed at high level serves the kitchen sink, the shower and the WC through a gravity feed. Waste from the kitchen and bathroom is dealt with via a filtration system using layers of rock of decreasing size, buried in an adjacent field.

The house epitomizes a passive sustainable design that perfectly fits the environment in which it is located. The permeability of the bamboo walls allows for natural ventilation to keep the interior cool at all times. Sunlight in the early morning and late afternoon shines directly into the home, bathing it in a warm glow and abolishing any chill from the night. As the sun gets higher and the day hotter, the large overhang of the corrugated steel roof shades the interior. A well-ventilated gap between the underside of the roof and the internal walls ensures that heat conducted through the corrugated sheet is blown away on the breeze.

The central courtyard acts as a semi-private outdoor space: an area for its owner to sit in the evenings. Unlike the two living modules it has no wooden floor covering. The floor is bare earth, into which Saxe Fernandez has planted an aloe vera bush. A large rock serves as a seat on which she sits while making long phone calls to her sons. Constructed from steel, bamboo and timber, the house was easy to build and very inexpensive, as well as a beautiful living space for Saxe Fernandez. The cost of building each living module was £12,500 ($20,000); with two modules the total cost of the house was approximately £25,000 ($40,000).

In addition to changing Saxe Fernandez's life, the home her son designed for her is an environmentally efficient system with far-reaching potential. The living modules are easily replicable: they can be added to or multiplied to create an array of configurations, extending the internal space and making the building adaptable to different sites and purposes. While this won't be necessary for his mother's home, Garcia Saxe has since been approached by several people and government agencies interested in using his living module design to create low-cost housing in developing countries and in building public schools in deprived areas of Latin America. *Will Jones*

Benjamin Garcia Saxe

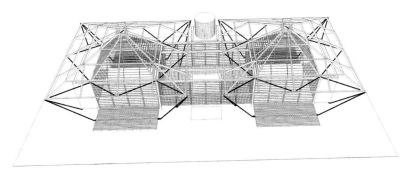
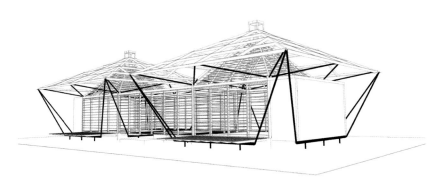
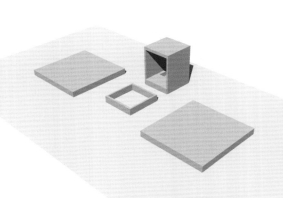
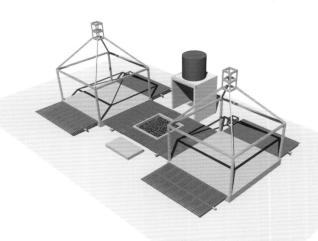
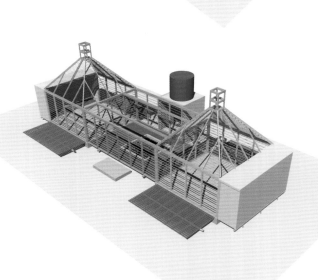
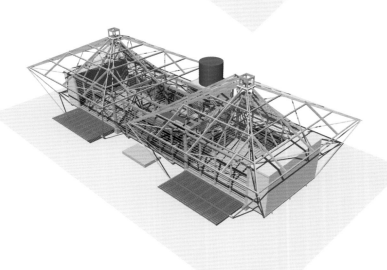

A Forest for a Moon Dazzler

Rainwater is collected,
stored and used in the house.
The skeleton of the building
has two main enclosed spaces
and a courtyard in between
(opposite). The porous facade
facilitates air circulation through
the home (top) and allows the
home to glow at night (bottom).

Benjamin Garcia Saxe

Covered with the largest green roof in the UK, the **Adnams Distribution Centre** needs no conventional mechanical equipment to cool all of the ale it stores.

The single-storey warehouse (opposite, top) is column free, which is made possible by the giant timber beams that arch over the space (opposite, centre right). This structure also supports a green roof.

The greenest warehouse in Britain, Adnams' brewery distribution centre, was completed in autumn 2006. The roof gives a hint that this is no ordinary warehouse. Covering an area of 6,000 m² (66,000 sq ft) of the structure is the largest green roof supported on the longest wooden beams ever installed in the UK. More impressive than the roof, however, is the building's pioneering wall construction. Instead of the crinkly metal facades typically associated with industrial warehouses, this building's cavity walls are constructed using hemp and lime blocks, with the cavity filled by hemp insulation. It is the first commercial building in the UK to utilize this technique.

The warehouse is used to store casks of real ale before trucking them to pubs around the region. To keep beer in peak condition it needs to be stored at a constant temperature of around 11°C (52°F) throughout the year. The traditional response to this requirement has been to store beer below ground; it is the reason that British pubs were traditionally built with large cool cellars. In circumstances where subterranean storage is not possible refrigeration is normally used.

Although the distribution centre is located in an old quarry, the cost of burying a huge 4,500 m² (49,000 sq ft) warehouse would have been prohibitive. Furthermore, the client's desire to minimize its operational energy consumption precluded the use of an energy-hungry mechanical refrigeration system to keep the beer cool. Aukett Fitzroy Robinson's innovative solution to this predicament has been to add weight to the building's walls and roof. The additional weight (known as thermal mass) enables the building's fabric to soak up heat during the daytime and to release it as the outside temperature cools overnight. The mass helps reduce daily temperature fluctuations to keep the interior – and the beer – at a constant temperature.

The roof is supported on a series of giant laminated and glued timber beams (known as glulam), which are more than 40 m (131 ft) long. These arch over the entire warehouse to create a flexible, column-free space beneath.

This innovative distribution centre demonstrates that a warehouse does not need an energy-guzzling mechanical cooling system to maintain suitable storage conditions for beer. In fact, Aukett Fitzroy Robinson's design has been so successful in its use of thermal mass that the building consumes only 30 per cent of the gas of a typical distribution centre. Even though the £5.8 million ($9.4 million) building cost 15 per cent more than a conventional industrial shed to construct, Adnams estimates that the scheme's low-energy design has cut its carbon emissions significantly and shaved around £49,000 ($80,000) a year from the brewer's annual energy bill.

In October 2010, the building's sustainability features expanded with the opening of a renewable energy centre on the site. This includes an anaerobic digestion plant and an array of solar thermal and photovoltaic panels. The energy centre has enabled the distribution warehouse to be powered by site-generated renewable energy. Meanwhile, the addition of the biodigester enables brewing and local food waste previously sent to landfill to be turned into biomethane gas, 40 per cent of which is used by the brewery with surplus injected into the national gas grid. The brewer even has plans to use the gas to power the distribution centre's fleet of delivery vehicles. The biodigester's virtuous circle is completed when the waste from the anaerobic digestion process is used as a liquid fertilizer on the farmland that grows the barley used to produce Adnams' beer – a sustainable initiative well worth raising a glass to.

Andy Pearson

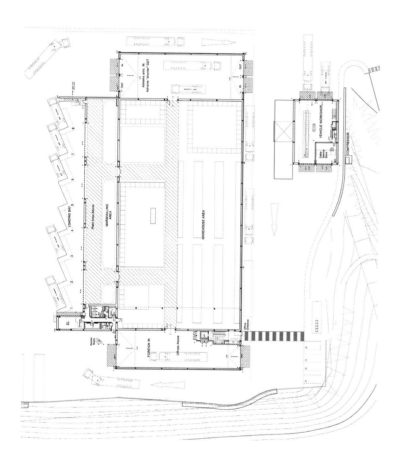

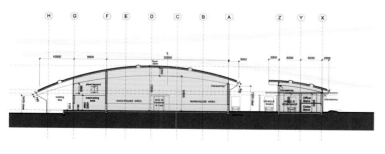

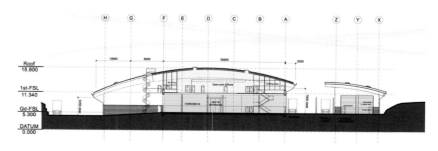

Aukett Fitzroy Robinson

Made entirely of indigenous materials including clay, rock salt, olive and palm tree woods, the **Adrère Amellal Desert Eco Lodge** uses no electricity.

Environmental
Quality
International
—
Siwa,
Egypt
—
2005

Adrère Amellal Desert Eco Lodge

The Eco Lodge sits near Siwa Oasis on the edge of the Western Desert (opposite). The walls were constructed out of a local clay and salt rock mixture called Kershef (bottom left). Structural beams and funishings are made from indiginous woods (bottom right).

Standing at the edge of Lake Siwa – a shimmering disc of water peppered with salt islands – and staring at the White Mountain cliffs, one could easily imagine that over the centuries the Adrère Amellal Eco Lodge had been shaped by the natural elements. Almost invisible against the desert-cliff backdrop, the walls are a combination of straight edges that could have been hewn from rock outcropping and sweeping curvilinear forms billowing out from the main site as if blown by the desert winds. These walls are punctuated by small, regular openings, and are made of Kershef – a mixture of local clay and salt rock. Building materials are scarce in the desert but this hotel has managed to adapt perfectly to its surroundings. The aesthetics of the lodge are in keeping with local building techniques, which is also why the rooms stay at a moderate temperature despite the intense desert heat. Windows and interior courtyard spaces are carefully arranged within the complex so that airflow is maximised, a tactic employed by the Siwa people for centuries. Visitors travel at great lengths to visit this site of outstanding natural beauty, which traces evidence of a human population as far back as 10,000 BC.

The Adrère Amellal Eco Lodge is the product of the goals set out by the Environmental Quality International (EQI) whose aim, since 1981, has been to promote and develop sustainable initiatives in Africa and the Middle East. The lodge at the Siwa Oasis is the crowning achievement of the organization and marks their move from consultation into investment and direct application of their ideas about microfinance and ecotourism. Local agriculture harnesses what little can be grown

in the harsh desert conditions and the EQI has encouraged resident farmers to sell high-quality produce under the banner of fully organic ranges, focusing primarily on olives and dates. They have also realised the potential of locally produced arts and crafts by the Siwan women. Their range of jewellery and embroidery is sold in a boutique shop on site but also in outlets throughout Western Europe. Therefore, the local people are able to bring money into the community without eroding their cultural heritage.

Energy costs are brought to an absolute minimum, as there is no electricity at the site; light is provided by locally sourced beeswax candles and temperature control is left to the natural surroundings. Building materials are entirely indigenous: structural beams are constructed of palm trees, and interior fixtures such as doors and window frames are made from olive wood. Even the chairs and tables are made of salt taken from deposits collected from the surrounding cliffs and lake. Waste water is carefully managed, with sedimentation tanks employed to contain and then slowly release waste into a sealed wetland. This is then utilised as a fertilizer for papyrus plants, ensuring that biodegradation is an entirely natural process. This lodge provides the luxury of the desert in ancient surroundings within an extremely low-impact building. The site of the hotel had been abandoned in the 1980s and heavy rainfalls had badly damaged what buildings remained. The EQI has found a way to adapt a site that had been left in disrepair by turning it into a sustainable development that is also a commercially viable asset.

Rob Fiehn

Andrea Air Purifier is a living air filter, leveraging the capacity of ordinary houseplants to clean toxins out of homes and offices.

A Peace Lily is the living component of the air purifier pictured here, however, many common house plants can be used.

There is a curious space on Rue du Bouloi in Paris called Le Laboratoire. As the name suggests, it is a laboratory of sorts, but not one filled with vials of bubbling liquids and test tubes. Instead, it is a laboratory for the mind, where scientists, artists and designers meet for discussions and experiments. The outcome of these get-togethers is usually hypothetical but at times it results in actual products: the Andrea Air Purifier is one such product. It was developed by French product designer Mathieu Lehanneur and Harvard professor and Le Laboratoire founder, American David Edwards. In short, it cleanses the indoor air from toxins with the help of an ordinary plant.

The first prototype of Andrea was made in 2007, though at that stage Lehanneur and Edwards did not have the intention to make the air purifier a commercial product. However, the interest that the product attracted from retailers and individuals was so overwhelming that the decision was almost made for them. It took two years of intense research and tests to have the product market-ready. Now it retails for £125 ($200) and is stocked in home-improvement stores and design boutiques. Some 15,000 purifiers have been sold since the launch in 2009.

The popularity of the product is proof of the growing concern over indoor air pollution. On average a person spends about 90 per cent of their life indoors and breathes in air that can be full of toxins. The plastic casing for electronics, glues and coatings on furniture, paint on walls, detergents and synthetic fabrics: all these emit different levels of Volatile Organic Compounds (VOC), of which there are about 900 known varieties. With new buildings being designed to be air-tight, to reduce energy consumption, many pollutants stay inside for longer, which can cause major health risks.

The Andrea Air Purifier works as a living filter that enhances a plant's natural ability to metabolize air pollution. A plant on a windowsill does this through its leaves, but in fact, the roots and soil of a plant are the most efficient toxin processors. Lehanneur and Edwards have addressed this by building a container that encases the plant, with a transparent top and an opaque base. A series of vertical slits encircle the top, where the airborne toxins enter the container and at this stage are processed through the plant's leaves and stem. With the help of a fan, the air is circulated from the leaves through the plant's roots and soil, and is then released, cleansed, into the air again through a vent on the container's side. This natural purifier provides a multi-stage system for clearing away toxins, and laboratory tests show that it is over 1,000 per cent faster than a plant at removing toxic gases from the air.

The first prototype of Andrea, then called Bel Air, was made from aluminium and glass, but when plans were drawn up to mass-produce the air purifier, it did not prove sustainable to continue manufacturing these materials and plastic was used instead. This may appear to be a contradiction, as the purifier is intended to counteract the effects of plastics on indoor air quality, but tests show that the purifier processes its own toxic air in less than 30 seconds. Additionally, because the product is now produced in China and shipped all over the world, plastic was the only option to meet the strict guidelines on freight weight and its impact on the environment. The plant is not included in the Andrea kit, mainly because it would not be sustainable to ship, but also because the plants that Andrea uses are very ordinary, everyday plants. Peace Lily, Red Edged Dragon Tree, Spider Plant and Aloe Vera have performed best in tests, and these can be picked up in almost any good nursery.

Maybe the most interesting aspect of the Andrea Air Purifier is that it is a truly hybrid project: a cross between design and science and between a think piece and a consumer product. Without the collaboration between Lehanneur and Edwards, and the environment of Le Laboratoire as a meeting place for different disciplines, Andrea would never have become a reality.

Johanna Agerman Ross

Mathieu Lehanneur

The walls of the **Ann Demeulemeester Shop** grow inside and out, insulating the store and improving urban air quality.

Between the facades, a moss wall and landscaping, 112 per cent of the total site area for the project is now planted.

A partnership between the Korean architecture firm Mass Studies and Ann Demeulemeester, a leading figure in fashion's avant-garde, resulted in a shop that challenges conventional thinking about the retail experience as well as the role of natural elements within the urban landscape. The new building in Seoul's Gangnam neighbourhood, which houses the shop as well as two other fashion stores, introduces previously unseen greenery into the urban fabric of Korea's capital and largest city.

The space is organized around a central courtyard and car park whose southern border opens onto the street. Under the supervision of landscaping experts Garden in Forest Co. Ltd and Vivaria Project, the exterior walls of the building, which enclose the courtyard and face the street, were transformed into a living facade. The exterior surface was covered with a geotextile and planted with pachysandra terminalis, an herbaceous perennial that grows in partial to deep shade. The plants have carpeted the building in lush greenery. By adding a layer of insulation, the foliage helps regulate the internal temperature of the building and reduces the consumption of energy used for artificial heating and cooling. The living facade not only makes the neighborhood more visually attractive, it also improves urban air quality by trapping carbon from the immediate surroundings and breathing clean air back into the city.

Shoppers are welcomed into the main store, located on the first floor, through an entrance on the western side of the courtyard. The colors, textures and layout of the shop were designed to reunite the interior space with the exterior environment. The space is flooded with sunlight from the expansive arched windows of varying sizes. The soaring ceiling, constructed of undulating dark brown exposed concrete, creates an organically shaped enclosure that reinforces the natural ambience generated by the space. The perimeter of the shop is punctuated by cylindrical columns finished with the same dark brown exposed concrete as the ceiling. The use of exposed concrete creates a lifetime of material and labour conservation by eliminating the need to repaint. In addition to the showroom on the western side of the building, an eastern wing houses fitting rooms, storage and bathrooms. This spatial organization facilitates a smooth customer experience and maintains the feeling that the shop is both open and connected.

Taking a step back out into the courtyard, visitors face a covered staircase that borders the eastern side of the open space. The staircase leads up to the first floor or down into the basement, each of which houses another clothing shop. The store on the first floor has access to a terrace. The separate but connected spaces create a warm, private and playful layout.

The staircase leading into the basement begins as a narrow, parallel, white passageway but transforms into an organic, moss-covered entrance as it connects the courtyard to the subterranean composite garden. Despite being 5.5 m (18 ft) below ground, the moss walls of the basement space are designed to reunite the indoors with the outdoors. By bringing the living facade inside whenever possible, the boundary between enclosed indoor space and the natural environment of the outdoors are blurred to the point of spatial ambiguity. By inviting shoppers, diners and designers to reconsider the way a building can reintroduce natural elements into the dense, often drab urban landscape, the Ann Demeulemeester Shop encourages creative thinking about new ways to bring the fabric of the city to life. *Bareket Kezwer*

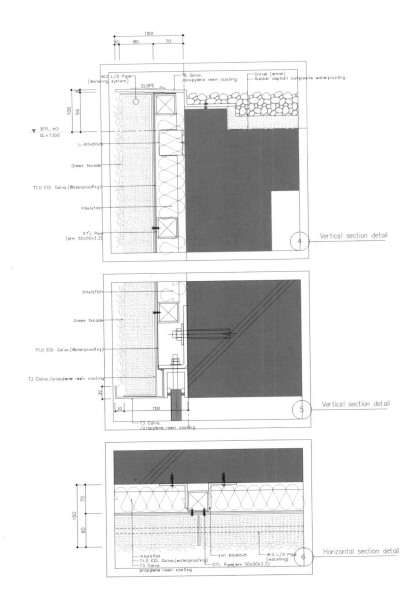

Vertical section detail ④

Vertical section detail ⑤

Horizontal section detail ⑥

Ann Demeulemeester Shop

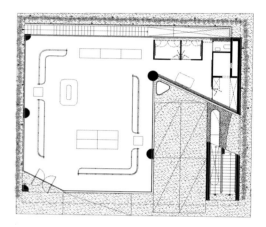

Plants cover most of the exterior of the building (opposite, top left). They were grown in a geotextile grid (opposite, top right) that is attached directly to the facade (opposite, bottom). Now full-grown, the greenery wraps the exterior walls surrounding the courtyard (top left) as well as the main staircase of the building (bottom left and right). The ground floor (top right) houses the shop.

The **BioLite Stove** captures energy from a wood-burning fire and turns it into an electrical current, cutting down on smoke emissions by 95 per cent.

Alexander Drummond and Jonathan Cedar
—
Berkeley, CA USA
—
2011

The BioLite HomeStove allows the user to reload fuel into the side of the stove while they continue cooking (opposite, top left and right). The CampStove (opposite, bottom left and right) is light and portable.

The development of the BioLite Stove is a twenty-first century enactment of the exhortation to 'think globally, act locally'. The co-founders of BioLite, Jonathan Cedar and Alexander Drummond, began their company together after being frustrated to find that all consumer camp stoves required either petroleum fuels or batteries. Acting locally as outdoor enthusiasts but thinking of the global problems associated with inefficient wood-burning cookstoves, Alexander and Jonathan set out to make a sustainable stove able to cook as quickly and cleanly as gas using nothing but scraps of wood.

For campers, open fires are comforting, but they are also inefficient, releasing more energy into the atmosphere than is useable. In a typical wood-burning fire, not enough oxygen is available to extract all the energy from the fuel; in this case, instead of producing heat and light, the burning wood produces chemical agents that mix into the smoke rising from the flames. Additional oxygen can be directed into the fire with fans, but these require electricity.

The core innovation of the BioLite Stove is a thermoelectric module that generates electricity from the fire's wasted heat and uses it to power combustion-improving fans that reduce smoke by 95 per cent while consuming half as much wood as an open fire. The stove creates a highly efficient fire that can bring 1 litre (1 quart) of water to the boil in 2.5 minutes, and it even produces excess energy of between one and two watts, which can be used to charge a cell phone or power an LED light.

Hikers using the BioLite CampStove don't have to bring petrol with them on trips, a neat convenience for people tallying up the weight in their backpacks, but the BioLite Stove model has also quickly emerged as a potential solution to the pollution produced by traditional wood-burning cooking. As the Partnership for Clean Indoor Air has noted, 'More than half of the world's population – three billion people – cook their food and heat their homes by burning coal and biomass, including wood, dung, and crop residues.' As a result, roughly half the world's women and children are inhaling highly polluted air in their own homes, leading to nearly two million premature deaths each year: twice as many as malaria. BioLite is working on a HomeStove, currently in field trials, which uses the same technology that is in the CampStove but is designed for interior use.

The BioLite HomeStove also addresses a larger planetary effect. The UN's Food and Agricultural Organization reports that 55 per cent of all trees cut down are for domestic purposes, contributing to mass deforestation. Project Surya, a UCLA-based organization dedicated to reducing the global effects of black carbon, has stated that the black carbon released from cooking fires is responsible for a large percentage of human-based global warming. BioLite Stoves, which use half as much fuel as a traditional fire, help reduce the need for wood.

BioLite's stoves offer a simple solution to a global problem, paring innovation with environmental stewardship and social responsibility. *Maya Suess*

Alexander Drummond and Jonathan Cedar

Handmade in Denmark from hollow bamboo tubes, the frame of the **Biomega RIO Bicycle** is stronger and more sustainable than steel.

Ross Lovegrove

—

Copenhagen, Denmark

—

2009

Biomega RIO Bicycle

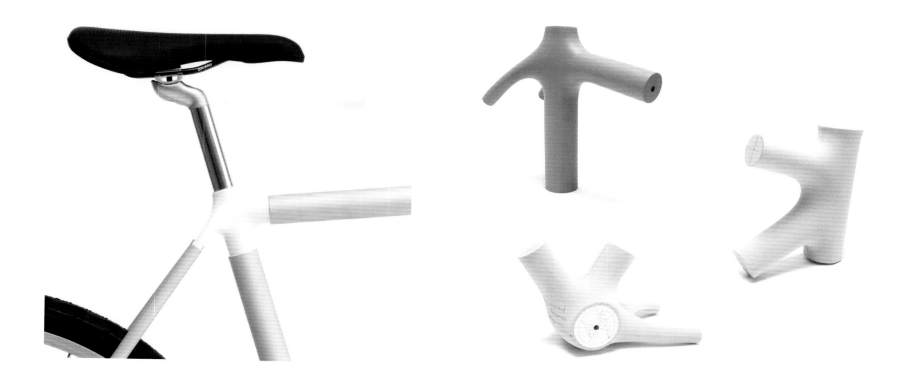

The frame of the Biomega RIO was deliberately made to look unmachined (opposite). It is held together with a unique joinery system that attaches to the interior of the hollow bamboo segments (this page).

The Biomega RIO Bicycle, by Welsh-born, London-based industrial designer Ross Lovegrove, isn't the first bamboo bicycle ever built. But with a world-famous designer and a design-led manufacturer behind it, it is the one with perhaps the greatest potential to alter the framework of urban life. Since Biomega's founding in 1998 by Danish designer Jens Martin Skibsted, the Copenhagen-based company's goal has been to usher in a new era of city living – to turn the bicycle into a viable and irresistible alternative that might begin to create quieter cities with less pollution, healthier inhabitants and greater civility. The company has sought to do so by inviting the world's top designers to collaborate in creating a series of luxury bikes that use design to breed desire, increase efficiency, and maximize the lifespan of a product.

Biomega began its collaboration with Lovegrove in 2001, even before the designer had begun work on his other sustainable projects, which include a solar-powered lighting tree for Artemide. In Lovegrove's practice, he has related to nature within a construct he calls 'organic essentialism', creating natural-looking forms from high-tech, avant-garde materials. His 1999 water bottle for the Welsh company Ty Nant, for example, looks like a torrent of rushing water but is fashioned from high-grade, moldable plastic. A table he designed for a 2007 solo exhibition at Phillips de Pury has the appearance of a gingko leaf but is made from carbon fibre. With the Biomega RIO bamboo bicycle, this relationship became more complex, as Lovegrove worked with a renewable material, harvested sustainably from the natural world, to improve on a classic form that has historically been regarded as futuristic.

The Biomega RIO bike is made by hand in Denmark, but it has taken years of experimentation to perfect. Fast-growing bamboo, when used correctly, is stronger and more sustainable than steel, with an incredibly high strength-to-weight ratio. (It's also quite flexible despite its strength, which makes for a smoother, more comfortable ride.) But because bamboo grows in an uncontrolled state, its stalks differ widely in diameter, which makes choosing pieces for production a difficult task. Once the pieces are selected, however, great pains are taken to retain the bamboo's essential character. The tubes are treated to prevent woodworm but also to retain their natural amber color, and the grasses' inherent knots and seams are left intact. Lovegrove realized that a bamboo bicycle would make more of an impact on the mind of a consumer if it actually looked like bamboo and not like a machined, overly manufactured product.

Bamboo provides the structural framework for the Biomega RIO, but the bike also contains smaller amounts of recyclable aluminium and stainless steel. Biomega and Lovegrove worked with Brazilian industrial designer and bamboo specialist Flavio Deslandes to invent a joinery system that would adhere the insides of the hollow bamboo frame to the bike's aluminium lugs. The bike boasts Biomega's shaft-drive system, which also contributes to the sustainability of the vehicle: shaft drives, which require less maintenance and last longer than chains, ensure the bikes have a reduced chance of making their way to the landfill. Biking is an inherently sustainable venture. But by using sustainable materials and injecting a bit of nature into city life, Lovegrove's bike marks a triumph of both substance and style that has all the potential to create a healthier world. *Jill Singer*

Ross Lovegrove

By weaving wicker and rattan together with broken plastic bins, **Bow Bins** rebuild waste into a new useful everyday item.

Cordula Kehrer

—

Zambales, Philippines

—

2011

Bow Bins

Bow Bins are made of old plastic bins woven together with wicker, rattan and weed. Each one is unique.

The concept of upcycling, as featured in William McDonouch's influential book *Cradle to Cradle*, is gaining plenty of traction. The fundamental premise is that instead of using virgin materials, or even recycled materials, new uses are invented for old objects without putting them through a process of deconstruction. Upcycling saves energy, reduces waste, fosters innovation and, in the hands of the right designer, fuels creativity.

Of course, upcycling is not a new idea: inventors have made beads out of magazines and built houses out of soda cans, but many of these projects are one-offs or DIY experiments. These can be remarkable, but it is perhaps more impressive to come up with an idea that is both compelling and flexible enough to support serial production and create employment in its manufacture. Bow Bins, created by German designer Cordula Kehrer, do exactly this.

Made from broken plastic baskets fused with sustainable rattan, Bow Bins offer consumers a utilitarian basket full of personality. The popping colour of the reclaimed plastic buckets playfully complements the intricately woven rattan, wicker or reeds. Originally made as one-of-a-kind items by German craftspeople, Kehrer has expanded her production by teaming up with New York-based experimental design house Areaware. Perfectly suited to Areaware's mission 'to create thoughtful products that encourage a dialogue between people and their everyday surroundings', Bow Bins remind us of the inherent potential of rubbish. They make us think twice before throwing out a broken object,

and their cheerful elegance is compelling evidence for the combination of disparate materials.

Kehrer describes Bow Bins as 'two completely different things that don't really match at first sight: artificial readymades, made of plastic, that stand for neglecting ecological responsibility – and a naturally growing sustainable material that is harvested locally and crafted by hand, keeping old traditions alive.' Drawing on tradition and ensuring that Bow Bins are produced as Fair Trade commercial items, Kehrer and Areaware have teamed up with the PREDA Foundation, a non-profit organization based in the Philippines. The mission of the PREDA Foundation is to empower the poor and to restore the rights of indigenous people; to this end it organizes multiple programmes, one of which is a micro-financing group that facilitates Fair Trade manufacturing projects.

The production of wicker and rattan has been central to the economies of South Asia for generations, but the industry has not always been run sustainably or without worker maltreatment. The PREDA Foundation is part of a movement to ensure an ethical industry and promote rattan and bamboo as sustainable alternatives to other lumber sources. Similar to bamboo, rattan stabilizes the earth and prevents erosion, grows in minimal soil and can regenerate degraded forests. By fusing sustainable rattan with plastic detritus, Kehrer's Bow Bins remind us there is a story behind every household item and that even the most mundane object – a garbage bin or a laundry hamper – can lead us towards a more responsible future. *Maya Suess*

The new **California Academy of Sciences** recycled 90 per cent of the materials from the original building and returned land to Golden Gate Park.

Renzo Piano
Design Workshop
—
San Francisco, CA
USA
—
2009

California Academy of Sciences

The band of 60,000 photovoltaic cells around the green roof of the new California Academy of Sciences is highly visible, enhancing awareness about the importance of shifting our energy supply to renewable sources (opposite). The green roof plants are grown in trays, arranged on a 7.5 x 7.5 m (24 x 24 ft) grid and separated by gabions (rock-filled wire baskets), which create a drainage system, keep the soil in place and provide footpaths for maintenance and exploration (this page). As the green roof plants grow, their roots will lock together the trays, which will then then slowly biodegrade as the roof becomes more stable.

Blending into the rolling hills of Golden Gate Park in San Francisco, the California Academy of Sciences (CAS), designed by architect Renzo Piano in consultation with Arup, Stantec Architecture and SWA Group, reflects the museum's mission to 'explore, explain and protect the natural world'. It embraces the important role of science in the twenty-first century and communicates the fact that science is a dynamic process while supporting the functional complexity of the Academy.

The CAS integrates the institution into the surrounding Golden Gate Park through its innovative green roof. The rolling hills of the roof suggest that a section of the park was lifted up and the building slipped underneath. Some 50,000 biodegradable coconut husk BioTrays, each filled with 15 cm (6 in) of soil and a combination of nine native Californian plants, cover the seven hills of the 1 hectare (2.5 acre) living roof. The fibres of the BioTrays are held together using natural latex. The lining, made up of 36 strains of fungi, supply nutrients to the plants, which will not require further fertilization or artificial irrigation.

The roof insulates the building, helping simultaneously to mitigate the urban heat island effect and keep the interior cool. Constructed with native vegetation, the roof restores biodiversity and provides a habitat for local wildlife. It absorbs 98 per cent of storm water, thereby preventing an annual 16 litres (3.6 gallons) of water from carrying pollutants into the ecosystem. The toilets use reclaimed water and the aquarium is filled with naturally filtered water from the Pacific. Both measures reduce the unnecessary use of potable water. The roof's perimeter is surrounded by a glass canopy, outfitted with 60,000 photovoltaic cells. The multi-crystalline cells are the most efficient cells

on the market and generate about 213,000 kW of energy per year, meeting approximately 10 per cent of CAS's needs.

CAS reduced its environmental impact through the creative use of recycled materials. Some 90 per cent of the materials from the demolition of the original building, which was severely damaged in the 1989 Loma Prieta earthquake, were recycled. Meanwhile, 9,000 tonnes of concrete were reused in road construction, 12,000 tonnes of steel were sent back to Schitzer Steel, 120 tonnes of green waste were recycled on site and 32,000 tonnes of sand from the excavation of the foundation were used in dune restoration projects in San Francisco.

Some 5 million kg (11 million lbs) of recycled steel, 95 per cent of the steel used in the construction, form the structural support. The floors were composed from 62 million kg (137 million lb) of locally sourced concrete, containing 15 per cent fly ash, a recycled coal by-product, and 35 per cent slag. Half of the lumber was harvested from FSC certified sustainable timber and 68 per cent of the insulation came from recycled blue jeans, a formaldehyde-free option made from post-industrial cotton waste. Meanwhile, 20 per cent of all building materials were manufactured within 926 km (500 miles) of CAS, reducing transportation needs and supporting the regional economy.

The ethereal building, organized around an open-air central glass courtyard, allows visitors to admire the vibrant colours of the park and reminds them of the need to tread lightly through the natural world. The museum itself stands as a permanent exhibition calling to attention the interconnectedness of humanity and nature. *Bareket Kezwer*

Skylights in the roof provide
natural light to the aquarium
and rainforest (opposite).
They automatically open to allow
hot air to escape from the interior.
A four-foot gap separating the
roof from the tops of the two
spheres housing the aquarium
and the planetarium (this page)
creates a stack effect, which
also helps draw hot air out of
the building when necessary.

Renzo Piano Design Workshop

The Morrison Planetarium, Steinhart Aquarium, Kimball Natural History Museum and research centre, which used to occupy 12 buildings, are all now underneath one roof. The more efficient layout of the new building includes a four-storey rainforest, and it also enabled CAS to return four hectares (one acre) of land to Golden Gate Park. The building also includes passive climate control to reduce the building's energy consumption, which falls 30 per cent below federal code requirement.

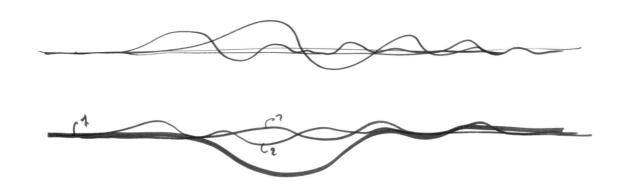

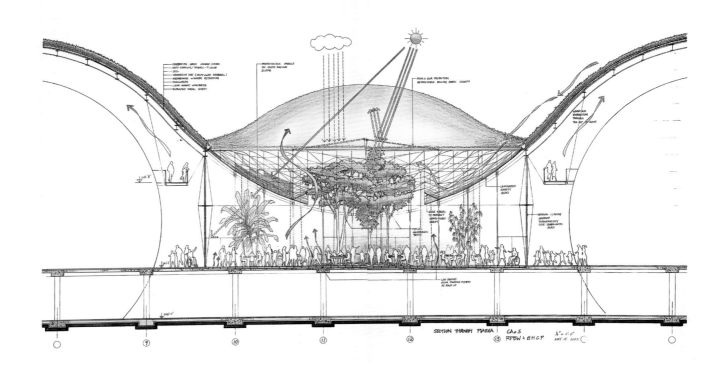

California Academy of Sciences

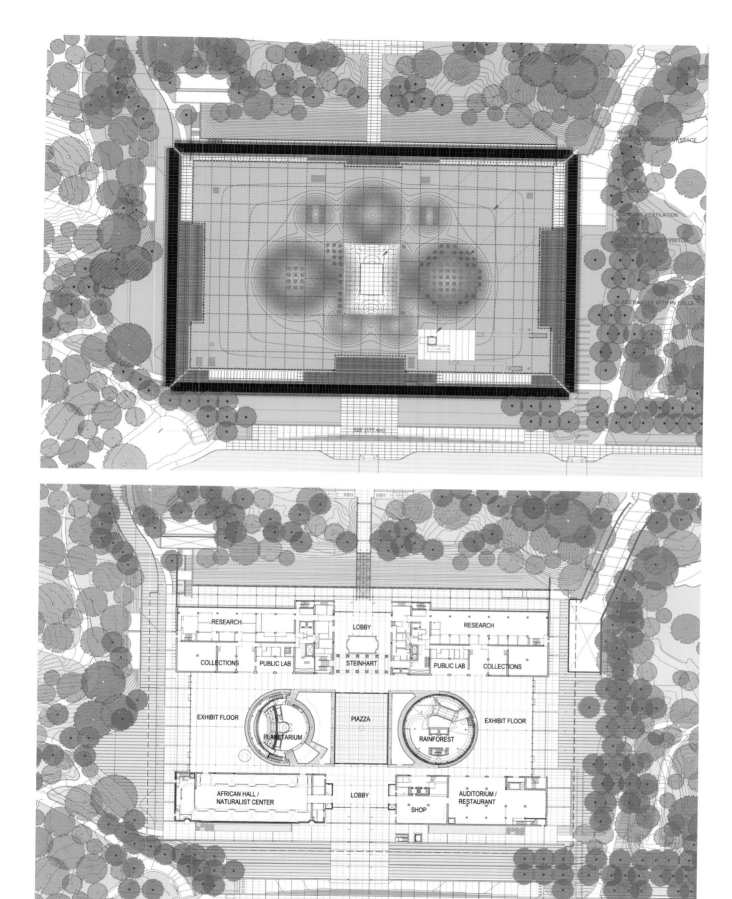

RESEARCH   LOBBY   RESEARCH

COLLECTIONS   PUBLIC LAB   STEINHART   PUBLIC LAB   COLLECTIONS

EXHIBIT FLOOR   PIAZZA   EXHIBIT FLOOR

PLANETARIUM   RAINFOREST

AFRICAN HALL / NATURALIST CENTER   LOBBY   AUDITORIUM / RESTAURANT

SHOP

MUSIC CONCOURSE DRIVE

Renzo Piano Design Workshop

The prefabricated components of the **Cellophane House™** eliminate conventional building waste, while its energy-harvesting skin allows it to perform off the grid.

KieranTimberlake

—

New York, NY USA

—

2008

MoMA's *Home Delivery* show in 2008 became a temporary site for the Cellophane House™, allowing for the house's assembly and disassembly in the middle of Manhattan.

Cellophane House™ is a five-storey, 167 m² (1,800 sq ft) prototype home commissioned for the *Home Delivery: Fabricating the Modern Dwelling* exhibition at the Museum of Modern Art in New York in 2008. In designing the two-bedroom, two-bathroom house, KieranTimberlake utilized the cradle-to-cradle philosophy, attributed to American architect William McDonough and German chemist Michael Braungart, which emphasizes positive ecological footprints through the reduction of waste in building life-cycles.

Several sustainable strategies appear in the Cellophane House™ project. First, the house is a kit of parts that can be easily assembled or taken apart. It was designed to be built of readily available materials and was fabricated off-site, with a modular construction process completed on-site. Unlike traditional, permanently fixed building components, the details of the home emphasize the assembly of its parts as a temporary process. The resulting flexibility offers the potential for disassembly instead of demolition, encouraging the recycling of building waste. Second, Cellophane House™ was modelled using Building Information Modelling computing software, a computer-aided design process that tracks building components and materials in real-time, allowing all members of a building construction team to work simultaneously on a design. Third, Cellophane House™ builds on the achievements of earlier KieranTimberlake projects and demonstrates the viability of their philosophy of performance research, using models that track a building's energy use over time. These research strategies have enabled KieranTimberlake to design highly efficient buildings as well as new, patented building materials. In Cellophane House™, the interior wall panels were made from SmartWrap™, a material that KieranTimberlake first demonstrated in the 2003 SmartWrap™ Pavilion, exhibited at the Cooper Hewitt Museum. At the time, SmartWrap™ was experimental and based on anticipated technology, but by developing the technology over a period of five years, KieranTimberlake was able to refine those early intentions and achieve a more viable product.

SmartWrap™ is a lightweight composite material system that integrates traditionally isolated functions of conventional building wall systems into thin layers. The external wall layer is a transparent membrane onto which different electronic smart materials, such as organic photovoltaic cells, are applied, while the interior wall layer of the system acts as a thermal membrane and insulator. An integrated technological system, the SmartWrap™ wall contains a series of smart components that act in tandem to regulate energy performance: OPV, which collect and convert sunlight; thin film batteries to store electrical energy; and conductive, printed circuits and organic thin film transistors (ODF) for distributing electricity and controlling functions.

It is this next-generation, multi-layer SmartWrap™ skin that encloses Cellophane House™ and harvests energy from the sun. An interior layer is laminated with 3M ultraviolet film, allowing light to enter the home while deflecting solar gain. Operating in conjunction with a passive ventilation system, these elements create a wall system that produces energy off the grid. During the exhibition, the home was also equipped with technology that monitored the environmental performance of the house during the MoMA show, acquiring data for future development of SmartWrap™ technology.

The Cellophane House™ is a successful reinterpretation of the prefabricated house as a sustainable home and an illustration of KieranTimberlake's general philosophy, which embraces a holistic approach towards building and emphasizes performance over image. *Lisa Tilder*

Cellophane House™

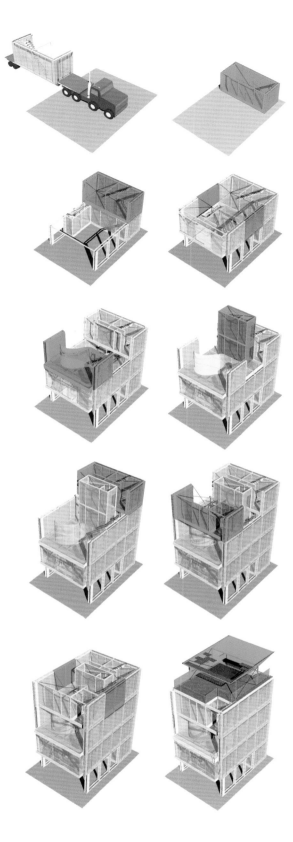

The components for the Cellophane House™ fit onto the back of a flat-bed truck. The kit unpacks (opposite) through a series of designed steps (left). The modular design allows for quick on-site construction of the entire house and its interior (top right), including partition walls and the kitchen (bottom right).

KieranTimberlake

Careful siting allows the **Center for Global Conservation** to minimize energy and resource use; red slate slabs from the Bronx Zoo's Lion House were reused in its construction.

FXFOWLE
—
The Bronx, NY
USA
—
2009

The long shape of the building helps control glare from the sun and facilitates natural ventilation (opposite). Exterior meeting spaces are adjacent to the sloped intensive green roof and the overhangs limit the amount of direct summer sunlight that enters the building (this page).

The Center for Global Conservation (CGC) houses the headquarters of the Wildlife Conservation Society (WCS), an organization dedicated to protecting wildlife and habitats worldwide. Designed by FXFOWLE, the CGC is located on the campus of the Bronx Zoo, the largest metropolitan zoo in the United States. Three mandates guided its design: first, to integrate the building sensitively with its site, second, to foster a greater sense of occupant well-being through strong connections to nature, and third, to minimize energy and resource use.

Carefully situated at the northern edge of a clearing surrounded by deciduous trees, the CGC bridges two existing rock outcroppings and nestles into a natural depression in the landscape, and its linear form is inflected to embrace significant trees. A stone path leads visitors through a reconstructed wetland to the building's entrance, defined by the bedrock outcropping at the eastern edge of the site. From a compact vestibule, a staircase opens onto communal spaces and offices designed to connect the occupants and the landscape: natural surroundings are visible from the office areas, interior meeting spaces are paired with exterior decks and terraces, and the ramped ground plane develops into a green roof, bringing grasses to the upper floors and linking the architectural promenade back to the landscape.

The design and orientation of the building maximize daylighting while controlling overheating, thus reducing energy consumption. The long rectangular floor plate, orientated east–west, controls glare and solar gain on east and west facades while optimizing north–south cross ventilation. Overhangs shade each facade differently, reducing heat and glare from the high-angle summer sun while capturing the low-angle winter sun, and double glazed low-e windows minimize thermal losses and solar gain. A coordinated daylight-dimming system and automatic window shading reduces the need for artificial lighting. Operable windows, a displacement air system, and the green roofs also reduce the building's energy consumption. Attention to space planning has helped to eliminate underused areas and oversized mechanical systems, and computer servers and other heat-generating equipment are located in below-grade spaces to mitigate temperature changes. A self-sufficient electric power operation was necessary for the site, which had no existing utility connections. The modular microturbine plant, designed by the electrical engineer, produces electricity, and waste heat from that process is used to heat and cool the building's water. An automated control system orchestrates the use of waste heat from the microturbine plant and maximizes energy efficiency; as a result, the CGC consumes about half of the energy used by a traditional building of the same size.

More unusual aspects of the building's sustainability include the use of reclaimed site materials, including red slate slabs from the Zoo's repurposed 1903 Lion House, and the use of extensive research – some of the first in the country – on how to mitigate bird mortality at the forested site. At the south, an exterior wooden screen creates a visible barrier above the sloped green roof. At the shadow of the overhang, the design team developed frit patterns, UV coatings, and vegetation options to discourage birds from flying into the glazing.

Sylvia Smith

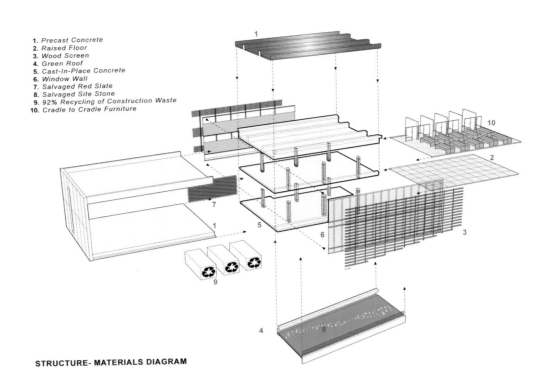

1. *Precast Concrete*
2. *Raised Floor*
3. *Wood Screen*
4. *Green Roof*
5. *Cast-In-Place Concrete*
6. *Window Wall*
7. *Salvaged Red Slate*
8. *Salvaged Site Stone*
9. *92% Recycling of Construction Waste*
10. *Cradle to Cradle Furniture*

STRUCTURE- MATERIALS DIAGRAM

1. *Copy Center*
2. *Informal Meeting*
3. *Outdoor Deck*
4. *Open Office*
5. *Office*
6. *Conference Room*
7. *Green Roof*

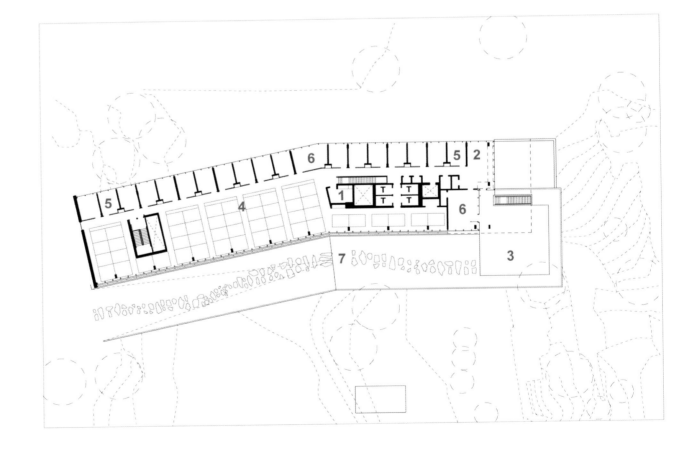

Third Floor Plan

Center for Global Conservation

1. *High Albedo Roof*
2. *Glazed Partitions*
3. *Return Air Plenum*
4. *High Efficiency lighting*
5. *Shading Control System*
6. *Operable Windows*
7. *Raised Floor System with Under Air Floor Air Distribution*
8. *Open Office Space*
9. *Intensive Green Roof*
10. *Cross Ventilation*
11. *Overhang*
12. *Wood Screen*
13. *Wetland*
14. *Light Colored Finish*
15. *Mechanical Space*

Summer Sun

Winter Sun

NORTH- SOUTH SECTION

1. *High Albedo Roof*
2. *Building Overhang for Shading*
3. *Bioclimatic Orientation: N/S to E/W Facade Relation*
4. *High Performance Low E Glazing for Daylight Maximization*
5. *Raised Floor System with Under Air Floor Air Distribution*
6. *Concrete Thermal Mass*
7. *Intensive Green Roof*
8. *Natural Cross Ventilation and Operable Windows*

Specialized materials come together to create the overall sustainable whole (opposite, top right). The green roof also functions as an accessible ramp (opposite, top left and bottom). Cross ventilation and daylighting were also closely considered in the building's sectional design (this page).

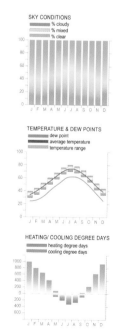

SKY CONDITIONS

TEMPERATURE & DEW POINTS

HEATING/ COOLING DEGREE DAYS

SECTIONAL RENDERING LOOKING WEST

FXFOWLE

The **Citigroup Data Centre** building uses 70 per cent less energy and 40 million litres (10 million gallons) less water than conventional data processing plants.

Arup Associates
—
Frankfurt, Germany
—
2009

The next time you search for a holiday destination online, think about the amount of carbon dioxide that you're generating. Computer data centres account for more than 1 per cent of all global carbon emissions, a figure certain to increase as the world continues to move online; Greenpeace estimates that by 2020 data centres will use more than the current amount consumed by France, Germany, Canada and Brazil. Which is why a new data centre for international financial services company Citi, designed by Arup Associates and built in the Am-Martinszehnten business park in the outskirts of Frankfurt, Germany, is so significant.

Data centres are needed to provide a secure location for IT servers – the specialized computers that deliver data to other computers 24 hours a day. Arup's starting point was to encourage Citi to minimize the energy consumed by its servers, which are housed in a 9,300 m² (100,100 sq ft), two-storey rectangular building. Traditionally, data centre servers are designed for a single dedicated function and kept in a permanent state of readiness, even though each server only operates when its dedicated function is needed. For this project, Citi has configured servers that can run several applications on a single machine, so fewer servers are needed. This innovation alone has reduced the power consumption of the data processing plant by more than 10 per cent.

To ensure performance, the servers have to be at a constant temperature between 22°C and 27°C (71°F and 81°F). It is not uncommon for data centre cooling systems to use up to a kilowatt of cooling for every kilowatt of electricity used by the IT equipment. In the Citi Data Centre, the reduction in the number of servers has itself resulted in a significant reduction of the cooling load, and the cooling system has been designed to save energy as well. Highly efficient air-conditioning units remove the heat from the server room, and a series of chillers and cooling towers reject this waste heat into the atmosphere. Two different piped chilled water circuits connect these components. One circuit links the chillers and cooling towers to the air-conditioning units; a second circuit links the cooling towers to the air-conditioning units, but bypasses the chillers. When the cooling loads are high, or when it is warm outside, the chillers are needed so the first circuit is used. However, on cool days, or when the cooling load is lower, the system will run without the chillers in 'free cooling mode'. Arup estimates that the scheme can run without the chillers for 63 per cent of the year.

The result of this design is that the 21,000 m² (226,000 sq ft) scheme uses only 30 per cent of the power typically required by a data centre, saving 11,750 tonnes of carbon dioxide emissions per annum. But this is not the only innovative feature of this building. Conventional cooling towers reject waste heat by evaporating water. As the water evaporates, dissolved impurities are left behind as solids and, to dilute the solution, a portion of this water is dumped and the cooling tower is topped up with fresh water. Here, the cooling water is treated using a reverse osmosis system, eliminating most of the impurities. This reduces the amount of waste water, saving up to 40 million litres (10 million gallons) of water a year. Because cooling tower water must be dosed with chemicals to inhibit the growth of potentially harmful bacteria, the amount of chemicals required is also reduced.

Water conservation is a feature of the building's exterior too. Green roofs with native plants cover 72 per cent of the roof area to reduce rainwater run-off, encourage biodiversity and help insulate the building. On the northeast elevation, this planting extends to the ground via a huge green wall measuring 55 m long and 12 m high (180 ft long and 39 ft high), which is irrigated using rainwater collected from the site. *Andy Pearson*

Although all data centre cooling systems consume large quantities of water, the cooling solution for this building uses considerably less than a conventional scheme. The water is stored in tanks on site.

Arup Associates

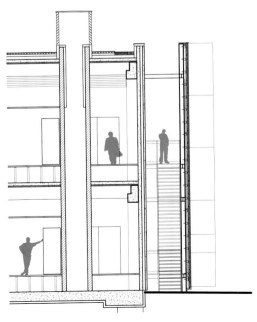

Citigroup Data Centre

The green wall of the building extends the entire length of the northeast facade (opposite). The mechanical rooms are key to meeting the building's cooling requirements (top) and the fenestrated window facade allows for natural lighting and ventilation (bottom).

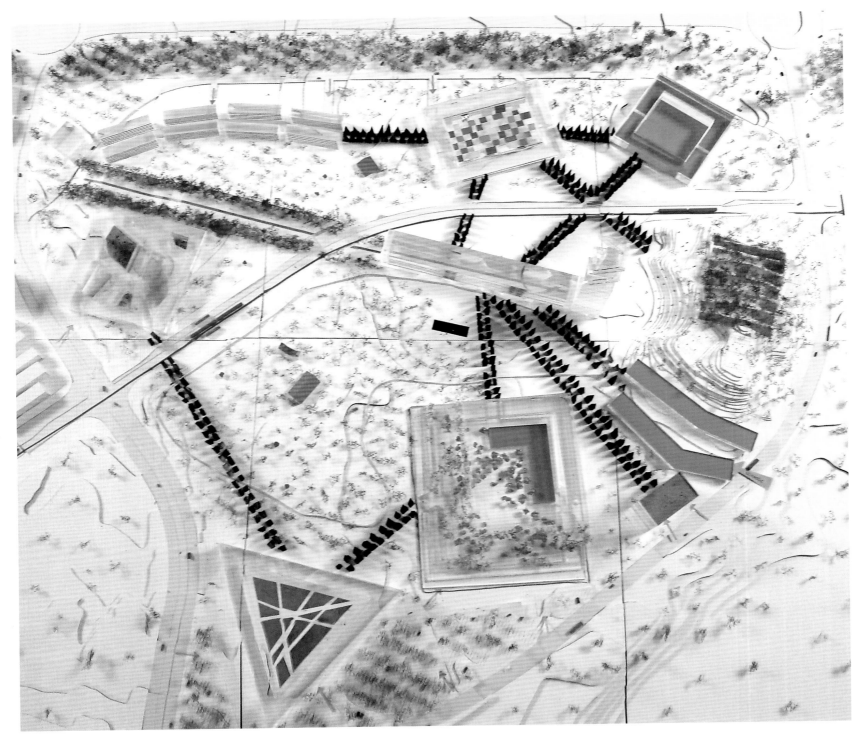

Submerged in soil excavated from the construction of new buildings around it, the **Colina de Deportes** arena is covered with flowering oleander plants.

Habiter
Autrement
with Ateliers
Jean Nouvel

Tolèdo, Spain

2009

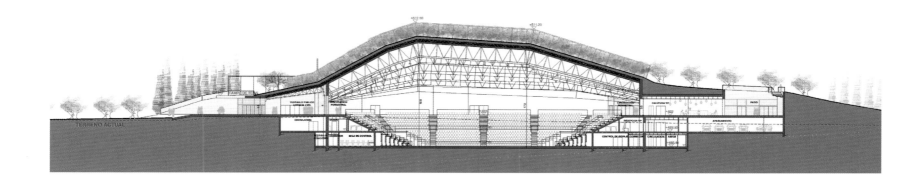

The masterplan for a new district on the outskirts of Tolèdo (opposite) comfortably integrates 2,000 units of social housing with the native landscape. The Colina des Deportes, a 6,500-seat arena (top), is visible in the masterplan model as a series of purple lines, representing the oleander shrubs that will grow on top of its roof trusses (bottom).

What differentiates architecture from landscape? How can the two be deployed together to enhance awareness of our relationship with nature? As cities increasingly seek ecologically responsible approaches to development and growth, these questions become ever more paramount. The Colina de Deportes, a project for a sports arena in Tolèdo, foregrounds this often contested relationship between architecture and landscape and offers a compelling model for integrating the two. Conceived as a component of a masterplan for a new urban district (also by the same design team), the 6,500-seat arena consists of a simple concrete box embedded in a giant, artificial *colina* (hill), the top of which serves both as roof of the arena and as planted gardens that link to the surrounding nighbourhood.

The masterplan, commissioned in 2007, proposes a new mixed-use zone of social housing and related programs for a 36 hectare (90 acre) site located in Tolèdo's urban periphery. In contrast to the typical and sometimes bleak suburban housing blocks that characterize the outskirts of European cities, the plan offers a new model for urban growth that seeks to extend the density and quality of the historic core while also maintaining a harmonious relationship between the built and natural environments. Taking a cue from the local biotope and the region's traditional agricultural heritage, the architects organized the new development with a grid of planted olive trees, which maintains a human scale but also integrates cultivation into the life of the new urban centre. A total of 2,000 housing units are distributed throughout ten separate buildings, each of which also incorporates supplementary programs such as a health centre, a nursery, and retail establishments.

Although the masterplan established the general massing and programming for each housing block, each building is designed by a different architect selected through a design competition process. The arena, located adjacent to the site's central plaza and retail complex, is one of the first scheduled for construction. Architect Mia Hägg of Habiter Autrement describes the project as a landscape project as much as an architectural project; indeed, the line between the two is hard to define. The artificial hill encasing the arena will be constructed from the soil excavated for the foundations of the new buildings throughout the site. The interior of the hill houses the arena and all its ancillary spaces: a cafeteria, locker rooms, administrative offices, VIP areas, and underground parking. The mound is carefully sculpted to incorporate several public courts for tennis and other outdoor sports, as well as a number of incisions providing access to the sunken arena.

The arena's roof structure consists of relatively generic, cost-effective steel trusses that span the width of the interior and form the crown of the hill. Each truss supports a linear strip of soil planted with oleander, a robust shrub with vibrant white and pink blossoms. Inspired by the gentle geography of the surrounding La Mancha countryside, the trusses vary slightly in shape to create a subtly curved, walkable landscape that, on the west side, facing the site's central plaza, doubles as an outdoor amphitheater. The planted groves alternate with longitudinal glass skylights that open to the arena below, providing natural daylight and ventilation to the interior and creating a dynamic visual dialogue between outside and inside. With a rich and complex interface between the landscape above and the arena activity below, the Colina de Deportes merges architectural and landscape strategies to challenge our assumptions of what is man-made and what is natural – and, in doing so, offers a compelling template for how the twenty-first century city can sustainably coexist with its environment. *Adam Marcus*

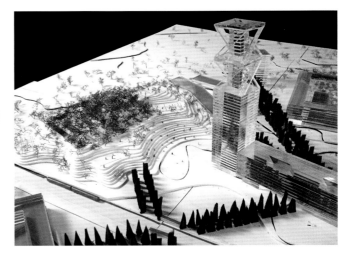

Made of non-toxic water-based ink and potato bio-plastic, the **DBA 98 Pen** reinvents the ballpoint pen so that it doesn't outlive its user.

DBA
—
New York, NY
USA
—
2010

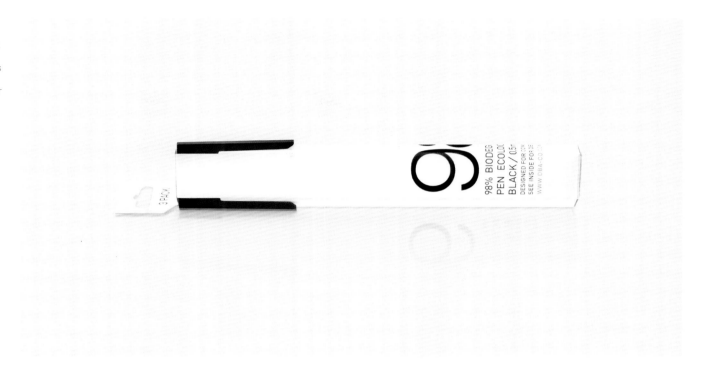

The DBA 98 Pen, from New York City-based sustainable product design consultancy DBA, gives an innovative spin to one of the world's most thoughtlessly discarded items: the petroleum-based plastic ballpoint pen. It's a writing instrument that challenges its users to think before they write.

More and more, our primary forms of communication no longer call for the archaic art of handwriting. Still, the ballpoint pen has not exactly vanished. Throwaway writing instruments continue to fill our drawers, our pockets and our purses. Ballpoint pens populate almost every room in our homes and surface in our workplaces. More than 100 billion disposable pens have been sold since 1950. When lined up end to end, these pens would circle the planet 348 times. And the toxic ink inside them? The liquid is enough to fill up 100 Olympic-size swimming pools. When these pens expire, they are discarded and enter the world's landfills – it is estimated that 1.6 billion disposable ballpoint pens are thrown away and enter landfills each year in the United States alone – where they remain, polluting the environment as they slowly decompose, for thousands of years. Even if disposable pens ever did become obsolete, they would continue to live on in trash heaps across the planet.

In contrast, the DBA 98 Pen is a disposable pen that does not outlive its user or pollute by leaching harmful chemicals into the ground: it is designed to be composted and to return safely to the earth within 180 days. An unfussy but thoughtfully designed 0.5 mm instrument, the DBA 98 Pen is composed of 98 per cent biodegradable materials. The constituent materials include an injection-moulded casing made from non-genetically modified potato-based bioplastic and water-based ink containing food-grade ingredients.

The only non-biodegradable exception is the pen's stainless steel nib. This one element, the remaining 2 per cent, is left behind during biodegradation.

The packaging for the DBA 98 Pen treads lightly on the environment as well. The pens are sold in sets of three and packaged in minimalist 100 per cent recycled and recyclable Forest Stewardship Council (FSC) certified paper boxes printed with vegetable inks. These stylish and sustainable boxes are a dramatic departure from the non-recyclable, poly vinyl chloride (PVC) blister packs in which disposable pens are commonly packaged. The price for a three-pack of DBA 98 Pens is only £5 ($8).

The DBA 98 Pen is also the result of an eco-friendly manufacturing process. DBA has partnered with Harbec Plastics Inc, in Ontario, New York, an ISO 14000-certified manufacturer, to produce the pens in an environmentally responsible factory that is powered by onsite wind turbines.

Officially unveiled in the spring of 2010, the 98 Pen is the signature product of DBA, a start-up founded in 2008 by Patrick Sarkissian, along with Leon Ransmeier and Erik Wysocan, both alumni of the Rhode Island School of Design. DBA has released the Endless Notebook, a 32-page notepad made from 100 per cent post-consumer recycled paper that is free of chlorine. Like the DBA 98 Pen, the Endless Notebook is manufactured in the United States using wind power, and DBA is currently working on other sustainable projects including a lightweight, energy-efficient heater constructed from recycled aluminum, a dish rack made of recycled polypropylene, a humidifier with an energy-efficient ultrasonic evaporation system and a PVC-free extension cord that does not release toxic substances through its production, use or disposal. *Matthew Hickman*

The **DESI School** for Bangladesh's future electricians combines modern alternative energy systems – it is 100 per cent solar powered – with traditional mud, bamboo and coco fibre building techniques.

Anna Heringer
—
Radrapur, Bangladesh
—
2008

Some 70 per cent of the population of low-lying Bangladesh live in homes constructed from the bamboo and mud readily available in the Ganges Delta. The form of these dwellings has evolved over the centuries, but recently, these single-storey houses have been shunned in favour of contemporary buildings of brick and concrete, which consume energy and displace traditional skills from the construction industry.

The Dipshikha Electrical Skill Improvement (DESI) school building, in Rudrapur, is a 300 m^2 (3,200 sq ft) mixed-use, vocational school for future electricians. Designed by German-born architect Anna Heringer, it integrates traditional methods of construction into a contemporary context. A two-storey design collects the school's functions into one building. The ground floor comprises a classroom with a veranda for practical lessons, two offices and storage space. The first floor contains a second classroom, an ornate veranda and two teachers' flats. The building's thick earthen walls and cross ventilation reflect traditional building patterns, while an upper storey, a covered stair and an erratic window pattern give the facility a modern flair.

The most significant refinements to the mud vernacular are hidden. Traditional mud-built buildings do not have foundations; as a result the walls are prone to vermin and soak up water, collapsing after about ten years. This school has a fired-brick foundation topped by a double layer of polythene sheeting to prevent moisture rising through the floor and walls. The ground floor walls are built using loam (a naturally occurring mixture of silt and clay), rice straw and water, trampled to a muddy consistency by the hooves of four water buffaloes.

The mud walls are built up in layers. Coco-fibre insulation is added to the inside surface of the walls, which is then finished with a plaster of light-coloured mud; the walls are left bare on the outside. The remainder of the building is constructed from bamboo. The first floor is formed from three layers of bamboo poles, laid in alternate directions to ensure loads are distributed evenly. The walls of the first-floor classroom have a simple woven bamboo structure, while those on the first-floor veranda have been intricately woven by craftsmen. A series of bamboo columns, each made from four poles bound together, rise up from the ground-floor walls to support the building's roof, which is created from sheets of corrugated iron attached to a bamboo frame.

These basic building methods are combined with modern, alternative-energy systems. Computer modelling was used to position the windows and openings to enable passive heating and cooling. Solar panels produce 100 per cent of the building's energy needs. A solar thermal heating system provides warm water while photovoltaic panels generate electricity from the sun to power a motor, which pumps water from a well into a roof-top storage tank; the panels also charge a series of batteries to store power for the electric lights at night. The students did the installation themselves as part of their electrical training. *Andy Pearson*

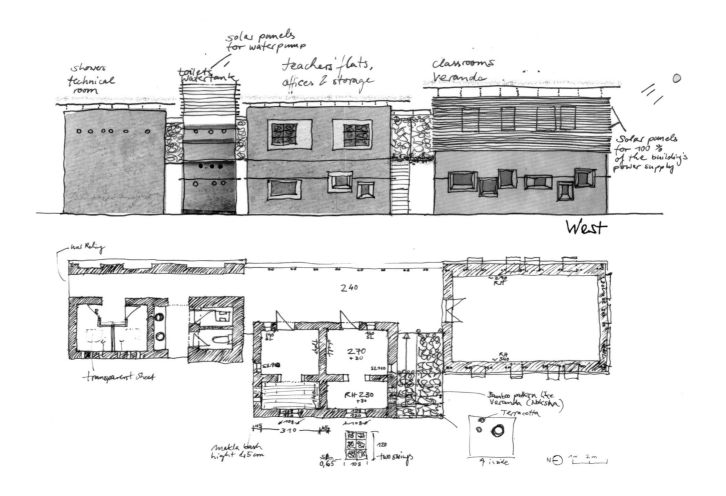

The following labels appear in the drawings:

showers
technical
room

solar panels
for waterpump

toilets
watertank

teachers' flats,
offices & storage

classrooms
veranda

solar panels
for 100%
of the building's
power supply

West

transparent sheet

240

270
+30

RH 2:30
+30

makta bash
hight 45cm

bamboo pattern like
veranda (naksha)
Terracotta

4 inside

N 1m 2m

The bamboo columns attach to the roof structure with a single bolt (opposite). The joint is then tied with nylon cord – locally produced coconut fibre rope was considered for the task, but this was found to be too weak for the main structural component. The intricately woven bamboo screens on the first-floor veranda (this page) are meant to ornament and distinguish the prestigious teachers' accomodation.

Anna Heringer

The **Design Indaba 10x10 Low-Cost Housing Project** required no electricity to construct its walls, which are ingeniously insulated with bags of sand filled on site.

Luyanda Mpahlwa

—

Cape Town, South Africa

—

2007

To address the urgent need for housing for some of South Africa's poorest residents, new two-storey homes were built in Freedom Park (opposite) by architect Luyanda Mpahlwa (this page), who used an ingenious and highly efficient construction method.

Cheerfully clad in bright colours, 10 houses by Luyanda Mpahlwa, a former partner and co-founder of MMA Architects in Cape Town, are the first buildings to result from the Design Indaba 10x10 Low-Cost Housing Project. Part of the celebrations of the 10th Design Indaba Conference in 2007, the project challenged 10 architectural teams to design affordable, attractive and innovative responses to the urgent need to house the urban poor. Sustainable design, construction and operation principles were encouraged. The project, which seeks to stimulate a wider debate around low-cost housing, as well as directly benefiting some of Cape Town's most impoverished families, is aligned with the organization's fundamental mission of making 'a better world through creativity'. Mpahlwa has since established an architecture and design firm Luyanda Mpahlwa DesignSpaceAfrica.

Luyanda Mpahlwa, who was arrested in 1981 for political reasons during the height of the anti-apartheid struggle in South Africa, pursued architectural studies despite adversity. He completed his National Architectural Diploma while serving a five-year prison term on Robben Island Prison, and later obtained

an architectural degree at the Technical University of Berlin, Germany, where he spent years in exile. Mpahlwa pursued his solution for the 10x10 housing project with a project team led by Kirsty Ronne, a young architect in the practice. Based on community engagement, Mpahlwa and the team designed homes that maximized the inherently social street front without giving up ample private space: for instance, the placement of the houses close to the street front makes space for private gardens in the back. The tight size of the plots (112 m² or 1,200 sq ft) necessitated a two-storey design. The upper floor accommodates a main bedroom and a children's room, which can fit two bunk beds, while the ground floor contains the living, kitchen/dining and wet areas. These are expected to be starter family homes; their design anticipates future expansion with additional external balconies supported by exposed eco-beams, which could be converted to an additional room.

Initially, teams were asked to meet the South African government's budget for low-cost housing, of ZAR50,000 (£4,450 or $7,000) per 40 m² (430 sq ft), but due to the fact that this was a pilot project of few

Luyanda Mpahlwa

Design Indaba 10x10 Low-Cost Housing Project

The insulating sandbags for the 10x10 Low-Cost Housing were filled on site (opposite, bottom right), before being placed into a structural frame (opposite, bottom left). Plaster is then applied to the house (this page) before it is painted (opposite, top).

units, and the factor of inflation resulting from the construction boom in the lead-up to the 2010 FIFA World Cup, the budget was forced up to ZAR75,000 (£6,650 or $10,500). To take advantage of economies of scale and to promote integrated urban planning, each team was asked to design a series of 10 houses. Notwithstanding the expanded budget, and the fact that traditional brick-and-mortar construction was too expensive, Luyanda Mpahlwa identified the need to explore alternative building materials and systems as a necessity to address the universal challenges facing building for the poor communities. As an alternative, Mpahlwa and team decided to use the Ecobeams system, which consists of a reinforced timber beam framework laid with a sandbag infill system.

Design Indaba funded the construction of the 10 houses in Freedom Park, a township in greater Cape Town. No electricity was needed on site for construction and local unskilled workers and the community of 10 beneficiaries – including many women and children – were employed in the construction to fill bags with sand. Latent benefits to this construction method include excellent sound absorption, improved thermal capacity against the semi-arid summers and soggy winters, waterproofing and enhanced wind resistance to the gale forces of the Cape as a natural result of the weight of a sand building. On hot Cape Town days the temperature difference between the interior and exterior could be 10–15°C (50–60°F). Following the completion of the 10x10 sandbag house pilot project in 2009, Luyanda Mpahlwa built a sandbag show house in Abu Dhabi, which was completed in June 2010.

Not only did the project create homes in which their occupants could take pride, the results have been presented to the South African Minister of Housing and are available in an open-source online manual, contributing to the global knowledge commons regarding the design and construction of low-cost housing. Looking ahead, the Design Indaba 10x10 Low-Cost Housing Project is ongoing, with buildings planned for South Africa, Abu Dhabi and Ghana.

Ravi Naidoo

Luyanda Mpahlwa

The highly efficient water and energy systems of the **DiGi Technology Operation Centre** are wrapped with a vertical green landscape, allowing butterflies and birds to co-exist with the flow of data.

T. R. Hamzah & Yeang Sdn. Bhd.
—
Shah Alam, Malaysia
—
2010

The DiGi Technology Operation Centre, located in Subang High Tech Park, Shah Alam, Malaysia, is a seminal example of a comprehensive ecological design approach applied to a large-scale data centre and telecommunications facility. Completed in July 2010, the 12,468 m² (134,200 sq ft) building was designed by T. R. Hamzah & Yeang Sdn. Bhd., an international architecture and planning firm based in Kuala Lumpur, Malaysia. For more than 30 years, they have pioneered a brand of ecological architecture known as 'bioclimatic skyscrapers', which seamlessly integrate designed systems within the natural environment.

The building's most dramatic design feature is a 1,460 m² (15,715 sq ft) vegetated green wall that wraps its exterior. This establishes a continuous ecological zone across all of the building's facades, enhancing the project's relationship with its natural context and increasing the biodiversity of the surrounding site by reintroducing plant life where the building now stands. The continuity of the vegetation effectively creates one large habitat, and microclimates within it are conducive to populations of butterflies and species of small birds. Five fresh air intakes are located just behind the trellis to capitalize on the particulate filtration and CO_2 sequestration afforded by their proximity to greenery. The plants, which cover over a third of the total surface area of the envelope, also improve insulation and shading, contributing to the building's overall thermal performance.

The extreme cooling loads of the data centre are mitigated by several systems. A highly efficient chiller system is linked to precision air-conditioning arrayed in a cold aisle containment system that establishes targeted cooling zones to meet the requirements of specific equipment, rather than cooling server rooms in a uniform manner. In addition to the large swathes of insulating green wall, the project's highly efficient building envelope features sun-shading, low-emissivity windows and a heat-reflective coating that reduces solar heat gain from exposed roof surfaces. Finally, 234 m² (2,520 sq ft) of photovoltaic panels on the roof feeds electricity into the municipal power grid, helping to offset the building's intensive energy demands. Together, these strategies account for a 30 per cent reduction in overall energy consumption.

All the landscaping, including the green walls, is irrigated via a gravity-fed drip system with rainwater harvested from the building's roof. Water-efficient fittings in all restrooms and pantries reduce overall consumption of potable water by more than 75 per cent. The project's sustainable drainage systems include ground-level bioswales and permeable grass pavers for all surface car parking, allowing surface rainwater run-off to replenish the site's local aquifer rather than being diverted out to sea through an external stormwater drain.

The design of the offices in the centre maximizes occupant access to daylight, which improves working conditions as well as reducing dependence on artificial lighting. Occupancy and daylight sensors throughout the building are linked to a central automation system, which also reduces the need for electricity; both strategies improve the project's energy consumption.

The DiGi Technology Operation Centre was awarded a Gold Rating by Malaysia's Green Building Index (GBI) sustainable building benchmark and is the first data centre in the country to be so recognized for its green design initiatives. Rather than relying entirely on 'bolt-on' green solutions, the project integrated sustainable strategies in concept designs from the earliest stages of development. The scheme pioneers sustainable building by interweaving fresh design initiatives, and in doing so it succeeds in overcoming many of the ecological challenges inherent in such an energy-intensive building type. *Mitch Gelber*

A green wall extending over all four sides of the building covers 33 per cent of the building's envelope, providing insulation and cleaning the air.

T. R. Hamzah & Yeang Sdn. Bhd.

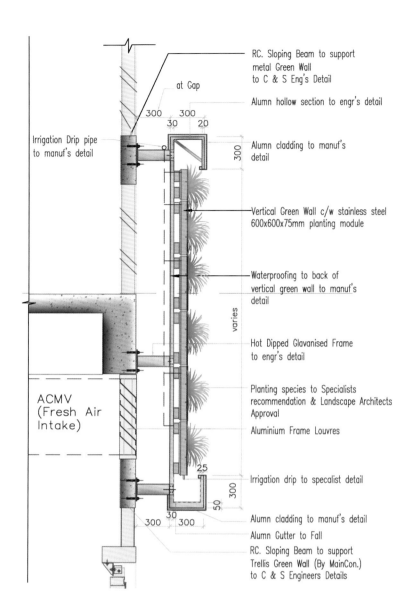

RC. Sloping Beam to support metal Green Wall to C & S Eng's Detail

Alumn hollow section to engr's detail

at Gap

Irrigation Drip pipe to manuf's detail

Alumn cladding to manuf's detail

Vertical Green Wall c/w stainless steel 600x600x75mm planting module

Waterproofing to back of vertical green wall to manuf's detail

Hot Dipped Glavanised Frame to engr's detail

ACMV (Fresh Air Intake)

Planting species to Specialists recommendation & Landscape Architects Approval

Aluminium Frame Louvres

Irrigation drip to specalist detail

Alumn cladding to manuf's detail

Alumn Gutter to Fall

RC. Sloping Beam to support Trellis Green Wall (By MainCon.) to C & S Engineers Details

Five fresh air intakes are located immediately behind the green wall trellis (left) so that the plants on the facade act as a natural air filter, cleaning the outside air before it enters into the building. The green landscape appears on all four sides of the building (right) and continues in the landscaping around the building (opposite).

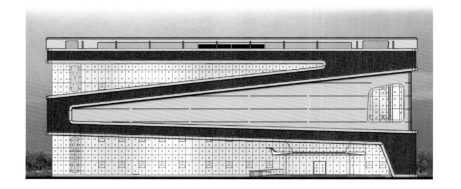

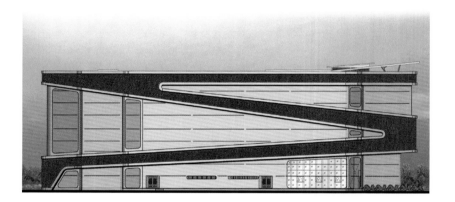

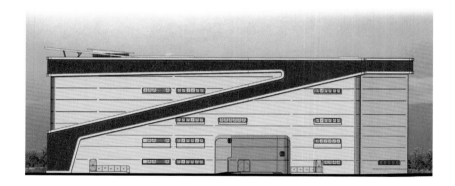

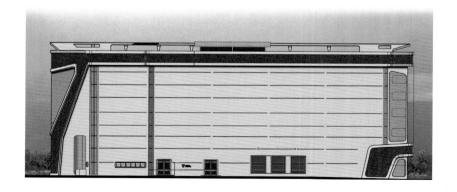

T. R. Hamzah & Yeang Sdn. Bhd.

71

The **Ecooler** is a silent clay tile screen and an energy-free substitute for air conditioning.

StudioKahn

Jerusalem, Israel

2010

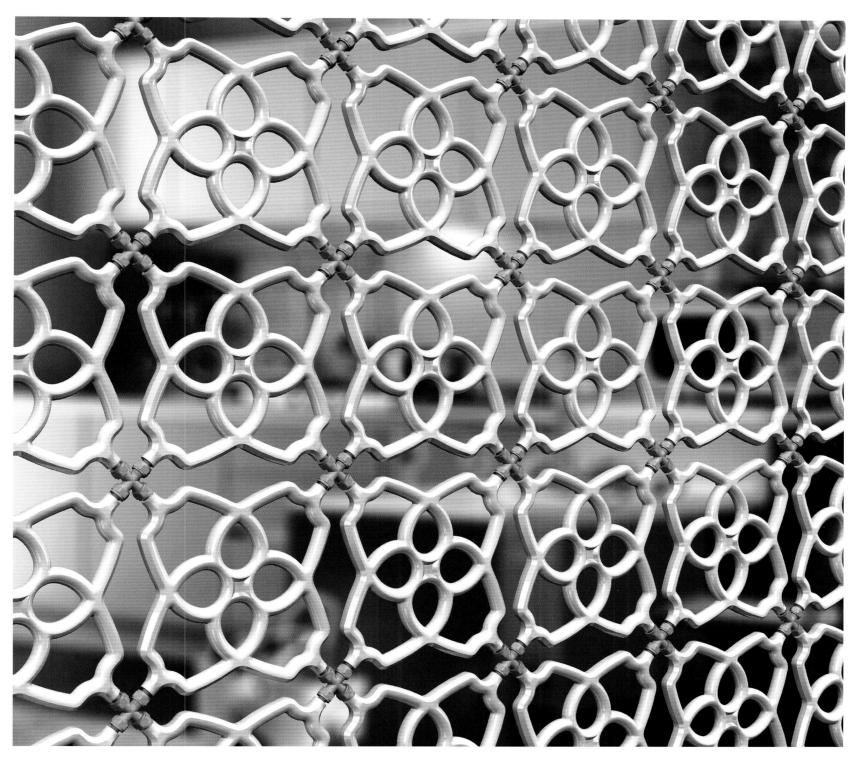

The boxy contraptions that hold air conditioning units have become a common sight in warmer climates. Stuck on to windows like sickly growths, they not only blight the urban landscape, they also produce unhealthy dry air and cold drafts. On top of that they use an unsustainable amount of electricity and contribute to raising temperatures outside.

These facts were the starting point for Jerusalem-based StudioKahn to produce a new system to cool houses and office buildings without the use of electricity. They call it the Ecooler. 'It's not only kind to planet earth but also to your neighbours as it doesn't make any noise', says Mey Kahn, co-founder of StudioKahn with partner Boaz. The challenge was to make a system that was cheap to produce, accessible to as many people as possible, and environmentally sensitive.

The Ecooler is a modular cooling system constructed from hollow ceramic tiles that sit in a metal frame, creating a screen. Each tile, made of hollow, twisting ceramic piping, is a 33 x 33 cm (13 x 13 in) square 2.7 cm (1 in) deep. They are connected to each other by brass valves. Water is then poured into one end and is distributed through the lattice-work screen. Each tile holds around 550 ml (28 fl oz) of water – the only thing needed to make the Ecooler function. The screen can be connected to plumbing or filled manually. The system requires available – though modest – amounts of water. This means it can't be used where water is in extremely short supply, but the designers are currently explorering the possibility of using grey water.

The cooling system is inspired by the age-old technology of the Jara jug, in which water is cooled inside a jug as the clay is infiltrated by the liquid and then evaporated from the outer surface. This cooling via evaporation is intensified when there is a breeze. The screen itself is inspired by the mashrabiya, a traditional Arabic wood-carved screen. Nowadays often made from concrete, it is used throughout the Middle East to shade homes from the blazing sunshine. The two combined together creates this air-cooling system. 'The fact that it's made from clay means that it is very inexpensive and easy to make', says Kahn. 'The only energy we use in the making of this is the electricity needed to fire the clay.' The Ecooler tiles are not glazed, so they require only one firing.

At the moment StudioKahn makes all Ecooler screens in their Jerusalem studio. It's a two-man job that uses moulds of forms delevoped through rapid prototyping to create intricate, swirling shapes. 'We looked at the shape for ages and were wondering if we should go for something more geometrical, but in the end we decided that this was less of a visual invasion', says Kahn. The brass valves are made in a factory in northern Israel and currently StudioKahn is trying to find a partner to mass manufacture the entire system even if it might mean changing the brass for plastic.

The first architectural applications using the Ecooler system will be on an organic Kibbutz in southern Israel and a hotel in the Swiss Alps. The Ecooler is particularly remarkable due to its relative cheapness, its use of natural materials and its ability to be produced almost anywhere. As well as being a sustainable solution to cooling air it also stands to change the urban landscape with its beautifully wrought shapes and its tranquility, in terms of sight, sound and touch. *Johanna Agerman Ross*

The Ecooler adapts the evaporative cooling techniques traditionally used by clay Jara jugs. The shape of the clay screen (opposite) is a modified version of the traditional mashrabiya tile, which allows for air circulation (this page).

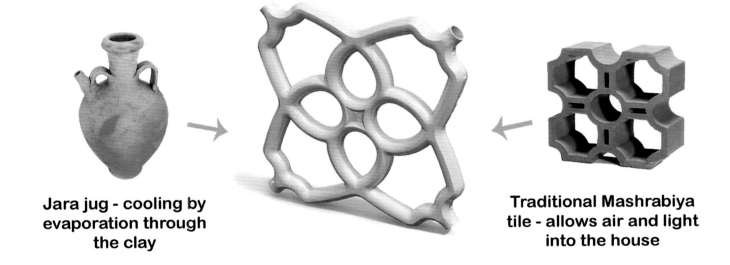

Jara jug - cooling by evaporation through the clay

Traditional Mashrabiya tile - allows air and light into the house

With half its mass submerged under the ground and the help of a sensor-operated canopy, **Ecopolis Plaza** self-regulates the energy it needs for heating and cooling.

Ecosistema Urbano

Rivas-Vaciamadrid, Spain

2010

Rivas-Vaciamadrid, a town just outside Madrid, is home to the newly constructed Ecopolis Plaza, a nursery school, public square and urban park. Designed by Ecosistema Urbano and situated next to an industrial area, amid a network of freeways with heavy truck traffic, the project has transformed a formerly vacant lot into a socially constructive space.

The architects began the design process with an energy simulation study of the performance of the building over one year, commissioned by the Thermodynamics Research Group at the Industrial Engineering School of Seville. This kind of study is intended to help apply the study of regional climate to urban planning. This process, called bioclimatic design, can be used to influence the choice of materials, the form of buildings and their orientation relative to the site and to each other. Working together, these factors can improve thermal comfort inside a space while maximizing the performance of the structure and its supporting systems.

Two main architectural elements were informed by the bioclimatic objectives. First, sinking half of the structure into the ground uses the land's thermal inertia – its ability to store heat during the day and release it at night – to stabilize the internal temperature. (It also ensures that the building does not overpower the outdoor space.) Second, a southern-facing glass facade helps control the building's internal temperature by allowing direct sunlight in during the winter, when the sun is lower in the sky. During the summer, when the sun is higher, heat is directed out of the building by a textile canopy.

The interior space of the nursery is contained within a concrete structure. The thermal mass of the concrete walls absorbs heat when the temperature rises and releases heat when it drops, a low-energy strategy that cools in the summer and warms in the winter. The space is filled with natural light that enters through light shafts including staircases and circular light tubes.

A bright yellow textile canopy, stretched over a skeletal steel framework, surrounds the concrete core. The canopy allows light in but blocks out the intensity of the sun, controlling the climate of the interior while providing shade to the outdoor spaces. Sections of the canopy, outfitted with sensors that adjust to the sun's position, roll up to provide the area with direct sunlight in the cooler months. The framework extends past the building, forming the structure for an outdoor playground.

The water management system is located in the public space outside of the building. A hexagonal lagoon located in a small valley collects both waste water from the building and rainwater directed by the hills. Inside the lagoon, the water is purified by macrophyte plants. The purified water is then stored in an underground gravel tank and used to irrigate to the plaza, reducing the amount of water entering the city sewage system. This small-scale, local model of sustainable water treatment in an urban context holds the potential to become a viable solution to resource management elsewhere in Europe – particularly in Spain, where the UN estimates 30 to 60 per cent of the country is currently at risk of desertification. *Bareket Kezwer*

The site has its own water
filtration system, which minimizes
the amount of water sent back
into the city's sewage system
(this page). The siting and
orientation of the building
(opposite, top) were influenced
by bioclimatic principles,
which helped create the bright,
sunny interior (opposite, bottom).

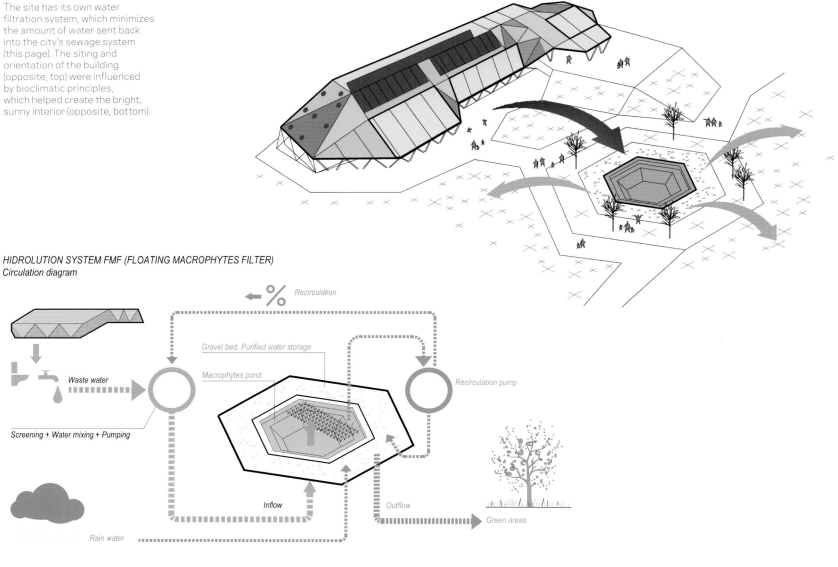

HIDROLUTION SYSTEM FMF (FLOATING MACROPHYTES FILTER)
Circulation diagram

Recirculation

Gravel bed. Purified water storage

Waste water

Macrophytes pond

Recirculation pump

Screening + Water mixing + Pumping

Inflow

Outflow

Green areas

Rain water

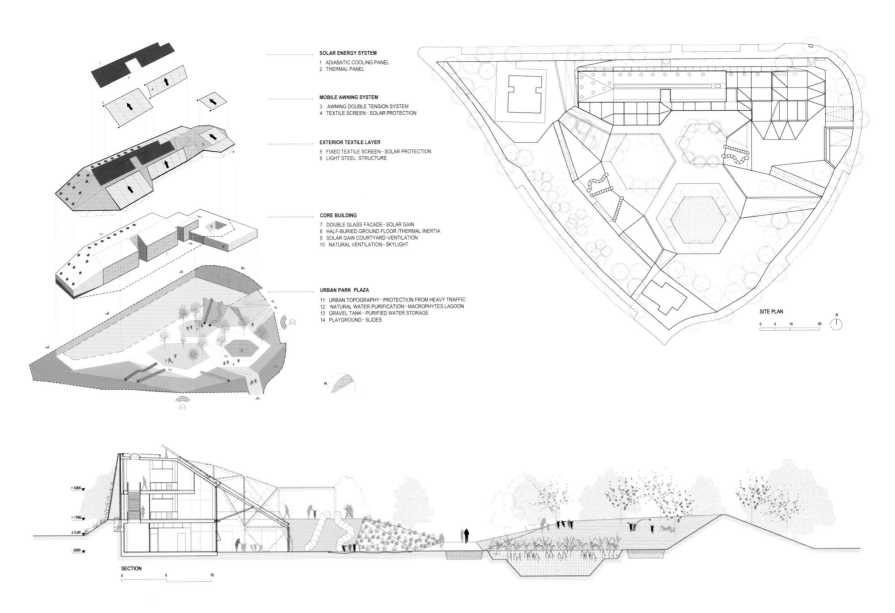

SOLAR ENERGY SYSTEM
1 ADIABATIC COOLING PANEL
2 THERMAL PANEL

MOBILE AWNING SYSTEM
3 AWNING DOUBLE TENSION SYSTEM
4 TEXTILE SCREEN– SOLAR PROTECTION

EXTERIOR TEXTILE LAYER
5 FIXED TEXTILE SCREEN– SOLAR PROTECTION
6 LIGHT STEEL STRUCTURE

CORE BUILDING
7 DOUBLE GLASS FACADE– SOLAR GAIN
8 HALF-BURIED GROUND FLOOR /THERMAL INERTIA
9 SOLAR GAIN COURTYARD– VENTILATION
10 NATURAL VENTILATION– SKYLIGHT

URBAN PARK PLAZA
11 URBAN TOPOGRAPHY– PROTECTION FROM HEAVY TRAFFIC
12 NATURAL WATER PURIFICATION– MACROPHYTES LAGOON
13 GRAVEL TANK– PURIFIED WATER STORAGE
14 PLAYGROUND– SLIDES

SITE PLAN

0 5 10 20 N

SECTION

0 5 10

The **Edible Estates** project has turned traditional and wasteful front lawns across the world into vegetable gardens and local food sources.

Fritz Haeg
—
Salina, KS
USA
—
2005

Today in the United States, an estimated 12 million hectares (30 million acres) of land is given over to green, manicured front lawns. This may be a form of symbolic decoration for the proud homeowner, but according to Fritz Haeg, a Los Angeles-based artist, designer, gardener and writer, it is also an utterly wasteful practice. Haeg is setting out to transform the way we use the groomed patches of grass that adorn many of our front yards. He is challenging people to rethink their ornamental lawns, to rip out their water-guzzling, chemical-dusted, gas-mowed turf and replace it with edible fruits, vegetable and herbs.

Edible Estates, Haeg's name for the project, have cropped up across the globe, from Maryland to California to London. Rather than a new phenomenon, this can be seen as a return to the early twentieth century, when lawns were mostly utilitarian, a place to grow food and to raise small livestock. During World War II, the federal government encouraged Americans to plant Victory Gardens to supplement strictly rationed produce and to contribute to the war effort. Haeg's project aims to resurrect the role of private land used for the public good.

Launched in 2005, Haeg's Edible Estates project was driven by his love of gardening and his desire to 'shift ideas of what is beautiful and acceptable in the landscape', as he puts it. It was also a reaction to the divisive election of 2004, the rising costs of food and the huge output of carbon that industrial food production and transportation releases into environment. In 1999, the Environmental Protection Agency estimated that the food system accounted for 16 per cent of total US energy consumption. Haeg aims to empower people to create their own food source, to inspire their neighbours, and to re-establish a relationship with the land that has largely been lost in urban and suburban areas.

He launched the project in Salina, Kansas, a city selected for its location in the centre of the United States. Haeg found his first clients, Stan and Priti Cox, through the Land Institute, a local organization dedicated to sustainable agriculture. In three days, he, the Coxes, and a handful of volunteers planted 80 m² (850 sq ft) of okra, corn, bitter gourd, pimento and curry trees. Like the Edible Estates that followed, this one was planted to suit its particular climate and growing zone. Each Edible Estate is markedly more sustainable and biodiverse than the monoculture it has replaced.

To date, Haeg has planted 10 Edible Estate prototypes, each in a different growing zone. In a South Californian neighbourhood, he helped a local family install a cornucopia of almost 200 different types of fruits and vegetables, including corn stalks, squash plants, dwarf curry trees and watermelons. He also mounted a small plaque declaring that: 'The empty front lawn requiring mowing, watering and weeding previously on this location has been removed.' In London in 2007, he created, along with local residents, a communal edible landscape on a triangular plot, bordered by two major roads, in front of an inner city housing project. Despite locals' misgivings that the garden would be vandalized or burgled, the lush plot remains bountiful, overflowing with tomatoes, Brussels sprouts and artichoke plants growing up to 2 m (6 ft) high.

In the US, where the trimming of grass front lawns can be subject to community regulation, not all neighbours are happy about the project. But Haeg intentionally dismisses the more discreet backyard in favour of the in-your-face front lawn. After all, as he writes in the preface of his book *Edible Estates: Attack on the Front Lawn*: 'By attacking the front lawn, an icon of the American Dream, my hope is to ignite a chain reaction of thoughts that question antiquated conventions of home, street, neighbourhood, city and global networks that we take for granted. If we see that our neighbour's typical lawn can be a beautiful food garden, perhaps we can begin to look at the city around us with new eyes … No matter what has been handed to us, each of us should be given licence to be an active part in the creation of the cities that we share, and in the process, our private land can be a public model for the world in which we would like to live.' *Jaime Gross*

The Tate Modern commissioned this Edible Estate in Southwark, London. Its design was inspired by the Royal Parks in London. It was first planted with apple trees, plum trees, aubergines, tomato plants, beans, peas, onions and sage, to name just a few of the many varieties.

Fritz Haeg

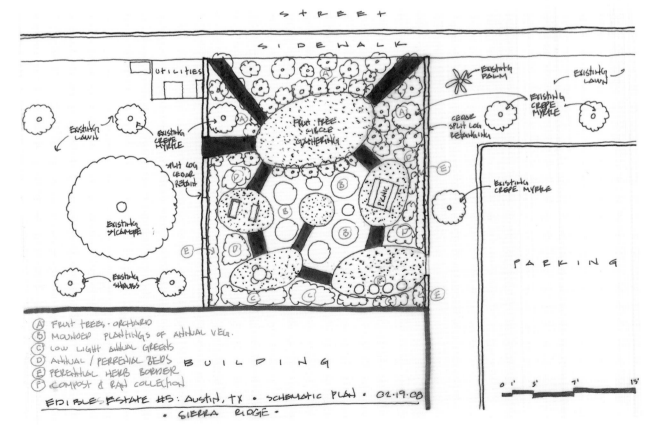

The transformation of the Southwark garden in London took place in only two days with plants purchased from local community gardens (top). In Austin, Texas, an Edible Estates garden was planted at an affordable housing complex. It bears peaches, pomegranates, figs, artichokes and peppers (bottom).

Ⓐ FRUIT TREES · ORCHARD
Ⓑ MOUNDED PLANTINGS OF ANNUAL VEG.
Ⓒ LOW LIGHT ANNUAL GREENS
Ⓓ ANNUAL / PERENNIAL BEDS
Ⓔ PERENNIAL HERB BORDER
Ⓕ COMPOST & RAIN COLLECTION

EDIBLE ESTATE #5: AUSTIN, TX · SCHEMATIC PLAN · 02.19.08
· SIERRA RIDGE ·

This garden in Baltimore was planted at the residence of Clarence and Rudine Ridgley, and was constructed by placing newspapers over the existing lawn and then covering them with large amounts of soil and compost. This trick keeps the existing grass (top left) from taking over the new garden (top right and bottom).

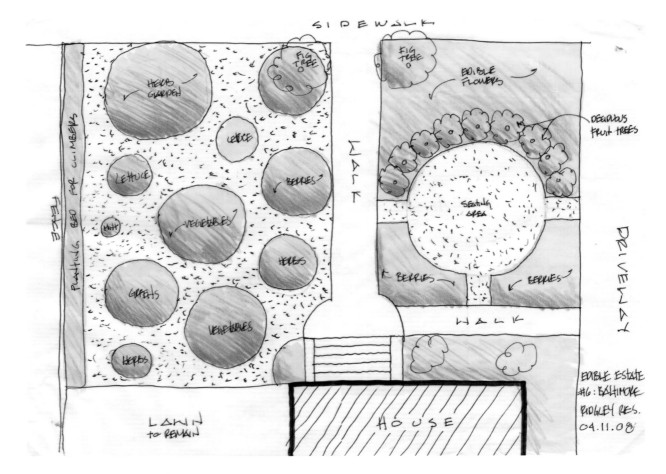

Fritz Haeg

Elm Park Urban Quarter reforms Dublin's suburban sprawl with a smartly executed, car-free mini-city.

Bucholz McEvoy Architects

—

Dublin, Ireland

—

2009

In 2006, Dublin, Ireland, was singled out by the author of a report by the European Environment Agency as a 'worst-case scenario' of urban planning, primarily due to the uncontrolled suburban sprawl of the city. This is the context in which Bucholz McEvoy Architects completed Elm Park, a high-density mini-city, in 2008. Situated near Dublin Bay and an 18-hole golf course on a six hectare (15 acre) site that once served as pastureland to the sisters of a nearby convent, Elm Park is a truly mixed-use development. The £300 million ($480 million) project packs in three large office blocks, 400 luxury apartments, a hotel, conference centre, hospital, senior citizen housing, leisure centre, crèche and other amenities amid abundant green space.

The project architects describe Elm Park as Dublin's 'green lung', because it includes expansive public gardens, nature reserves and biking trails. With a gross area of 10 hectares (25 acres), the development is around six times denser than its sprawling surroundings. The six major structures, each eight storeys high, are finger-like: long, thin and orientated in the same direction on a north–south axis. Making optimum use of the site's breezy and mild marine microclimate, these east-facing and west-facing structures are designed to make use of natural daylight through passive solar design strategies – and to take advantage of unobstructed views of the Dublin Mountains.

This orientation was also designed in order to harness the westerly winds as a low-energy source of heating and cooling. The buildings, clad in timber-supported breathing skins, have no air-conditioning or mechanical ventilation systems. In each office block, wind is drawn in through vents on the east facade and travels through the building to a thin atrium lining the west side, where it exits the structure. On sunny days, these atriums act as solar chimneys, and on cold days, when the buildings need to be heated, air moving in through the east facade passes over hot water pipes. In the residential blocks, individual units stretch across the entire width of the building, allowing for ample natural cross-ventilation.

There's one thing that is noticeably absent at Elm Park: vehicular traffic. To allow for green space and give pedestrians and cyclists free reign, the development's parking facilities are all located underground. The basement car park, like the structures above ground, is naturally ventilated and lit by large wells that also provide access to the buildings. The decision to keep Elm Park car-free renders the bustling development a giant park dotted with buildings.

To further maximize the amount of green space and to bring the development down to a human scale, large segments of Elm Park's buildings are elevated above the ground on huge stilts. The gently rolling landscape or 'urban carpet' at Elm Park, designed by Paris-based architects Neveux-Rouyer Paysagistes, includes indigenous grasses, shrubs and ferns alongside mature fir and pine trees imported from Scandinavia. Overlooking Elm Park's gardens is a public concourse that connects all the buildings. And although the hidden parking makes Elm Park easily accessible by car, the use of public transportation from Dublin's city centre is encouraged.

Prefabricated building components were used at Elm Park: concrete walls and stairs were factory-built for optimum efficiency, speed and reduction of construction waste. The electricity needs of Elm Park's office blocks are supplied by an on-site heat and power plant that recycles heat into power through co-generation. In lieu of a fossil fuel-based system, a woodchip boiler supplies the office and residential blocks with hot water. An energy-management system circulates energy around the development, according to demand, ensuring that no energy is wasted.

With Elm Park, Bucholz McEvoy proves that even within the sprawling European capital of Dublin, a smartly executed mini-city can reinvent an urban framework.

Matthew Hickman

The six major structures of Elm Park are orientated on a north–south axis to optimize the site's breezes and to make the most of natural daylight.

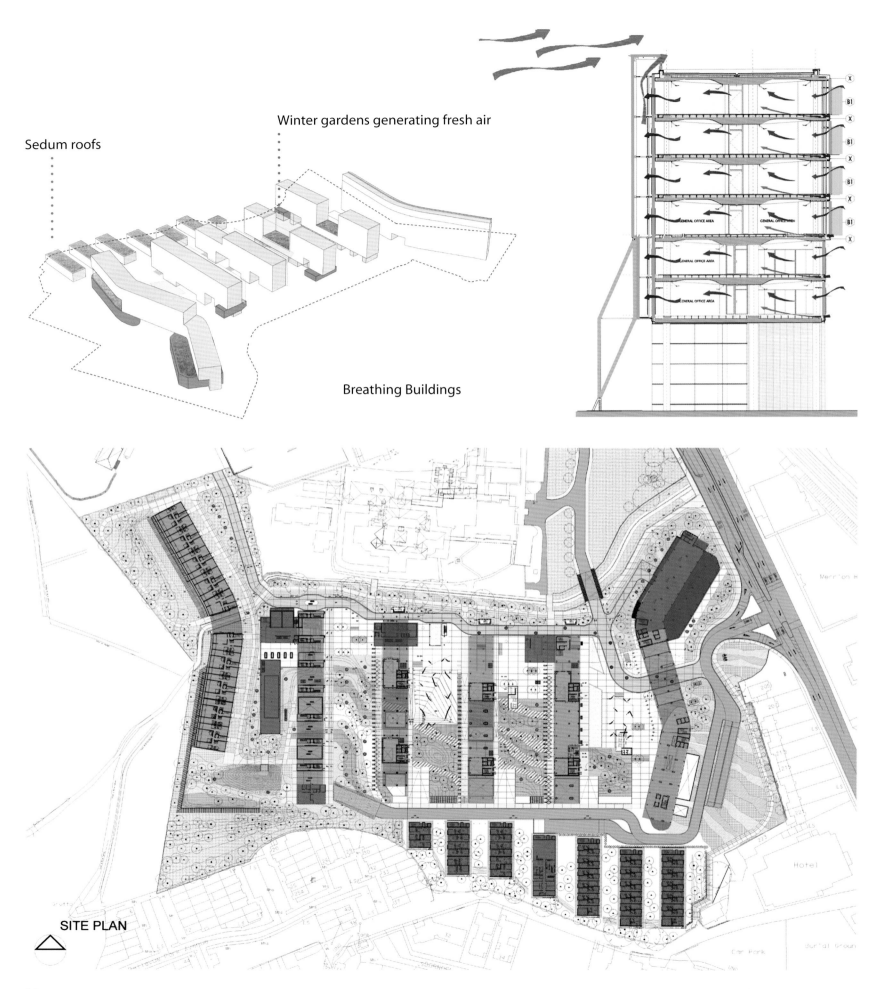

Sedum roofs

Winter gardens generating fresh air

Breathing Buildings

SITE PLAN

Feasibility studies were completed for the entire masterplan to determine the optimum building height for each structure as well as the optimum dimensions for the interior spaces. This information informed a design that ensured comfort for both the external public spaces and interiors of the buildings (opposite). Key parts of the facade were built to scale in a factory before being constructed on site, to ensure that it was built correctly (this page).

The **Embrace Infant Warmer**
uses no electricity, eliminating
one of the leading causes of infant
mortality at less than 1 per cent
of the cost of traditional incubators.

Reducing electricity usage is frequently thought of as a worthy goal with an indefinite future impact but in some situations, it can be a matter of life and death. For a newborn baby, staying warm is vital. In their first and most vulnerable moments, many babies are unable to maintain a healthy body temperature on their own. A drop of even a few degrees can cause long-term adverse health and mental conditions, and often results in a loss of life if medical treatment is not received. Tragically, hypothermia affects more than 20 million babies and their parents annually, and is one of the most common causes of infant mortality; however, it is also one of the most preventable.

Neonatal hypothermia can be avoided through the use of incubators, but this equipment can cost up to £15,000 ($20,000) and requires a steady supply of power, making it both unaffordable and unsuitable for populations in the developing world that do not have regular access to electricity. As a result, in areas where births most often take place in the home, parents often resort to archaic warming methods, such as placing hot water bottles near babies, or putting the babies directly under heat lamps, techniques that are both ineffective and dangerous.

The Embrace Infant Warmer is a solution to this widespread problem: a socially aware and affordable alternative to a traditional incubator, resembling both a kangaroo's pouch and a mother's loving hug. It is essentially a miniature, hooded sleeping bag into which a tiny newborn baby can be tucked away and kept warm, but while apparently simple, the Embrace is the result of advanced technologies.

The key to the Embrace is a wax-like substance that has a melting point of 37°C (98.6° F), which is precisely the body temperature necessary for healthy neonatal growth. A sealed pouch of this phase-change material can be heated electronically or placed into a hot water heater where electricity is unavailable or unaffordable.

The pouch is then slipped into a pocket located at the back of the sleeping bag, which can be secured around the child's body. The wax maintains a constant temperature for four to six hours, naturally releasing heat if the child is too cold or absorbing it if the child is too warm. After a few hours, a mechanism indicates when the pouch has cooled, and the wax can then be reheated.

The pouch interior is waterproof and durable, and is designed without any interior seams so that the Embrace can be easily sterilized and reused for long periods of time and for multiple users. Significantly, the pouch is also lightweight, intuitive and transportable, allowing babies to be safely taken to medical facilities if needed, and providing parents with the psychological benefit of being able to hold their child in their arms. Most importantly, the Embrace costs a fraction of traditional incubators and doesn't require power. At less than £125 ($200), the Embrace Infant Warmer costs less than 1 per cent of a traditional incubator, making the product accessible to populations and clinics that would otherwise not have access to dependable medical amenities.

The Embrace Infant Warmer was initially developed in 2007 as part of a graduate level course at Stanford University's Design School in California. The co-founders of Embrace include Jane Chen, Rahul Panicker, Naganand Murty, Linus Liang and Razmig Hovaghimian who, as part of their research, travelled to Nepal in the hope of providing low-cost incubators to local clinics. They quickly realized that a solution to neonatal warmth would have to be found by accommodating the existing practices and rural facilities of local populations who are often without the means to travel to medical facilities in urban centres. Embrace aims to save the lives of more than 100,000 babies by 2013 and prevent long-term health conditions for over 800,000, as well as continuing to provide low-cost technological solutions for medical problems in the developing world. *Daniel Ayat*

These waterproof and durable sleeping bag-like incubators 'embrace' newborns needing incubation. They require little energy to heat in comparison to costly neonatal hospital equipment. Embrace Infant Warmers can be used in rural areas and homes not near medical facilities, allowing this innovative technology to serve some of the world's poorest populations.

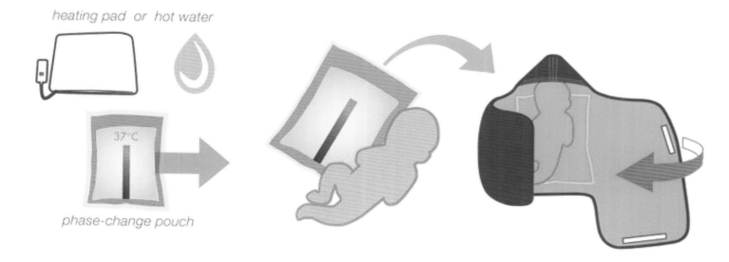

heating pad or hot water

37°C

phase-change pouch

The 1 km (0.6 mile) facade of the **Federal Environmental Agency** minimizes the offices' heat loss, and the building as a whole performs 50 per cent better than energy conservation law requirements.

The new home for the Federal Environment Agency and Europe's largest library of information on the environment is built on the former 'Gasviertel', the quarter where the industrialization of Dessau began. The empty factories and warehouses have been replaced with a vibrant new four-storey headquarters in a fluctuating palette of reds, oranges, yellows, blues and greens. Composed of bands of coloured and transparent glass, which alternate with larch-clad spandrel areas, the assortment of colours breaks up the expanse of the 1 km (0.6 mile) facade.

Most employees at the Federal Environment Agency have their own 12 m² (130 sq ft) office. The architects placed these offices on either side of a corridor, then took this line of offices and turned it in upon itself to create a relatively compact building. This solution enables the scheme to fit comfortably on the site; it also allows the inward-facing facades to be sheltered beneath a vast, glazed atrium roof.

Heat loss from the external offices is minimized through the use of triple-glazed windows and high levels of insulation. Prefabricating the facade with sustainably sourced timber and covering the highly insulated roof with soil and vegetation limits the heat lost from top-floor offices. Every office has a large tilt-and-turn window, which opens either to the outside, or to the atrium, reducing energy consumption by allowing the offices to be naturally ventilated in spring and autumn. To prevent sunlight from overheating the offices, horizontal blinds in the triple-glazed windows provide retractable solar shading and exterior-facing windows are recessed to create shading from the midday sun. The atrium also has mechanically operated roller blinds to provide shade beneath its saw-tooth roof, which is naturally ventilated to ensure a comfortable interior temperature. Low-level louvres bring fresh air into the atrium while roof vents allow the warmed air to escape.

On days when the air temperature is below 5°C (41°F) or above 22°C (72°F), the building switches to a mechanical ventilation system, incorporating the world's largest geothermal air heat exchanger. The heat exchanger comprises more than 5 km (3 miles) of interconnected pipes, some as large as 150 cm (60 in) in diameter, which are buried in the earth surrounding the building to take advantage of the constant 13°C (55°F) ground temperature a short distance below the surface. Air-handling units draw air from five sculpted air intakes around the site's perimeter, bringing it through the heat exchanger and into the building. The heat exchanger normalizes the temperature of the fresh air supply. In winter, the air is warmed on its subterranean journey. In summer, the ground absorbs heat from the warm outside air as it passes through the exchanger. There is no mechanical cooling in the offices; instead the building is ventilated at night to cool the building's concrete frame and ceilings. External vents, adjacent to the office windows, open to allow cold night air to flow through the offices to the atrium and out through its roof.

In the summer the building's conference room and data processing areas rely on the sun to keep them cool. A solar-powered air conditioning system uses a roof-mounted, vacuum-tube solar collector to heat water. This drives an absorption chiller – a complex system that creates a vacuum, which is used to produce cool air. When the sun does not generate sufficient heat to power the chiller, the district heating system is again used to provide top-up heat. The building holds 400 m² (4,300 sq ft) of photovoltaic panels on the atrium's roof, which can generate up to 31 kW of electricity. *Andy Pearson*

Sauerbruch Hutton

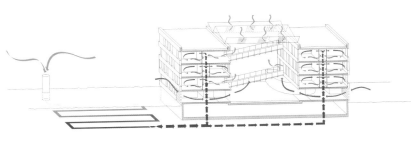

ventilation, summer

night cooling, summer

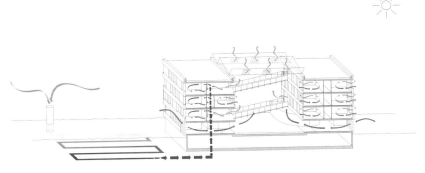

ventilation, autumn and spring

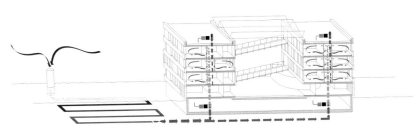

ventilation, winter

The heating and cooling systems of the Federal Environmental Agency make use of fresh air, when permitted by the outdoor air temperature, and minimize the use of mechanical ventilation (top). This strategy relies in part on the atrium, which was formed by wrapping the long building back on itself (bottom). Windows overlooking the atrium are as large as possible (opposite), and reflective surfaces in the atrium help maximize the amount of daylight reaching the surrounding offices. The ceiling, walls and furniture in the offices are light in colour, in order to better reflect interior light, and a sophisticated lighting control system ensures the minimal use of artificial light.

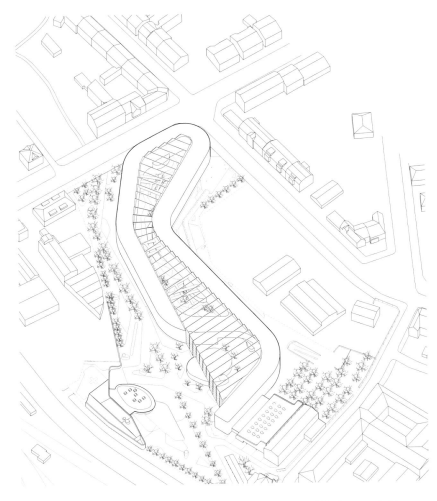

Federal Environmental Agency

Sauerbruch Hutton

The solar-powered fleet of **Floating Community Lifeboats** is built from converted boats and locally available materials, eliminating the need to rebuild permanent structures damaged by pervasive flooding.

Shidhulai Swanirvar Sangstha

—

Rajshahi Division, Bangladesh

—

1998–present

Using a fleet of converted boats, Shidhulai Swanirvar Sangstha, a non-profit organization founded in 1998, has transformed over 4,828 km (3,000 miles) of rivers in Bangladesh's northern Rajshahi Division into channels for education, information and technology.

Shidhulai Swanirvar Sangstha is the brainchild of Mohammed Rezwan, a native Bangladeshi architect. Alarmed by the fact that by 2050, 17 per cent of Bangladesh will be under water and 20 million Bangladeshis will become climate refugees, Rezwan redirected his professional practice. Using a fleet of boats, Shidhulai improves quality of life by bringing services to riverside communities. Under Rezwan's direction, Shidhulai, which means self-reliance, is helping 90,000 families improve their livelihoods through access to education, information, communication technology and portable solar-powered lighting.

Shidhulai currently owns and manages 88 boats with a paid staff of approximately 180 and 2,000 volunteers. Of the 42 boats that are operational, 21 are functioning schools, libraries, and battery charging stations, five run onboard agricultural training centres, four screen educational programs, five are mobile healthcare clinics, and seven are used for workshops, transportation and waste management. These boats make three to four hour stops six days a week. The remaining 46 boats are in the process of being converted into climate shelters for flood victims.

Shidhulai's fleet of boats is specifically designed to withstand Bangladesh's severe climate while serving user needs. The flat bottoms allow easy passage through shallow rivers and over flooded land. The multi-layered waterproof roofs keep out the monsoon rain and heat while side windows provide ventilation.

A metal truss supports the weight of the roof, allowing the interior to remain open. The fleet, which is estimated to last between 10–15 years, was constructed entirely using locally available materials.

The fleet of boats is powered exclusively using the renewable energy of the sun. Photovoltaic (PV) modules are installed on the roofs of the boats. Each PV module can generate between 200 Wp and 2 kWp of power, depending on the electrical demand. The energy generated through the PV modules is stored in rechargeable lead-acid batteries. To maximize the life of the PV system, Shidhulai manufactures the charge controller and battery chargers and has an in-house engineer and technician do the installation and maintenance. The PV modules are imported to Bangladesh and bought from local markets and have an expected lifetime of 15 years.

Increased flooding in Bangladesh has led to a greater number of students – those who live too far from a local school or who fear drowning in the monsoon floods, and who tend to be female – who stop attending regular school. By picking students up at their homes, the travelling school ensures that children remain actively involved in their education. Each school boat runs three to four classes a day. The classroom comfortably sits 30 to 35 students and is equipped with a small library of a few hundred books, a computer or laptop with an internet connection, electronic resources, a printer, and mobile phones. Other boats contain training centres that educate adults on sustainable agricultural practices. Surveys suggest that since Shidhulai began bringing their programming to these waterside communities, farmers have on average increased their income by 45 per cent, while the average use of synthetic pesticides has decreased by 60 per cent, with about one third of farmers eliminating their use altogether. *Bareket Kezwer*

Constructed of salvaged steel, repurposed wood from wine barrels and recycled slag, the **Ford Calumet Environmental Center** creates a living laboratory on a post-industrial site.

Studio Gang and SCAPE

—

Chicago, IL USA

—

2004–present

Reclaimed steel forms enclosed exterior porches (opposite). The building rests within the Hegewisch Marsh wetland (this page).

The Ford Calumet Environmental Center will be located within the Hegewisch Marsh wetland of Chicago's Calumet Region, a 72 km (45 mile) sweep of terrain at the southern end of Lake Michigan that boasts some of the region's most ecologically diverse prairies, savannahs, forests and endangered species habitats. Within this extraordinary natural landscape is another, industrial one: numerous abandoned or underused rail yards, factories and steel mills occupy the area. During the twentieth century, the Calumet region is said to have refined more steel than most industrial nations.

The region is currently undergoing environmental remediation and the Ford Calumet Environmental Center will be a research and education hub for this process. Designed by Studio Gang, the Chicago architecture firm led by Jeanne Gang and Mark Schendel, and New York-based landscape architects SCAPE, the Center is sponsored by the Illinois Department of Natural Resources, the City of Chicago Department of Environment, Chicago's Environmental Fund and the Ford Motor Company.

Both natural and industrial histories of the region coexist in the Studio Gang design. Measuring 2,500 m² (27,000 sq ft), the Center is dubbed the 'Best Nest' for the way it mimics a bird's use of local flora to assemble its home. It will be largely composed of locally salvaged materials, including steel and other remnants from the Calumet industrial region. More than 930 m² (10,000 sq ft) of steel will be used to form enclosed porches. The textured sculptural appearance of the steel beams,

along with patterns in the exterior glass, will help to prevent bird collisions.

Passive environmental strategies, such as considering the building's angle in relationship to the sun, are employed to make the Center more energy-effcent. Terrazzo flooring will be composed of recycled slag, the by-product of metal purification. Reused wood is used for exterior siding and decking and other recyclable materials such as glass bottles, bar stock and rebar will also be used in the construction.

In addition, there are many active green technologies in the design. A stormwater collection system will collect and route up to 90,000 litres (24,000 gallons) of water to an underground storage system. A filtering system uses plants, bugs and microbes working together to clean waste water; the treated water is then recycled back into the wetland. Geothermal heat pumps and earth tubes draw upon the earth's temperature to heat and cool the structure. Invasive plants such as buckthorn are used as heat, fuelling a biomass boiler.

As a space for environmental research and education, it is natural that the building itself will be integrated into on-site educational lessons. Science laboratories will have workspace to test and analyze specimens and samples, and classrooms will contain 'wet' workstations. Intended to host researchers, industry leaders, staff and students, the Ford Calumet Environmental Center will be a living laboratory for environmental research and innovation. *Helen Babbs*

Studio Gang and SCAPE

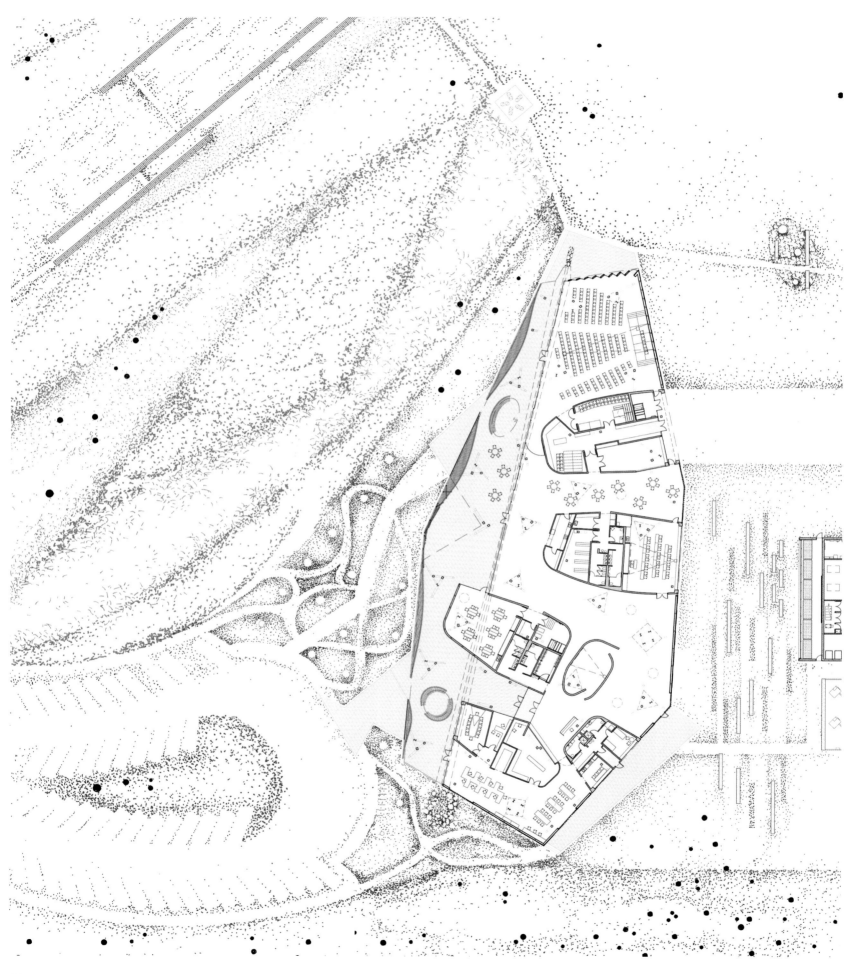

The surrounding site of the Center is being ecologically restored and exterior porches allow visitors to observe this transformation (opposite). Geothermal heat pumps regulate the interior temperature, rainwater is collected via the building's roof, and bio-fuel supplies energy (this page).

The **Ford Point** project salvaged 95 per cent of a dilapidated Ford factory building shell. It now meets the electrical needs of new tenants with a one-mega-watt solar panel installation.

**Marcy Wong
Donn Logan
Architects**
—
**Richmond, CA
USA**
—
2009

The renovated shell of the Ford Assembly Building was carefully reconstructed to meet earthquake-resistant building standards, which were not yet in place at the time of the factory's original construction.

One of California's most important landmark buildings, the Ford Assembly Building, has been transformed into a valuable development for the City of Richmond: Ford Point, which was completed in 2009. Architects Marcy Wong and Donn Logan of Berkeley, California, reinvented the dilapidated 48,774 m² (525,000 sq ft) factory, creating a new set of active spaces for local businesses, manufacturing and community events.

The factory was originally designed by Albert Kahn, the main architect for Henry Ford, who designed most of the company's plants around the world. Built in the 1930s along the edge of San Francisco Bay, the building's maximization of sunlight and open, flexible space was key to facilitating the ever-evolving efficiency of the assembly line production of automobiles. Historically, assembly buildings were the spaces where all the components that make up the automobile came together to form the final product. At this plant in Richmond, parts that came from Ford's main factory in Dearborn, Michigan – the Rouge River Factory – were assembled and sold to the local market.

At its peak, this Assembly Building employed approximately 3,500 people. The factory was closed in 1956, and the site was essentially abandonded. With today's renovation, 600 jobs have now been created on the site. The River Rouge Factory was also renovated in the early twenty-first century, but it remained a centre for the manufacturing of conventional cars – specifically F-150 trucks. In contrast, Ford Point is innovative in that it reuses the existing building to create new possibilities for emerging sustainable business. It now houses a diverse set of sustainably minded tenants, recruited by the project's developer and owner, Eddie Orton of Orton Development Inc, including SunPower Corporation (a leading photovoltaics manufacturer); Vetrazzo (a company that creates countertops out of recycled glass); and Mountain Hardwear, which

produces high-tech clothing from organic cotton, wool, hemp, recycled polyester and REVA (recycled EVA foam).

Marcy Wong and Donn Logan were able to salvage 95 per cent of the Ford Assembly Building's shell. After the 1989 Loma Prieta earthquake damaged the building, seismic upgrades were implemented into the renovation of the shell and the original – but damaged – limestone parapet was repurposed into benches. The 1 MW solar panel installation on the roof sits on the opaque saw-tooth south-facing sides of the building's skylights (an original architectural feature designed by Albert Kahn) and now supplies SunPower and Mountain Hardware with 100 per cent of their on-site power needs for manufacturing and office use. The north-facing skylights provide ample natural lighting for the new tenants, and in Wong and Logan's office design for SunPower, potted trees sit under these skylights to bring greenery into the office interior and divide up the vast interior space. Other materials, such as plyboo (a bamboo product), recycled carpets and non-PVC (polyvinyl chloride) plastics complement the sustainably sourced materials used to construct the interior.

Recreational and historical programmes complement the commerical activies on the site. The 3,700 m² (40,000 sq ft) Craneway Pavilion, which housed not only the assembly of early cars but also tank construction during World War II, a Rosie the Riveter Vistor Center, the BoilerHouse Restaurant, and the San Francisco Bay Trail are all located along the site's southern water-facing end, and serve as public amenities so that the community can now enjoy the waterfront location and expansive views. The Ford Point scheme is a part of a larger redevelopment plan for Richmond and a ferry service to San Francisco is planned from a ferry terminal nearby.
Lori Gibbs

Ford Point, originally a Ford
assembly building (top)
is now a commerical and public
space on the San Francisco
Bay (bottom). Offices benefit
from the light coming in through
the sawtooth skylights designed
for the factory (opposite, top left).
The BoilerHouse Restaurant
sits within the factory's original
boiler room (opposite, top right).
The equipment and fittings have
been painted silver and still occupy
the space (opposite, bottom).

FREITAG rescues discarded industrial materials from landfills and gives them a new life as messenger bags, wallets, and backpacks.

FREITAG
—
Zurich, Switzerland
—
1993–present

Each FREITAG bag is made from a single piece of a recycled truck tarpaulin stitched together and then affixed across the front flap with a strip of Velcro. Every bag is photographed after it is made, as no two are identical.

The bicycle has long reigned as one of the most practical, cheap, efficient and sustainable forms of transportation, especially in urban environments. It is therefore not surprising that couriers, in need of simple and functional equipment, use bikes to navigate cities quickly. Their bikes are usually lightweight with a single gear for the best possible ratio between speed and physical effort. These couriers are instantly recognizable around the world, not because of their bikes or clothing, but by the FREITAG messenger bags slung across their backs.

Adorned with colourful, asymmetric designs, no two bags are identical. Made of a single piece of tarpaulin, the bags have a large, wedge-shaped front flap that has evolved to suit cyclists who need quick and easy access to their packages. The tarpaulin – lightweight with an incredible tensile strength – is recycled from old truck covers and would otherwise be impossible to reuse. Other parts of the bag are constructed from reclaimed materials originally designed to be strong and durable: the edging is made from old bike inner tubes and the strap is a former car seat belt. FREITAG bags last for many years, despite the rough treatment that they are likely to endure.

The Freitag brothers, Markus and Daniel, were graphic designers who, in the early 1990s, evolved the concept of a waterproof bag to transport their work around their hometown, Zurich. Living in a flat overlooking a highway, they were inspired by the brightly coloured lorries that rumbled past their window. It dawned on them that the tarpaulins covering these vehicles fulfilled the design criteria for their perfect bag: strength, water repellence and longevity. There was no need to recreate a material that already existed and the process of recycling would make their designs sustainable as well. What started out as a personal project soon developed into a business and then an internationally recognized brand that now includes messenger bags, carrier bags, backpacks, wallets and protective covers for electronics.

The company's values are echoed in the design and construction of their flagship store in Zurich, built by Spillmann Echsle Architekten. The store is made up of 19 shipping containers, selected from a yard in Hamburg and repurposed for the current site in Zurich.

With the same view that inspired the brothers, the shop is set in an industrial site between the motorway and a railway. Nine containers are stacked on top of one another to form the main tower, housing 1,600 bags and products for sale. To the left of the tower, six containers arranged in a cube formation enclose the main entrance and cash desks; and to the right of the tower another four containers, arranged vertically, accommodate a sales area. Glazing has replaced the container doors on the sales levels to give a light, transparent feel to the metal structure and allow in natural light. At night, internal lighting illuminates the tower and turns the structure into a local landmark. Like the bags, the store reuses durable materials to create something new and aesthetically pleasing, while celebrating the industrial heritage of the products. Apart from designs stencilled onto the top four containers, the building materials have been left as found.

The bags themselves are constructed in Zurich; FREITAG is one of few industrial manufacturers remaining there. Work on the bags begins in a warehouse in the downtown area with the arrival of old tarpaulins that have been carefully selected for vibrant designs. The truck coverings are usually costly to dispose of and so freight companies are happy to supply the main construction material for FREITAG products. The tarpaulins are cut into manageable sizes and washed in super-size laundry machines before being brushed flat so that they can be divided into different bags. Transparent stencils are used for the final cutting process so that the design on the front of the bag can be selected. The addition of the inner-tube edging, seatbelt strap and final stitching is completed by specialists working in Switzerland, France, Portugal and Tunisia. The materials are not easy to assemble due to the hard-wearing properties that make them so durable. Each unique bag is photographed for sales purposes.

FREITAG has extended beyond simple bag manufacturing; the company has become a byword for utility, industry and high design. Perfectly designed for the needs of cyclists, FREITAG products have become a favourite of non-cyclists as well, due to their spare form, functionality and use of hardy materials that would otherwise become waste. *Rob Fiehn*

FREITAG

The FREITAG flagship store in Zurich was built of 19 modified shipping containers, stacked and reused by architects Spillman Echsle. The main tower of the store is made with nine stacked containers; the door on the end of each container was replaced with glazing (opposite). The bags sold inside are made of old truck tarpaulin material, which is removed and trimmed (bottom) and then cut to size using a transparent stencil (top). This single piece is then stitched together to form the bag.

G Park Blue Planet in Chatterley Valley is a carbon-positive distribution building, heated by the sun and powered by energy captured from vehicles entering and leaving the warehouse.

Chetwoods Architects
—
Staffordshire, UK
—
2009

Designed by UK-based Chetwoods Architects for global logistics provider Gazeley, and completed in 2009, the G Park Blue Planet is located on a 12.5 hectare (30 acre) Chatterley Valley site, adjacent to the M6 motorway in Staffordshire. The project incorporates multiple sustainable technologies to create a carbon-positive development: all the energy required to heat and power the building is supplied entirely from renewable sources, and the scheme is endowed with so many sustainable power sources that it returns a surplus of electricity to the National Grid.

Chetwoods' use of curves and graded green facades in the project's design helps to soften the profile of this giant steel-framed building, so that it sits unobtrusively in its valley setting. The warehouse has been orientated to minimize disturbance to the nearby residents by hiding the delivery yard, loading bays and the occupier's potentially noisy activities behind the building's southern side. On the building's northern aspect, the arching roof curves gently down towards a newly created park in a series of sculpted curves.

The vast roof has been designed to enable natural light to penetrate deep into the warehouse's core. Over 15 per cent of the roof's surface area is transparent, formed of 16 rows of ethylene tetrafluoroethylene (ETFE) roof-lights spaced evenly along its 272 m (890 ft) length. ETFE is a transparent, recyclable plastic foil, which has been assembled into air-filled pillows

to improve the material's thermal properties. Three layers of foil form the pillows, which are kept inflated with a small, continuous flow of air. Solar photovoltaic laminates have been welded to the inner face of the pillow's outer skin on two of the rows of roof-lights. The photovoltaics generate up to 17 kW of electrical power, which is enough to drive the air pumps that inflate the pillows, saving almost 32 tonnes of carbon dioxide emissions a year. To enhance the natural light from the roof-lights in the area where it is needed most, the building also features a 2 m (6.5 ft) high strip of translucent cladding above the delivery docks on the southern side of the warehouse. However, a building of this scale requires significant amounts of lighting, and so an artificial lighting system supplements the daylight when needed, but is dimmed when conditions allow, in order to save energy. Meanwhile, movement detectors ensure that lighting is turned off in unoccupied areas. In a traditional scheme, this artificial lighting would emanate from the warehouse after dark. At G Park Blue Planet, the ETFE rooflights that allow natural light into the building during the day also limit light released from the warehouse at night: adjusting the air pressure in the pillows activates a dot pattern printed on the ETFE foil layers, forming a barrier that reflects light back into the building and minimizes neighbourhood light pollution.

In addition to lighting the warehouse, the sun also helps to heat it. A 3,800 m² (40,900 sq ft) solar absorbing wall is incorporated into the building's southern facade,

The design of the warehouse shields the noise and activities of the loading docks from surrounding neighbours, while high-tech transparent bands along the roof surface allow ample natural light into the space below (opposite). The dark green colour of the exterior walls absorbs heat from the sun and uses it to meet the heating needs of the interior (this page).

An environmental public park surrounds the warehouse, which is also strategically located near a main railway for the delivery and dispersal of goods (this page). All of the timber used is FSC certified (opposite, top). The curved steel roof structure can be seen in the interior of the space, which is brightly lit by the sun during the day (opposite, bottom).

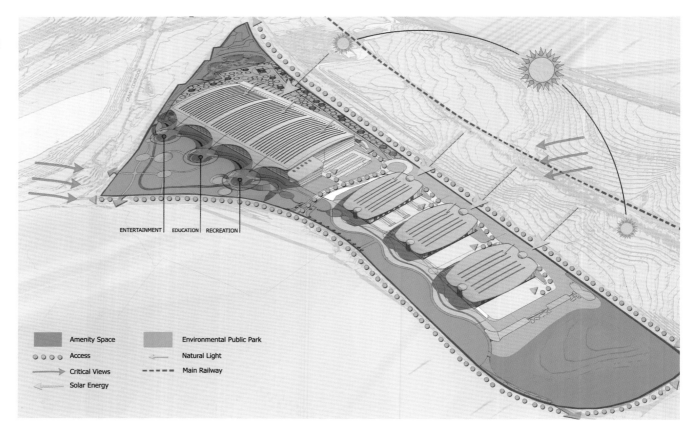

ENTERTAINMENT EDUCATION RECREATION

▨ Amenity Space	▨ Environmental Public Park
○○○○ Access	⇐ Natural Light
→ Critical Views	--- Main Railway
⇐ Solar Energy	

above the translucent cladding and loading docks. This dark green area of wall is designed so that as the metal facade soaks up heat from the sun, it warms air enclosed in a plenum behind. Fans then draw the warmed air into the building, where it is distributed at a high level to provide 'free' background heat, supplementing the underfloor heating pipework, which is fed by the biomass boilers.

Perhaps the most unusual technology used at G Park Blue Planet is buried in the access road that leads to the warehouse yards. Two pits, in the future, will incorporate 16 electro-kinetic plates that generate electricity from vehicles entering or leaving the site. The plates will be sited close to the gatehouse at the warehouse's entrance at a strategic point on the road, where the vehicles have to slow down. The plates work by converting the energy stored in a moving vehicle (kinetic energy) into electrical energy. They will generate up to 96 kW of power, which will help to power the warehouse's external lighting. There is also potential to use this power in the future to charge an electric bus to bring workers to the site.

The most critical technology in ensuring this development is carbon positive is the biomass-fuelled combined heat and power (CHP) system. The system has yet to be installed, because it needs to be tailored to match the energy demands of the building's occupier. However, G Park Blue Planet's mini-power station provides sufficient heat and electrical power for the warehouse, generates a surplus to heat and power surrounding buildings, and exports power to the National Grid.

The CHP system will also provide heat and power to the warehouse's offices. These are located in a separate four-storey, 1,500 m² (16,150 sq ft) building linked to the main 34,000 m² (366,000 sq ft) warehouse by G Park Blue Planet's enveloping roof. Separating the office area has enabled Chetwoods Architects to increase the amount of natural light entering the space and to soften its appearance by supplementing the industrial insulated composite panel cladding system with western red cedar cladding, solar shading and high performance windows.

The roof above the offices is home to a 14 kW solar thermal system, which heats hot water for the cloakrooms and kitchen. Beneath the roof is a 20,000 litre (5,000 gallon) water tank that stores rainwater for flushing toilets. However, the bulk of the rain falling on the roof is channelled into a series of ponds embedded within the site's landscaping. This water helps to enhance the diversity of the site's flora and fauna and provides sufficient water attenuation to cater for a 1 in 110 year flood.

G Park Blue Planet's design is the first to be rated 'outstanding' under the Building Research Establishment Environmental Assessment Method (BREEAM) rating system. The developer estimates that the warehouse's environmental features will reduce the building's running cost by almost 40 per cent, when compared to a typical industrial warehouse, which could amount to savings of £3 million ($4,800,000) over a 10-year occupancy. *Jaime Gross*

Chetwoods Architects

The automated systems of the **Glenburn House** monitor temperature, lighting and energy consumption; wind energy, used to power the house, is stored in a battery bank that can be adjusted with a remote control.

Sean Godsell Architects

—

Glenburn, VIC Australia

—

2007

Glenburn House

The adjustable rusted-steel screens on the exterior of the house span the length of the earth-embedded home (opposite). The landscape becomes an integral aspect of the house, which is entered either through the garage (this page) or the formal entry which cuts through the long axis of the plan.

In the Glenburn House, designed by Sean Godsell Architects and located in the Yarra valley, 90 minutes' drive northeast of Melbourne, architecture and landscape are fused and the result is beneficial to both. The house is directly embedded into a slope, on 20 hectares (50 acres) of re-invigorated farmland, adjacent to a national forest and overlooking panoramic views of the vast Australian landscape. The northwest and southeast sides of the rectangular property are buried in the valley floor, protected from the area's strong winds and the excessive heat. The outer skin of the building is rusted steel, which provides adjustable shade and contains integrated solar collectors capable of gathering electricity and heating water. These collectors are subtly integrated into the facades, reflecting the architect's belief that sustainable elements should be woven into the fabric of contemporary buildings.

Sean Godsell's spare, industrial aesthetic can be traced to the influence of modern masters from Kazuo Shinohara and Tadao Ando to Le Corbusier and Alvar Aalto, but his fresh approach comes from the use and re-use of materials and new technologies. Working alongside the solar collectors on the exterior, a wind generator provides power that can be stored in a battery bank. The battery supplies are monitored by a digital control system and, in a low-energy situation, can minimize power usage. This system enables the remote control of power and lighting and, if necessary, the whole house can be 'shut down'. The adjustable screens on the exterior mean that natural light and cross-ventilation mitigate the need for excessive lighting or air conditioning.

Water is a scarce commodity in this remote landscape and so rainwater is harvested in a 100,000 litre (26,000 gallon) tank buried below ground, where it is kept cool. The architect also uses the earth to regulate the temperature of the entire house. Drought-tolerant plants were selected for the exterior landscaping, preventing an unnecessary burden on the water reserves. Sewage and waste water drain away into a treatment system placed in the grounds of the house, and are then used through run-off irrigation. Floorboards and decking are formed of a durable Australian hardwood, tallowwood, reclaimed from a warehouse building in Sydney. The gap between this timber flooring and the structural floor slab is filled with a high-density polystyrene that supplements the natural insulation provided by ground submersion. The computer-controlled system accesses information from in-slab sensors, which relay building temperature and levels of energy consumption to prevents unnecessary heating of the interior. This house is also one of the few residences in Australia to use double-glazing to eliminate thermal bridging (the process by which heat is allowed to escape).

A forward-thinker in sustainable architecture, Godsell demonstrates that simple concepts teamed with innovative design and construction will drive the future for buildings everywhere. In the Glenburn House, he shows that built-in computer technology, intelligent landscaping and new approaches to moderating energy consumption can be united in projects as small as private residences to make a large impact. *Rob Fiehn*

Sean Godsell Architects

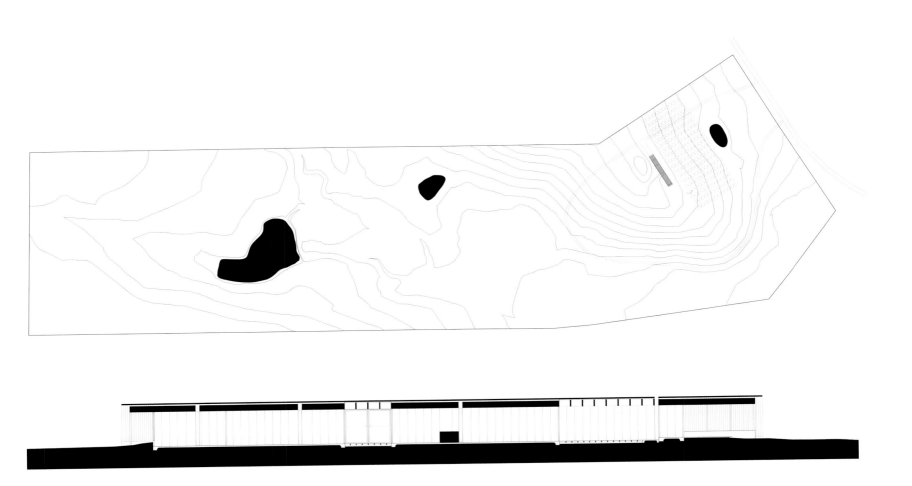

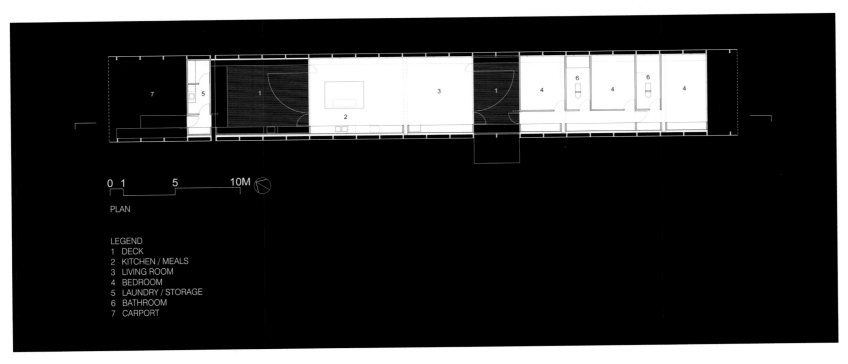

0 1   5   10M

PLAN

LEGEND
1 DECK
2 KITCHEN / MEALS
3 LIVING ROOM
4 BEDROOM
5 LAUNDRY / STORAGE
6 BATHROOM
7 CARPORT

Glenburn House

The bedrooms and bathrooms of the Glenburn House sit at the southwest end of the linear building. A more public space, containing the living room (top) and kitchen (bottom left), is set between this more private area and a deck (bottom right), creating a continuous band of space segemented by glazed doors.

Sean Godsell Architects

A natural ventilation stack effect is used to bring fresh air into the **Green Lighthouse** – Denmark's first carbon-neutral public building.

The building's cylindrical shape effectively dissipates the cold north facing winds that blow against it (opposite). Its orientation also maximizes sunlight and energy collection (this page).

Designed and built for the Danish University and Property Agency as a showcase for sustainable building at the United Nations' Climate Conference in Copenhagen, the Green Lighthouse is Denmark's first carbon-neutral public building. Designed by Christensen & Co., it is home to the Faculty of Science at the University of Copenhagen.

The building takes the sun as its inspiration. Shaped like a sundial, the orientation of the 950 m² (10,220 sq ft), three-storey building is designed to reap the most energy possible from the sun. Its cylindrical shape effectively removed the cold north-facing facade possessed by every rectilinear northern hemisphere building. An array of photovoltaic panels adorns the south-facing sloped roof. Glazed apertures in the building's external walls and roof are positioned to allow in maximum light but minimize the ingress of solar radiation. Solar energy is stored when not required, and is even used to assist in cooling the building during the summer months. However, while sunlight is a great free resource, it comes with its own set of challenges – namely solar radiation, or heat. For the design of the Green Lighthouse, the architect mapped the path of the sun at all times

of day over an entire year in order to be able to calculate where windows and skylights were best positioned on the external facade as well as how big or small they should be. This allows for the illumination of the internal environment while ensuring that the building doesn't lose heat and consume more energy than necessary. In addition, window and door openings are recessed to block the entry of solar radiation from the high sun in the summertime, while allowing in the cooler light of the lower winter sun. All doors and windows also have automatic solar shades and louvres, which operate in response to the light and heat levels at any time on any particular day.

The building is used as a student advisory, administration and faculty lounge. The interior is dominated by a central atrium, which allows light to travel down from skylights into the very heart of the building. In addition to providing a great space for social interaction, this open space functions as a channel for warm stale air to rise up through the building and escape via vents in the roof. Low-level motorised intake vents allow in cooler fresh air and a ventilation cycle described as a natural stack effect develops: warm air rises and escapes and,

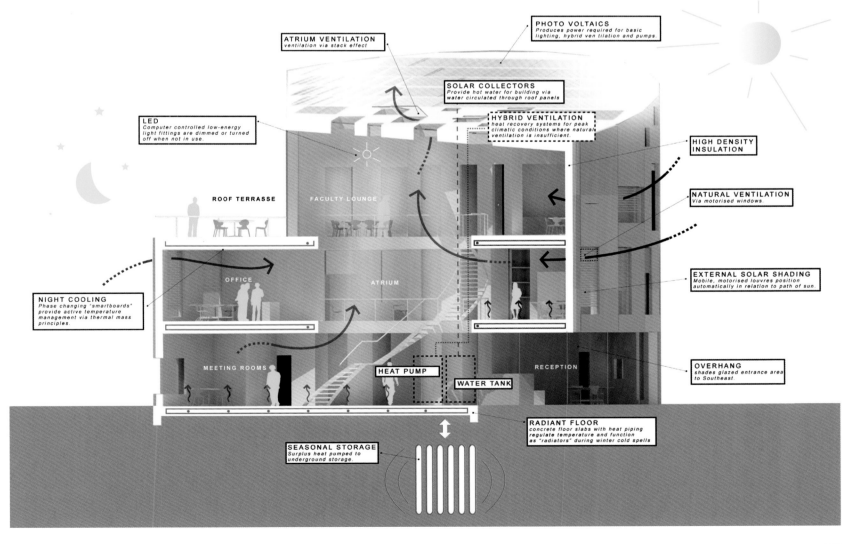

ATRIUM VENTILATION
ventilation via stack effect

PHOTO VOLTAICS
Produces power required for basic lighting, hybrid ventilation and pumps.

SOLAR COLLECTORS
Provide hot water for building via water circulated through roof panels

LED
Computer controlled low-energy light fittings are dimmed or turned off when not in use.

HYBRID VENTILATION
heat recovery systems for peak climatic conditions where natural ventilation is insufficient

HIGH DENSITY INSULATION

ROOF TERRASSE

FACULTY LOUNGE

NATURAL VENTILATION
Via motorised windows.

OFFICE

ATRIUM

NIGHT COOLING
Phase changing "smartboards" provide active temperature management via thermal mass principles.

EXTERNAL SOLAR SHADING
Mobile, motorised louvres position automatically in relation to path of sun.

MEETING ROOMS

HEAT PUMP

WATER TANK

RECEPTION

OVERHANG
shades glazed entrance area to Southeast.

RADIANT FLOOR
concrete floor slabs with heat piping regulate temperature and function as "radiators" during winter cold spells

SEASONAL STORAGE
Surplus heat pumped to underground storage.

The open interior atrium of the building allows hot air to rise up and escape through the roof (opposite). The skylights above also allow for natural light to shine down into the interior space, which also functions as a communal gathering space (this page).

in doing so, pulls in clean fresh air below it. The internal environment is thus heated and cooled without the need for any air conditioning. And, when the weather is particularly pleasant, an outdoor terrace provides a semi-private external space detached from the general university campus.

In addition to the passive environmental aspects of the Green Lighthouse's architectural design, Christensen & Co. has implemented a raft of active (technology-driven) sustainable elements. A 45 m² (485 sq ft) photovoltaic array on the roof converts solar energy into electrical power. This electricity is used for lighting, motorised ventilation vents, cooling requirements in summer and heat pumps. During the summer, when there is excess solar energy, it is stored in a geothermal system underground.

The architect estimates that 35 per cent of the building's heating requirement will be met with solar energy and 55 per cent from the geothermal network, with the remainder coming from the district heating

network. In total, approximately 50 per cent of the building's energy will be generated from renewable sources. Together with the lower energy requirements due to the architectural design, this results in a saving of 80 per cent over conventional construction methods.

Finally, lighting that utilises light emitting diodes (LED) is installed throughout the building. This type of lighting is far more energy efficient, both in the fact that it uses less power and because the light sources last up to 100,000 hours.

The design of the Green Lighthouse is positive proof that sustainable design is not merely a question of integrating as much expensive technology as possible. In fact, if not combined with intelligent architectural design, green technologies will not produce the results predicted by their manufacturers. Instead, the best way to achieve carbon neutrality in construction is to combine active and passive techniques for reducing carbon emissions and maximizing energy efficiency. *Will Jones*

Home to the largest bamboo building in the world, the **Green School** required no site excavation.

John and Cynthia Hardy
—
Bali, Indonesia
—
2008

The bamboo structures of both the Green School and the nearby Green Village (opposite) are open to Bali's elements.

Ecologically sustainable design is based on the idea that we should work with nature instead of against it. This is not a new proposition; many designers are looking backwards, putting contemporary spins on ancient methods. Green School, set along the Ayung River in Bali, Indonesia, is an example where traditional techniques are fused with new forms to create a holistic design and visually stunning architecture.

The founders of Green School, John and Cynthia Hardy (partners in life, business and design) moved to Bali over three decades ago. On settling into the Balinese way of living green and falling in love with the mastery of artisans in the region, they established a community based around elemental principles of sustainability: be local, let the environment lead and think about what your grandchildren will need.

The heart of this community is Green School. Housing classrooms, a library, offices and social spaces, Green School is a series of monumental structures made by Balinese artisans. The graceful central building named 'Heart of School' is a collection of three spiralling rooftops, arching aloft an intricate bamboo skeleton. The school buildings have no walls, only the lush tapestry of tropical forest surrounding them. The Green School curriculum includes three areas: academic studies, environmental studies and the creative arts. Reflected in the school buildings is Green School's mission to encourage leadership in all these areas.

Green School is a leader in sustainable design because of the building's near-ubiquitous use of bamboo. Bamboo produces 35 per cent more oxygen then an equivalent grove of trees and prevents soil erosion. It can grow by up to one metre per day, reaching full maturity within four years. It doesn't need to be replanted, as new shoots will spring from an extensive root structure often called the 'mother'. A commercially viable yield can be harvested in a far less destructive manner, using much less energy than other lumber products, and is a good replacement for hardwoods. Bamboo is nearly as strong as soft steel, making it a highly reliable building material.

The Hardys' mission is a holistic one, and their vision is expanding. Their daughter Elora Hardy has returned to Bali to lead the development of a surrounding Green Village. Attracting residents from all over the world, the Green Village offers homes to like-minded people, who want to experience a life in harmony with the natural world. Though currently living on the grid, Green School and Village are working toward energy self-sufficiency, integrating solar, micro-hydro and bio-diesel systems. All their water comes from natural springs found on the property and grey water is passed into water gardens, where papaya and other fruit trees are planted. Composting toilets are also used to reduce water usage. Abstaining from any form of excavation, buildings follow the contours of the land. At Green School, the result is a collection of buildings that sit lightly on the 9 hectares (23 acres) of the site, on which gardens grow food for the 250 students – a number that is itself continuing to grow. *Maya Suess*

John and Cynthia Hardy

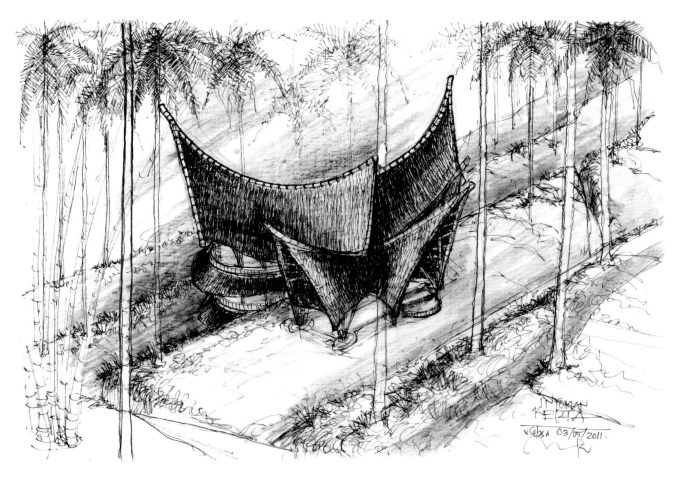

Bamboo is a flexible building
material and can be used to
create linear structures, such as
some of the individual houses in
Green Village (this page) as well as
the circular spaces of the Green
School (opposite).

Green School

John and Cynthia Hardy

Green Toys™ products are made entirely from recycled milk jugs, saving energy and ensuring they are free from toxic components.

Robert von Goeben
and Laurie Hyman
—
San Francisco, CA
USA
—
2007–present

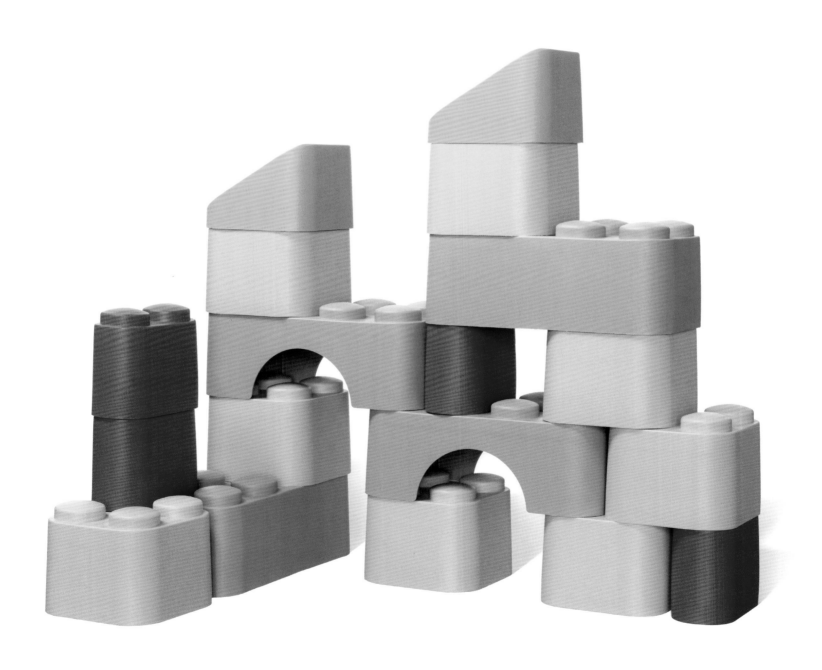

Amid recurring recalls, toxic paints and choking dangers, buying toys can seem like a hazardous activity. For parents, the safety of their children is paramount, but they are also increasingly concerned that the consumer choices they make today will impact negatively on their children's future world. It is in this new marketplace, in which environmental concerns play a growing role, that Green Toys Inc. aims to make a difference with toys and other child-friendly products that parents know are safe and which are made exclusively from recycled plastics.

Green Toys Inc. is the brainchild of Robert von Goeben and Laurie Hyman. Recognizing that toys can be fun and safe as well as environmentally and ethically responsible, they set out to make products with a positive impact on human and environmental health. The company is based in San Francisco, California, home to strict laws concerning product safety and environmental standards. The toys are produced locally, from local materials. Taking advantage of California's sophisticated recycling infrastructure, the raw plastic material is collected from discarded milk jugs, processed by local recycling companies and converted into one of the safest, cleanest and most non-polluting plastics available, called high-density polyethylene.

This raw plastic is then sent to a manufacturer also located in California. The concentration of manufacturing processes in California means that transportation costs are cut down and the number of miles that each toy travels to market is drastically reduced, lowering the energy required for distribution. This serves to limit the level of CO_2 and other greenhouse emissions of traditional toy manufacturing and shipping processes.

The toys are sold in recycled and recyclable corrugated boxes that minimize the use of material and feature no additional plastic wrapping. In addition to providing fun, high-quality products, part of the success of the business model comes from filling a void caused by customer dissatisfaction with cheap and often unsafe toys. Green Toys Inc. demonstrates a level of transparency in the manufacturing process, unique in the mainstream toy industry, by offering easy access to independent certifications of the toys' safety and environmental benefits.

Green Toys Inc. products include brightly coloured classics such as building blocks and kitchen sets and a number of stout trucks, boats and fire engines, with a small number of moving parts. They have no external paint coatings, minimizing possible contaminations of lead-based paint chips. The designs avoid the use of batteries, which are often filled with potentially noxious chemicals and heavy metals. Some products emphasize the underlying ecological mission of the company: the Indoor Gardening Kit is packaged with organic seeds for 'young green thumbs', and the Recycling Truck comes complete with sorting bins ('sort bottles, cans and paper or just have a blast', advises the Green Toys Inc. website.)

The innovation of Green Toys Inc. lies in its ability to use green technologies effectively on a local scale to provide a high-quality product that can compete in a multi-national toy industry. In price, its toy line is comparable to other brand-name toys that are often produced internationally and shipped large distances before finally reaching the consumer. The Green Toys Inc. approach shows the economic viability of innovative and sustainable thinking, where local ingenuity and resources can provide commercial, social, economic and environmental advantages for companies and consumers. *Daniel Ayat*

Robert von Goeben and Laurie Hyman

GreenPix Zero Energy Media Wall
is the world's largest carbon-neutral LED display. It runs at night using only the energy it collects during the day.

Simone Giostra & Partners
—
Beijing, China
—
2008

Unlike other large LED facades, each pixel of the GreenPix Media Wall is 3 x 3 ft (1 x 1 m) and displays at a low resolution, which means that GreenPix is not well suited for commercial advertising. The pointillist-inspired wall is better suited to abstract displays.

The facade of the Xicui Entertainment Complex in Beijing, known as GreenPix Zero Energy Media Wall, boasts the world's largest carbon-neutral LED display. Unveiled in 2008, the building comprises 2,292 RGB LED lights that transform the 2,230 m² (24,000 sq ft) envelope into a self-sufficient low-resolution media display. The scale of the installation makes it highly visible from great distances.

The net-zero spectacle of lights was designed by New York-based architecture firm Simone Giostra & Partners Architects (SGPA); global engineering firm Arup provided lighting and structural advice for the project. To achieve the massive low-resolution screen, SGPA and Arup, along with German manufacturing firms Schüco and SunWays, developed a new technology that laminates polycrystalline photovoltaic cells and embeds them into a glass curtain wall. Under the supervision of the design team, Chinese manufacturer SunTech produced the first glass solar panels that make up GreenPix.

The 550 m² (6,000 sq ft) of photovoltaic cells are distributed over the 12-storey building at varying densities to maximize natural light and shade where required. The photovoltaic cells transform excessive solar radiation during the day into energy that is used to power GreenPix at night. This not only reduces heat gain within the structure, but it also allows the media wall to be a self-supporting organic system that consumes no energy from the grid. Because the power of the display is dependent on weather conditions, GreenPix visually reinforces the delicate balance between resources and the scale and pace of production.

The urban intervention achieves its poetic commentary by engaging the public through its dynamic site-specific and locally relevant content, as well as its responsive light display. The screen is controlled through a flexible computer program that has three display modes. The first mode is based on simple visitor interactions. Infrared cameras translate human movement into abstract visual designs. The second mode is based on the environment. The pressure-sensitive glass panel feeds input, such as the speed and direction of the wind, into the program to create a fluid display.

The software allows the first two modes to display real-time reaction. By enabling the display to communicate information about the unique circumstances of a specific moment in time, GreenPix establishes a new relationship between facade and environment while bringing to life the activity and behaviour of the building. The third mode plays video art by Chinese, Japanese, European and American artists. The fluid light patterns of the default video, a piece by the artist Jeremy Ratsztain, mirrors the daily energy performance of the system. Located near the site of the Beijing Olympics, GreenPix was designed to reinforce Beijing's image as an innovative urban centre. *Bareket Kezwer*

Simone Giostra & Partners

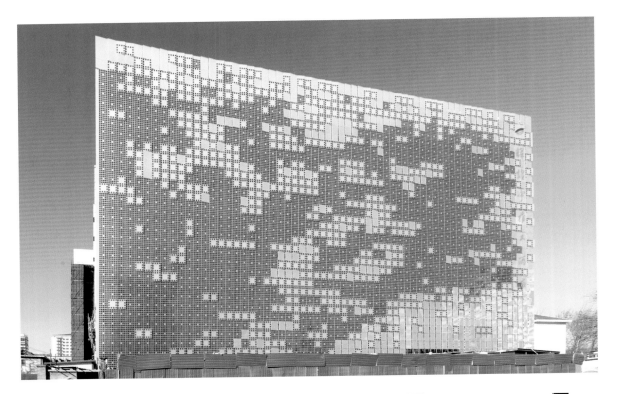

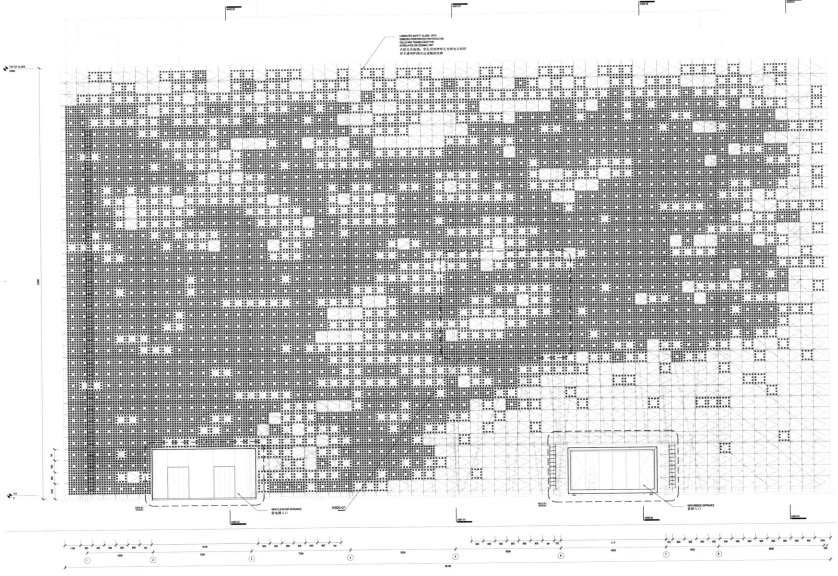

GreenPix Zero Energy Media Wall

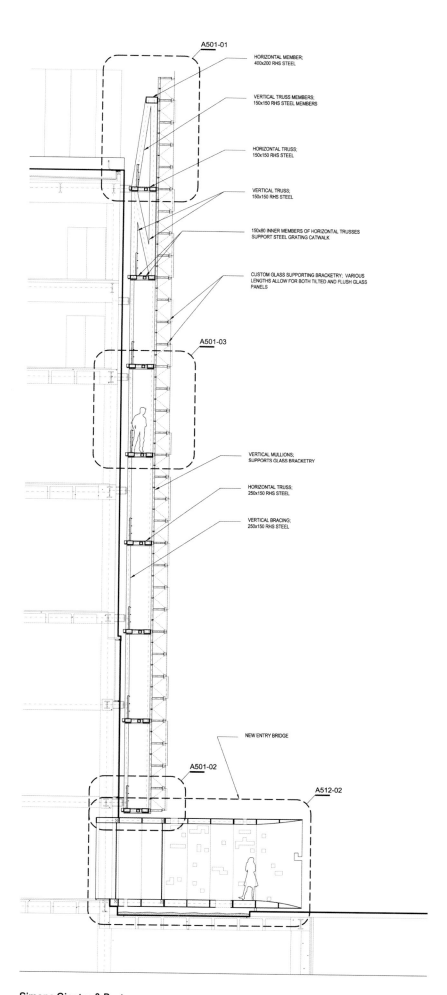

A501-01

HORIZONTAL MEMBER;
400x200 RHS STEEL

VERTICAL TRUSS MEMBERS;
150x150 RHS STEEL MEMBERS

HORIZONTAL TRUSS;
150x150 RHS STEEL

VERTICAL TRUSS;
150x150 RHS STEEL

150x80 INNER MEMBERS OF HORIZONTAL TRUSSES
SUPPORT STEEL GRATING CATWALK

CUSTOM GLASS SUPPORTING BRACKETRY; VARIOUS
LENGTHS ALLOW FOR BOTH TILTED AND FLUSH GLASS
PANELS

A501-03

VERTICAL MULLIONS;
SUPPORTS GLASS BRACKETRY

HORIZONTAL TRUSS;
250x150 RHS STEEL

VERTICAL BRACING;
250x150 RHS STEEL

NEW ENTRY BRIDGE

A501-02

A512-02

Simone Giostra & Partners

The layout of the photovoltaic cells optimizes the building performance by reducing the energy required to maintain a comfortable internal temperature. The photovoltaic cells are strategically distributed over the 12-storey building facade.

Built of bamboo, sand, coconut palm fronds and reclaimed rubble, the **Guludo Eco Resort** meets the luxury requirements of its guests without using electricity.

Kilburn
Nightingale
Architects
—
Quirimbas
National Park,
Mozambique
—
2006

Bandas serve as guest rooms at the resort (opposite). The frames of the buildings are made of bamboo and the roof is made of coconut palm fronds (this page).

Guludo Beach Lodge, located in Quirimbas National Park, along the northern coast of Mozambique, promotes co-founders Amy and Neal Carter James's belief that high-quality low-quantity tourism can protect the ecosystem while alleviating rural poverty through sustainable development.

The resort is designed to create the minimum environmental impact while helping the local economy by using regionally sourced materials, methods and labour. British firm Kilburn Nightingale Architects designed the resort according to the vernacular building tradition. The local community was consulted throughout the design process to gain local insight and ensure the scale and materials of the resort were appropriate and respectful of Guludo's culture and landscape.

The resort is laid out along the beach in a similar pattern to the layout of the local village. A series of *bandas*, free standing huts, radiate north and south along the beach from a cluster of public buildings organized around a central courtyard. A covered dining hall gives travellers a panoramic view of the ocean as they dine on local cuisine. Each *banda* includes a bedroom and lounge area which opens onto a shaded verandah looking onto the sea. The large shaded interior of each structure has no interior walls to allow the breeze to flow unobstructed through the open area. The roof is made from coconut palm fronds, tied into a batten and laid down like tiles. The walls are built either from sun-dried mud blocks or from a bamboo framework filled with reclaimed rubble, sand and lime; both techniques have been developed from local traditions.

The bamboo is tied together either using woven grass or a fibre made from the nylon reinforcement of discarded car-tyres. These techniques are durable, but also familiar to the locals so repairs can be made quickly and easily if needed. The structural bases are made from a stand of woven bamboo and a thin layer of the lime cement. Ceramic floors are made with tiles crafted by local women's groups. The walls of the bedroom area are layered with woven grass screens and mosquito nets. All the furniture in the resort is made on site in the lodge's workshop. The alfresco bathroom facilities include an outdoor shower enclosure made from perforated coconut shells, which allow water to trickle through. Rather than using taps, the water comes from a borehole and is warmed by the sun. Dry composting toilets, purpose designed and locally made, allow human waste to be used as a fertilizer. The position of each *banda* optimizes the cooling effects of the sea breeze and maximizes natural ventilation and shading. Independent from any service or energy infrastructure, effective passive design allows Guludo to meet the guests' comfort requirements without using electricity, air conditioning or plumbing.

Through a commitment to sustainable and fair labour and development, Guludo ensures the local population benefits from tourism. By purchasing locally, employing locals, providing positive working conditions and creating opportunities for skill development, Guludo demonstrates how tourism, the world's biggest industry, can be a catalyst of sustainable development that nourishes local communities and respects the ecosystem. *Bareket Kezwar*

Habana Outpost is one of the greenest restaurants in the world, creating an eco-friendly dining experience for all.

Sean Meenan
—
New York, NY
USA
—
2005

Diners at Habana Outpost pick up their meals at a red food truck in the courtyard (opposite). The solar-panel awning and roof of the restaurant collect rainwater, which is reused to flush the bathroom's toilets and to water plants both inside (left) and outside the restaurant. Orders can be placed and ideas given to the staff at the counter (right).

'You get more bees with honey', says Sean Meenan. That's how he describes his approach to sustainable design and the restaurant business, which can be seen in a holistic project at Habana Outpost, his Mexican-Cuban 'eco-eatery' in Brooklyn. 'People really enjoy being here', he continues. 'They're having fun, smiling – that's how you hook people. When people try to be righteous about environmentalism, it can turn people off. That's the opposite of what we do here.'

Meenan opened Habana Outpost in 2005, in Fort Greene, Brooklyn. He hadn't originally planned to create one of New York City's greenest restaurants – at first, he just wanted to install solar panels on the awning over the parking lot-turned-dining-patio: 'The sun's there, it's free, it makes energy', as he puts it. 'It's a no-brainer.' He also knew he wanted the restaurant to be a community gathering place, where people from all corners of the city and all walks of life would feel welcome. As it turned out, installing the photovoltaic array served as a kind of beacon to the neighbourhood, drawing eco-minded locals to the building site with suggestions for ways in which to create a better, greener restaurant. Meenan welcomed the input from the community. 'People came to me, enthusiastic', he says. 'It snowballed.'

As a result, Habana Outpost evolved into a sort of eco-incubator, where any feasible idea could be put into action and tested. The interior showcases a slew of recycled materials, including 'retired' racing sails and reclaimed wooden doors from a South American monastery. The front entrance is panelled in wheatboard, a material that resembles plywood and is made from wheat stalks and water-based glue. All the tableware is biodegradable: the plates are made of sugarcane fibre; the cups are PLA, a 'plastic' made of corn, and the cutlery is crafted from potato starch. After diners finish eating, they are asked to bring their tableware and food scraps to the do-it-yourself composting and recycling station, tucked under the solar array.

The restaurant collects, sanitizes, filters and stores rainwater from its roof and solar panels, using it to flush toilets and water the on-site garden. This water recycling system was designed and built by local architecture students participating in Urban Studio Brooklyn – a programme sponsored by Meenan to give students hands-on experience of designing and building green structures.

Meenan sees Habana Outpost as an ongoing project, and continues to respond to community input and push green technologies forward. In 2006, he installed a light pipe chandelier, designed by Atom Cianfarani, which uses panels mounted on the restaurant's storefront to focus sunlight into cables made of optical fibres. A special lens then radiates the light inside, without the use of electricity or bulbs. More recently, the restaurant made the switch from state-of-the-art fluorescent lights – which are up to 10 times more energy-efficient than traditional incandescent bulbs – to an even more energy-efficient cold cathode lighting system, a new generation of neon lighting with a fuller, warmer spectrum of light that requires just 15 per cent of the electricity required by incandescent bulbs.

The green mission has carried over into Meenan's personal life as well. These days, he drives a restored 1965 Lincoln Continental convertible that runs on discarded vegetable oil from his restaurants. 'When people realize that it smells like French fries, they start asking questions', he says. That gives him an opening – a chance to talk about his eco-eatery's mission and the car's environmental perks. It gets 48 km (30 miles) to the gallon, and its emissions contain no sulphur and low levels of carbon monoxide. 'My car gets a lot of love', Meenan reports. 'It gives people a sense of hope, and opens up possibilities that are off most people's radar. It's a win-win situation.' Much like Habana Outpost itself.

Jaime Gross

Sean Meenan

The **Halley VI British Scientific Research Station** is the greenest building in Antarctica. It can be moved across the rapidly changing landscape and, at the end of its lifespan, removed without a trace.

Hugh Broughton Architects
—
Brunt Ice Shelf, Antarctica
—
2006–12

Halley VI British Scientific Research Station

Halley is the most southerly research station operated by the British Antarctic Survey (BAS). Evidence of a man-made hole in the ozone layer was first discovered here in 1985. The station is located on the 150 m (490 ft) thick Brunt Ice Shelf where temperatures drop to –50°C (–58°F) in winter, and hardly ever rise above freezing in summer. Its coastal location means the site is regularly buffeted by winds in excess of 100 kph (62 mph). In addition to the cold, there is the dark; the sun does not rise above the horizon for 105 days of the year.

Designed by engineer AECOM and Hugh Broughton Architects, Halley VI will sustain the lives of the scientists permanently occupying one of the most hostile and remote places on earth. In addition to coping with the extreme climate, Halley VI also complies with the strict requirements of the Protocol on Environmental Protection to the Antarctic Treaty, so its environmental impact is minimal. As a result, the research station generates its own heat and power, consumes a minimal amount of water and processes all of the waste it generates. And when the station finally reaches the end of its life, it is designed to be removed without leaving a trace.

Construction of Halley VI is due to finish in January 2012. As its name suggests, Halley VI is the sixth incarnation of the research station that has been present on the continent since 1956. The first four bases were devised to be buried by snow, over 1 m (3 ft) of which falls on the site each year. These bases lasted approximately 10 years apiece before becoming entombed. The fifth incarnation was completed in 1992, yet unlike its predecessors, it was built on extendable legs so that it can be raised above the snow. Although successful as a design, this base is located on an ice shelf that flows out to sea at a rate of 400 m (1,300 ft) a year.

After almost 20 years, Halley V is now so far from the mainland that the ice shelf is in danger of 'calving', with the distinct possibility that the station will end up on an iceberg, giving rise to the need for Halley VI.

The important difference between Halley VI and its predecessors is that the new station is built on hydraulic legs, which are mounted on giant skis. The station comprises seven blue accommodation, science and life support modules, each with a floor area of 150 m^2 (1,600 sq ft). These highly insulated modules are designed to be adaptable to allow for easy conversion as the research programme evolves. At the heart of the station lies a red, two-storey, 470 m^2 (5,000 sq ft) communal module. This is clad with vertical and inclined glazing and translucent silica-based insulation panels to provide a comfortable space for group dining and socializing.

Each module's extendable legs will enable it to climb out of the snow, and modules can be towed on their skis so that the station can periodically be relocated further inland. This sustainable solution gives the research centre a far longer life than any of its forerunners.

The station's modules are arranged in a straight line, perpendicular to the prevailing wind; the science laboratories are at one end of the row and the accommodation modules are at the other. This arrangement ensures that the wind-driven snow accumulates in long tails on the module's leeward side, while the windward side is kept clear for access. The orientation also keeps the skis free of snow as a result of the scouring effect of the wind beneath the station. A total of 52 scientists and maintenance staff will occupy the base during summer. In winter, this number will decrease to a hardcore

The construction of Halley VI was under way in the 2009–10 season (opposite). The research station's modular design allows for easier assembly on site: the support modules were erected separately and then joined with the other modules to create the entire research centre (this page).

The interior of Halley VI is carefully designed to support both scientific research and the communal life of the scientists during their long stay. The colour selection and lighting of the interiors are designed to support the occupant's psychological well-being during the sunless months. The red central module (this page and opposite) provides a place for communal dining and socializing within the station.

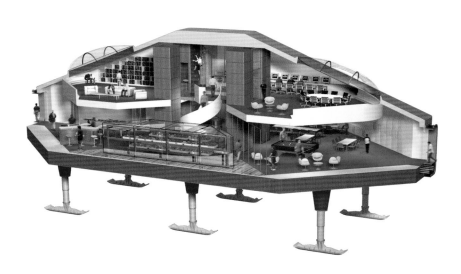

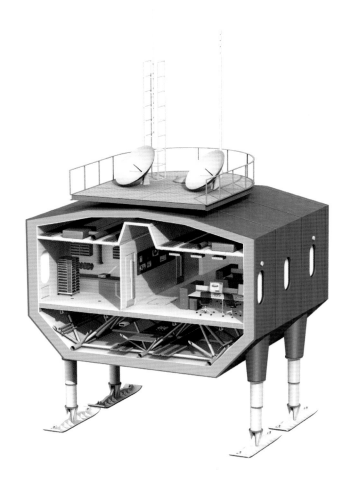

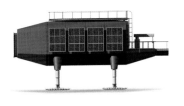

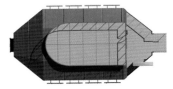

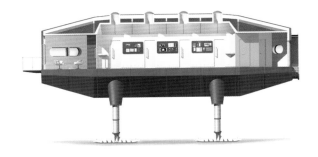

Halley VI British Scientific Research Station

staff of 16, who will remain at the station, cut off from the world for up to 10 months a year.

In such harsh conditions, technology is critical to the occupants' survival. The station has two energy modules, housing generators, electrical equipment, fire suppression systems, a water and sewage plant, as well as space for fuel storage. The modules are linked to enable the plant to operate efficiently. However, if a catastrophic fire were to destroy one of the modules, the remaining units would have sufficient capacity to keep the station running.

Six generators provide the station's electrical power. They burn aviation fuel, which remains liquid down to a temperature of –47°C (–52.6°F), yet provides 90 per cent of the energy of conventional diesel. Fuel for the generators is transported across thousands of miles, so the designers have minimized the base's energy use. Cooling water from the generators is reused to heat the accommodation through the radiators and ventilation system.

Heat from the generators melts snow in a purpose-built tank to produce water for the station. This process adds to the base's energy footprint, so even though Halley VI is built on ice, water conservation is a key consideration. Scientists on this station will consume about 50 litres (11 gallons) of water per day – about half the level of its predecessor. To minimize water use, aerating taps and showers with reduced flow heads are fitted; consumption is also reduced via a vacuum toilet system, similar to the type used on aircraft. Even the station's laundry has

been designed to be water-efficient. There is provision for the installation of solar panels and if tests are successful, they will heat water in the summer months, when the station is fully occupied and bathed in continual daylight. During the winter, however, there is insufficient light for the units to function effectively.

The base's lighting system also minimizes energy use. LED lamps provide external lighting, but because of the low temperatures, the lamps appear up to 30 per cent brighter than usual. The latest long-life fluorescent lamps illuminate the interior because they are more energy-efficient and produce a better quality light. To maintain the scientists' psychological well-being, every bunk is provided with a wall-mounted bed-head panel fitted with a special lamp that simulates daylight as part of the user's wake-up call. These lamps stimulate the body's production of mood-enhancing serotonin.

Under the Protocol on Environmental Protection to the Antarctic Treaty, the dumping of waste on land or sea is prohibited. Therefore, both human and food waste is dried in special centrifuges, before being burned in an incinerator; the heat produced by the process is used to heat the station. Recyclable waste is separated, compacted and bagged for transport so that it can be shipped off the continent annually by the supply ship. In fact, the design treads so lightly on the frozen continent that the only waste left on the ice is treated waste water, but even this is purified to European bathing standards before being discharged. *Andy Pearson*

Harmonia 57 has an exterior that literally grows with the surrounding city of São Paulo, breathing fresh air into one of the world's largest metropolitan areas.

Triptyque
—
São Paulo, Brazil
—
2008

Harmonia 57 opens up
to the neighbourhood with
its adjustable exterior screens
(opposite) and its interior
courtyard allows for sunlight
and air circulation throughout
the building (this page).

The French-Brazilian architects of Harmonia 57, a shop that was originally built as an artist's studio in a creative neighbourhood on the western side of São Paulo, derived the name of their firm from the term 'triptych', which describes an artwork divided into three sections, parts or panels. Both Triptyque's practice and their projects strive for a complexity that comes from distinct elements that, working together, form a greater whole.

Acting like a living, breathing organism, Harmonia 57 forms a complex ecosystem that treats and reuses rainwater on site, mitigating some of the high temperatures of the tropical climate and utilizing Brazil's heavy rainfall to its advantage. The building is divided into two main blocks joined by a metal footbridge above an internal plaza, which opens like a clearing and acts as a meeting place. The front block is raised and floats above the ground on piers, whereas the rear block is solid, with a smaller volume, almost like a bird-house, perched on the roof.

Large, operable windows and shutters, as well as many terraces, give the building a feeling of openness. The structure is made of organic concrete, which absorbs water with pore-like niches that hold a variety of plant species. As a result, the entire building has a planted facade, irrigated by a misting system. This external vegetal layer acts like an additional skin, buffering the interior against external noise and heat. The choice of plant species for the walls was dictated by both practical and aesthetic considerations: some species create shade whereas others crawl over the surface of the building to provide a buffer of humidity for other plants.

Harmonia 57 also has a fully integrated, yet technically simple, hydro-system of pipes, collectors and tanks, which are integral to the architecture. Pipes take the form of handrails, for example, allowing the building's rainwater and grey water to be reused for the irrigation system and toilets, and to prevent uncontrolled run-off from seeping into the ground. Any surplus of water is collected and stored in three shells located on the ground, which prevent water from flooding the street during periods of intense rainfall.

The building's interiors are exposed through porous facades and although the interior spaces are well-finished with clear and luminous surfaces, the structure appears to be inside-out, with the pipelines running like veins and arteries across the exterior walls. A green roof generates fresh air and provides for comfortable thermal conditions inside the building, reducing the need for air conditioning. The building's environmental performance here develops into a new aesthetic: a sophisticated low-tech approach in which the performance becomes integral to the architecture.

Harmonia 57 is a building that breathes, sweats and adjusts itself. The plants and the concrete substrate they occupy create a dialogue between the built and the natural. Clearly, Triptyque's evocation of the building as a living creature is not merely a poetic statement. The name of the building comes from the Harmonia street, where it is located, but fortuitously, it is also a harmonious work of art – an arrangement of parallel narratives that present a continuous and progressive story. *Lukas Feireiss*

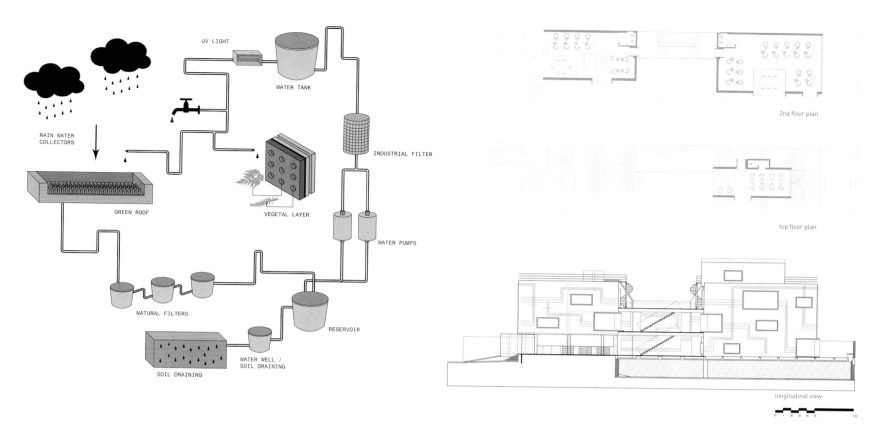

RAIN WATER COLLECTORS

UV LIGHT

WATER TANK

INDUSTRIAL FILTER

GREEN ROOF

VEGETAL LAYER

WATER PUMPS

NATURAL FILTERS

SOIL DRAINING

WATER WELL / SOIL DRAINING

RESERVOIR

2nd floor plan

top floor plan

longitudinal view

Triptyque

The **Hawaii Preparatory Academy Energy Lab** is 100 per cent water neutral and it uses only 8 per cent of the electricity it produces.

Flansburgh
Architects
—
Kamuela, HI
USA
—
2010

Being sustainable not only means developing new systems that work in harmony with the natural world, but also passing on environmental stewardship to future generations. Educational institutions that teach programmes in sustainability are beginning to practice what they preach by erecting facilities that are pioneers of green design. One such example is the graceful Energy Lab at the Hawaii Preparatory Academy, designed by Boston-based architectural firm Flansburgh Architects.

A high-school science building focusing on the study of alternative energy, the Energy Lab stands on the cutting-edge of sustainability – and is only the third building to be awarded the Living Building Certification from the International Living Future Institute. The Living Building Challenge is an emerging framework, philosophy and tool for designers and architects to define and execute advanced measures of sustainability in any project scale or type.

Originally a grey field area where the Hawaii Preparatory Academy dumped construction waste, the land is now a site of environmental restoration. Set on a steep hillside outside of Waimae, on Hawaii's big island, the lab is integrated into the majestic landscape, utilizing all of the natural benefits of its location. Its due-south orientation, combined with abundant trade winds that grace the hillside, create the ideal environment for highly efficient windmills, and thermal and photovoltaic panels.

Functioning at zero net energy, the 'Zero Plus' Energy Lab earns its nickname by using only 8 per cent of the energy that it produces, directing the remaining wattage into the campus grid. Energy usage at the lab is highly monitored by an intricate system of 480 sensors, which control various systems that adjust natural daylight and airflow. Through an integrated network of skylights, wood sun-screens and interior roller shades, light and heat are carefully monitored and controlled. Instead of traditional air-conditioners, the lab is cooled on hot days by an experimental radiant cooling system; water is transferred through thermal rooftop panels during cool evenings, then stored below ground until needed to cool the warm daytime air. In addition, ventilation systems adjust temperature and humidity to maintain maximum comfort and efficiency during every minute of the day.

Comprised of small project rooms, a laboratory and a large research centre, the Zero Plus Energy Lab serves as an unlimited tool for learning. Each innovative system offers a hands-on educational experience. In all the cutting-edge systems that the designers at Flansburgh Architects have developed for the Zero Plus Energy Lab, they have displayed an outstanding commitment to residents. Every encounter within the lab engages the highest level of ecologically sound design – the structure even captures and filters 25,000 litres (6,600 gallons) of rainwater a year for all of its potable drinking and waste water. With each school day at the Zero Plus Energy Lab, the students gain a deeper understanding of what it means to live in harmony with the planet, and know by experience that living sustainably is within reach. *Maya Suess*

The ohia wood column was reused (opposite). Wooden sun-screens control light and heat entering the building (left) and rainwater is stored in a white barrel under the building (right).

Hawaii Preparatory Academy Energy Lab

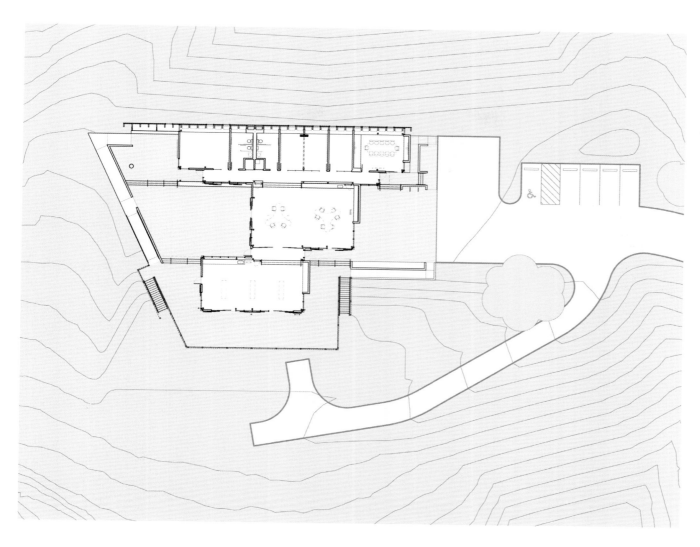

The southern orientation of the building allows for collection of solar energy from the roof (opposite). Outdoor areas are sheltered from the northeast trade winds, which are harnessed for the building's ventilation system (bottom).

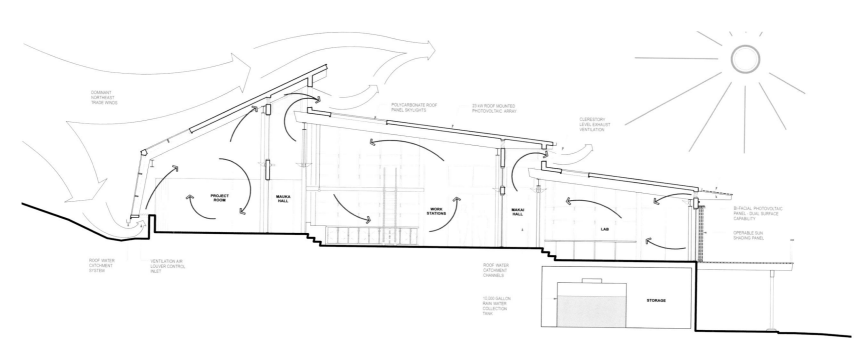

DOMINANT NORTHEAST TRADE WINDS

POLYCARBONATE ROOF PANEL SKYLIGHTS

23 kW ROOF MOUNTED PHOTOVOLTAIC ARRAY

CLERESTORY LEVEL EXHAUST VENTILATION

BI-FACIAL PHOTOVOLTAIC PANEL - DUAL SURFACE CAPABILITY

OPERABLE SUN SHADING PANEL

PROJECT ROOM

MAUKA HALL

WORK STATIONS

MAKAI HALL

LAB

ROOF WATER CATCHMENT SYSTEM

VENTILATION AIR LOUVER CONTROL INLET

ROOF WATER CATCHMENT CHANNELS

10,000 GALLON RAIN WATER COLLECTION TANK

STORAGE

Flansburgh Architects

The **High Line** reclaims 22 blocks of abandoned railway in downtown New York, turning it into an elevated urban park and a vital public space.

James Corner Field Operations and Diller Scofidio + Renfro

—

New York, NY USA

—

2009–present

Snaking through 22 blocks of downtown New York, the High Line park is a unique reuse of a decrepit industrial folly: the High Line Railway, built in 1934. The line was commissioned when the West Side Cowboys – employed to ride in front of street-level trains with warning flags – failed to prevent 10th Avenue from turning into 'Death Avenue'. This 20 km (13 mile) long line travelled through buildings, so that goods could be transported directly inside warehouses. Eventually, the effects of the Great Depression and interstate trucking rendered the line obsolete. Services continued to run as late as 1980, but after its last delivery of frozen turkeys, the High Line closed its tracks.

In the 1990s, the line became famous among more adventurous New York explorers and drought-tolerant grasses, bushes and even trees sprouted through the gravel on the tracks. Two such explorers, Robert Hammond and Joshua David, formed the Friends of the High Line in 1999, to block Mayor Rudy Guiliani's demolition plans and turn the High Line into a raised park stretching throughout the city. Some 720 teams from 36 countries entered the competition to transform the railway, which was won by landscape architects James Corner Field Operations and architects Diller Scofidio + Renfro. Both firms are well known for their interdisciplinary approaches, and they were joined on the project by the influential Dutch garden designer, Piet Oudolf, who focuses on the structure of plants rather than their colour, and factors the ageing and changing of plants over seasons into his horticultural arrangements.

The design took the wild growth forming along the line as inspiration, offering grasslands, sundecks, water features, public spaces, art installations and even performance spaces – creating not only a park, but a cultural focal point in New York. The High Line Park has been described as a key example of 'agri-tecture', the fusion of agriculture and architecture. Building methods and engineering were considered alongside decisions that incorporate the choice and arrangement of plants into a harmonious whole. Particular species of plants were chosen for the park to reflect the natural landscape of the east coast of the United States, and to make this less manicured and closer to the wilderness that originally took over the tracks.

Rails were removed but their locations were carefully mapped so that their elements could be returned to their original locations, and new materials were not required. Benches, which appear to emerge from sleepers, are formed of Ipe timber and have been carefully sourced from maintained forests, certified by the Forest Stewardship Council, ensuring that materials come from a sustainable source and will not have a detrimental impact on the ecology of another area. Energy-efficient LED lights illuminate the park and the street below.

Offering previously unobtainable views of the Hudson River, the park provides urban regeneration to the surrounding areas and proves that nature, architecture and landscape design can have the most environmental and social benefits when designed together. *Rob Fiehn*

James Corner Field Operations and Diller Scofidio + Renfro

Plants on the High Line are sustainably fertilized with a compost tea, which is brewed from a mixture of natural fish fertilizer and flour or molasses. The original railway tracks are retained in some places. Set around them are new, tapered concrete planks, which allow the plants to grow without blocking access (opposite). This recreational atmosphere is a welcome addition to the neighbourhood, which contains both commercial (top) and residential (bottom) buildings.

James Corner Field Operations and Diller Scofidio + Renfro

The vast public park underneath the **Horizontal Skyscraper Vanke Centre** has a network of pools that recycle the building's grey water.

Steven Holl
Architects
—
Shenzen,
China
—
2009

The landscaping of the site plays an integral role in the complex (opposite). Grass-covered mounds house interior spaces including cafés, auditoriums and restaurants (this page).

Suspended on eight cores, spaced 50 m (164 ft) apart, the Horizontal Skyscraper in Shenzen, designed by Steven Holl Architects, climbs across the South China countryside. With 360-degree views afforded from glass cubes that are suspended underneath the structure, the building floats above a landscaped garden, featuring a network of inhabitable mounds, pools, walkways and colourful seating areas. Small restaurants and cafes are also set among the garden. With moisture emanating from the pools and the overhanging building forming a kind of canopy, a microclimate is formed within the garden space, encouraging the proliferation of plant life. Underneath this lush area, a conference centre, a spa and underground parking take advantage of the space below grade.

The structure of building is a high-strength concrete frame, supported by tension cables, bearing a load of 3,200 tonnes. Fully glazed facades afford views of lakes and mountains, while shading from solar gain is created with a system of dynamically controlled louvres. The eight legs that elevate this structure to its 35 m (115 ft) height limit also provide access to the different sections. Inside, the building is divided into three main programmes: a hotel, apartments and office space, all of which are connected by garden paths.

The roof of the building is covered by 130 m² (1,400 sq ft) of photovoltaic panels, enough to provide the facility with 12.5 per cent of its power. Areas not covered by solar panels feature large swathes of green roof. Water conservation was a key issue in such a verdant landscape and so the network of pools that help create the microclimate are provided by a system of grey water recycling. There is also an extensive rainwater harvesting system that irrigates the flora. Local materials, such as bamboo, have been used as much as possible and renewable materials were selected for the doors, floors and furniture throughout the building.

Steven Holl is concerned with a phenomenological approach to architecture – the experience of materials and our perception of their sensory properties. Therefore, Holl begins each project by exploring the specific site and examining the ways in which he can anchor an architectural intervention to its landscape. In this project, this approach has led to the careful selection of materials, for both their effect on experience and their impact on the environment. It has also led to the creation of an immense public garden, covering three quarters of the site area, inseparable from the experience of walking under the enormous building: a remarkable confluence of architecture and landscape. *Rob Fiehn*

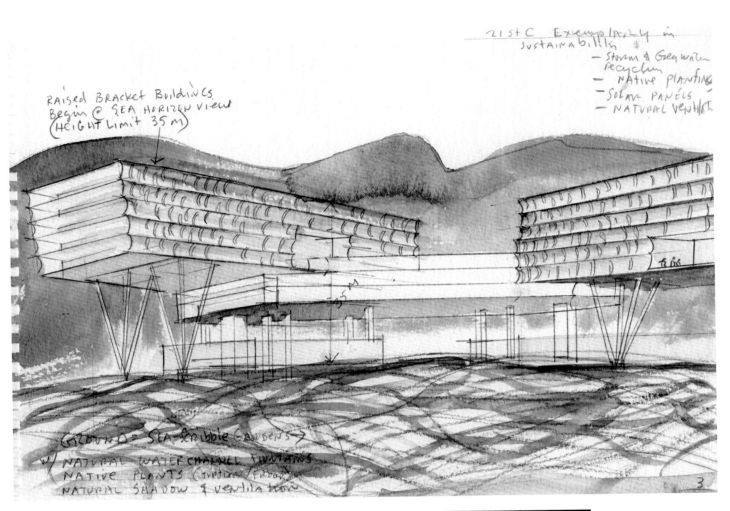

Raised Bracket Buildings.
Begin @ SEA HORIZON view
(HEIGHT Limit 35 m)

21st C Exemplary in
Sustainability
— Storm & Greywater
recycling
— NATIVE PLANTING
— Solar PANELS
— NATURAL VENTH

35 m

GROUND = SEA-scribble GARDENS
w/ NATURAL WATER CHANNEL "iwatiing
NATIVE PLANTS (water / frog)
NATURAL SHADOW & ventilation

3

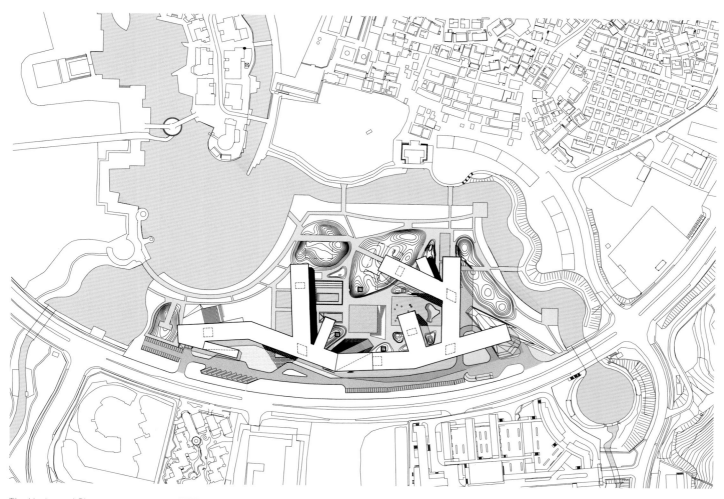

The Horizontal Skyscraper was designed to appear as if it were once floating on a higher sea that has now subsided (opposite, top). The concrete structure of the complex is supported on eight cores (opposite, bottom). A network of pools populate the gardens at ground level (top); public spaces are submerged below the gardens (bottom).

Steven Holl Architects

The **Hybrid Muscle** pavilion generates all the electrical power it needs from the work of a single large ox.

R&Sie(n)
with Philippe Parreno
—
Chang Mai,
Thailand
—
2003

In a dark Thai rice paddy, something is coming to life. Grunting and groaning, it flickers like a swarm of fireflies. Light begins seeping from an unidentified source, and a large structure starts to take shape against the night sky. This is the opening scene from Philippe Parreno's 2003 film *The Boy from Mars*, and it shows an awakening both mechanical and animal in nature: a large ox, tethered by a series of ropes and pulleys to a large, open pavilion clad in a semi-transparent flesh-like skin. This project, called Hybrid Muscle, is built entirely off the grid. The ox lifts a two-ton weight that, when dropped, causes compression in a generator that transfers mechanical energy into enough electrical power for 10 light bulbs, a laptop and cell phones.

The conceptual phase of the design is a result of a collaboration between the artist Philippe Parreno and the architectural firm R&Sie(n), commissioned by Rirkrit Tiravanija to occupy a plot of land that he owns as part of an artists' retreat. The space is intentionally designed to create a clash of worlds. Typical of Tiravanija's approach to art, the pavilion operates outside of the conventional institutional limits of the museum or gallery, and in what has been described by French art critic Nicolas Bourriaud as 'relational aesthetics', it serves to marry the art object to social interactions and daily life. While the project was designed to have the preliminary function as the set for Parreno's film, it was then intended to become a social centre open to locals and visiting artists.

Built on nine solid concrete slabs, the structure is designed for both solidity and comfort. Large wooden beams emerge at irregular angles from the concrete base, which is necessary for stability on the moist soil of a rice paddy. A porous skin made of sheets of elastomer is then stretched over these beams, shielding users from the elements and providing the natural ventilation that is all but obligatory in the Thai humidity. Like a giant lung, the skin of the pavilion heaves and flutters in the wind as users rest underneath it.

The hybrid approach to this structure is typical of the work of R&Sie(n). Established by François Roche in 1989, the firm's other partners are Stéphanie Lavaux and Jean Navarro, but they refuse individual attribution of their work, even going so far as to create a fictional architect figure for their firm: a pictorial morphosis of photographs of their faces into a single genderless form. R&Sie(n) often seek to challenge the term sustainability: working at the theoretical threshold of what constitutes the organic, their projects balance an environmental outlook with technological, mechanical and artistic inputs. In Hybrid Muscle, the architectural approach is described as a game between Parreno's film, Tiravanija's brief, and the structural requirements of creating a usable and comfortable space. The outcome of the game also depends on a dialogue with the organic elements of the environment, the idea of the animal as an engine, and the requirements for electrical power. As a result, it is hard to pin down whether the end result is more art than architecture, animal than structural, social than spatial, or organic than inorganic – but it is a structure that challenges architectural boundaries and the role of sustainable practices in shaping these boundaries. *Daniel Ayat*

The energy to light the pavilion comes from the ox's hard work (opposite). Elastomer sheets stretch over the skeleton of the pavilion, allowing it to glow after dark (this page).

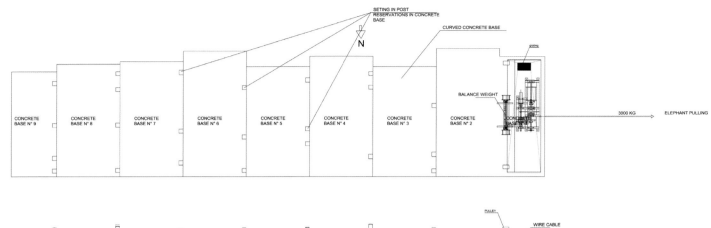

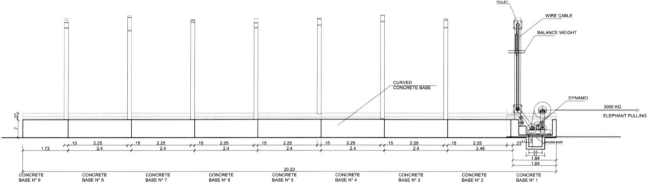

Wooden beams emerge from the curved concrete slab flooring that anchors the pavilion to the rice paddy (this page). The energy generated by the ox pulling against the anchored structure is stored and later fed to the lighting and mechanical equipment (opposite).

Hybrid Muscle

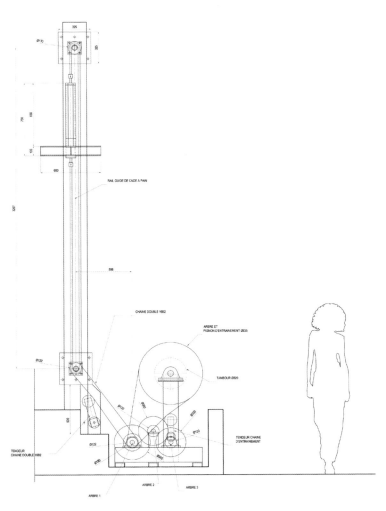

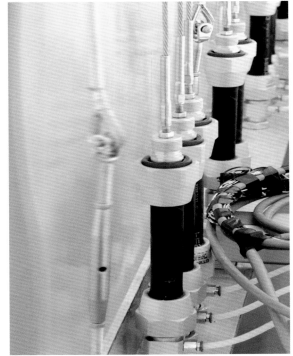

The **Impossible Wood Chair** is made with liquid wood, a recyclable fusion of plastic and wood fibres that can be melted down and re-moulded at the end of its life.

Doshi Levien
—
Udine,
Italy
—
2011

The overlapping bands of the chair are formed through injection-moulding, which creates a continuous form incorporating back, seat, and arms.

It is hard to imagine our world without plastic. It is everywhere and in everything – from milk jugs to mobile phones. Not to mention our landfills, waterways and soil. Our consistent short-term use of this durable material has resulted in a backlog of synthetic materials in the environment. This is the backdrop to the introduction of the Impossible Wood Chair by the London-based design team Nipa Doshi and Jonathan Levien of Doshi Levien – a chair that utilizes the positive elements of plastic (re-usability, durability and flexibility) while reducing its negative impact on the planet. By harnessing plastic's good qualities, Doshi Levien have managed to turn a synthetic, cold and environmentally destructive material into something fresh, beautiful and alive.

The chair is made of a moldable part-plastic part-wood material with unique visual and tactile properties. It offers a depth and texture that exhibits radically different aesthetic qualities to plastic; instead of a slick, homogenous surface, the Impossible Wood Chair has a worn-in, raw and earthy quality. It even emits the comforting smell of wood. The moldable wood material is a thermoplastic composite made of 80 per cent wood fibre and 20 per cent polypropylene. The chair is made through a conventional injection moulding process. The pressure and heat from the mould releases moisture contained in the wooden fibres, generating the smell and texture of the material. Essentially, thermoplastic composites are created by diverting old plastic into new materials that can be used for a wide range of products. At the end of their lifespan, these products can easily be melted down and reformed into new structural elements every bit as strong and beautiful as the original. The result is a continued cycle of production, construction, use, demolition and recovery, utilizing less energy and providing more value.

Impossible Wood Chair was designed for the Italian-based furniture company Moroso. Moroso believes that there is a close connection between the quality of an item and its impact on the environment. All of their products use clean, non-polluting production processes and materials that are natural or recyclable. This is underpinned by the concept that if you put enough thought into how a product is produced and what it looks like, you can influence a shift away from the short-term use of disposable household items into products that can be passed down from generation to generation.

By utilizing the recycling process to create something beautiful, functional and environmentally sound, the Impossible Wood Chair reminds us that the innovative and creative re-use of plastic is essential for cleaning up our earth. *Melanie Dowler*

Doshi Levien

The **Improved Clay Stove** is 60 per cent more efficient than a typical Sudanese stove, reducing smoke and air pollution and cutting the time needed for wood collection in half.

Practical
Action Sudan
—
Darfur,
Sudan
—
2001–present

Traditionally, Sudanese cooking is done on an open flame, a method of food preparation that has become increasingly problematic. The indoor air pollution caused by the smoke produced through open-flame cooking has become a leading cause of respiratory illness. The demand for firewood required to fuel cooking fires has depleted wood resources. As firewood has become increasingly sparse, women, the primary wood collectors, have faced an increased risk of getting attacked as they have ventured further out in search of firewood.

In 2001, Practical Action Sudan, a Sudanese-based NGO, began promoting the simple technology of the Improved Clay Stove to address these growing environmental and social concerns. The stove was adapted from an existing regional stove, and Practical Action standardized the indigenous practices and trained women and local pottery associations in the technique. Rather than creating a commercially available product that many would not be able to afford, the Improved Clay Stove is an affordable and accessible construction method, which allows the manufacturing and dissemination to be done safely and quickly.

The Stove provides Sudanese women with a method for constructing a stove specifically suited to their current cooking pot. The stove is made by gathering clay and mixing in an additive. The clay is built around the pot, on a base of three bricks (or one brick divided into three), which support the pot during cooking. After the pot has been removed, the surface of the stove is smoothed and after the stove has baked in the sun for about half an hour, an exhaust hole is cut in the side of the stove. This exhaust hole makes the stove more efficient by increasing airflow and allowing wood to be added during cooking without removing the pot. The stove does not require firing and is left to dry naturally.

The only requirements to construct an Improved Clay Stove are clay and one brick, making it a viable technology for those living in extreme poverty. By the end of 2003, more than 100,000 families had adopted the stove. But while the Improved Clay Stove was an improvement over traditional open-fire cooking, quality remained a concern. Practical Action worked with the stakeholders through their process of 'participatory technology development' to enhance the stove. Many stoves were producing an unsafe level of smoke, which was addressed by specifying that the distance between the bottom of the pot and the bottom of the stove be half the diameter of the pot. This minor adjustment ensures that the stove reduces smoke and air. The improvements also included a re-evaluation of the clay mixture used to create the stove. New guidelines take into account the natural make-up of the local clay and provide regional clay-to-additive ratios.

The combination of best cooking practices and a properly constructed stove is 60 per cent more efficient than any previous stove, cutting wood collection time by 50 per cent, or producing financial savings for those who purchase wood. By 2007, Practical Action had trained more than 3,000 Sudanese women in villages and camps, reducing the pressure on the depleting wood resources and contributing to the improved and sustainable livelihoods of the poorest communities. *Bareket Kezwer*

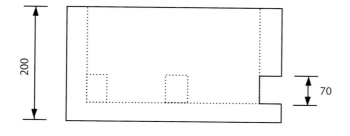

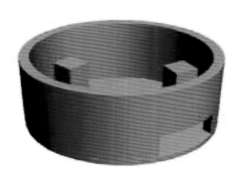

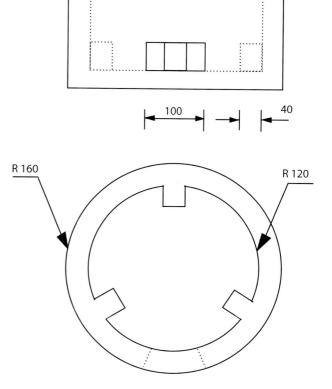

Made of three shipping containers and insulated with recycled cellulose and cork, the prefabricated **Infiniski Manifesto House** meets 70 per cent of its own energy needs.

James & Mau
Architects
—
Curacaví,
Chile
—
2009

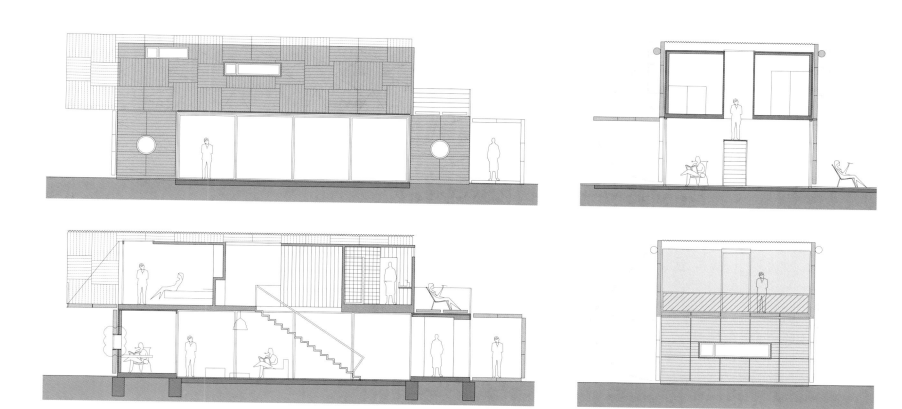

Wooden panels, covering stacked shipping containers, comprise the facade of the Infiniski Manifesto House.

The Infiniski Manifesto House, designed by James & Mau Architects, exemplifies the prefabricated modular system of Infiniski, a concept company specializing in sustainable architecture and construction. James & Mau's lead architects on the project, Jaime Gaztelu and Mauricio Galeano, are the founders of Infiniski.

Built in 2009, the 160 m² (1,720 sq ft) house incorporates recycled, reused and non-polluting materials. Three weather-resistant recycled maritime containers comprise its two-levels. One 12.2 m (40 ft) container on the ground floor has been cut into two parts and supports the two containers of the first floor. Thermo-glass panelling seals the central space formed by this bridge-like structure, thereby fashioning light-filled living and dining spaces. These glass walls slide open to the paved outdoor patio. The enclosed spaces created by the smaller containers serve as the kitchen, laundry and bathroom. Three bedrooms and one bathroom are located on the upper floor.

Situated in the coastal mountain range of central Chile's Melipilla Province, the surrounding climate is mild Mediterranean with a long and hot dry season in the summer and low temperatures and rainfall in winter. Bioclimatically designed, the house runs mostly on renewable solar energy. Wooden panels sourced from sustainable forests cover one side of the house and recycled mobile pallets cover the other; the pallets are self-opening and controlled by the temperature.

In cold weather they open, allowing the sun to heat the metal container walls. On warmer days, they close to keep the space cool. External solar covers are installed along the rooftop. Geothermal heat pumps help to facilitate heating and cooling. As a result of its alternative materials and systems, the house provides roughly 70 per cent of the energy it needs.

Among the house's many eco-friendly features is recycled cellulose and cork insulation. Other cast-off and environmentally mindful materials include recycled aluminium, iron, steel and paper; ecological painting and eco-label ceramics. Gaztelu and Galeano's minimalist design further integrates with the environment by way of minimal landscaping and complementary vegetation; in effect, enhancing the 'organic' appearance of the house. Adding to the modern look and feel are furnishings provided by the interior design companies Cómodo Studio and gt_2P, both based in Santiago de Chile.

Taking only 90 days to build, the Infiniski Manifesto House answers the call for innovative as well as efficient sustainable architecture. Infiniski's prefabrication system is faster than most other construction methods, reducing on-site pollution and other costs to the environment, such as fuel usage for material transport. Adaptive reuse of maritime containers also reduces costs to the client; in total the project cost £72,000 ($118,200) to build. What's more, in the future, the structure can be easily modified or enlarged as desired. *Nicole Caruth*

Infiniski Manifesto House

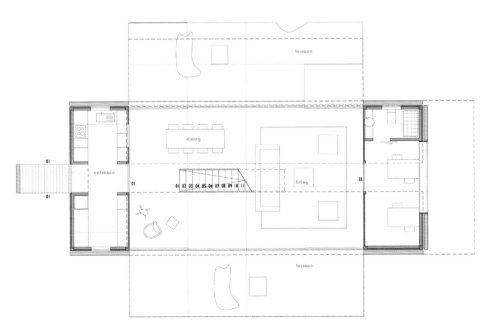

The public spaces of the house are located on the ground floor. The sides of the shipping containers on this floor have been partially removed and filled in with glass panels, some of which slide open, allowing the occupants to take advantage of the Mediterranean climate (opposite). When the sun is too intense, the wooden panels of the facade can be adjusted to provide shade (this page).

The **Integral House** is heated and cooled by 23 geothermal wells and the wood used in its construction was carefully selected using life cycle cost calculations.

Shim-Sutcliffe
Architects
—
Toronto,
Canada
—
2008

A reflecting pool wraps around the curved plan of the house, accentuating the fluidity of the plan layout (opposite). The fins of the facade prevent excessive heat from the sun from entering the house (this page).

Established in 1994, Shim-Sutcliffe Architects focus on the relationships between buildings and their natural surroundings. This extends to the larger environment, and their Integral House demonstrates a commitment to sustainable solutions for building requirements. The integral – the process whereby a curvilinear form is defined by a series of vertical line – is one of the definitive operations of calculus. The symbol of this theory is a thin, sweeping 'S' shape, the summa, which also resembles the F-hole of a violin. Built for the mathematician James Stewart, who is passionate about music and plays the violin, the Integral House can also be used as a performance space.

The house takes its name from the rear elevation, formed by a five-storey, undulating wall that faces a steep ravine. These curves are fully glazed and delineated by a system of linear wooden fins, providing solar shading and breaking up the view of the surrounding landscape. This elevation was nicknamed the 'summa wall' by the architects at an early stage in the design phase. Comparatively, the front of the house is a modest two-storey composition of an opaque, etched glass facade perched on top of a wooden base. The staggering of floors down the ravine side is testament to the ingenuity of the architects and echoes the forest paths that wind their way down the steep hillsides.

Upon entering the house, the visitor immediately encounters the double-height living room that also functions as the performance space. A grand staircase leads down to this area, with ample room allowing 150 guests access to this intimate concert hall. Visitors can also view performances from overlooking dining and living spaces that act as theatre-like balconies. Three concrete elements punctuate all five storeys of the house: a stairwell, a lift shaft and a chimney, reinforcing the mathematical relationship between the curve and vertical.

The heating and cooling of the house is provided by 23 geothermal wells bored into the ground. The ravine-facing facade is triple glazed, which optimizes energy efficiency (and also manages the acoustic requirements of a concert hall, located in a residential area), and solar gain is further mitigated by the vertical fins on the transparent walls. The wood that is used on the exterior and interior of the house was selected on life cycle cost calculations, which assess the environmental impact of a product based on its energy input and carbon footprint. The house engages with its immediate surrounding landscape by straddling the hillside and utilising the gradient to create dramatic interior spaces, while managing a sustainable relationship with the larger environmental context as well. *Rob Fiehn*

Integral House

The wood used on both the interior and exterior of the building echoes the surrounding forest and visually engages the surrounding landscape (opposite). Concrete elements punctuate the interior of the house and support the double height space that functions as both a living room and a performance space (this page).

The **Kamakura Passive House** introduces Japan to low-carbon living and uses only one fourth of the energy of a conventionally designed home.

Key Architects

Kamakura, Japan

2009

Kamakura Passive House

When Miwa Mori of Key Architects was hired to design a house for the Hasumi family in Kamakura City, she was presented with a creative challenge. Her client required that his house be powered exclusively by electricity, a stipulation of the mortgage he received from his employer: the Tokyo Electric Power Company. To meet the needs of her client, Mori arrived at the solution of constructing Japan's first Passive House.

The Kamakura Passive House brings the efficient use of natural resources, already characteristic of traditional Japanese architecture, into the twenty-first century. Contemporary Japanese homes have thin walls, typically constructed from particle board and single-pane glass windows in aluminum frames. Heating these structures during the winter and cooling them during the summer is energy-intensive and expensive. By contrast, the Passive House, a well-insulated building that maintains a comfortable internal temperature, eliminates the need for active heating and cooling systems.

Passive House, or Passivhaus as it is referred to at the Passivhaus Institut in Germany, is a special architectural certification, which requires the building to meet a specific kWh/m^2 per year energy profile, and uses about a quarter of the annual energy consumed by the average newly constructed home. To receive certification, a Passive House must meet budget restrictions, and is only considered cost-effective when the cost of construction, design, installation and operation of the house for 30 years does not exceed the cost of building a new home. The combination of energy conservation targets and budget requirements that is integral to Passive House standards creates an economically affordable model for constructing energy-efficient homes.

Each house is orientated to maximize exposure to the winter sun, while window overhangs prevent solar gain in the summer. Hot water is heated using renewable energy. A Passive House is constructed with thick walls to maximize insulation. The wooden exterior of the Kamakura House is insulated with organic wood, wool and foil to prevent the growth of mould during the humid season. The windows in the Kamakura House are triple-pane, fitted into wooden frames, and designed with minimum exterior joints to prevent heat loss. The tight seal captures naturally occurring heat from residents' bodies and heat from the building's energy-saving appliances.

To make sure the house does not fill with stale, recirculated air, a Passive House employs a mechanical ventilation system. Cool air is pumped into the house and warmed inside by the hot air being pumped out to a Heat Recovery Unit. The heat recovery rate is more than 80 per cent. As the ventilation system uses filters, the indoor air quality in a Passive House is excellent. Since moving into their new home, the Hasumi family noticed a dramatic drop in the frequency of asthma attacks. The higher cost of construction has been quickly recouped as the Kamakura Passive House only consumes about one third of the energy involved in running a typical house in Japan.

With one million new residential homes built annually in Japan and no current energy-efficiency requirements for these new homes, Mori hopes that the success of the Kamakura Passive House will encourage policy-makers to legislate well-insulated homes as the new standard in Japan. *Bareket Kezwer*

A staircase, accessed from the dining area, leads up to a roof deck (bottom left and opposite). The interior of the house (bottom right) maintains a comfortable temperature without active heating and cooling.

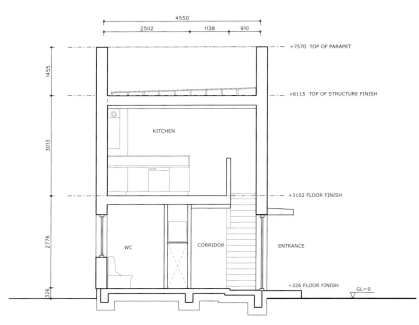

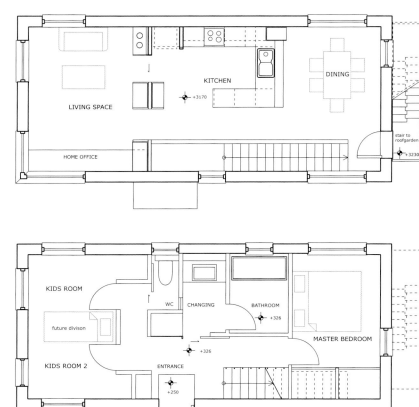

Old cardboard is ground down into a pulp and moulded in order to make the **Kraft and Solo Benches** and give the recycled material a new life.

Domingos Tótora
—
Brazil
—
2008–present

The use of material varies within Domingos Tótora's work: the Kraft Bench (opposite, top) celebrates its rough material, while the Solo Bench (opposite, bottom) is almost unidentifiable as cardboard.

Domingos Tótora, a Brazilian designer and native of the mountain town Maria da Fe, has a nearly obsessive interest in cardboard and the possibilites of its reuse.

One of his most widely known pieces, the Kraft Bench, exemplifies this devotion to sustainability by barely hiding the material. Slices of recycled cardboard pulp, 1 cm (½ in) in thickness, are held together with a water-based glue, proudly proclaiming their origins. The bench varies in width depending on the number of slices of cardboard used. Viewing the piece one can easily imagine the source material being put out on the streets of cities across Brazil for recycling: one man's trash is always another man's treasure. With a little imagination and care this refuse has been beautifully transformed into work that gracefully walks the line between art, craft and design.

Other work, like the Solo Bench – which was recently a nominee for Design of the Year by the Design Museum London – showcases the malleability and potential of the material and its ability to easily change form and texture. The Solo Bench has been finished and sanded so finely that it takes on the appearance of stone. Even on close inspection it is difficult to pick up on the fact that what you're seeing and touching is recycled cardboard. Only the color, a brownish hue familiar to anyone who has ever taken out the trash, hints at its origins.

Tótora has described the process by which his designs are realized as such: 'In a certified sustainable process, recycled cardboard is broken up into small pieces and turned into a pulp that serves as the base material for furniture, objects and sculptural pieces that are molded by hand, dried in the sun and finished to perfection. In this beautiful and labor-intensive process, the cardboard, which originated as wood, is essentially brought back full cycle by taking on a wood-like quality again. We believe sustainability happens through actions and not words'.

This practice might be seen as an outgrowth of Brazil's recent identity as the centre of a design practice focused on creative reuse, of which the most famous practioners are probably the Sao Pãulo-based Campana Brothers, Fernando and Humberto. Their Bambu Lamp, produced by the Italian manufacturer Fontana Arte, incorporated bamboo and industrially sourced metal and put Brazil back on the international design map, after it had largely disappeared in the 1970s and 1980s when the country had begun large scale production of cheap plastic pieces. The kind of work the Campanas did – a witty mix of Brazil's mid-century glory years and its more recent past as a maker of knock-offs – included not-so-subtle moves toward green design through the use of locally sourced materials.

Tótora's designs draw on this heritage, but both literally and figuratively smooth it out, dispensing with clever juxtapositions in favour of a clean elegance that only sometimes reveals its origins. The results hint at a future where waste might not exist. Could it be that there is a use for everything? In the hands of Domingos Tótora it certainly seems to be possible. *Andrew Wagner*

Craftsmen create the Solo Bench pieces by moulding them into place and sanding them smooth (this page). In the Kraft Bench, thin slices of recycled cardboard are pressed together and held with a water-based glue (opposite).

Domingos Tótora

Revitalizing a brownfield site, **Kroon Hall** replaces a decommissioned power plant and its bioclimatic design responds to seasonal changes.

Hopkins Architects
—
New Haven, CT USA
—
2009

The building's sophisticated lighting system keeps it bright when needed but turns off when no one is occupying the space.

Yale University's School of Forestry and Environmental Studies (FES) was founded in 1900. Today it is a leading centre for the academic investigation of the environment. Kroon Hall, the new FES building that opened in 2009, embodies the values of the school and its diversity of research and programmes. A global team of leaders in sustainable architecture and design including Hopkins Architects, Centerbrook Architects and Planners, Arup, Atelier Ten and Olin Partnership among others, worked together to create Kroon Hall, which demonstrates the latest in green building technology. The building, which was awarded a Platinum Leadership in Energy & Environmental Design (LEED) rating, uses approximately 50 per cent of the energy of a conventionally designed building of the same size. Kroon Hall, which has masonry on the outside and a timber box on the inside, includes office space for over 50 faculty and staff, three classrooms, a 175-seat lecture hall, a library, conference centre and a café. Similar functioning spaces are grouped together to reduce redundancy and the offices are modular to allow for future modification. The ribbed cathedral-like roof is built of douglas fir boards which were shaped using hydraulic pressure.

The demolition materials from the Pierson Sage Power Plant, the decommissioned building which previously occupied the site, were recycled. Kroon Hall is designed to minimize environmental impact and energy requirements through the use of recycled and future recyclable materials as well as sustainably harvested and manufactured materials. The stone used on the exterior of the building was harvested within 500 miles of campus. By replacing a former brownfield site, Kroon Hall enabled the creation of two new courtyard spaces for public gathering and discussion. All of the lumber used is FSC (Forest Stewardship Council) certified and the majority of it comes from Yale's own forest. The concrete is thermally inactive, the glass and insulation are low-e (low emissivity), and the paint is low impact.

The bioclimatic building requires user interaction and participation to optimize its performance, and responds to seasonal weather changes. The southern facing glass wall creates solar gain in the winter and is angled in a way to avoid direct sunlight during the summer. The north side of the lowest level of the building is underground, optimizing the inertia of thermal mass (which absorbs energy and regulates the building's inside temperature). The high thermal retention of Kroon Hall lowers the overall energy needs of the building. The design integrates a geothermal energy system that includes ground source heat pumps and a displacement air system. The arched roof is outfitted with south-facing photovoltaic solar panels and the building's water is heated using solar power. The glass walls on the northern and southern ends of the building ensure that the building is flooded with natural light. As the sun sets, an intelligently controlled artificial lighting system maintains a constant light level while sensors ensure lights are not on when no one is present. Manually operable windows increase natural air circulation.

The design also includes a rainwater harvesting system and cleaning pond to reduce the water consumption of the building. Rainwater runoff from the roof and ground are collected and then moved to a storage tank where it is mixed with extra water from geothermal wells. The water from the storage tank is recirculated through a surface treatment pond where aquatic plants further clean it. The water is then filtered and disinfected before it is used to flush toilets or irrigate the surrounding lawns.

The transformation revitalized the area of campus and creates a sense of unity among the existing FES buildings. Kroon Hall not only provides a centre for research and academic activity, but also acts as an inspiration to the entire Yale University campus. *Bareket Kezwer*

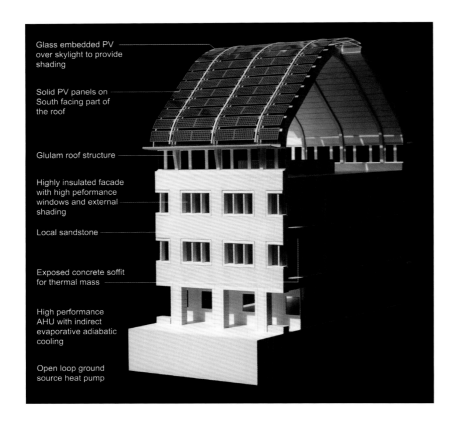

Glass embedded PV over skylight to provide shading

Solid PV panels on South facing part of the roof

Glulam roof structure

Highly insulated facade with high peformance windows and external shading

Local sandstone

Exposed concrete soffit for thermal mass

High performance AHU with indirect evaporative adiabatic cooling

Open loop ground source heat pump

Many of the materials in Kroon Hall (top left) were selected for their sustainability. The south-facing sloped roof is lined with solar panels (opposite, top). The pond is an active part of the stormwater reclamation system (opposite, bottom left). The narrow plan facilitates the building's ventilation (opposite, bottom right).

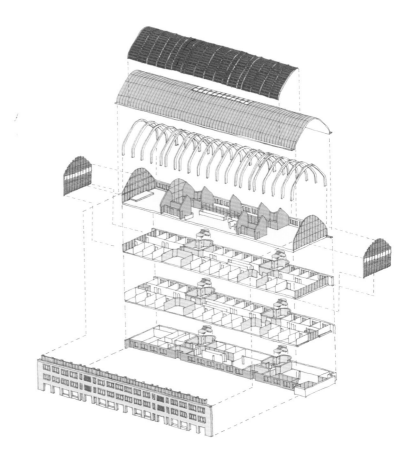

Key

1 Classroom
2 Core
3 Meeting room
4 Learning Centre
5 Library

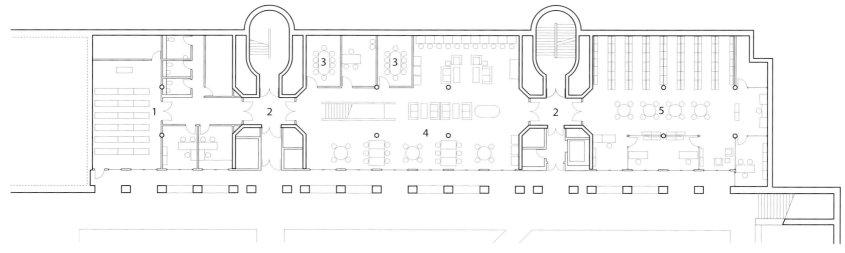

Landscape Park Duisburg Nord

reinvents a derelict and decaying industrial landscape, creating a vibrant, healthy communal asset: a public park.

The Landscape Park Duisburg Nord, designed by Latz + Partner, transforms an industrial blast furnace plant and its grounds into a new urban landscape and public park. Through careful intervention, Latz + Partner maintained the site's industrial heritage, while drastically rejuvenating its landscape into one that is both ecologically productive and culturally engaging.

The Landscape Park grew out of a state-sponsored initiative to redevelop a series of brownfield sites – contaminated, abandoned lands previously used for industrial purposes – which have the potential to be reused. Duisburg is situated in the Ruhr Valley in northwestern Germany.

The state government of North Rhine–Westphalia created the International Building Exhibition (IBA) at Emscher Park in order to address the need for large-scale brownfield redevelopment across the region and to mitigate the environmental damage left behind from heavy industry throughout the valley. Instead of implementing a top-down, centralized redevelopment strategy, IBA proposed the reuse of many dispersed sites within the Ruhr region. The Landscape Park Duisburg Nord is one of these projects.

The Landscape Park occupies almost 200 hectares (500 acres) of open land between the suburbs of Meiderich and Hamborn within Emscher Park. Here, the iconography of the ironworks and the Thyssen ironworks symbolize the region's industrial past. Among the objects occupying the site at first were blast furnaces, a gasometer, cooling tanks, railroad tracks and slag heaps. By re-imagining the potential for these artefacts, park visitors can gain an appreciation of the past while engaging with a sequence of regenerative landscapes, which create fresh recreational experiences as a result of the ecological transformation of the land.

Instead of demolishing the blast furnace tower, its reuse allows visitors to climb 70 m (230 ft) for a panoramic view of the park. A refurbished gasometer is now one of the largest artificial diving centres in Europe, and its cooling tanks have been transformed into lily ponds, complete with remediating plant ecologies. Alpine climbing gardens have been created inside former ore storage bunkers; railroad tracks have been converted into bicycle paths. A water park promotes the ecological regeneration of the Emscher Canal system, promenades and parks along railway lines connect the park with adjoining cities, and an active museum preserves the unique identity of the monumental steelworks. The Park even has its own farm, complete with goats and horses that graze next to a mill. A wilderness area originally abandoned as a no man's land between two highways has been preserved as one of the most advanced biotopes in the park.

Latz + Partner's poetic reuse strategies for the Landscape Park Duisburg Nord intentionally play upon the ambiguity between industrial and landscape park, creating an opportunity for visitors not only to reconsider industrial sites but more importantly to understand, through experience, the ways in which landscape architecture can define a sense of sustainable place.

Lisa Tilder

Latz + Partner

The Piazza Metallica (this page) is a prime example of the transformations in the park. Iron plates once used to cover casting moulds in the iron works now line the floor of the piazza. Other monumental artefacts include the blast furnices (opposite, top). Before the park was created, a ribbon of railroad ran through the site (opposite, bottom left); now the effects of the renovation can be viewed from the surrounding neighbourhoods (opposite, bottom right).

Landscape Park Duisburg Nord

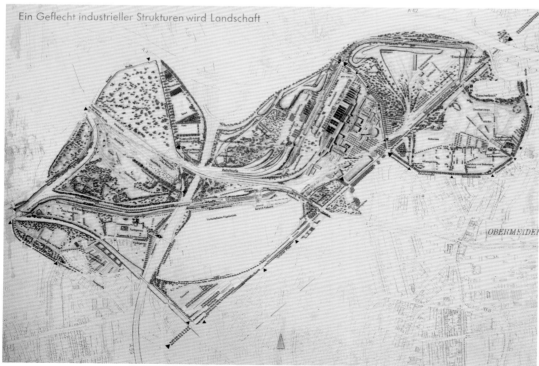

Ein Geflecht industrieller Strukturen wird Landschaft

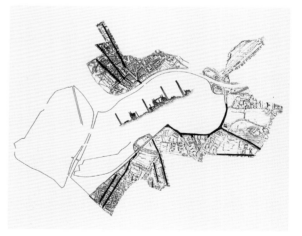

Latz + Partner

Using parabolic cooking dishes solely powered by the sun, the **Lapin Kulta Solar Restaurant** serves a menu that follows the path of the sun across the Arctic Circle.

Martí Guixé and Antto Melasniemi

—

Summer 2011

The parabolic-shaped cooking dishes prepare food directly with the sun's rays.

The Lapin Kulta Solar Restaurant is an epicurean celebration of the sun. The eatery and artistic installation is the brainchild of Martí Guixé, the self-proclaimed ex-designer who works in Barcelona and Berlin, and Antto Melasniemi, the Finnish hospitality and culinary expert. The restaurant made its debut in April during Milan Design Week at the Milan Triennale Design Museum. During the summer of 2011, the restaurant featured a menu that changed daily, according to the strength and path of the sun as it travelled across the Arctic Circle of Europe to Helsinki and Stockholm.

The kitchen consisted of a series of parabolic solar cooking dishes constructed by Guixé, Melasniemi and a team of volunteers. Each dish took five hours to make and could be used to prepare food for about 15 people. The design of the reflective parabolic aluminium dish directed sunlight on to the central cooking spot; by concentrating the sun's rays on to a smaller area, a higher temperature could be reached, allowing faster and more even cooking of the food when placed in a pot or pan in the centre of the cooking dish.

This method of cooking required direct sunlight and the dishes had to be manually repositioned to track the sun. The energy-conserving preparation method of the Solar Kitchen not only allowed the restaurant to function independently of the power grid, but also presented diners with food that incorporated the alternative energy structure into the meal. Using the sun instead of a traditional gas flame or oven changed both the taste and texture of the food produced, because the heat source fully immersed the food, rather than warming it from beneath as in a traditional stove.

The restaurant's concept required diners to approach their meal with a sense of flexibility and adaptability. Because the solar cooking dishes required direct sunlight, diners were subject to the improvisation of the chefs as they responded to the changes in daily weather conditions. Although local fare was always served, on a sunny day the restaurant's patrons could expect barbequed food, whereas on an overcast day tartar, sashimi or salad were on the menu. The restaurant was closed on rainy days. The immediacy of the cooking method created a model in which each meal at the restaurant provided a unique dining experience. Diners were invited to watch the cooking process and were introduced to a new culinary experience.

By cooking exclusively with the energy of the sun, Lapin Kulta Solar Kitchen Restaurant renegotiated the relationship between food and nature and allowed diners to observe the real-time response to food preparation. Lapin Kulta Solar Kitchen Restaurant succeeded in bringing together gourmet food, beer and art into an environmental experiment that challenged traditional perceptions of the kitchen. *Bareket Kezwer*

Martí Guixé and Antto Melasniemi

Lapin Kulta Solar Restaurant

The centre of the parabolic cooking dish can heat up cooking pots (opposite, top right) or containers for hot drinks (opposite, bottom). Chefs can easily check the progress of dishes (top left) and the resulting meals vary from day to day with the strength of the sun (top right). In April 2011, Lapin Kulta set up outside the Milan Triennale Design Museum (bottom).

Martí Guixé and Antto Melasniemi

The **Lean + Green Lightweight Wine Bottles** are designed to save 20,000 tonnes of glass a year and are 18 per cent lighter than conventional wine bottles.

O-I
—
Perrysburg, OH
USA
—
2009–present

A glass of wine a day may be considered good for you, but its glass bottle is bad news for the environment. Bottles consume raw materials during manufacture and energy in the course of the bottling and distribution process. When you throw the bottle away, it creates waste that needs to be recycled.

Yet a fine vintage remains a source of pleasure, so a vast number of bottles are shipped across the world. They are the most common form of packaging used by manufacturers. About 90 per cent of wine packaging consists of glass bottles. At a global level, the Waste & Resources Action Programme (WRAP) estimates that this is equivalent to 8.5 billion tonnes of glass.

In view of growing retailer and consumer demand for sustainably produced and packaged wine, the glass manufacturer O-I has introduced its Lean + Green lightweight wine bottle range. The breakthrough success in the traditional realm of the wine packaging industry stems from O-I's holistic view of sustainability and challenging environmental standards.

O-I was committed to designing wine bottles that would deliver long-term value for customers. In collaboration with the marketing department, an internal team of designers applied the latest technology to produce bottles to optimum levels of lightness, while retaining the appearance and function of the heavier bottles they replaced. Studies by research and consultancy company Ipsos concluded that the tapered shoulders and height proved key for consumers at the point of sale.

The company used a process called 'Narrow Neck Press and Blow', originally perfected in the 1990s for smaller beer bottles and refined in recent years to include the larger 750 ml (26.4 fl oz) format wine bottles. The process enables the better distribution of glass in bottles, allowing for lighter weight designs to meet glass strength specifications of customers.

O-I has reduced in size three tiers of glass bottles: Reference (Prestigious Wines); Caractere (Premium Wines) and ECO (High Value Wines). The Reference has dropped in weight from 550 g (20 oz) to 460 g (16 oz), the Caractere from 460 g (16 oz) to 410 g (15 oz) and the ECO from 400 g (14 oz) to 345 g (12 oz). In 2011, it will launch an even lighter, Bordeaux-style container for cork and screw-tops, with a weight of only 300 g (11 oz).

As well as achieving a sustainable design through a reduction in weight, the Lean + Green bottles are made with a high level of recycled content and label protection. Usually divisions and sprays are required to protect bottle labels. But the in-built label protection of these lightweight wine bottles has removed the necessity for secondary packaging, and thus lowered their environmental impact. At the end of their life cycle, the bottles are fully recyclable.

Between 2009 and the end of 2011, O-I will have produced over 650 million Lean + Green lightweight wine bottles in Europe alone, saving more than 40,000 tonnes of glass and over 25,000 tonnes of carbon dioxide. Equivalent versions of the eco-friendly containers have been produced for the Australasian, North American and Latin American markets. The bottles thus preserve both the wine inside them and the environment around them. *Nicola Homer*

The Bordeaux-style bottles (opposite) are ultra-light and weigh in at 345 g (12 oz) and 460 g (16 oz) respectively, while providing the same proportions of the traditional wine bottle (this page).

Lean + Green Lightweight Wine Bottles

The **Living Wall at the Musée du Quai Branly** is the world's first vertical garden constructed on a massive scale.

Patrick Blanc with Gilles Clément and Ateliers Jean Nouvel
—
Paris, France
—
2006

Living Wall at the Musée du Quai Branly

Situated within the urban framework of Paris, the museum and its vertical gardens bring biodiversity into the streets, and extend to the greenery lining the Seine river.

To say that Jean Nouvel's Musée du Quai Branly in Paris is out of the ordinary is an understatement. But it isn't simply an oddball; it is a building that points to the future of architecture by wearing its commitment to the environment on its sleeve, in an unusual manner. In fact, strolling down Quai Branly (the street after which the museum, dedicated to indigenous arts and culture, is named), one might not even notice the 76,500 m² (823,000 sq ft) structure lightly placed amid the Gilles Clément-designed public gardens, because the museum's facade consists of a Living Wall. Designed by Patrick Blanc, this vertical garden measures a striking 200 m (650 ft) wide and 12 m (40 ft) tall. A metal frame provides a soil-free self-supporting system light enough to be hung on the wall or even suspended in the air, weighing less than 30 kg per m² (6 lbs per sq ft). This frame also keeps the far-reaching foliage from becoming enmeshed with the windows or building structure. However, its visual integration into the structure has created a wild, yet clean, effect.

Botanist Patrick Blanc has long been inspired by the verdant plant life that occupies the cliffs, caves and crevices throughout the world. Noticing that plant life thrives on almost any moisture-laden surface, Blanc began experimenting with ways in which to re-create similar circumstances. Could he transport this life indoors, encouraging the vegetation to creep up interior walls? Could he bring such a structure to the centre of a thriving city where even the hardiest of plants must be carefully maintained in order to survive?

Blanc was convinced that through biodiversity he could create these living, vertical gardens that would not only enliven urban streetscapes, but that could actually change the face of cities and towns – adapting them to the twenty-first century – without altering their charm.

Blanc spent years as a resident at the Centre National de la Recherche Scientifique (CNRS), where he perfected his patented growing system: two layers of polyamide felt stapled to plates of expanded PVC with a thickness of 10 mm (0.4 in) are affixed to metal scaffolding. The felt layer, with its strong water-retaining capacities, allows planting at a remarkable density of 20 to 30 plants per m² (2 to 3 per sq ft). A drip irrigation system at the top delivers a diluted fertilizer mixture, allowing the transplanted vegetation to flourish.

While Blanc's indoor gardens have typically contained tropical plants with the ability to withstand low light, the Quai Branly has presented the challenge of bringing these indoor gardens outside into an urban environment. The Living Wall facade looks north, shielding the vertical garden from the harshest sun rays and allowing the growth of Blanc's carefully curated collection of plant species, including Bergonias, Pachysandras, Heucheras, Ferns, Sedges, Mosses and Liverworts.

Five years after its completion, Blanc's vertical garden remains a testament to what the future of urbanism might hold. The attention that this project has attracted serious debate about how to bring more green space to cities around the world. As the earth's human population expands, dense urban environments remain the most eco-friendly solution to creating hospitable human-centric environments. If we are to achieve the maintenance of the natural world while providing for the masses of humanity, cities must be viewed as preferred choices of habitat across social strata and cities of all sizes will have to not be only high-functioning but physically attractive. Nouvel, Clément and Blanc's work points to a new, lush vision of the city – one that is appetizing enough for all eyes to feast upon.

Andrew Wagner

Patrick Blanc with Gilles Clément and Ateliers Jean Nouvel

Living Wall at the Musée du Quai Branly

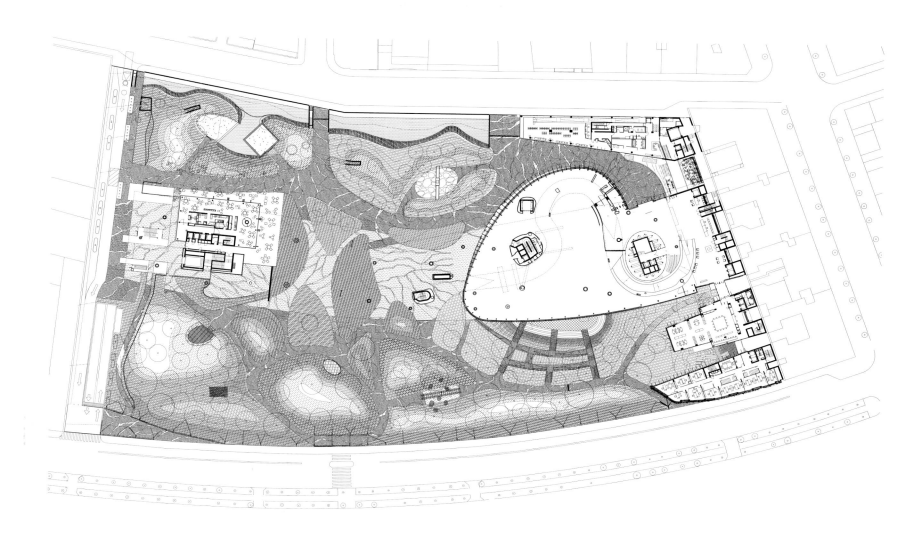

The living wall is a vertical extension of the horizontal gardens, which completely surround the museum at ground level (opposite). The wall itself is situated to face north, so as not to over-dry the plants in the direct southern sunlight (bottom).

Patrick Blanc with Gilles Clément and Ateliers Jean Nouvel

Lucy / Carpet House is made from 72,000 reused carpet tiles and it stays cool without air conditioning in Alabama's sweltering summers.

Rural Studio
—
Hale County, AL
USA
—
2002

The Lucy / Carpet House – the result of a unique blend of sponsorship, architectural experimentation, and a philosophy of social improvement – can be found in the small community of Mason's Bend. Located in Hale County, Alabama, this town still bears the scars of the long and brutal practices of slavery: one third of inhabitants live below the poverty line. But Hale County is also the location of many projects created by the acclaimed architectural group Rural Studio. Set up in 1993 by the late Samuel Mockbee and Dennis K. Ruth, professors at Auburn University, the studio has been improving the living conditions in rural Alabama while training young architects. Students rotate through different projects while they attend the university and are carefully overseen by their teachers, providing them with the practical experience of taking designs through to the construction process.

Built for Lucy Harris and her family, the aim of this project was to construct a house using low-cost materials that could also function as a tornado shelter. It is part of Rural Studio's Outreach Program, which brings students into direct contact with those for whom they design and construct buildings – Mockbee was keen to impress on his students that 'it's not about your greatness as an architect, but your compassion'. Students are taught to find ways to solve the problems of social housing without large budgets, and this includes fund-raising and donations as well as the use of innovative building techniques and recycled materials. In the Lucy / Carpet House, the architects worked with Interface Carpets to utilize leftover products for construction materials; unused carpet tiles were chosen for their insulation properties. Interface donated

72,000 carpet tiles, which were compressed together by a heavy wooden ring beam and stabilized by steel columns to make up the walls of the house. These non-recyclable tiles provide excellent insulation and their dense mass ensures that they remain impervious to water and fire. They had been warehoused for a sufficient amount of time (seven years) to allow all noxious gases to dissipate, and they underwent treatment to prevent microbiological growth and tests to ensure their resistance to fire and water damage.

The house is composed of a single-storey structure containing a main living area with an adjoining tower. Upstairs there is a master bedroom and below a tornado shelter, built of concrete for maximum shelter for storm damage, which doubles as a family room for everyday use. To keep the non-air conditioned interior as cool as possible, the front of the house is orientated east, with one large, main window allowing air to flow into the building and an overhanging roof providing shade from solar gain. There are few openings in the walls and so most cooling breezes enter through the main window on the east facade. Ceiling fans circulate air through the main living space and, to keep the house temperate, hot air is vented by attic fans. The house cost £20,000 ($32,000) and, like all Rural Studio projects, was donated to the Harris family. The house continues Mockbee's legacy of providing 'shelter for the soul', creating a vital set of educational experiences for young architects that encourages them to use leftover materials in an innovative way and to change the built environment by making connections between those who design it and those who occupy it.

Rob Fiehn

The wood beam structure of the Lucy / Carpet house (opposite) secures the carpet tiles in place, allowing them to function properly as a building material (this page).

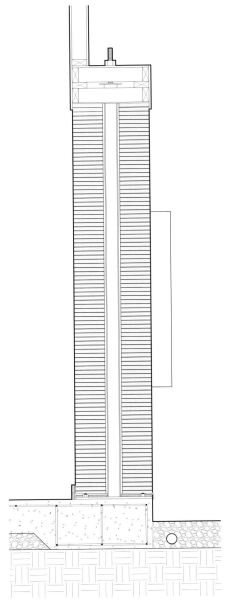

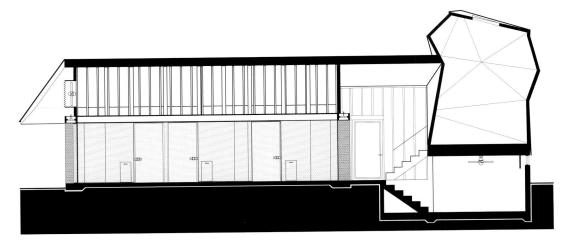

Section

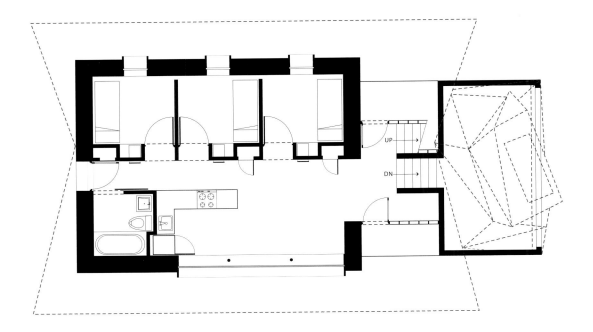

Wall Section Detail

Plan

Lucy / Carpet House

The master bedroom, with
an angular ceiling and skylight
(opposite, top left and right),
sits above the concrete tornado
shelter, which is anchored into
the ground. In the hot climate,
the large roof overhang (top)
is combined with large windows
(bottom) and an internal
programme that regulates air flow
to keep the house comfortable.

Rural Studio

Lunar Resonant Streetlights

convert existing streetlamps to adjust to moonlight levels, saving energy while minimizing light pollution and glare.

Civil Twilight Collective
—
San Francisco, CA USA
—
2007

Every evening as the sun sets on streets across the world, artificial light floods the landscape. Urban dwellers no longer expect to look up and see stars. In 2007, design collective Civil Twilight proposed an alternative: Lunar Resonant Streetlights. The current standard for American streetlamps is a cobra-headed fixture with a sodium bulb and a sunlight-sensitive sensor. The lights power on at sunset and power off at sunrise. Rather than replacing the existing infrastructure, Lunar Resonant Streetlights would retrofit these existing streetlamps. Standard sodium bulbs, which cannot be dimmed, would be replaced with clusters of high-efficiency, dimmable white LED lights. Solar sensors would be replaced with highly-sensitive photocells that can detect the varying intensity of moonlight throughout its monthly cycle, as well as daily changes in atmospheric conditions, and adjust the intensity of the LEDs accordingly.

The concept for Lunar Resonant Streetlights was created by Civil Twilight founders Kate Lydon, an architect and graphic designer; Christina Seely, an artist and photographer; and Anton Willis, an architect, along with an engineer and a team of advisors. During their research, Civil Twilight discovered that streetlights account for 38 per cent of electricity used for lighting in the United States, accounting for 300 billion tonnes of carbon emissions annually. Switching to Lunar Resonant Streetlights would decrease energy demand. Coupled with the high efficiency of LEDs, this reduction could save between 90 and 95 per cent of the energy used for street-lighting: between 270 million and 285 million tonnes of carbon emissions annually.

More shocking than the astronomical amount of energy used to light the streets, or the two-thirds of people in the United States who cannot see moonlight, is the historical reason for this situation. In the 1930s, as the United States underwent rural electrification and the consolidation of utilities, power generation plants could not be switched on and off easily, so the government had to find ways to increase power usage during off-peak evening and night-time hours in order to ensure a constant energy demand to keep plants running efficiently. Street lights were used to offload excess during this time, but although the need for offloading ended in the 1970s, the light level was never revised.

The intensity of current streetlights is not only a leftover of an obsolete energy practice, it is actually a safety liability. The human eye evolved to see the environment even on moonless nights, but not to jump quickly between uneven light levels. Turning from a brightly lit street onto an unlit street poses a safety risk because the human eye cannot adjust at the speed of the moving vehicle. Lunar Resonant Streetlights, sensitive to the need for evenly dispersed lighting, could create safer roads by restoring the evenness of streetlighting and thereby improving night-time visibility.

Civil Twilight believes that sustainability will be encouraged not by making people feel guilty about their choices, but by reconnecting them with nature on a personal level. Practically, Lunar Resonant Streetlights reduce energy usage and carbon emissions while improving road safety at the same time. Poetically, they would hold the capacity to bring the experience of star-gazing back to the city, using the beauty of the natural world to remind people of their place in the universe. *Bareket Kezwer*

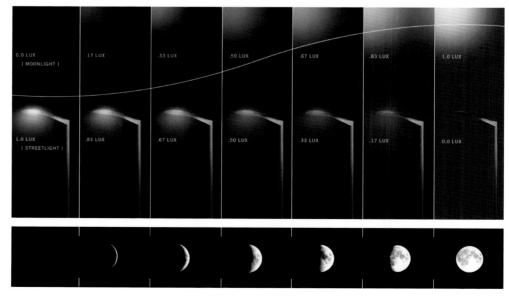

Lunar Resonant Streetlights automatically adjust to the natural light of the moon – which fluctuates night by night – making the level of lighting on the street safer and more comfortable for the human eye.

Civil Twilight Collective

Two 23 m (75 ft) waterfalls regulate the humidity of the air flowing through **Manitoba Hydro Place** and it is passively ventilated with the help of a solar chimney.

The Manitoba Hydro Place complex has rejuvenated the local economy by bringing more than 2,000 new employees into the area every day.

Manitoba Hydro Place, located in downtown Winnipeg, is one of North America's most complex energy efficient large-scale buildings and the first of the next generation of bioclimatic architecture. Manitoba Hydro (MB Hydro) set an ambitious goal for its new building to achieve 60 per cent above the Canadian Model National Energy Code for Buildings (MNECB), while providing a healthy work environment filled with 100 per cent fresh air for more than 2,000 employees, in an extreme climate where temperatures typically fluctuate from -35°C (-30°F) to 35°C (95°F) over the year.

The 65,000 m² (700,000 sq ft), 21-storey office tower occupies a full urban block in the centre of the city. The site was selected for its proximity to the city's transit system and a local network of raised walkways. The 'Capital A' form, made up of two towers set on a shared three-storey podium, proved to be the most dynamic solution to make use of Winnipeg's abundant sunlight and strong gusting southerly wind. The two towers come together at the north and are fused by a 115 m (377 ft) tall solar chimney, a key element in the passive ventilation system and a new landmark on the urban skyline. At the south, the towers open for maximum southern exposure. On this side, three six-storey stacked winter gardens become the lungs of the building and at the same time provide spectacular meeting spaces. Each features a 23 m (75 ft) tall waterfall, which humidify or dehumidify incoming air depending on the season. The towers are set back on the podium to reduce shadow impact on Portage Avenue, the city's historic main shopping street. The placing of the south end of the building on a 21° angle also created space for a new urban park on the Graham Street transit corridor.

Inside the podium, which has green roofs, a three-storey, light-filled public Galleria also serves as a lobby for 2,000 occupants. A sheltered pedestrian route through the site accessed at both north and south ends, the Galleria is now the focal point for downtown activity and an indoor public event space that can accommodate over 1,500 people for benefits, concerts, markets, and orientation for downtown walking tours. In the former suburban offices, the majority of MB Hydro employees drove alone to work. Less than a year after opening the new building, 90 per cent of the employees working there were taking public transport.

The tower floors are designed as 11.5 m (38 ft) deep column-free open spaces, to achieve maximum space for future growth, and to ensure everyone receives access to views and natural light. Each floor is organized into three-storey 'neighborhoods' – smaller sections organized around shared, stacked atria with connecting stairs and lounges. This organization aims to reduce elevator use, catalyze face-to-face communication and facilitate interaction between departments.

While the form maximizes southern exposure, double facades on the east and west provide buffers from the cold, winter climate. The curtain-wall system forms a 1 m (3 ft) wide buffer zone between a double-glazed outer facade and a single-glazed inner wall to insulate the building against heat and cold. Automated louvre shades in the cavity control glare and heat gain. Motorized operable windows open and close in response to changes in light and temperature.

A comprehensive collection of meters and sensors – for systems including lighting, plug loads, water heating, HVAC energy – allow for the verification and optimization of the energy targets. Building Management System (BMS) points allow MB Hydro to observe building performance in close detail, and fine-tune systems as required. This BMS is unique due to the sheer number of observation points (over 25,000 at last count, more than a major medical complex). It also enables employee feedback through custom web-based computer interfaces to control aspects of lighting and solar shading. In addition, the BMS monitors local climate using two on-site weather stations, and uses climate data to automatically adjust slab temperatures, operable window positions and shade positions, dynamically creating the optimum conditions for both energy efficiency and occupant comfort. *Matthias Schuler*

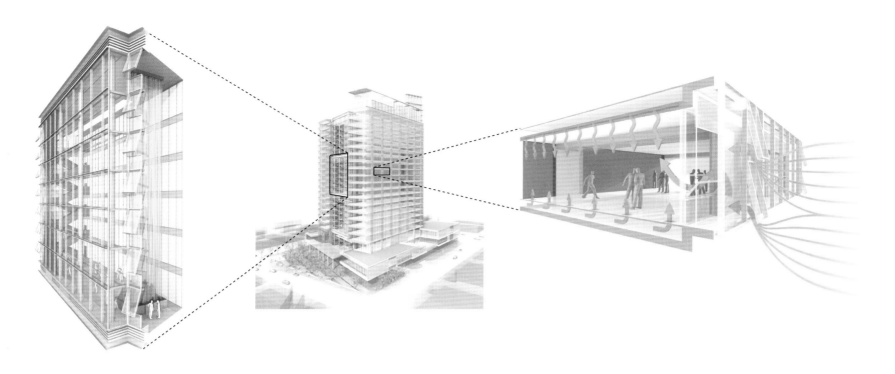

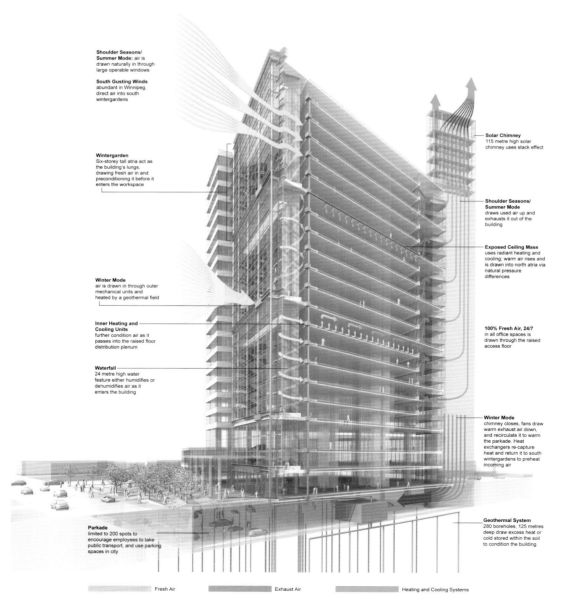

**Shoulder Seasons/
Summer Mode:** air is
drawn naturally in through
large operable windows

South Gusting Winds
abundant in Winnipeg,
direct air into south
wintergardens

Wintergarden
Six-storey tall atria act as
the building's lungs,
drawing fresh air in and
preconditioning it before it
enters the workspace

Winter Mode
air is drawn in through outer
mechanical units and
heated by a geothermal field

**Inner Heating and
Cooling Units**
further condition air as it
passes into the raised floor
distribution plenum

Waterfall
24 metre high water
feature either humidifies or
dehumidifies air as it
enters the building

Parkade
limited to 200 spots to
encourage employees to take
public transport, and use parking
spaces in city

Solar Chimney
115 metre high solar
chimney uses stack effect

**Shoulder Seasons/
Summer Mode**
draws used air up and
exhausts it out of the
building

Exposed Ceiling Mass
uses radiant heating and
cooling; warm air rises and
is drawn into north atria via
natural pressure
differences

100% Fresh Air, 24/7
in all office spaces is
drawn through the raised
access floor

Winter Mode
chimney closes, fans draw
warm exhaust air down,
and recirculate it to warm
the parkade. Heat
exchangers re-capture
heat and return it to south
wintergardens to preheat
incoming air

Geothermal System
280 boreholes, 125 metres
deep draw excess heat or
cold stored within the soil
to condition the building.

Fresh Air   Exhaust Air   Heating and Cooling Systems

Manitoba Hydro Place

Fresh air is drawn into the building and past the waterfalls (opposite, top); exhaust air is drawn up and out of the building's solar chimney (opposite, bottom). The solar chimney is a distinctive addition to the Manitoba skyline (top). A limited number of parking spaces below grade encourage building users to commute to work on mass transit and the 280 boreholes of the geothermal system heat and cool the building as needed (bottom).

Office lofts

Hanging
wood screens

Access
bridges

Water
features

Green roof

South grove

Geothermal
well field

Parkade

Public plaza

The unfired earth tiles that make up the **Mapungubwe Interpretation Centre** use 75 per cent less energy than reinforced concrete, are made with a hand-press machine and are ready to use within one week.

Designed by Peter Rich Architects, the 1,650 m² (17,760 sq ft) Mapungubwe Interpretation Centre is an inspiring building, all the more remarkable when you consider that its slender, curved and domed roofs are constructed from nothing more than unfired earth tiles. To create this impressive feat of structural engineering, the architect worked with structural specialists Michael Ramage of Cambridge University and John Ochsendorf of Massachusetts Institute of Technology.

The technique underlying this project, of kiln-fired terracotta tiles overlaid to create roof vaults, has been used for centuries. What is new at Mapungubwe, however, is the adaptation of the technique to work with unfired earth tiles, which are weaker in compression than fired tiles, and which are incapable of supporting any tensile load. The key lay in perfecting the shells' structural form. For each span, the vault's form has been developed using sophisticated digital structural models, ensuring that only compressive forces are present in the structure's thin shell. The resulting structure is highly efficient and, because the earth tiles only have to deal with compression forces, the vaults and domes do not require steel reinforcement. These thin shells generate small forces on the supporting structure below, requiring minimal buttresses and further simplifying the building's construction.

Ease of assembly was important because the project was intended to transfer skills into the local community, for which the labour-intensive use of earth tiles was perfect. The building's 200,000 tiles are fabricated with 95 per cent soil and 5 per cent cement, formed in a hand-press machine modified from local brick-making equipment, and dried for a week. The vaults are self-supporting, even under construction, and require temporary formwork only at the beginning of the job. The shells are constructed from overlapping layers of thin tiles laid on edge. The first layer is assembled using fast-setting gypsum mortar; all subsequent layers are attached using a mix of sand and cement. The number of tile layers varied depending on the length of span. The completed structures are finished with a surface of local stone rubble to subtly set the building into its magnificent surroundings.

Using unfired soil without the need for steel reinforcement meant no need to transport materials from Johannesburg, 10 hours' drive away. With the exception of cement, all materials came from within a few kilometres of the site, and there was no need for construction machinery. The cost is estimated to be at least 30 per cent cheaper than if the scheme had been built using reinforced concrete. Equally important from an economic perspective, it was constructed by about 160 local labourers and tile-makers who left the project with the construction skills necessary to enable them to continue working. The thermal mass exposed on the underside of the vaults helps moderate daily temperature swings inside the building to reduce the need for cooling. The earthen tiles soak up heat during the day. At night, when the temperature drops, the tiles release this heat back into the building. An extra energy-saving benefit of the high vaulted ceilings is that they enable daylight to penetrate deep into the building's interior, reducing the need for artificial lighting. *Andy Pearson*

These self-supporting domes blend into the South African landscape and rely purely upon the inherent strength of the earth tile itself (opposite). A model of this dome construction technique was built for the 2010 Earth Awards in London (top).

Peter Rich Architects

The interior spaces created by the domes are not hindered by columns (this page). The building's construction required the production of 200,000 pressed tiles, which employed a dozen people for a year (opposite, top, centre left and centre right). Mockups were constructed both before and after the building's completion (opposite, bottom).

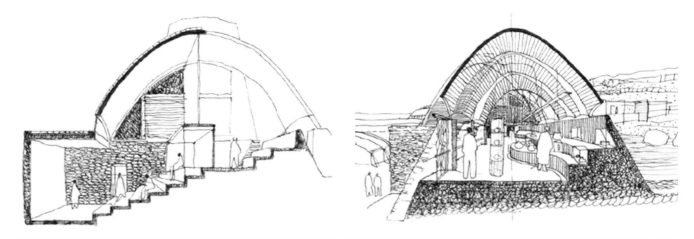

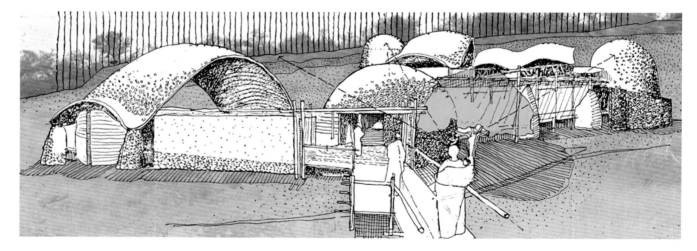

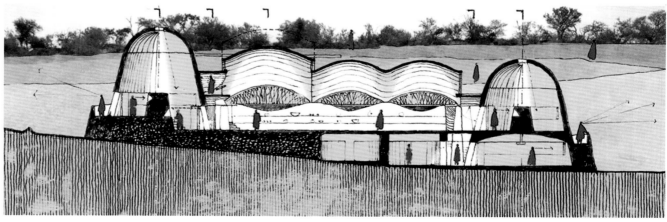

Masdar City is the world's first carbon-neutral city and is designed to create a 'cold island' in the middle of the UAE desert.

Foster + Partners
—
Abu Dhabi, UAE
—
2006–present

Masdar City is envisioned as the world's first carbon-neutral city development. When completed, it will provide 50,000 people with homes and also contain some 1,000 businesses and a university. The primary goal of the project is to show that a carbon-neutral development is possible today and to initiate development in renewable energy components.

To understand the importance of the planning and building activity in the United Arab Emirates, one has to keep in mind the extraordinary urban growth seen in the past and expected in the future – 10 per cent in 1900, 50 per cent in 2007 and 75 per cent in 2050 – as well as the fact that a high percentage of energy consumption and emissions derive from buildings and cities.

The multidisciplinary team designing Masdar City includes architect Foster + Partners with climate engineers Transsolar as well as urban designers, landscape architects, traffic consultants, infrastructure experts, renewable systems experts, Islam experts and building system experts. A key element to creating a carbon-neutral city is to reduce demands and improve systems in order to supply all the energy required from on-site production. To reach this goal, Masdar aims to combat the urban 'heat island' – or build-up of heat around the city – by creating a 'cold island', keeping the city cooler than the surrounding desert.

This required shading the streets to keep hot winds out during the day, yet allowing a breeze to hold temperatures at a comfortable level during the night. This is achieved through well-positioned wind towers and homogeneous building heights, which prevent hot winds from being redirected into the streets. Street and courtyard dimensions and orientation guidelines for the buildings optimize shading but allow in enough daylight. The narrow streets – as found in traditional cities here – are the pedestrian urban spaces, and small private rapid transport systems are set below ground. To minimize the external heating loads on the buildings, high-level building envelope requirements for insulation, air tightness, shading and window quality were mandated. The building system uses cooling and dehumidification based on a liquid desiccant system. The guidelines also define rules for specifying equipment, lighting and elevators, to limit electricity consumption.

The first part of Masdar City is now built. The existing buildings are orientated to provide optimum shade and reduce cooling loads, and shaded colonnades at podium level exploit the benefits of exposed thermal mass. Facades respond to their orientation and carefully positioned photovoltaic panels also shade streets and buildings. The public spaces are further cooled by green landscaping and water to provide evaporative cooling in the desert climate. *Matthias Schuler*

Abu Dhabi is investing £15.5 ($25) million into the development of Masdar City, which is engineered to be a cold island in the middle of the surrounding desert climate (opposite). The first completed section (this page) is the Masdar Institute, a research-driven graduate instition that focuses on the science and engineering of advanced alternative energy, environmental technologies and sustainability.

The Masdar Institute (top) is the first completed part of Masdar City. In most cities in the UAE, the harsh climate necessitates a focus on interior urban spaces, which require air conditioning. In Masdar, a wind tower (bottom left) directs breezes through the streets, which have been designed with the optimum width for this purpose (bottom right). Solar panels on top of the buildings double as shading for the courtyards (opposite, top left) and narrow streets (opposite, top right) that separate the Masdar Institute's laboratory buildings from the terracotta facades of the student accomodation. Private rapid transport systems (opposite, bottom right) are set below ground to make the street level more pedestrian-friendly.

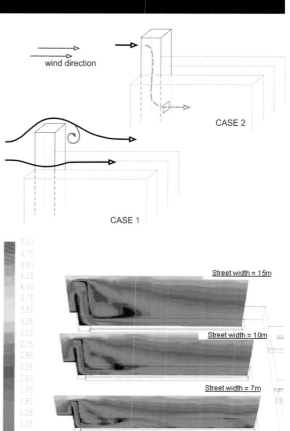

wind direction

CASE 2

CASE 1

Street width = 15m

Street width = 10m

Street width = 7m

Larger wind towers

The nitrogen-filled ETFE pillows on the facade of the **Media-TIC** building eliminate the need for air conditioning and reduce its carbon footprint by 20 per cent.

On the southeast facade of the building (opposite) 104 ETFE cushions (this page) can inflate and deflate according to the sun's strength, which greatly reduces the need for air conditioning in Spain's infamous heat.

The facade of the Media-TIC in Barcelona is covered in plastic pillows that inflate or deflate depending on the heat of the sun. The pillowed structure eschews traditional heating and air-conditioning systems by using new technology to control the interior climate of the building. This is the attempt of Catalonian architect Enric Ruiz-Geli of Cloud 9 to make a building that minimizes its carbon footprint in a manner that could soon be expected of all new buildings.

The Media-TIC office complex is suspended in 22@ Barcelona, a science and IT village found in Barcelona's Poblenou district. 'Suspended' is accurate, as the building's upper floors hang from a truss at the top of the building, creating a column-free interior in the ground floor. A digital technology hub, the Media-TIC is light and airy; it's light green steel structure playfully suggests its 'green' credentials.

Cloud 9's design solution for the temperature control of the offices is remarkably elegant. The Catalonian sun naturally heats the building while the polymer plastic ethylene tetrafluoroethylene (ETFE) pillows, fixed within the triangular framework of the southeastern facade, serve as both insulators and a barrier against excess heat. The pillows are fitted with sensors to measure the heat and angle of the sun, and, fully solar-powered, are able to inflate and deflate to regulate sunlight entering the building. ETFE has some interesting qualities – besides being an excellent insulator, it is also lightweight,

durable and an anti-adherent, which means it is easy and inexpensive to maintain.

On the southwest facade the ETFE pillows also include a system that rapidly floods them with nitrogen. The nitrogen forms a 'cloud' sunscreen that quickly lowers solar penetration into the building. The system's innovation lies in its sheer flexibility. In winter the clear ETFE allows sunlight to naturally heat the building; in summer, or during warmer periods of the day, nitrogen restricts solar penetration. It's a clever design – an effective natural cooling and heating system that abandons fossil fuels and reduces the building's carbon footprint by as much as 20 per cent.

The Media-TIC's ecological technologies are impressive, but equally important is the way in which the emphasis upon sustainability has been integrated into the building's aesthetic. The technologies Cloud 9 uses to create a green architecture aren't hidden away: instead they are on clear display, forming an important part of the design. The building's exterior is bare and its steel structure is exposed and thrust centre-stage. Green steel beams run down from the building's apex and, on the building's southeastern and southwestern sides, resolve into a system of concave and convex triangular segments plumped up with the ETFE pillows. It's a striking tableau: in Media-TIC, ornamentation and ecological function have become indistinguishable.

Johanna Agerman Ross

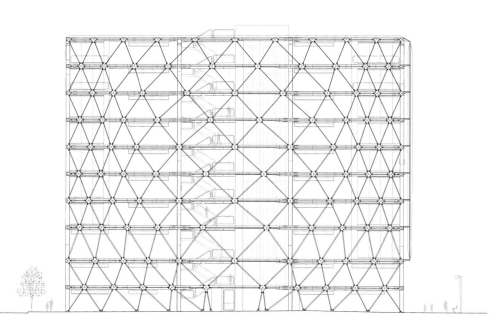

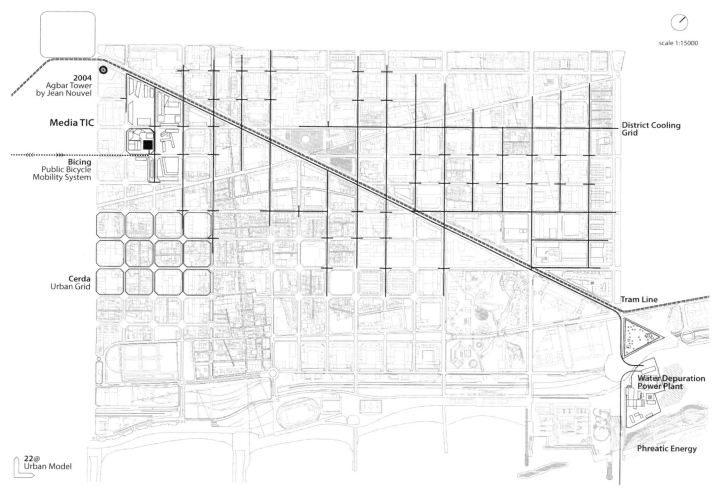

scale 1:15000

2004
Agbar Tower
by Jean Nouvel

Media TIC

District Cooling
Grid

Bicing
Public Bicycle
Mobility System

Cerda
Urban Grid

Tram Line

Water Depuration
Power Plant

22@
Urban Model

Phreatic Energy

Media-TIC

The interior of the Media-TIC is largely column-free (opposite, top right), which is the result of the suspended structure of the building (top left). The ETFE panels on the facade (top right) attach to a triangulated steel framework (bottom).

Minimally invasive to the fabric of their informal settlement site, **Metro Cable** stations provide social services in addition to public transport and will eventually give power back to the grid.

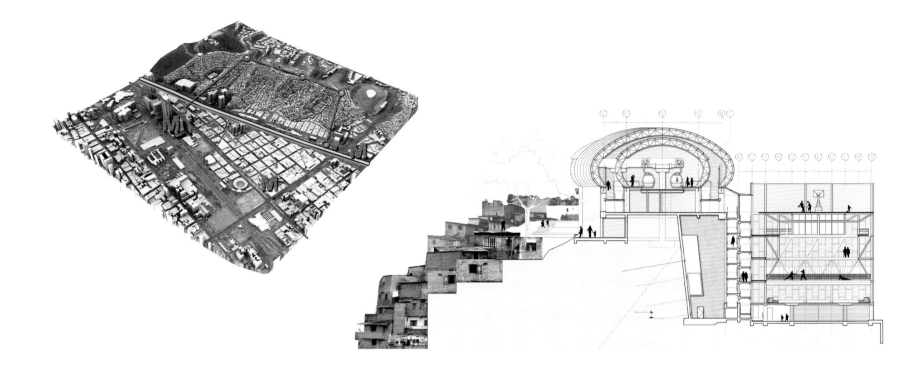

The Metro Cable system connects the hilltop *barrios* (opposite) with the city's metro network (top left). The La Cieba station (top right) can eventually include space for education, health, sports, arts and music.

During the industrial boom of the 1970s and 80s, Venezuela's rural poor flocked to Caracas in search of employment. Many of the new urban residents settled on untenured land in the hills surrounding the valley of central Caracas. It is estimated that of the city's 5 million inhabitants, 60 per cent live in informal settlements, known in Venezuela as *barrios*. Residents face conditions of extreme poverty, inadequate infrastructure and insufficient public space. Because the *barrios* are located in the hills, it is difficult to connect them to the public transit network. Long bus journeys to work are the norm and keep *barrio* residents trapped in the cycle of poverty as well as adding to urban air pollution.

In 2005, Alfredo Brillembourg and Hubert Klumpner, co-founders of Urban-Think Tank (U-TT), a Venezuelan based architecture firm founded in 1993, began to re-evaluate the government plan to connect the *barrios* to Caracas's urban centre. The government proposed the construction of a series of new roads between the city centre and the *barrios* that would serve as the infrastructure for new bus routes. Brillembourg and Klumpner held a public symposium at the Central University of Venezuela in Caracas to explore their concerns about the cost of the government solution, the number of barrio residents that would be displaced by the construction of the new roads and the destruction of buildings and attendant waste that would be generated. Architects, planners, activists and *barrio* community leaders gathered to discuss the government's plan and devise an alternative proposal. After evaluating the limitations presented by the terrain and the existing community structure and needs, a U-TT-led task force proposed an elevated cable car. By elevating the system, the solution

guaranteed minimal displacement of existing houses and structures and greatly reduced the amount of pollution that would have been generated by the construction of new roads and the ongoing traffic of new bus routes.

In 2006, President Hugo Chávez set up a joint venture with an Austrian firm that specializes in building cable cars for mountains. Construction began in 2007, and the first line, which connects the barrio of San Agustín to Parque Central terminal on the state-run Metro de Caracas, began full service in 2010. The 2.1 km (1.3 mile) route has five stations; two stations in the valley connect to the main Caracas transit system and three additional stations provide access to residents on the mountain ridge. The stations have common platform levels, access ramps, circulation patterns, materials, structural elements, and signage. Their shape differs depending on the topographic conditions and the additional cultural functions the station will house. A library is currently under construction at La Ceiba station with plans to build a gym, supermarket, and daycare at other stations in the future. While the cable system currently draws energy from the city's grid, the installation of wind turbines and photovoltaic arrays on the stations will eventually power not only the Metro Cable system itself, but could supply energy to all of San Agustín, much of which currently lacks electricity.

Passengers are transported along the Metro Cable in eight-person gondolas. The system can transport 1,200 people per hour in each direction and is currently transporting 15,000 people a day. The Metro Cable connects approximately 40,000 hillside residents to Caracas's commercial and urban centre and reduced the average commute from the *barrio* from 2.5 hours to 20 minutes. *Bareket Kezwer*

The **Mission One** is the world's first battery-powered motorcycle that can recharge in two hours from a 240-volt outlet and travel 241km (150 miles) on one charge.

Yves Béhar
—
San Francisco, CA
USA
—
2010

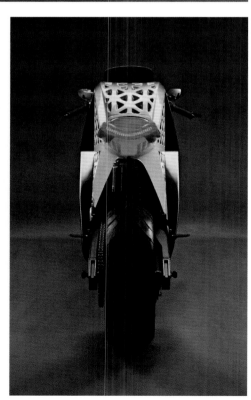

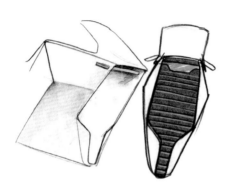

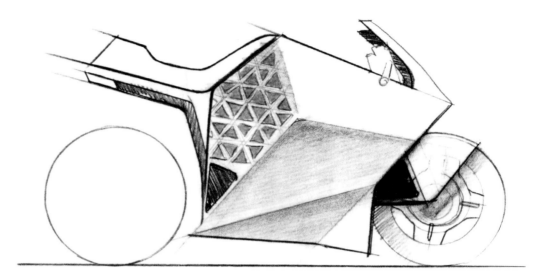

Mission One is wireless-enabled: a real-time data acquisition system allows riders to capture data on speed, location, throttle position and lean angle, which can be analyzed after each ride.

The Mission One is the first model from San Francisco company Mission Motors, who began the project by building an electric version of a converted Ducati 900SS motorcycle. With this starting point, the company aimed to develop a desirable and environmentally friendly superbike that would be accepted by bikers and powered by alternative energy.

Yves Béhar, a San Francisco-based Swiss designer who founded the company fuseproject in 1999, designed the Mission One. 'This project is a statement about how design can make performance and sustainability come together without compromise', says Béhar of the project. 'Just because you create an electrical motorbike doesn't mean that you have to suddenly downgrade the experience to something sluggish and boring. The motorcycle is being sold on performance first. The fact that it's electric is an added benefit.'

The Mission One is built to express speed and efficiency through its sharp lines. The bulk and weight of a traditional motorbike – a combustion engine, crankshaft, exhaust system, cylinders and a fuel tank – has been replaced by a high-energy, lithium ion battery pack, which produces zero emissions. The 136 horsepower electric motor is the size of a football and there are no gears, which means that the acceleration from 0 to 257.5 kph (0 to 160 mph) happens in one smooth movement and is much quieter than a gasoline motor,

virtually eliminating both fuel and sound pollution. At 240 kg (525 lbs), it's a bulky machine, but its design and detailing emphasize lightness. The battery pack and motor, as well as all the mechanical elements of the bike, are covered in a honeycomb-textured skin with a unique decorative quality. The seat ducktails from the main body of the bike and counter-levers out over the back wheel, providing a sporty forward-leaning position for the rider; recesses for the rider's legs increase the aerodynamic efficiency.

The breaking system is regenerative; it recaptures the kinetic energy produced while stopping, which prolongs the overall battery life. The battery takes two hours to be recharged through a standard wall socket. The electrical energy is much more efficient than gasoline: the Mission One can travel 240 km (150 miles) on one charge (costing only about £1.25 ($2) in electricity consumption), whereas a traditional motorcycle could only travel 24–32 km (15–20 miles) using the equivalent energy in gasoline.

A successful exercise in how to market a product through its design, the Mission One is one of the most talked about electric bikes on the market and it hasn't even launched yet. But the ultimate reach of the project is still theoretical: the first Mission One motorbike is set to be a highly luxurious product with a price tag of £43,000 ($70,000), although a £9,350 ($15,000) bike is also in the works. *Johanna Agerman Ross*

Yves Béhar

Modec Trucks
are 98 per cent recyclable, save nine tonnes in CO_2 emissions annually, and cost only £0.5 ($0.8) per mile to operate.

Modec
—
Coventry, United Kingdom
—
2007-present

Tesco, FedEx, Marks & Spencer, and UPS use the zero-emissions trucks for their business needs. Dealers for the Modec Truck are located in the UK, the Netherlands, Ireland, France, Spain, Denmark, Switzerland and the United States.

The Modec Truck is a clean and quiet commercial vehicle, powered completely by batteries, which can travel 160 km (100 miles) after an overnight charge. Capable of carrying a two-tonne load while travelling at up to 80 kph (50 mph), the electric vehicle appeals to big companies with plenty of deliveries to make. One Modec truck can save nine tonnes of CO_2 a year, as compared to a diesel equivalent, and operates with a fuel cost of only £0.5 ($0.8) per mile. The vehicle is particularly effective in cities, as its motor does not idle in stop-and-go traffic like a traditional engine. The truck is also 98 per cent recyclable, which means that it can be kept out of landfill when it reaches the end of its life.

The company was founded in 2004 and started producing trucks in 2007, after investing £30 million ($50 million) in research. The company attracted some big players in the automotive industry and quickly picked up an impressive list of clients. The firm set its sights on the overseas market, establishing dealerships in the United States and across Europe. The trucks come in various shapes and sizes, and have been adapted to suit clients' needs. There is a box van, one with dropped sides, a tail lift truck, a tipper and a refrigerated version. What makes Modec most interesting is the vehicle's use of cutting-edge battery technology.

The truck has two battery options – 85 kWh Zebra batteries, which provide 160 km (100 miles) of drive time, and Li-ion 52 kWh batteries, which offer 97 km (60 miles). The Zebra is a molten salt battery and uses sodium nickel chloride. It was developed specifically for high-energy storage and high-power draw applications. The Li-ion uses lithium iron phosphate and offers more stability, but has lower levels of energy storage and power delivery when compared with less stable batteries. The batteries sit inside a 'cassette' that is resilient to piercing, over-charging, over-discharging, short-circuit, gasoline fire and a 50 kph (30 mph) impact. When the battery is dead, it can be disposed of in the same way as an ordinary AA battery – many local authorities have battery-recycling schemes.

The Modec's motor has just three moving parts and the unit is permanently sealed, unlike internal combustion engines. A high-strength steel chassis is home to the vehicle's battery pack, and it is designed so that the battery is fairly easy to remove: an empty battery can be swapped for a fully charged one in about 20 minutes. The battery can easily be upgraded and the vehicle also has the potential to house fuel cell units in the future.

The company employed around 70 people at its base in Coventry before it was forced to make redundancies. The West Midlands town was chosen because it was considered the heartland of the UK automotive industry, with easily accessible local suppliers and a skilled workforce. Founder Lord Jamie Borwick's hope is to find someone to buy the flagging company and continue the good work. *Helen Babbs*

The **Open-Air Library** was built from the repurposed cladding of a nearby warehouse; it houses books donated by neighbourhood residents.

KARO*
architekten
—
Magdeburg,
Germany
—
2007

The Open-Air Library is just what it sounds like: a library open to the elements, with a 24 hour, seven-day-a-week lending policy. It's the result of a close collaboration between the citizens of Magdeburg and the architecture practices KARO* architekten and Architektur+Netzwerk. Magdeburg, in Eastern Germany, is a post-industrial town: much of the local area's manufacturing has ended and its citizens have suffered high unemployment and big cuts to public services. In some parts of town, up to 80 per cent of existing buildings sit abandoned.

In 2005, Leipzig-based KARO* architeken and local firm Architektur+Netzwerk led a public enquiry to determine how the fallow site of the former public library could be used. The library burnt down in the 1980s and there was no money in the local government to build a new one. This first consultation resulted in a 1:1 scale of the proposal for the site – a library and place for social interaction – created from beer crates borrowed from a local brewery and filled with book donations from the community. 'It was meant to be a social sculpture', says Stefan Rettich of KARO*. 'The aim was to create new and to enhance existing social networks.' The project was a success. The community continued running a library in a nearby abandoned shop and discussed how to take the project further, eventually obtaining funding from the federal government to build a more permanent structure. 'We spent almost another year in consulting with the community on the function, shape and material of the place', says Rettich. 'The biggest challenge was to make architecture out of all these ideas.'

The project is now known by its local nickname: The Bookmark. Located on a triangular site, The Open-Air Library is slightly raised, creating a clear division from the street while remaining accessible from all sides. A slightly taller structure on the northern end contains a stage and café. This is the only part of the architecture that has a door – it leads to backstage storage that holds equipment for book readings and performances by local bands. The book wall runs along one entire side of the site. It has a small roof for protection from the elements, an alcove with windows and seating overlooking the street outside. The most dominant part of the Open-Air Library is a lawn with a seating platform in the middle, creating a garden for reading.

The facade is built from the recycled cladding of a demolished 1960s warehouse nearby: white, square panels set into a metal grid. 'People wanted us to use recycled material as part of the architecture so when I heard of this warehouse I asked if we could re-use parts of it', says Rettich. 'The funny thing was that its shape made reference to the beer crates that we first used in this project and people liked that.'

Keeping the library open means that the construction costs were low and that the space avoids the energy consumption of air conditioning and heating. The absence of a sealed enclosure also contributes to the feeling of the library being both of the neighbourhood and for the neighbourhood. Of course, architecture can't solve all problems: 'There have been two cases of vandalism of the library already', says Rettich. 'And it means that what we have done in the community is not enough, there is still big unemployment and many issues that the local government needs to deal with.' But the Open-Air Library does prove that community interaction and ambitious architecture can be pursued at the same time. *Johanna Agerman Ross*

The **Organic Jewellery Collection** is made entirely of Tecbor, a natural Amazonian latex rubber, which requires no complex machinery, no energy and a minimal amount of water to produce.

Flavia Amadeu

Brazil

2004–present

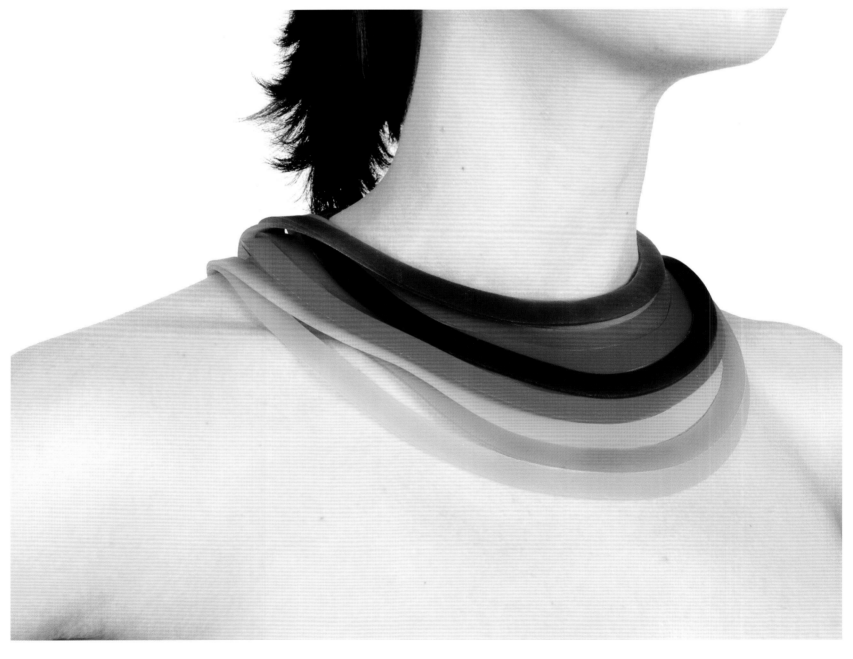

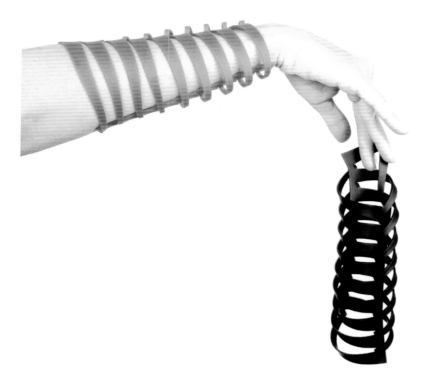

Pieces of Tecbor can be cut into necklaces (opposite and right) and arm bands (left) as well as many other shapes.

Flavia Amadeu's Organic Jewellery Collection is bright, bold, fashionable and sustainable: all the pieces in the collection are made from Tecbor, a natural latex rubber produced by native communities in the Amazon Rainforest.

Covering 6 million km² (2.3 million sq mi), the Amazon is the largest tropical rainforest in the world, and it contains an estimated 300 million rubber trees. Rubber tapping is the process of extracting latex from rubber trees by cutting into the tree bark and collecting the latex that oozes out. When done properly, the process does not cause lasting damage to the trees. From 1900 until 1920, 97 per cent of all internationally traded rubber came from the Amazon, and rubber tapping has long been an economic mainstay of native Amazonians.

Since the 1920s, however, the demand for Brazilian rubber has steadily declined as Brazilian prices were undercut by the introduction of monocultured rubber tree plantations in Southeast Asia. As a result of the decreasing economic rewards of rubber tapping as well as the deforestation of the Amazon, driven by the increased resources required for global industrialization during the twentieth century, native Amazonian communities face both economic displacement and environmental devastation. Local rubber tapping families increasingly need to either participate in deforestation or relocate from the forest to the peripheries of cities to find paid labour.

Rubber production in the Amazon also had serious health consequences. Most of the rubber produced has been smoked sheet rubber, which is created by coagulating latex with formic acid, a toxic compound. The coagulate is rolled into sheets and dried over an open wood fire. Long term exposure to formic acid has been associated with mutations, liver and kidney damage and skin allergy. Tecbor technology was developed by Professor Floriano

Pasture, a chemist at Lateq, the University of Brasilia's Chemistry Technology Laboratory, who wanted to find a way to produce natural rubber that could be inexpensively, simply and safely produced by native rubber tapping communities in Amazon.

Tecbor is air dried, and congeals latex using pyroligneous acid, also known as wood vinegar, a byproduct of the production of charcoal from wood. Eliminating the need for fire drying reduces the resources required to produce the rubber and removes the health risks associated with smoke inhalation. Producing Tecbor requires no electricity or complex machinery and minimal water. The new process not only lowers health risks formerly associated with rubber production, the simplicity and low production costs also make it accessible to a wider community. Tecbor rubber sheets are industry ready.

Once the Tecbor technology was perfected, Lateq partnered with the National Council for Rubber Tappers, the National Centre of Traditional Populations and Greenpeace to train local rubber tapping families. Hundreds of local rubber tapping communities have learned the Tecbor technology and, with some adaptations based on local conditions, are experiencing economic growth through the production of Tecbor.

Amadeu's Organic Jewellery Collection was one of the earliest initiatives to use Tecbor. Amadeu incorporated the naturally malleable, resistant and colourful quality of Tecbor into the design of the collection. The elasticity of the rubber allowed Amadeu to create pieces that can be worn in a variety of ways. Each piece can be readjusted to fit different parts of the body. The bold bands of solid colour can be worn as bracelets, armbands or anklets – beautiful objects that promote environmental, economic and social sustainability. *Bareket Kezwer*

The **Oru Kayak** is made with 70 per cent less plastic than conventional kayaks and re-engages urbanites with a forgotten form of public space in major cities: the waterway.

Civil Twilight Collective

—

San Francisco, California

—

2010

Oru Kayak

In just five minutes, the Oru Kayak can be unfolded into a full-sized kayak (opposite) from a case so compact that it can be taken on public transport (this page).

A commuter facing the wall of traffic crossing the Golden Gate Bridge in San Francisco or the Bosphrous Bridge in Istanbul would quickly understand the utility of the Oru Kayak. Designed by local collective Civil Twilight, the Oru uses principles drawn from origami to expand out of a portable case into a high-performance watercraft in less than five minutes. It's so quick to assemble that zipping to work underneath the morning rush hour could soon become a reality.

The compact Oru is designed for urban dwellers: it can easily be stored in small apartments, and travels well on public transport systems. At a weight of only 7 kg (16 lbs), you can tote it over your shoulder on the train, and pack it into a rucksack on longer trips. The kayak pares back the strap-and-gadget appearance of most outdoor equipment to achieve a sleek and minimal aesthetic.

When the Oru is assembled, the monocoque shell folds out from a seamless sheet of twin-walled plastic. This fold pattern lends the kayak great rigidity without an internal skeleton. This was inspired by the field of computational origami, pioneered by engineers and mathematicians including Robert Lang and Erik Demaine, who developed models generating volumetric forms out of flat sheets. This use of fluid forms, rather than the angular forms of traditional origami, is crucial to the kayak's performance in the water.

The Oru is a sustainable design in both a physical and philosophical sense. The kayak is produced with machinery widely used in the packaging industry. As a result of its folding structure, the watercraft uses 70 per cent less plastic than a typical moulded kayak and is fully recyclable. On delivery, the product's compact size makes shipping and logistics efficient. In addition to saving energy through its manufacturing processes, the Oru Kayak encourages city dwellers to appreciate waterways as a form and opens up the possibilities for water-based sustainable transport.

The Oru follows a persistent strand of enquiry in Civil Twilight's work: it re-examines the relationship between natural and built environments in work spanning art, architecture, design and engineering. A spirit of collaboration has proved key to its founders, Anton Willis, Kate Lydon and Christina Seely.

The studio addresses sustainability through diverse projects such as the Mycofarmhouse, where mushrooms recycle wooden buildings into compost for urban farming, and a book entitled *Reservoir*, facilitating meditation on the need for a balanced relationship with water. Now with the Oru Kayak, it encourages people not only to use waterways as a sustainable means of transport, but to discover the joys of paddling across the world. *Nicola Homer*

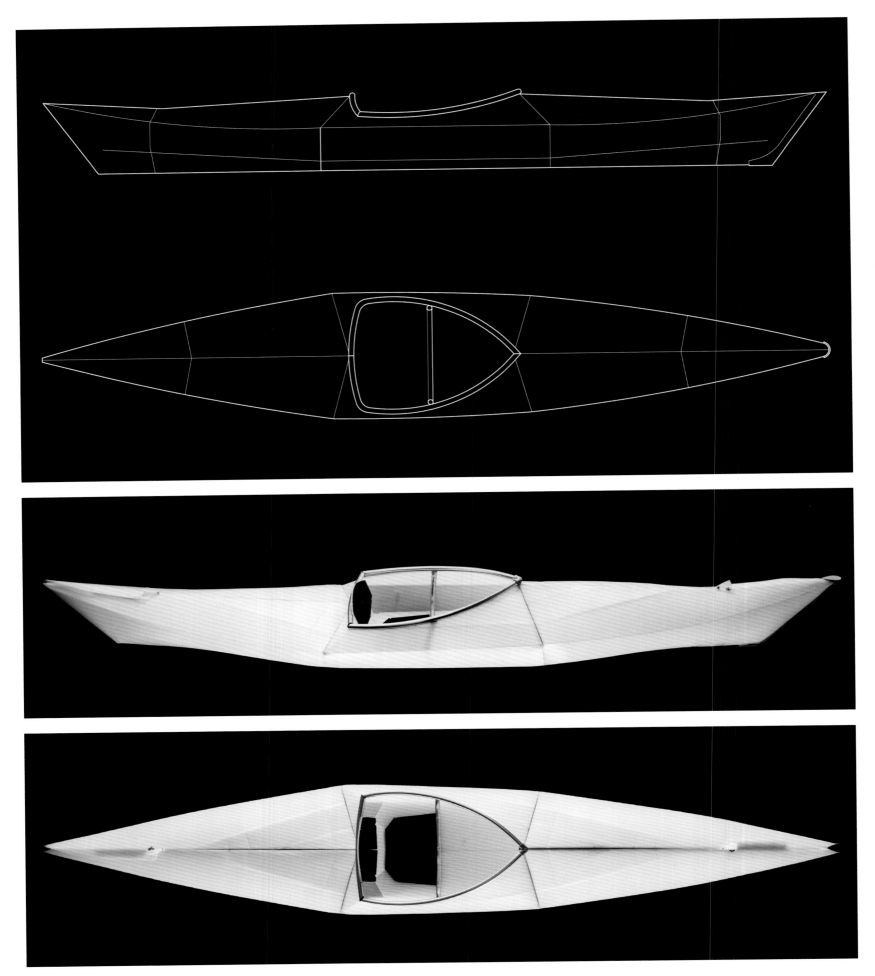

Oru Kayak

Side and top views of the kayak illustrate the simple folds in the seamless sheet of twin-walled plastic (opposite). The carrying case for the kayak holds all the components for the boat and is light enough to be carried easily (this page).

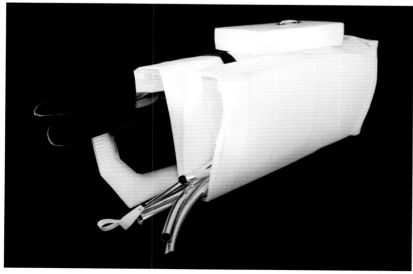

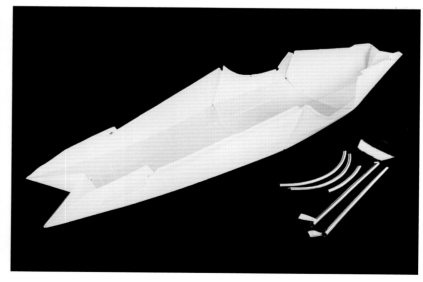

Civil Twilight Collective

Made from 12,500 plastic bottles, the **Plastiki Boat** is the world's first fully recyclable boat.

MYOO (formerly Adventure Ecology)
—
San Francisco, CA USA
—
2010

The Plastiki Boat embodies a cradle-to-cradle approach to design, in which materials and objects have more than a single useful life.

On 26 July 2010, the Plastiki catamaran docked in Sydney harbour, having completed a voyage of 8,000 nautical miles. The innovation of British adventurer and environmentalist David de Rothschild and his organization MYOO (previously Adventure Ecology), the Plastiki expedition began her adventure following a report issued by UNEP, called 'Ecosystems and Biodiversity in Deep Waters and High Seas', which called attention to the environmental problems resulting from the expanding human footprint, and by taking inspiration from Thor Heyerdahl's 1947 Kon-Tiki expedition in which he sailed a balsa-wood raft across the South Pacific.

The Plastiki is a one-of-a-kind catamaran constructed of 12,500 reclaimed plastic bottles and a newly developed recyclable material. Engineered by a team of experts, the Plastiki was intended to showcase the cradle-to-cradle philosophy that is prevalent in nature. Taking inspiration from bio-mimicry, Michael Pawlyn, the Plastiki's concept architect, determined early on that the reused plastic bottles should be configured in the segmented style of a pomegranate along the pontoons of the catamaran, to give the vessel strength and buoyancy. Inspired by Buckminster Fuller, Nathaniel Corum from Architecture for Humanity designed the detachable geodesic cabin, which contained six bunks and a small kitchen that would become the six-person crew's living space for their three months at sea.

The ambition was to construct the entire vessel out of recycled PET (polyethylene terephthalate) bottles; MYOO approached the team behind the product development and incubation company, Level 2 Industries, to experiment with the material. After research and testing, the Plastiki hull was fitted with 12,500 half-gallon (two-litre) PET plastic bottles filled with carbon dioxide to make them more rigid, providing 68 per cent of the boat's buoyancy. A specially developed technology incorporating recycled PET called Seretex was used to engineer the superstructure of the boat, replacing the commonly used unrecyclable fibreglass or costly carbon fibre. Seretex is a revolutionary technology devoted to creating closed loop solutions for recovering and repurposing the PET plastic waste stream.

The two masts, measuring 12 and 18 m (40 and 60 ft) tall, are made from reclaimed aluminium irrigation pipes; the sails are hand-made from recycled PET cloth. Even the bonding agent, made from sugar cane and cashew nut husks, is recycled and 100 per cent biodegradable. This makes the Plastiki the world's first fully recyclable boat. She measures 18 m (60 ft) by 7 m (23 ft), weighs 12 tonnes and achieves an average speed of 5 knots.

In March 2010, the Plastiki set sail from under the San Francisco Golden Gate Bridge. It was an adventurous voyage with giant waves, high winds and brutal temperatures. The team relied solely on renewable energy, including solar panels, wind and propeller turbines and bicycle-powered electricity generators, for all their energy needs on-board. A satellite linkup allowed the Plastiki and her crew to share their experiences of life at sea. This was crucial to the second aim of the expedition: to shift public thinking on plastic waste and to demonstrate how plastics can become part of the solution to wasteful consumption. The Plastiki crew would see plastic waste littering the Pacific throughout their journey, from jerry cans, trays and bottles to microscopic plastic nurdles. Such plastic is ingested throughout the marine food chain, damaging and often killing marine life. By managing the feat of constructing an elegant and 100 per cent recyclable sailing vessel from the plastic waste that it would encounter, the Plastiki demonstrates that creative design can address even enormous problems.

Although building and sailing the Plastiki is an extraordinary achievement, its legacy is what really matters. There were plans to recycle the vessel, but its message seems to be more evocative with the Plastiki catamaran intact. So it will, for now, continue touring the oceans to deliver its message. *Johanna Agerman Ross*

MYOO (formerly Adventure Ecology)

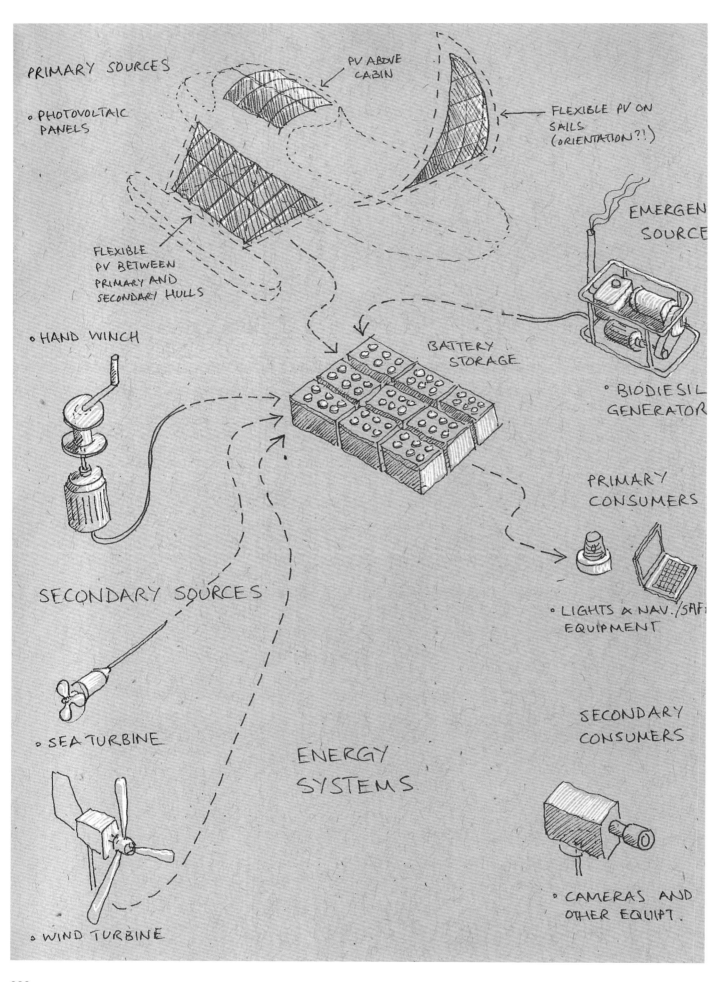

PRIMARY SOURCES

PV ABOVE CABIN

FLEXIBLE PV ON SAILS (ORIENTATION?!)

° PHOTOVOLTAIC PANELS

EMERGENCY SOURCE

FLEXIBLE PV BETWEEN PRIMARY AND SECONDARY HULLS

° HAND WINCH

BATTERY STORAGE

° BIODIESIL GENERATOR

PRIMARY CONSUMERS

° LIGHTS & NAV./SAFETY EQUIPMENT

SECONDARY SOURCES

SECONDARY CONSUMERS

° SEA TURBINE

ENERGY SYSTEMS

° CAMERAS AND OTHER EQUIPT.

° WIND TURBINE

The Plastiki crew used only on-board renewable energy during the 2010 expedition. Photovoltaic panels, a hand winch, a wind turbine and a sea turbine are all connected to a centralized battery storage pack (opposite). Photovoltaic panels are the primary energy source (top) for this vessel, which floats on 12,500 PET bottles (bottom).

The **Plumen 001** bulb uses 80 per cent less electricity than incandescent bulbs and its yellow hue is designed to be softer on the eyes.

Samuel Wilkinson

—

London, UK

—

2011

  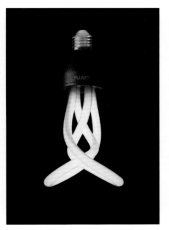  

The tubes of the light bulb have a dynamic shape, which changes in appearance when one turns the bulb around to see all sides.

Most energy-saving bulbs offer little in the way of either aesthetics or visual comfort. British industrial designer Samuel Wilkinson and London-based sustainable design company Hulger set out together to create a more inspiring design for compact fluorescent lamp (CFL) energy-saving light bulbs. To develop the Plumen 001, the design team began by acknowledging that while original incandescent light bulbs have a simple beauty, the environmentally sensitive CFL lacked that same aesthetic appeal.

Through the design team's research, they found that most people had a problem with either the way the CFL bulbs look, or with the harsh white light the bulbs emit. After thoroughly analyzing the manufacturing process of the standard CFL, it soon became clear that to radically change the shape of the bulb, they would have to develop new methods of manufacturing. The glass tubes of the Plumen 001 proved to be the biggest design challenge. The process of heating and moulding its tubes is a restrictive and delicate process, and the phosphorescent coating can only be applied in a particular way. In the end, however, it was these manufacturing challenges that helped to facilitate the inspired and elegant final design.

Once the mechanics of manufacturing were sorted out, the hue of the light was tackled. Essentially, a light that produces a more yellow tint was developed to deal with the harshness of the original CFL bulbs. By utilizing this yellow tint, the Plumen 001 produces a softer feel on the eyes while casting off a bright light quality from the grade-A rated bulb. The look and colouring of the bulb design offers an organized complexity. That is to say that at first glance the tubes of the bulb can appear quite random in shape, but as you take a closer look at the bulb it becomes more rational, recognizable and beautiful.

The Plumen 001 uses 80 per cent less energy than an incandescent light bulb, and its average life span is eight times longer that of an incandescent. While these bulbs are more expensive up front, they save consumers money in the long-term, as the bulb's overall energy use is much lower.

The Plumen 001 is more than just a design-savvy bulb. It also has the potential to reduce greenhouse gasses in a measurable way. A large percentage of the total energy consumed in the world today is used to generate domestic electricity, which powers appliances and lights our homes. Most electricity is still produced by fossil fuels, a major ongoing challenge in reducing pollutants in our environment. Turning to an efficient lighting unit is one of the most cost-effective ways to reduce electricity use and greenhouse gas emissions.

Just as energy-efficient light bulbs are essential to sustainable living, light is essential to design. By merging the latest technology with innovative design, the Plumen 001 is a beautiful product that celebrates environmental stewardship for everyday use. *Melanie Dowler*

The **Power House** turns an abandoned Detroit home into an energy cell supplying electricity to its neighbours and creating a self-reliant power network.

Design 99

Detroit, MI
USA

2005

Detroit, Michigan is in a dire economic situation, with the problems of the credit crunch and the fallout of the US housing market adding to the century-long decline of the automobile industry, which has historically been the area's primary economic driver. Detroit itself has become a symbol of the decline of the American Dream: the population of the city that once promised a good job and a family home has fallen from its peak of more than two million in 1945, to 951,000 by 2000 and 790,000 at the last census in 2010.

Since 2005, there have been an estimated 55,000 foreclosures. The city has made efforts to plan for its own abandonment, decommissioning neighbourhoods and tearing down homes, but even demolition doesn't come cheap. This costs an estimated £4,500 ($7,500) per house, so for over 12,000 vacant buildings, it would amount to about £55 million ($90 million), and material from the demolished houses would end up in landfills.

This urban decay has been a subject of media fascination; the city has been portrayed as a sublime contemporary ruin by rappers, fashion photographers, academics and journalists. But most of Detroit's inhabitants don't produce or consume this image of the city; instead they deal every day with desolation, depleted civic services, drugs, homelessness and other conditions of urban malaise. Despite this, Detroit has a rising number of organizations at work to better the city and improve its environment. Fuelled and incensed by Detroit's constant media battering, these groups are striving to make real changes and to create a positive image for Detroit.

Design 99 is one of these pioneering organizations. In 2005, artist and gallerist Mitch Cope and his wife, architect Gina Reichert, moved to a new home in the most ethnically diverse neighbourhood in the Detroit area. They found a property that was formerly a Polish deli, complete with a shop front and a house at the back. It bears witness to the historical base of Polish and African-American workers in the city, who have formed part of a diverse mix of immigrants from the 1970s onward, the largest number of which has come from Bangladesh.

Over the next few years, the financial crisis exacerbated Detroit's problems, increasing foreclosures and vacancies and, along with them, looting and arson. Homes were stripped of any components that could be sold: copper pipes, electrical cable, remaining fixtures and fittings. In 2008, Design 99 invested in a former drug house just around the corner from their home – the price was only £1,150 ($1,900). Two vacant lots adjacent to the property were negotiated for an additional £1,800 ($3,000). A house next door became available for £300 ($500), which was snapped up and sold to artist friends, and another close by was bought for only £60 ($100).

Cope and Reichert renamed the original £1,150 ($1,900) home the Power House. They fitted it with solar panels and a wind turbine to supply DC electricity for low-energy fittings. The roof was packed with insulation and vinyl siding removed to expose the cedar siding underneath. The original aim of the project, which is piecemeal, self-funded and self-driven, was to make the house into an energy cell that can supply energy to its neighbours and create an off-grid, self-reliant network. The house, through a match-funding arrangement with Fonds BKVB, is now home to an artist-in-residency programme for Dutch artists and architects, and the two adjacent lots have become a community garden.

Through this transparent method of working – visible to the entire neighbourhood – the project encourages comments, questions and community involvement. Furthering their role as neighbourhood curators, Design 99 has worked with *Juxtapoz* art magazine to purchase additional homes for one-off art commissions, as site-specific spaces and immersive art environments. Future ideas for fostering a sustainable community include the conversion of alleys into bike paths and skate parks, setting up micro-economic craft workshops and developing a retrofit collection of parts as a tool-kit for other abandoned homes. The relatively modest, DIY spirit of Design 99 reflects Cope and Reichert's ideas that the project's long-term sustainability, and indeed the reversal of Detroit's urban decay, will necessitate a diversity of approaches and support from political and economic sectors. *Joshua Bolchover*

The Power House is outfitted with solar panels and a wind turbine (opposite) and is only one part of the broader effort to revitalize the surrounding neighbourhood (this page).

The windows of the Power House are made of coloured acrylic cut into half-inch strips and stacked one on top of another inside a wooden frame (opposite and top). The material was reclaimed from a museum exhibition and functions as a security system for neighbourhood houses, using colour, light and pattern to confuse potential vandals. The 'hoodcat' is a mobile tool for reclaiming, reconstructing and reconsidering neighbourhoods. It is an extension of the concepts and work of the Power House, which is why it shares a similar paint scheme (bottom).

The nomadic **Prinzessinnengärten** adapts to the ever-changing urban landscape of Berlin, providing locals with organic foods while minimizing the use of waste, labour and financial resources.

Robert Shaw and Marco Clausen
—
Berlin, Germany
—
2009

The gardens are tended to by local gardeners at pop-up sites.

Founded by documentary film-maker Robert Shaw and photographer Marco Clausen, Prinzessinnengärten (Princess Gardens) is a movable organic garden based in the Kreuzberg neighbourhood of Berlin. In the summer of 2009, Shaw and Clausen formed the non-profit organization Nomadisch Grün (Nomadic Green) and leased a 6,000 m² (64,600 sq ft) vacant lot in Moritzplatz, an area of Kreuzberg considered wasteland for more than 50 years and once obscured by the Berlin Wall. It was here that the Prinzessinnengärten was born.

Designed to 'pop-up' in unused or abandoned spaces with relative ease, the plants, vegetables and herbs of Prinzessinnengärten are sown in recycled plastic crates, Tetra Paks and rice sacks. Vegetation can move from one location to another, nearly unscathed. All produce is grown in compost soil and without the use of pesticides or artificial fertilizer. Honeybees kept by an on-site beekeeper add to the garden's biodiversity, as they feed on the nectar of plants. During the harsh winter months, the various sections of Prinzessinnengärten are either stored or relocated. In 2011, the garden was temporarily housed in the Eisenbahnmarkthalle, an old covered market and public centre of Kreuzberg.

Shaw and Clausen have created an innovative model of sustainable agriculture that can adapt to the ever-changing urban environment. With cities and their real estate markets constantly in flux, community gardens have at times faced permanent destruction or the high costs of relocation when their land leases expire. Prinzessinnengärten is a viable, forward-thinking solution for such circumstances. Conceived on the basis of impermanence, the mobile garden minimizes waste and the need for capital, labour and other resources as it moves from one site to another.

Prinzessinnengärten is about creative green design and it is also about building a sense of community; fostering relationships among the participants and to the natural environment are both essential to the project. Local residents can participate in educational garden workshops, partake in communal dinners made with the garden's harvests, or simply take in the greenery with neighbours. People of all ages serve as environmental stewards, volunteering time and labour to help establish and maintain the garden. The nutrient-rich produce of their labour is available for purchase on-site. Hence, the social impact of Prinzessinnengärten is far-reaching, including a long-term positive impact on the health of local residents through healthy organic food options.

Prinzessinnengärten alters any location to which it travels, not only visually and socially, but also ecologically: the garden plants absorb pollutants in the air by increasing levels of carbon dioxide; capture radiation from the sun, in effect cooling the area; and reduce fuel consumption and greenhouse gas emissions related to the transport of fruits and vegetables. The mobile garden also offers a new habitat for birds and other living organisms to feed on, inhabit and thrive within. Through adaptive reuse of space, the mobile garden reinvents parking lots, rooftops and other empty spaces with environmental incentives. *Nicole Caruth*

Robert Shaw and Marco Clausen

The garden can be moved
to any location (opposite).
Vegetables and produce
are grown and harvested,
then they are served to the
local community (this page).

Public Farm 1 occupied a museum courtyard, creating a place for agricultural and food production within the confines of a formerly industrial neighbourhood.

WORK ac
—
New York, NY
USA
—
2008

In PF 1, fruit and herbs grow within cardboard tubes. In the middle of the structure is a pool that allows for visitors to interact, socialize and cool off.

In 1968, Paris played host to one of the world's most culturally significant urban uprisings. Students took to the streets of the city, brandishing slogans including 'sous les paves la plage', or 'under the pavement, the beach'. Forty years later, when WORK ac decided to bring revolution back to the city landscape, their call was: 'sur les paves la ferme', or, 'over the pavement the farm'. Their project, Public Farm 1, was installed at the experimental art space PS 1, which was founded by Alanna Heiss in 1971 as the Institute for Art and Urban Resources, an organization that explored the reuse and development of derelict spaces in New York for cultural purposes. Acquired by the Museum of Modern Art in 1999, PS 1 has long been known for showcasing and encouraging experimental art and artists. One of the spaces regularly repurposed is the outdoor courtyard, which is host every summer to a different architecture installation.

In Public Farm 1 (PF 1), which was installed in the courtyard in the summer of 2008, a plunging hillside of recycled cardboard tubes twisted and climbed again to form an inverted V-shape, creating a shaded area below and one of the strangest lawns ever imagined above. The sturdy cardboard tubes were bolted together and contained a variety of vegetables, fruit and herbs; fresh produce was available for harvesting and chickens lived on site. Some of the taller tubes – rising as high as 9 m (30 ft) – were employed as structural columns but also housed functions to serve and entertain. One column contained a solar-powered phone charging station, another a soundscape of farmyard animals, curated by Michael Horan. One tube was employed as a comment on New York's light pollution: a starry sky was created inside by an array of small, low-powered lights installed in the ceiling. While looking up at this fake cosmic firmament visitors could hear the chirping of crickets, as if they had been transported away from the city. A pool was carved out of the middle of the structure and acted as a focal point for visitors. Tubes set on their sides created benches and a juice bar further reinforced the installation's function as a social space. A cardboard tube tribute to Vladimir Tatlin, the modernist painter and architect, also decorated the site, recalling the Soviet folly of replacing small farms with a centralized system of agricultural production.

The overall form was designed by WORK ac, but the finished product was the result of a series of collaborations. Construction team Art Domanty were joined by 100 volunteers to assemble this petal-inspired network of planting containers. The rainwater harvesting system employed to ensure that the plant irrigation was sustainable was overseen by Atlantic Irrigation Specialties and advice was obtained from a host of institutional bodies, including the Horticultural Society of New York and the Council on the Environment of New York.

PF 1 acts as a manifesto for the attitude of WORK ac. Founded by Amale Andaos and Dan Wood, the studio's projects span a vast range of scales, ranging from an urban dog house to the masterplanning of entire cities. PF 1 embodies their idea that even small spaces can be playfully reinterpreted to improve the look of urban areas and to serve both their neighbourhoods and the larger world: if public farms were built throughout cities, the provision of food could be freed of the economic and environmental costs of transportation. PF 1 was a temporary structure but the architects ensured that it performed as a working farm, overcoming the assumption that urban and agricultural environments are separate in anticipation of a world where cities are growing and expanding and new solutions must be investigated to address food production. With PF 1, WORK ac has proven that intelligent sustainable design can help provide these solutions, by reintroducing the city dweller and the natural world to each other.

Rob Fiehn

Many different edible plants are grown in PF 1 (top). The incline in the design allows for rainwater collected in a cistern to pass down through the planting beds (bottom). The cardboard tubes are both physical structure and planting containers (opposite, top left and right); some support the structure while others can be accessed from below when necessary (opposite, bottom left and right).

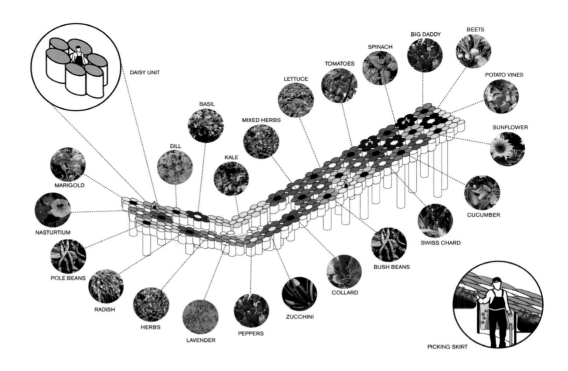

DAISY UNIT

BEETS
SPINACH
BIG DADDY
TOMATOES
POTATO VINES
LETTUCE
BASIL
MIXED HERBS
SUNFLOWER
DILL
KALE
MARIGOLD
CUCUMBER
NASTURTIUM
SWISS CHARD
POLE BEANS
BUSH BEANS
RADISH
COLLARD
HERBS
ZUCCHINI
LAVENDER
PEPPERS

PICKING SKIRT

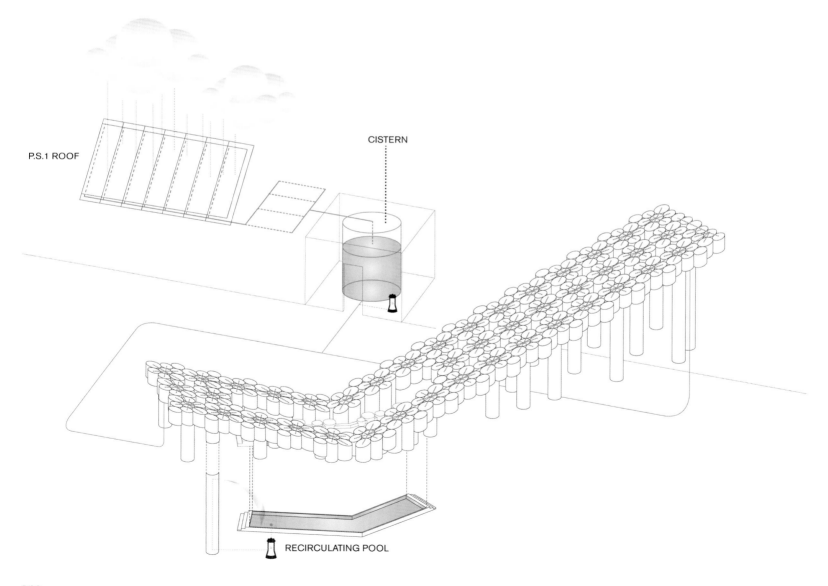

P.S.1 ROOF

CISTERN

RECIRCULATING POOL

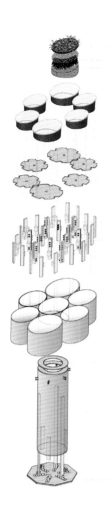

PLANT
2" COMPOST
JUTE EROSION CONTROL FABRIC
GAIA SOIL GROWING MEDIUM

SMART POTS

PLYWOOD PLANTER SHELVES

7/8" x 5-1/2" BOLTS

2 x 4 REINFORCING

KEY BLOCKS

CUT SONOTUBES / DAISY MODULE

PLYWOOD TOP RINGS

CARDBOARD COLUMN

2 x 4 REINFORCING

3-1/2" x 7/8" BOLTS
STEEL BRACKETS

WORK ac

PUMA's Clever Little Bag

is a sustainable substitute for the ubiquitous and wasteful shoebox.

Yves Béhar

—

Herzogenaurach, Germany

—

2010

The Clever Little Bag not only saves materials used for making shoeboxes (opposite), it can also be reused as a tote bag (this page).

The humble shoebox already has a whiff of sustainability about it. When their delicate parcels are removed, shoeboxes are often repurposed as places to stash love letters, photographs, receipts, or other mementos. They are even used as cases in which to stage childhood dioramas. But in fact, the manufacture of these little boxes is an incredible drain on materials, water and energy, accounting for millions of tonnes of waste each year. And the paper wastage reaches a striking extent in this age of digital images, emailed missives and electronic receipts.

PUMA observed this damage to the environment. The German athletic and sportswear company, which sells millions of pairs of shoes per year, has been working for over a decade to reduce its footprint, to improve its sustainability and remove supply-chain excesses under a concept called PUMA.Safe (Social Accountability and Fundamental Environmental standards). The company has succeeded on many levels, reducing the size of its tags to save tonnes of paper, swapping environmentally unfriendly apparel materials for organic cotton and recycled polyester, and fabricating its shopping bags from biodegradable cornstarch. But PUMA's most comprehensive initiative has been an attempt to redesign its packaging and distribution system that is based on the shoebox.

The resulting framework, called Clever Little Bag, made its debut in 2010. The industrial designer behind it was Yves Béhar of San Francisco's fuseproject. With PUMA, fuseproject worked for 21 months, analyzing the structure of boxes, brainstorming over 2,000 solutions, and creating more than 40 prototypes before realizing that the paradigm-shift in packaging would not actually lead to a shoebox. Instead, its designers created a non-woven bag wrapped around a three-sided, die-cut cardboard frame that uses 65 per cent less cardboard than the standard shoebox.

Clever Little Bag's innovations go well beyond its reduction in the use of paper. Béhar did away with traditional laminated printing, which makes shoeboxes shiny but interferes with their end-use recycling. The bag that surrounds the cardboard frame is non-woven and heat-stitched, and as a result requires less energy to produce at the outset. And because the bag is made from recycled Polyethylene Terephthalate (PET), it is recyclable at the end of its natural life cycle. The bag is used to stack, ship and display shoes at retail outlets, but it is can also used as a shopping bag at the check-out because it is branded with PUMA's name and logo. This alone saves up to 275 tonnes of plastic per year. The whole package is lighter than a traditional shoebox, which means that it saves 500,000 litres (132,000 gallons) of diesel during the transportation process.

In comparison to using shoeboxes for packaging and distribution, PUMA estimates that the bag reduces water, energy and fuel consumption at the manufacturing level by 60 per cent – which translates into savings of 8,500 tonnes of paper, 20 million megajoules of electricity and 1 million litres (265,000 gallons) of water per year – the equivalent of flushing your toilet 100,000 times. The fact that the bag is also reusable is an added bonus. *Jill Singer*

The **Quinmo Village Project** educates rural Chinese residents on eco-household agricultural techniques to sustain and promote the village's thriving independence.

Joshua
Bolchover
and John Lin

—

Guangdong
Province,
China

—

2006–present

China's economic reformation has restructured the relationship between the countryside and the city, creating hundreds of new cities at unprecedented speeds and leading to the amalgamation of urban hinterlands into vast regional sprawls. The most remote villages become enclaves for only the very young and the elderly, and are reliant upon income sent back from migrant workers. Farming becomes secondary rather than a key economic imperative. This dependency on migrant labour ultimately is not sustainable and increases the chasm between the rural poor and the urban rich.

Quinmo Village, located in the northwest of Guangdong Province, has been affected by these drastic changes. The village has an estimated population of 1,800, who grow rice and keep pigs and chickens. The long-term sustainable development of the village aims gradually to shift the village into economic self-sufficiency, by educating the inhabitants and changing their methods of agricultural production. The village now offers young people viable alternatives to factory work and the economic pull of the city.

The first project constructed in Quinmo was a school building, taking the form of a terraced landscape. It blends into the existing rice terraces and curvilinear contours of the terrain. The terraces form a theatrical public space orientated towards the village and used for large events. The concrete steps have open risers that filter light to avoid excessive solar gain and allow cross ventilation through the classrooms, drawing air into the space. The building is constructed from the cheapest materials available – concrete beams and columns with brick infill – which is the standard construction method for schools across China. To engage the villagers in the process of construction, the bricks have been hand-painted in fluorescent colours.

The library is designed as a landscape of cut-out islands within a raised floor, forming voids for sitting and reading.

With the creation of the new school, the old school – a traditional courtyard building – became vacant. John Lin and Joshua Bolchover, with Kadoorie Farm and Botanic Garden, adapted the old school to house an agricultural research organization: an exemplary eco-household and education centre for agricultural techniques. Here, in a complete ecological cycle, household food waste becomes feed for pigs and chickens, which in turn produces manure for plant beds, allowing for the testing of new plant varieties. A greenhouse nurtures seedlings and the kitchen garden contains herbs for daily use.

The agricultural programme extends to a farm outside the village and experiments with economically profitable products, such as premium chicken and tea-tree oil. This system aims to open up additional markets, creating the possibility for Quinmo's financial autonomy, as opposed to a continued dependence on migrant incomes.

The old school has grown into an informal community centre for the village – kids spend their lunch breaks reading and playing in the courtyard, while the village head uses one room as his office and the open dining area for larger group meetings. Throughout the year, a non-profit organization organizes several camps for children, who are sponsored to go to school and receive higher education. These students return to the village and teach the younger children about their experiences.

The promotion of sustainable and holistic agricultural practices in Quinmo Village can incrementally renew an interest in rural productivity, while furthering the educational possibilities for its children and providing alternative options to working in cities. *Joshua Bolchover*

Joshua Bolchover and John Lin

EDUCATION LOOP
Quinmo Village

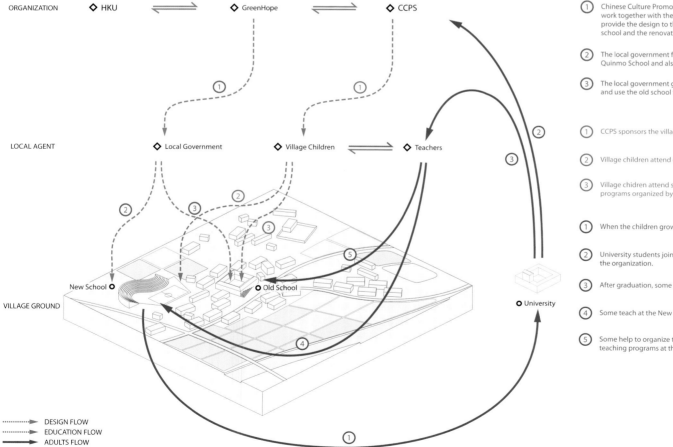

ORGANIZATION ◇ HKU ⇄ ◇ GreenHope ⇄ ◇ CCPS

LOCAL AGENT ◇ Local Government ◇ Village Children ⇄ ◇ Teachers

VILLAGE GROUND New School ○ ○ Old School ○ University

⋯⋯▸ DESIGN FLOW
⋯⋯▸ EDUCATION FLOW
——▸ ADULTS FLOW

① Chinese Culture Promotion Society (CCPS) and Greenhope work together with the University of Hong Kong (HKU) to provide the design to the local government for the new school and the renovation of the old school.

② The local government funds the construction of the New Quinmo School and also provides education for the children.

③ The local government gives CCPSS permission to renovate and use the old school for cultural center purposes.

① CCPS sponsors the village children's education.

② Village children attend classes at New Quinmo School.

③ Village chidren attend summer camp and winter teaching programs organized by the CCPS at the old school.

① When the children grow up, they go to university.

② University students join the CCPS and take part in the organization.

③ After graduation, some become teachers.

④ Some teach at the New Quinmo School.

⑤ Some help to organize the summer camp and winter teaching programs at the old school.

The new school in Quinmo Village (opposite, top) is part of a network of organizations, people and projects that are transforming the economic and social life of the village (opposite, bottom). The open public space of the new school houses New Year lion dance performances, morning assemblies and basketball games (top). Much of the construction of the new school was done by village residents, including the brightly painted facade (bottom right), and the completion of that building allowed the old school to house new recreational and educational facilites (bottom left).

Joshua Bolchover and John Lin

253

Recyclable Loofah Panel Houses

are constructed for £1.85 per m² (33¢ per sq ft), in just three to four days, reusing plastic fibre and loofah plant waste in Paraguay where wood is scarce.

Pedro Pedrós
and Elsa
Zalvídar
—
Paraguay
—
2008

Panels are installed on homes (opposite) after the loofah plant is harvested and processed into sheets (this page).

In 1992, Paraguayan community activist and organizer Elsa Zalvídar initiated a programme to increase the earning potential of rural women by cultivating loofah. A simple crop, loofah is a cucumber-like edible vegetable before it fully ripens; after it ripens, loofah can be dried into a rough scrubber. Zalvídar taught regional women to grow and harvest loofah, and to produce cosmetic sponges, mats, insoles and slippers from the vegetable. By the mid-2000s, almost 200 women were growing loofah, and Zalvídar saw the success that the programme brought in terms of alleviating poverty.

Despite the ecological growing methods of loofah, which ensure that the quality of the harvest is higher than the yield of loofahs grown in plantations, approximately one-third of the crop did not achieve a high enough quality for exportation. This agricultural waste, plus the 30 per cent of each loofah trimmed off during its transformation into a product is now used by Zalvídar to create panels which can be used to build housing for some of the 300,000 families in Paraguay who lack adequate housing.

The housing inadequacy is closely related to the growing scarcity of wood in Paraguay. In recent decades, deforestation has devastated Paraguay, leaving the country with less than 10 per cent of its virgin forest. Addressing the diminishing supply of lumber, as well as the need to reduce agricultural waste and plastic that would otherwise be added to landfill, Zalvídar teamed up with Pedro Pedrós, a Spanish industrial engineer, to create a low-cost alternative construction material.

After months of experimentation, Zalvídar and Pedrós created loofah panels by mixing agricultural waste with reground plastic. The panels are sustainable, strong, durable, flexible, lightweight and versatile. They can be used as floors, walls and roofs and are easily joined by metal connectors to construct homes at £1.85 per m² (33¢ per sq ft) in three to four days. The panels are appropriate for the earthquake-prone region. Because they are light and flexible, they bend and don't break. In the event that a structure does collapse during an earthquake, people will be significantly less likely to get hurt.

The panels are extruded by a machine, which can produce a panel of 0.5 m (16 ft) by 120 m (390 ft) in half an hour. The simple technology, which involves a melter, a mixer, an extruder and a cutter, allows different ratios of agricultural waste and plastic to be mixed, creating panels of differing densities, flexibilities, weights and insulative qualities so they can be adapted to varied construction needs. Colour can be added during the process, saving money and time by eliminating the need to paint. The panels are easily recyclable, can be melted and used to create new panels, or reused in other construction projects. The plastic used is specifically selected, so it can be re-melted, mixed with more agricultural fibre and made into new panels. When they become too rich in vegetable fibres to be recycled anymore, they can be used as high-energy fuel.

The greatest strength of Zalvídar's initiative is the integrated system of cultivation, recycling, production and distribution. Local growers, plastic gatherers and factory workers collaborate to stimulate the economy, reduce deforestation and raise the standard of living. The model, which requires only recycled plastic and agricultural fibres, is easily reproducible in other parts of the world, where other locally available agricultural fibres, such as corn husk or palm trees, could replace loofah. Recyclable Loofah Panel Houses demonstrate the power of using locally abundant organic and recycled material in sustainable housing alternatives for the urban and rural poor. Bareket Kezwer

Pedro Pedrós and Elsa Zalvídar

Rolling Huts return what was once an asphalt-covered trailer park to a natural landscape through its site-sensitive design and use of raw and renewable materials.

Olson Kundig Architects

—

Mazama, WA USA

—

2007

The Rolling Huts form an alternative type of campground in Methow Valley (opposite). The huts are arranged in a small group of six, and all have views of the surrounding landscape (this page).

In a time when undeveloped environments are continually at risk of becoming sprawling developments, Rolling Huts show that it is possible to reverse this trend. Faced with an asphalt-covered site, Tom Kundig of Seattle-based Olson Kundig Architects took a former RV campground in Washington State's Methow Valley and returned it to its natural state. The Pacific Northwest firm, founded by architect Jim Olson in the late 1960s, is known for its continual exploration of the relationship between architecture and landscape.

Mindful of the sensitive alpine river valley ecology – the native grasses and shrubs – Kundig created six small, wheeled cabins. He re-conceptualized mobile homes as innovative Walden-like escapes. The low-tech Rolling Huts are designed to create minimal impact on the environment and remediate previous damage done to the landscape by development. Raising the shelters on wheels protects the meadow floor and allows unobstructed views of the surrounding North Cascade Mountains.

Each Rolling Hut is built of a steel-clad box on a steel and wood platform. Lifted up on large, custom dual steel wheels, the huts sit on a chassis that supports external and internal living areas. A 22 m² (240 sq ft) deck made from renewable Ipe hardwood surrounds a 19 m² (200 sq ft) steel box. For the construction, Kundig chose raw and renewable materials such as steel, plywood and car-decking. These durable, low-maintenance materials weather over time and take on a natural patina.

The Rolling Huts are designed to work holistically with the seasons. An asymmetrical roof shelters each hut. Supported on wood beams, the canopy extends beyond the interior steel box to provide shade for the deck in the summer. As the corrugated roof slopes upwards in an inverted 'V' shape, clerestory windows fill in the gap between wall and ceiling, letting in light and providing distant views. Snow collects on the roof during the winter; with the spring thaw, it melts and percolates naturally back into the long grasses.

The Rolling Huts' interiors are efficiently beautiful. In the meadow, time is spent outside. Each cabin houses a small bedroom, a living room and a petite kitchen, with just enough space for a bar-sized fridge, microwave and coffee pot. Conscious of excessive heat gain in the small spaces, north-facing double-paned sliding glass doors open to the deck for exterior access and ventilation. The tight space requires only a wood-burning stove for heat during the winter. Toilets and showers are located nearby at the larger main barn.

Inside, renewable cork is used on all the floors. Inexpensive plywood covers the walls and ceiling. Left unfinished, it is shaped into utilitarian furniture – bed platforms, benches, shelving and even reconfigurable cubes for seating, dining and storage. Kundig brings an eco-mindedness into every part of the building process, from the large-scale site of Methow Valley to the small-scale details of everyday life. *Mimi Zeiger*

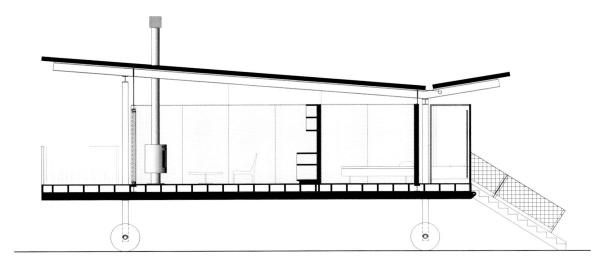

Each hut can sleep two, and its wheels lift the space above the ground, which provide better views of the surrounding wilderness (opposite, top). This also protects the meadow floor (opposite, bottom).

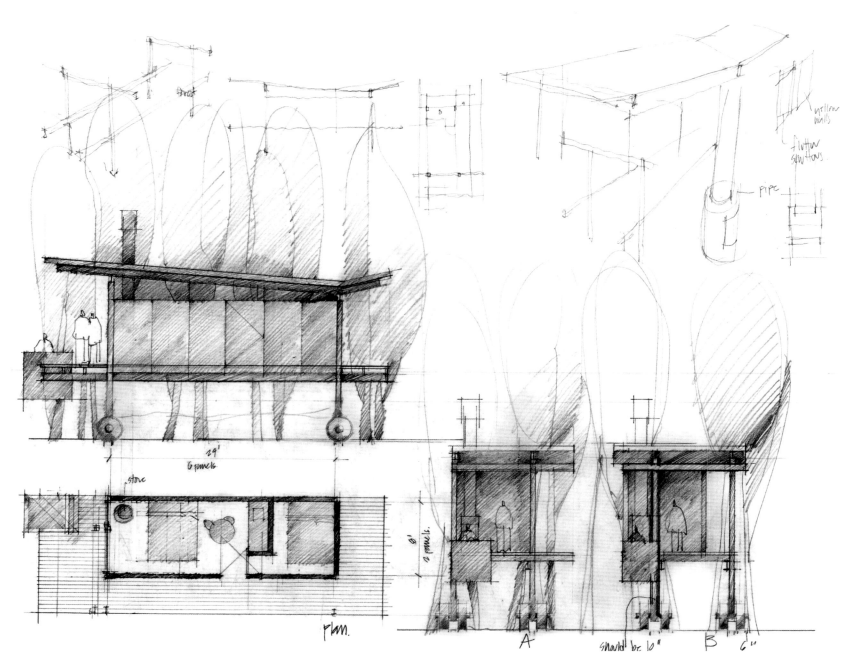

The **SAYL Chair** is 93 per cent recyclable at the end of its lifespan, throughout which it provides maximum comfort and support to the human body.

Yves Béhar
—
Holland, MI USA
—
2010

The steel and aluminium components of the SAYL office chair are 100 per cent recyclable and the plastic components used are not made from the harmful PVC (polyvinyl chloride) material, so they can be recycled at the end of the chair's life too.

The SAYL Chair was designed by Yves Béhar of San Francisco-based design and branding firm fuseproject. The Swiss-born Béhar does not confine himself to one genre of design: his portfolio includes organic cotton PACT underwear, the GE WattStation electric vehicle charger and the One Laptop Per Child project, which aims to bring low-cost laptops to children in developing nations. SAYL is produced by Herman Miller, a Michigan-based furniture manufacturer for whom Béhar has previously conceived three low-energy LED task lamps. This is Béhar's first ergonomic desk chair, an object for which the Herman Miller brand is famed.

Following a three-year long design process, SAYL made its public debut at the Museum of Contemporary Art, Chicago, in October 2010. The chair garnered attention not only for its fresh use of largely recycled and recyclable materials, but also for its sticker price. The most basic SAYL model starts at £250 ($399), making it the most affordable member of Herman Miller's roster of beloved work chairs, which also includes the Aeron and Ergon.

The SAYL family of chairs – which features both a work chair and a side chair – are manufactured with no extraneous materials. This process makes the chair lightweight and affordable and places less of a burden on the environment. Of the materials used to create the SAYL work chair, 10 per cent are recycled, while the entire chair is 93 per cent recyclable at the end of its life. The SAYL side chair comprises up to 21 per cent recycled materials and is 92 per cent recyclable. Although plastic is a constituent element of both chairs, this does not include environmentally harmful polyvinyl chloride (PVC) and the plastic can also be recycled at the end of the chair's life.

SAYL is manufactured without air or water emissions in Holland, Michigan, at the GreenHouse, Herman Miller's production facility, which is driven entirely by green power (50 per cent from wind power, 50 per cent from captured landfill off-gassing). Designed by architect William McDonough, the GreenHouse was selected as a pilot project in the development of the U.S. Green Building Council (USGBC) Leadership in Energy and Environmental Design (LEED) certification protocol in 1995. Herman Miller has been involved with the USGBC council since its infancy, having helped to fund the organization when it started up in 1993. Today, the GreenHouse maintains LEED 'Pioneer' status.

Béhar not only designed SAYL to have minimal environmental impact but to provide maximum comfort and support to the human body. The streamlined concept was inspired by a building project completed in 1937 in Béhar's adopted home of San Francisco: the Golden Gate Bridge. Using 3D Intelligent Suspension Technology, the chair's elastomer suspension framework is stretched from the 'Y-Tower' back support structure, which resembles the sail of a boat – hence the name SAYL. Like cables linking the towers of a suspension bridge, SAYL's flexible suspension material can vary in thickness, applying tension wherever it is most needed. Allowing for a wide range of movement and offering superior lumbar, sacral and spinal support, SAYL's unique suspension back material also keeps its sitter cool for long stretches of time.

In addition to the eco-friendly attributes of the chair, Béhar and Herman Miller have also taken into account shipping and packaging. The ready-to-assemble SAYL is shipped in two pieces in a single corrugated cardboard box, which is half the chair's size and meant to be recycled repeatedly as part of a closed-loop recycling system. Inspired by a feat of classic, durable engineering on the Pacific Coast and manufactured in an efficient, environmentally friendly manner in America's midwest, SAYL elegantly and radically redefines the ergonomic work chair. *Matthew Hickman*

Yves Béhar

The **SMA Solar Academy** is completely energy self-sufficient: it relies on bio-gas, photovoltaic panels and diffused silicon cells in its glass windows.

HHS
Architekten
—
Niestetal,
Germany
—
2011

The building is lifted on columns because it is located within a flood plain (opposite). The south-facing wall of the building is covered with diffused silicon cells, which collect energy and create a shaded pattern of natural light on the interior (this page).

Many buildings claim to generate much of their energy from renewable resources. However, almost all of them are connected in some way to the public power network, either by drawing off a small percentage constantly or relying on it as a back-up when on-site renewables don't produce enough energy. SMA, a leading manufacturer of solar technology, designs, manufactures and sells photovoltaic systems worldwide, with a focus on the developing world, where a reliable connection to a power grid is often impossible to achieve.

Naturally, when the need to build a new training centre arose, SMA took the bold step of commissioning an architect to design a completely energy self-sufficient building at its base in Niestetal, Germany. The SMA Solar Academy, a £4.2 million ($7 million), 1,600 m² (17,000 sq ft) facility is an exercise in the integration of renewable energy sources and a lesson in how to design and construct a building that is independent of any fossil-fuelled energy sources.

The Academy is powered and heated predominantly by solar power. The entire roof and south-facing wall of the building are clad in large photovoltaic panels. In addition, sun-tracking photovoltaic arrays are mounted at ground level around the building. As the sun shines, the photovoltaic panels that adorn the building are constantly capturing solar power, while inverters are converting it into electricity. If they produce more energy than is required, any excess is stored in an internal battery bank, also located on the main floor of the building.

However, even this battery bank can run dry. HHS Architekten's solution is to heavily insulate the solid walls and roof to minimize the energy required to heat the building in winter and to keep it cool internally in the summer. To meet the challenge of creating power when there is little solar activity, the architect has also integrated a combined heat and power system in the uppermost floor of the academy. Powered by bio-gas, an electric turbine creates power by spinning. The resulting heat is used to warm the building's interior. In summer, cooling is provided by a heat exchanger connected to an underground borehole installation.

All of the equipment used to generate renewable energy has been made accessible for display in this teaching building. The main floor of the building includes a central reception and social space with four meeting rooms in the wings. A demonstration space displays the building's solar inverters, usually hidden from view, for inspection by an estimated 15,000 students annually. The corridor to the meeting rooms also serves as a live demonstration. The south-facing glazed wall of this space is covered in diffuse silicon cells, adhered to the glass. Providing a degree of shading in the day, the energy they draw from the sun also illuminates and heats the space when required. In the main reception space, a large digital display indicates the building's current energy consumption and the corresponding amount of CO_2 that is being saved. The battery room and inverters can also be observed from this space, as can a digital display showing the state of charge of the batteries.

The size and visibility of the new building, set within a relatively flat landscape, prompted HHS Architekten to taper the mass toward its extremities. As such, the main bulk of the building – reception, technology centre and battery room – lies in the middle, while the meeting and seminar rooms are pushed to the narrower edges. By elevating the building on columns, the architect creates the impression that it is floating above the landscape, thereby giving a sense of lightness to the building. This move also lifts the building above the flood plain on which it is located and negates potential flooding in the winter. First and foremost, however, the building is positioned and spatially designed to ensure its optimal energy-efficient function.

Although the SMA Solar Academy only uses a minimal amount of energy, it does not forgo any conveniences of a twenty-first century educational establishment. The building is kept at a comfortable temperature and is well ventilated all year around. In addition, all the seminar rooms have modern equipment, such as digital boards and workstations, for students to engage with individual projects or devices.

As a consequence of its intelligent design, the building is self-sufficient: it operates independently and is not connected to any public power network in any way. SMA calls this an 'island solution', a concept that can be applied anywhere in the world, regardless of the location's remoteness or regional energy instability. Pushing these environmental limits and illustrating just what renewable technologies such as solar power can achieve is important to the future of the renewable energy industry. However, perhaps more pressing is the need to demonstrate this technology to design professionals and potential clients. Only when solar power is better understood will it become more commonly used. SMA's new solar academy is an imaginative and exciting step towards a future powered by cleaner, greener fuel. *Will Jones*

The central core of the building houses the combined heat and power plant.

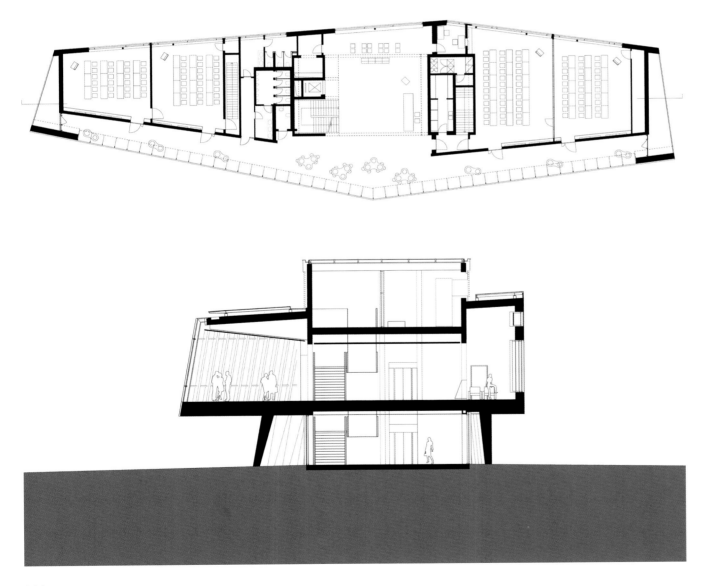

SOFT Rockers collect and store the sun's energy to create a user-friendly recharging station open both day and night.

Kennedy &
Violich
Architecture
—
Boston, MA
USA
—
2011

This outdoor piece of furniture sits in MIT's Killian Court (opposite). The SOFT Rocker was built by professor Sheila Kennedy and a team of students at MIT (left). Now in use, it charges small electronics such as cell phones (right).

The energy-generating SOFT Rockers debuted at MIT's Festival of Art, Science and Technology (FAST), an event celebrating 150 years of creative innovation at the university. Outdoor rocking lounges filled the campus's Killian Courtyard, where the furniture provided much needed seating and clean energy charging stations where students could power-up their gadgets. The SOFT Rocker is the result of an interdisciplinary collaboration of designers and engineers led by architect Sheila Kennedy and Jungmin Nam of Kennedy & Violich Architecture Ltd (KVA). Principle of Boston-based KVA, Kennedy is known for her research and design of mobile and embedded technologies, including the founding of the non-profit the Portable Light Project, a global initiative to bring energy-harvesting solar textiles to developing countries. Combining high-tech manufacturing strategies with low-tech, user-friendly implementation, the SOFT Rocker is a direct outgrowth of Kennedy's earlier investigations.

The project's innovation comes from combining an emerging fabrication process with a sustainable vision for small scale, off-grid energy production. The design team was sensitive to the amount of time, labour, and materials traditionally required to create thin, moulded wood forms. (For example, the kind of curvatures found on Eames plywood furniture.) Instead, they adapted a mass-customization technique called Zipshape to create the SOFT Rocker's unique teardrop form. Developed in 2009 by German architect Christoph Schindler, this wood joining method speeds the process and reduces costs. The team shaped the rockers out of medium-density fiberboard (MDF)

– composed of fast-growing, ecologically sensitive wood. A lightweight Kuka robotic arm cuts the softwood panels. Parametric software digitally controls the cutting process and the Kuka robotic arm carves precise grooves in the MDF, which allows each panel to bend. When two panels are specially cut to interlock together, they create the SOFT Rocker's curved surface.

SOFT Rockers are part of a holistic, sustainable energy system. Unlike standard outlets that draw energy directly from the grid, these lounge chairs are independent power stations and are free from the constraints of conventional hard-wired infrastructure. Each loop-shaped SOFT Rocker is equipped with a flexible photovoltaic panel, which collects enough solar energy to power any small electronic device with a USB port such as a cell phone, computer, or even a cooler. The lounge's design works in conjunction with the human body and the environment. For the 1.5 axis, 35 watt solar tracking system to operate at optimum performance, it requires that a person occupy the lounge and use his weight to orientate the rocker towards the sun. By tilting back in the chair, the user can calibrate the alignment.

Designed to be lively and engaging places for college students to hang out any time, the SOFT Rockers operate both day and night. During the day, harvested sunlight charges a solar array and the energy is stored in a 12 ampere-hour battery. At night, thin strips of electroluminescent lighting tape bathe the lounge in a futuristic glow – perfect for socializing, relaxing, and recharging. *Mimi Zeiger*

The **Solar Handbag** generates two watts of electricity, which can be used to charge mobile devices or to illuminate its interior with optical fibres.

DIFFUS
Design
—
Copenhagen,
Denmark
—
2011

The solar collectors are sewn right onto the exterior surface of the handbag.

The Solar Handbag is a black tote bag with an ingenious twist. It was created by Danish design studio DIFFUS (founded by Hanne-Louise Johannesen and Michel Guglielmi), in collaboration with the Alexandra Institute and Centre for Software Innovation. It has 100 silicon solar cells or 'power stations', which collect daytime sunlight and generate two watts of usable energy – enough to run a mobile device. Thus the carrier can keep his or her electronic devices charged throughout the day, even with low levels of sunlight exposure. At night, opening the the bag activates a set of interior optical fibres, shaped like cooking whisks, which glow to assist the user in his or her search for objects.

The handbag's solar 'sequins' have been woven into this self-conductive embroidery, which transmits all harvested energy to a rechargeable lithium ion battery tucked inside a small compartment. These components were developed through a joint research effort between Forster Rohner AG, a Swiss embroidery company, and two regional schools: the University of Applied Sciences Rapperswil and the NTB Interstate University of Applied Sciences of Technology, Buchs, Switzerland (also known as NTB Buchs). By turning monocrystalline silicon – the most efficient photovoltaic material in existence today – into these miniature decorative adornments and utilizing traditional textile-making techniques, DIFFUS and its partners have increased the material's possibilities for use in future textile products.

At present, many textile-based solar products are limited in efficiency and aesthetics due to the number of solar cells that the exterior and interior surface can hold. The Solar Handbag is an important step forward in green fashion; its energy-harvesting surface maximizes design freedom as well as usefulness. Its trendy shape is more than simply fashion forward: the handbag was designed to mimic an eclipse, alluding to the relationship between the sun and moon, between the light source and the enlightened.

In addition to art and design technologies, DIFFUS works with theoretical and practical applications of architecture. The designers compare the merger of function and design in the Solar Handbag to the work of nineteenth-century French architect Gustave Eiffel, famous for designing the Eiffel Tower, in which the armature is part of the splendour.

Where fashion and environmental concerns once seemed at odds, the fashion industry suggests that green clothing and accessories are just as important (and trendy) as the overall effort to improve and save our habitat. Indeed, as DIFFUS and its partners confirm, portable fashions that utilize sunlight to create electricity can play a significant role in our overall sense of well-being. Other innovations from DIFFUS include the Climate Dress, a garment with sensors and LED lights woven into the fabric. *Nicole Caruth*

The flexible, modular and recyclable plastic leaves of **Solar Ivy** harness energy through photovoltaic cells, providing shade and power to the buildings they 'grow' on.

SMIT: Sam and Teresita Cochran

—

Brooklyn, NY USA

—

2009

Solar Ivy

A biomimetic form of the natural ivy plant, Solar Ivy functions as a lightweight, solar-powered, energy-collecting cover for building facades (opposite). Each leaf captures sunlight, and can store a half-watt of power in embedded Konarka Power Plastic organic photovoltaic cells (this page).

Move over Wisteria, Kudzu and Morning Glory: there's a new climbing plant in town. Giving emerging technology a boost of verdant appeal is Solar Ivy from Sustainably Minded Interactive Technology (SMIT), a multi-disciplinary sustainable design firm based in the Brooklyn Navy Yard, New York. The principals of the firm are the brother and sister team of Sam and Teresita Cochran, born in St Louis, Missouri, and architectural designer Benjamin Wheeler Howes.

Initially a wind and solar device dubbed GROW, Solar Ivy was conceived as Sam Cochran's thesis project while an undergraduate student in Industrial Design at the Pratt Institute in Brooklyn. Taking on the biomimetic form of ivy, each modular 'leaf' is made from recyclable, UV-stable polyethylene, which is capable of harnessing energy – about half a watt of power – through embedded Konarka Power Plastic organic photovoltaic cells.

Like natural ivy, Solar Ivy can 'grow' prolifically on a variety of building typologies and facades, whether atop a garage or a garden shed, on the rooftop of a commercial building or gracing the front facade of a home. The leaves themselves are embedded into a flexible yet durable stainless steel mesh framework that can be anchored onto various vertical building surfaces.

Once rooted into the framework, the lightweight leaves are free to naturally flutter, flit and flail about in the wind, capturing sunlight from various angles. From there, the energy collected by each leaf is transferred to the existing electrical grid through a grid tie inverter,

or stored in on-site batteries for later use. In addition to providing dramatic visual flair by way of a highly adaptable alternative energy system, Solar Ivy, like a strategically placed tree, also provides shade to a structure, further reducing energy costs by controlling heat gain.

Just as Solar Ivy can be installed on a variety of facades, it is designed to be highly customizable. The leaves can be produced in a variety of colours: they can mimic Solar Ivy's natural counterpart, in deep green or the rich reds and yellows of autumn foliage, or when used in advertising applications, Solar Ivy can be ordered to coordinate with an organization's trademark colours.

The density of Solar Ivy can also be customized to meet aesthetic or energy needs. A homeowner can 'prune' Solar Ivy by lowering the density of the array: like a string of holiday lights, an individual leaf can easily be removed or replaced without disrupting the entire network. Solar Ivy can also be produced with different types of photovoltaic material to suit a client's particular needs, and be made to have varying levels of pitch. Designed with a complete life-cycle analysis in mind, the photovoltaics, leaves and other elements of Solar Ivy incorporate recycled and recyclable materials whenever possible.

SMIT is also developing another flexible, modular alternative energy system: a new version of GROW capable of producing solar energy while also harnessing kinetic energy through the movement of individual leaves as they dance in the wind. *Matthew Hickman*

The density and colour of the Solar Ivy leaves, made from recyclable UV-stable polyethylene, can be customized to suit a building's exterior (opposite). Solar Ivy can also provide varying levels of shading to a building's interior (top and bottom).

SMIT: Sam and Teresita Cochran

Made of recycled steel, Homasote, and reclaimed concrete, the **Solar Umbrella House** is nearly 100 per cent solar powered.

Brooks + Scarpa Architects

Venice, CA USA

2005

Brooks + Scarpa
Solar Umbrella House

Located in a typically snug Venice plot, the Solar Umbrella House is a remodelled bungalow designed by and for Lawrence Scarpa and Angela Brooks, principals of Brooks + Scarpa Architects. Originally a low-rise, 1920s villa, the architects have added a two-storey structure to the south end and reorientated the house to take advantage of the abundant Californian sunlight. The house is inspired by and named after Paul Rudolph's Umbrella House (1953). Rudolph's iconic modernist villa in Florida is characterized by a wooden trellis 'umbrella' that screens the occupants from the intense subtropical sun. Scarpa – a former employee of Rudolph – created his own shading 'umbrella' for this house but, in a twenty-first century twist, the 89 photovoltaic solar panels that wrap the roof and the south facade of the building also provide nearly all of the house's electricity.

Brooks + Scarpa is a leading practitioner of sustainable design, and this ethos is central to the Solar Umbrella House. The bright blue polycrystalline solar panels, which form the canopy over the house, were partly chosen for their intrinsic beauty. They are connected to the local grid as part of a net-metered system; the architects are effectively 'selling' electricity to the utility company as it accumulates throughout the day and then 'buying' it back at night. The building extension and the installation of the solar panels cost £240,000 ($390,000) and the payback period is expected to take 10 years from completion of the house. There are also three solar hydronic panels, which pre-heat domestic water and a small pool. The remodelling has halved gas consumption, which is even more impressive when you consider that the house is now 2.5 times its original size.

More passive measures have also been taken to improve climate control: orientation of glazing, concrete sink wells and an overhanging lantern in the kitchen that is employed as a heat chimney and allows natural light to enter the building.

The selection of sustainable materials was of paramount importance to the architects, who looked for materials that were durable, recyclable where possible, free of formaldehyde, sourced locally and low in maintenance. Recycled steel was used for structural elements and left unadorned, creating an industrial aesthetic. For a wall finish, the architects used Homasote, made from recycled paper and glue that is compressed under extreme pressure and heat. Orientated strand board (formed of wooden strips layered together for strength) was used for flooring in the remodelled areas of the house, with unadorned concrete for the addition. This concrete was formed largely of reclaimed material and the stucco on the exterior of the building contains a coloured pigment, requiring no repainting.

Energy is also saved through the relationship between exterior and interior spaces: cross ventilation keeps the rooms of the house naturally cool, while the passage of heat is encouraged by elements such as a perforated steel staircase. The cool temperature is maintained by operable shutters and skylights, which also enable natural light to filter throughout the house. The landscape has been designed to tolerate drought and allow water to percolate easily into the ground. Stormwater is retained and a drip irrigation system is in place, which can be adjusted to differing seasonal requirements.

Rob Fiehn

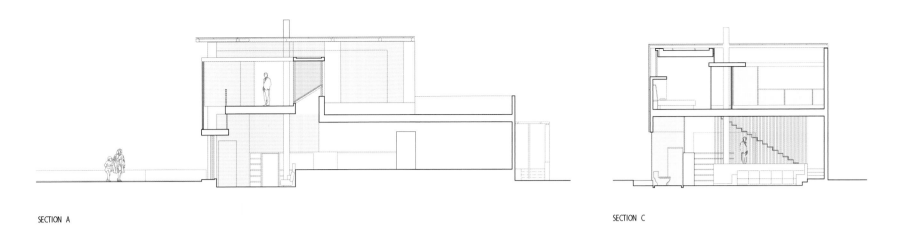

SECTION A

SECTION C

FIRST FLOOR PLAN

1. LIVING
2. (E) DINING
3. (E) KITCHEN
4. (E) BEDROOM
5. (E) STUDY
6. (E) BATHROOM
7. (E) CLOSET
8. WATER POND
9. BAMBOO PLANTER
10. BATH
11. LAUNDRY
12. A.V. CENTER

BOCCACCIO AVENUE

WOODLAWN AVENUE

SCALE IN FEET
0 1 3   6   10   15

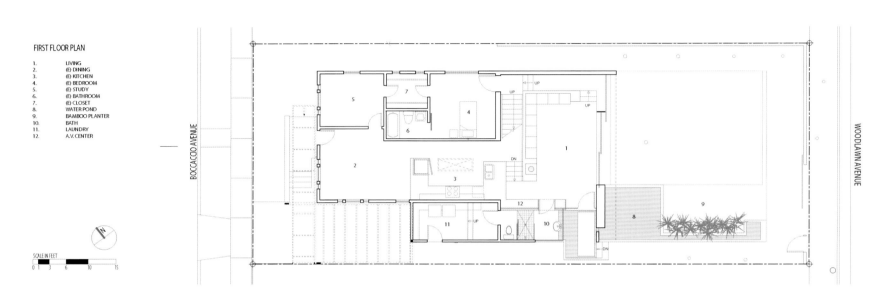

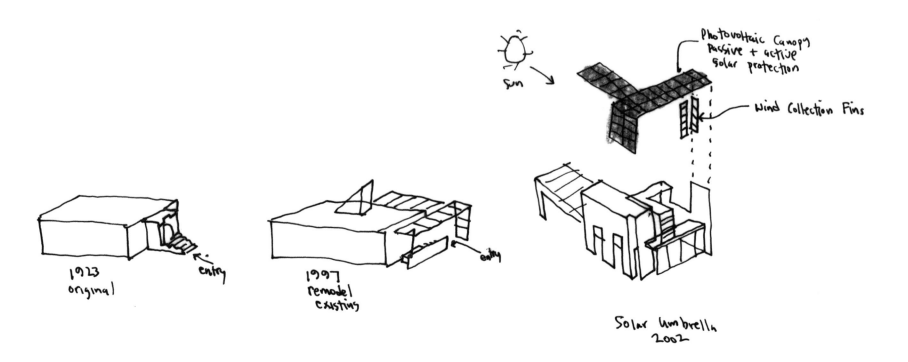

1923
original

entry

1997
remodel
existing

entry

Photovoltaic Canopy
passive + active
solar protection

Wind Collection Fins

sun

Solar Umbrella
2002

The renovation of the house had to take into account an earlier remodelling (opposite, bottom). The new design (opposite, top) allows for ample natural light to flow into the interior and patio spaces, blurring the boundaries between what is outside and inside. Recycled steel structural elements were used in construction (top left and right) and glazing on the interior walls allows for natural light to illuminate the living area (bottom).

Brooks + Scarpa Architects

Solarsiedlung has an advanced solar-powered design that produces a surplus of energy, which can be sold back to the grid.

Rolf Disch Solar Architecture
—
Freiburg im Breisgau, Germany
—
2000–06

Rolf Disch Solar Architecture has been building with solar energy for more than 40 years, and its work represents a marriage of technological innovation and social initiatives. Disch has been a forerunner in implementing solar panels as an integral part of building practices. Reflecting the scale of the environmental problems they tackle, the firm operates on a multitude of levels, from architecture and urban planning, to renovations and retrofitting, as well as product development and business consulting.

The Solarsiedlung project, completed in 2006 in the German city of Freiburg, can be seen as the prime example of this approach. At first glance, the Solarsiedlung resembles any other upmarket housing complex. It comprises 50 brightly painted family housing units framing open green spaces and a large commercial structure. Called the 'Sun Ship', this three-storey structure is built of reinforced concrete with a wooden facade, which serves to shield the housing areas from a main road. An eco-supermarket and green bank are located in the Sun Ship along with the German Eco Institute and about a dozen other companies; atop the structure, nine penthouses nestle amid a landscaped roof garden. Each building in the Solarsiedlung features large-scale photovoltaic panels glistening on the roof.

What is most innovative about this housing project is Disch's commitment to a goal that he calls 'PlusEnergy'. This requires a commitment to developing purely renewable energy sources, as well as to CO_2-neutral building. But more importantly, the buildings must produce more energy than they require, thus effectively acting as small-scale power plants. Based on extensive studies, the Solarsiedlung was the first full-scale test of PlusEnergy principles. The housing units at the Solarsiedlung produce 420,000 kWh of solar energy per year, saving roughly 200,000 litres (44,000 gallons) of oil and reducing CO_2 emissions by 500 tonnes.

The south facades of the Solarsiedlung buildings feature glass that is triple-glazed, with argon between the three panes. An infrared reflection layer on the interior pane prevents long-wave heat rays from leaving the building.

Thermal insulation is used to trap heat in the winter months. Along with the plentiful solar panels and a careful awareness of Freiburg's climatic conditions, these innovations can provide a space that is not only environmentally progressive, but is also economically viable. The energy produces by the Solarsiedlung creates a surplus of up to 36 kWh per m^2 a year (about 3.3 kWh per sq ft) annually. Not only does this mean the Solarsiedlung homes have almost no heating costs, but the excess energy can be sold back to the grid.

The Solarsiedlung is remarkable for its attention to the notion that being green is not only a technological concern, but also a social and economic issue for designers. The project adds twenty-first century technological solutions to the traditional German concept of the 'siedlung' as a community housing space in the search for the most effective forms of living. In accordance with ecological principles, the layout of the Solarsiedlung is determined primarily in relation to its exposure to sunlight, but it also incorporates public transportation, bike and pedestrian paths, as well as controlled traffic management. Car usage is reduced for the residents of the Solarsiedlung through a well-organized car-share program, further limiting energy usage.

In concert with the research and development of the Solarsiedlung, Disch has also established ethically responsible, ecological real-estate investment funds: another example of the idea that green investments can be good for everyone. The success of the Solarsiedlung has made the project an exemplar for a number of developments across Germany. The project shows that battling climate change is feasible through building, but only if this practice takes into account its social and economic consequences. By balancing an applied technological approach to the needs of the inhabitant, Disch is able to create a successful model for communal living that doesn't take for granted the form of the architectural project over its social function. As a model for ecological architecture that is economically viable, Disch leaves the possibility of green living looking pretty sunny. *Daniel Ayat*

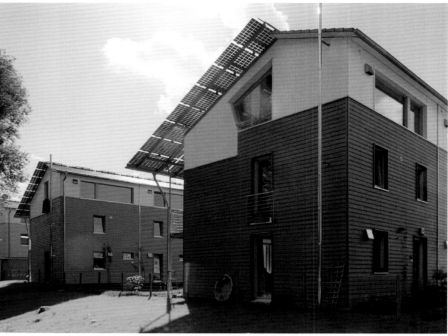

Solarsiedlung

The PlusEnergy development is designed to contribute both economically and ecologically through its incorporation of solar panels (opposite, top left) and garden areas (opposite, top right and bottom). Along the street-facing edge of the complex an eco-grocery store and bank buffer the residential area from traffic (this page).

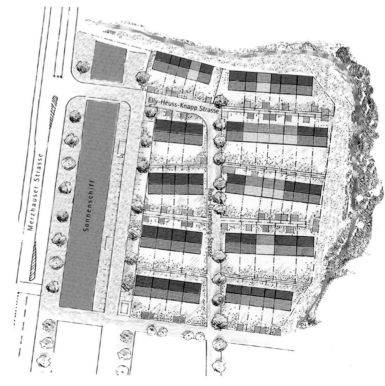

The **Southport Broadwater Parklands** was once a car park and brownfield site. It is now home to 3 km (1.9 miles) of foreshore parklands and 3,500 new trees.

AECOM and Whitearchitecture
—
Queensland, Australia
—
2009

The redevelopment of the Gold Coast (opposite) includes a major events lawn (this page), bathing boxes, barbecue shelters, play equipment, walking and cycling path networks, an extended pier, constructed wetlands and bio-retention basins.

The Southport Broadwater Parklands, an urban park and event space along the eastern coast of Australia, transformed a former car park for 900 vehicles into a spectacular gateway to the Gold Coast. The masterplan, created by AECOM, revitalized the former brownfield site into an active green waterfront. A pedestrian crossing replaced the underpass, visually and physically linking Nerang Street in the Central Business District (CBD) to the parkland area. By reconnecting Southport CBD with the foreshore and harbour area, the Parklands celebrate Queensland's regional identity.

The complex project included masterplanning, landscape architecture, civil and structural engineering, the construction of a stormwater drainage system, and mechanical and electric services for the stretch of foreshore parklands. Two new events lawns, the Great Lawn and the Little Lawn, accommodate large events and include transitional areas to manage crowd flow and spectator seating. Power and water are brought into the site underground so they have less impact on the lawns, which contain integrated access points for the temporary water and power as well as for sewers.

The Great Lawn was elevated to accommodate stormwater. At its peak, the lawn rises by 2 m (6.5 ft); it tapers down toward the shoreline. The Porch, a public stage with a sheltered area and a large outdoor screen was built for film screenings and community theatre. A pier was erected, which reaches 105 m (344 ft) out into the Broadwater.

All of the Parklands structures were designed by Australian firm Whitearchitecture. The buildings are covered in a white perforated skin that allows natural light in during the day. At night, artificial light illuminates the buildings, which become beacons for the Parklands. The Pier Pavilion, the site's display gallery and visitor centre, includes public toilets and showers as well as bike lockers. The dual-skin screening facade treatment prevents the building from overheating. The flexible internal division allows for adaptable use if future retail or commercial use is desired. The building is topped with a green rooftop deck that provides insulation.

The layout of the buildings is designed to accommodate crowd flow during large public events. The buildings and other elements within the park are linked by a network of interwoven paved pathways that disperse crowds while providing the excitement of navigational choices. Brightly coloured public furniture, made entirely of recycled plastic, invites visitors to make themselves at home.

A second phase of the project enhanced the Parklands with a children's water park, a memorial and a new building. Rockpools, the water park, uses saltwater from the Broadwater instead of potable water.

The sustainable landscaping of the Broadwater Parklands places ecosystem preservation at the forefront of the agenda. Some 3,500 new trees were planted, 200 m (656 ft) of dune and beach were created, and the water supply of the Parklands was

AECOM and Whitearchitecture

Photovoltaic panels are integrated into the roofs of brightly coloured pavilions throughout the development (top). Storm water run-off is captured and cleaned in a terraced wetland (bottom and opposite).

Southport Broadwater Parklands

turned into a self-sufficient system. Furthermore, 255 photovoltaic panels were integrated into the roofs of a series of shade shelters, to provide enough power to meet the electricity needs of the inhabitants of the Parklands.

The stormwater management system reduced the annual gross pollutants load by 90 per cent. The foundation of the system is a central urban wetland with bioretention basins. Stormwater and upstream catchments from Southport CBD are collected in the wetland and filtered through weeds and terraces before re-entering the Broadwater. Pedestrian walkways and bridges traverse the wetland, which is located between the two main events lawns, directing water as well as allowing visitors

to explore the innovative urban stormwater management system.

Some of the treated water is reused for non-potable needs such as passive irrigation. The irrigation infrastructure has been designed with adaptability in mind, to allow future developments in the use of the water distribution system. A newly created 1.2 hectare (4 acre) mangrove wetland, which supports sedimentation that increases pollutant uptake, further improves the quality of the stormwater and reduces pollution that enters the Broadwater. The 22,000 newly planted mangrove seedlings and sea grass beds create a habitat for coastal fish and crustaceans, and improve biodiversity along the Broadwater foreshore. *Bareket Kezwer*

Made of local materials – red earth, sand, straw, cement and bamboo – **Sra Pou Vocational School** required no machine-made or prefabricated components.

Sra Pou Vocational School is a professional training centre and community building, located in the village of Sra Pou in Oudong (central Cambodia). In January 2010, residents of Sra Pou were evicted from a slum in the capital city of Phnom Penh (about 50 km or 30 miles away) and relocated to this rural shanty town. Resources here are scarce and sometimes foreign to former city dwellers. Additionally, the village lacks basic infrastructure, sturdy housing and means to improve economic activity. The school teaches residents useful skills to apply to their new environment and encourages them to earn their living by launching sustainable businesses together.

In the spring of 2010, Finnish students Hilla Rudanko and Anssi Kankkunen travelled to Cambodia with an Aalto University group in search of design tasks with a local non-governmental organization (NGO). They made contact with the organization Blue Tent and, with their help, came to understand the urgent need for a school. Rudanko and Kankkunen embarked on the project soon afterward, and their Helsinki-based architecture firm, Rudanko + Kankkunen, was founded during the design phase. In its practice, Rudanko emphasizes research, concept design and urban design. Kankkunen focuses on building design, visualization and modelling.

Completed in the spring of 2011, the two-level 200m² (2,150 sq ft) building comprises an open multi-purpose space and two classrooms. Courses are led by a local NGO, but the school's lessons in self-sufficiency and sustainability begin with its construction: the school was built by regional labourers and with locally sourced materials. Nothing in the structure was machine-made

or prefabricated; all the construction techniques were transferable and did not necessitate the use of special tools.

The school's brick-like walls – made by mixing the surrounding red earth with sand, straw, cement and water – were moulded on site and then left to dry in the sun. Bamboo sticks and wooden planks were used as support beams or flooring. Local handicraft workers made the brightly coloured woven fibre doors and window shutters. Some of the decorative details were functional: small holes in the soil block on the north and east walls were designed to allow sunlight and wind to illuminate and cool the space, respectively. The interior and outdoor awning offered a safe retreat from sun or rain.

Land is the only asset that many poor people have. It creates opportunities for income and engenders a sense of security. Rudanko + Kankkunen have used the land and its natural resources to empower the people of Sra Pou; their sustainable architectural design is a means of making broader social change. By employing residents in the construction of the school, the architects have ostensibly imparted not just a sense of ownership, but also practical knowledge that might be applied to developing low-cost community spaces and homes in Sra Pou. Through this space for learning, adults and children might acquire the necessary skills to build an economically sustainable future.

Following the school's completion, Rudanko + Kankkunen joined the Finnish NGO Ukumbi, which offers architectural services for communities in need. *Nicole Caruth*

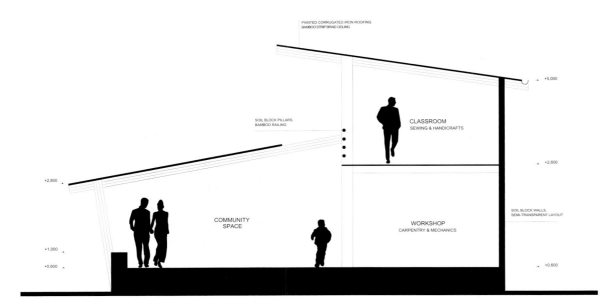

PAINTED CORRUGATED IRON ROOFING
BAMBOO STRIP BRAD CEILING

SOIL BLOCK PILLARS,
BAMBOO RAILING

CLASSROOM
SEWING & HANDICRAFTS

+5,000

+2,600

+2,800

COMMUNITY
SPACE

WORKSHOP
CARPENTRY & MECHANICS

SOIL BLOCK WALLS,
SEMI-TRANSPARENT LAYOUT

+1,000

+0,600

+0,600

The coloured screens open
easily from the veranda area,
and light pours in through
planned openings in the
brick-like wall (opposite).
A single staircase leads to the
second floor of the school.

ENTRANCE FROM
STREET
▼

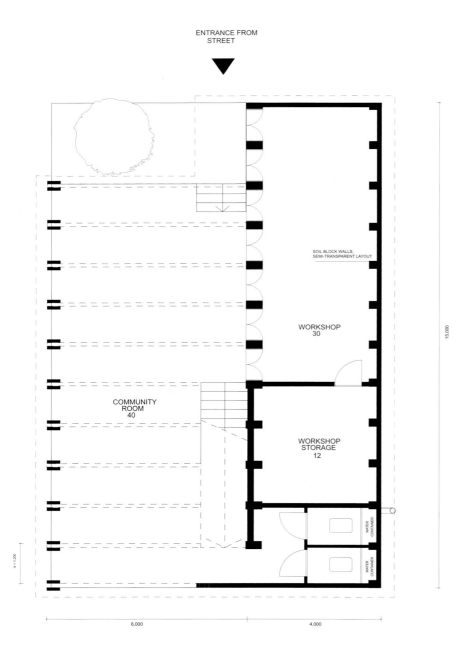

SOIL BLOCK WALLS,
SEMI-TRANSPARENT LAYOUT

WORKSHOP
30

COMMUNITY
ROOM
40

WORKSHOP
STORAGE
12

WATER CONTAINER

WATER CONTAINER

15,000

h = 1,200

6,000

4,000

Rudanko + Kankkunen

The distributed elements of the **Stockholm Energy Systems** project are designed to gather energy from the sun and the wind.

The Stockholm Energy Systems project began as a pavilion commissioned in 2009 for the Stockholm Exhibition, a multi-year urban initiative directed by Swedish curator Jan Åman and funded by the city of Stockholm. Åman invited architect Mia Hägg of Paris office Habiter Autrement to design a temporary pavilion addressing themes of energy consumption and conservation, particularly as they relate to new sustainable building technologies. The event's organizers drew inspiration from an important historical precedent: the landmark Stockholm Exhibition, which celebrated the ideals of functionalism and standardized mass production that fueled the rise of modernism in the 1930s. By consciously invoking the memory of the event, the implication is that our current moment – also one of vast technological innovation – can learn from the visionary optimism that characterized the modern movement at its inception.

The site selected for the exhibition – a barren, 2.5 km (1.5 mile) wide stretch of undeveloped land surrounded by a number of isolated suburban neighbourhoods – presented a fitting opportunity to test the ambitious curatorial agenda. The adjacent neighbourhoods of Husby, Kista, Tensta, and Rinkeby are largely immigrant communities with rich cultural vitality, but they nevertheless represent some of the city's most problematic areas in terms of crime and urban connectivity. Faced with this challenging context, Hägg was joined by filmmaker Maris Mezulis to study the surrounding neighbourhoods and solicit input from the residents to gain a better understanding of the project conditions.

Their research led them to rethink the original notion of the pavilion as merely a freestanding building in the landscape. Rather, it became evident that the project itself could become an instrument of positive change for the four surrounding neighbourhoods – and that the project's use of sustainable building technologies could serve not only an expository function, but could also be used to actively improve the quality of life for the area's residents. With this in mind, Hägg and Mezulis reconceived the project as a system of small-scale interventions to be implemented incrementally throughout both the landscape and the surrounding urban context, with the distributed infrastructure of sustainability becoming a kind of connective tissue uniting the disparate neighbourhoods.

Elements include the addition of 'winter gardens' to existing apartment blocks, retrofitting individual apartments to improve energy efficiency, recycling heat from a local shopping mall and distributing it to the surrounding residences, and a smart playground that captures kinetic energy as children play on the equipment.

For the vast field in the centre of the site, Hägg and her team developed a series of modular architectural elements (dubbed 'sprouts') to be deployed over time throughout the landscape, delineating new pathways connecting the four neighbourhoods. The sprouts, fabricated from flexible yet robust glass fiber-reinforced plastic, collect energy during the day and illuminate the walkways at night, creating a soft glow that promotes a more welcoming and secure environment. The sprouts come in two variations: the solar sprout is capped with a photovoltaic panel 'petal' that collects energy from the sun, and the wind sprout harvests kinetic energy through gentle oscillations in the breeze. The electricity is fed back into a central battery, which, at night, powers LEDs that are embedded in the stalk of each sprout.

At the centre of the landscape, the illuminated walkways converge at a small pavilion. The building, like the sprouts, is constructed largely of slender poles topped with solar panels, and it also integrates information displays and rainwater collection systems. This 'observatory' becomes the nerve centre for the entire project, accumulating live data from each of the components and conveying information about energy usage throughout the system. The project becomes a platform for interaction between residents and the infrastructure of the city itself, with the hope that providing a mechanism for feedback will foster greater awareness about energy consumption and encourage conservation. It is this aspect, together with the process of civic engagement that has characterized the project from the start, that has led to the project's evolution from a temporary exhibition piece to a longer-term city planning initiative, winning political support from the neighbourhoods and the city government alike. This pragmatic approach – working with existing infrastructures, designing and building incrementally, incorporating community input – offers an alternative and perhaps more realistic model for designing the 21st century sustainable city.

Adam Marcus

The pavilion canopy is designed to recycle grey water as well as to receive information from the distributed 'sprouts' (this page). The sprouts, which connect four neighbourhoods (opposite, centre left) come in two varieties, one that collects wind energy (opposite, top left) and another that collects solar energy (opposite, top right).

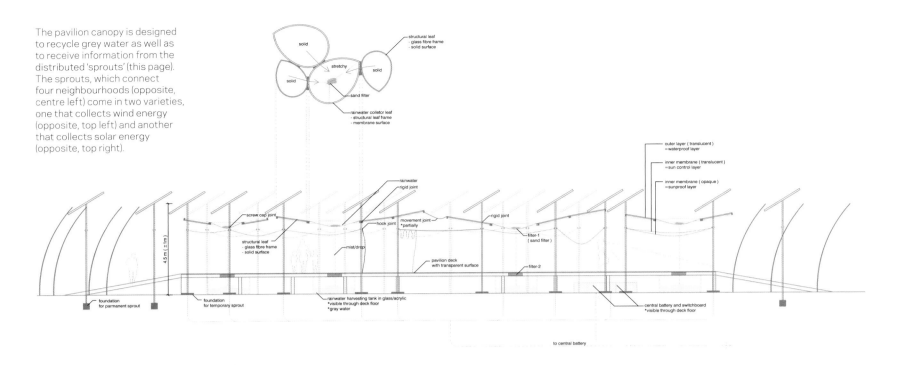

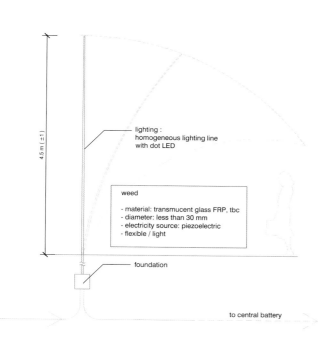

lighting :
homogeneous lighting line
with dot LED

4.5 m (±1)

weed

- material: transmucent glass FRP, tbc
- diameter: less than 30 mm
- electricity source: piezoelectric
- flexible / light

foundation

to central battery

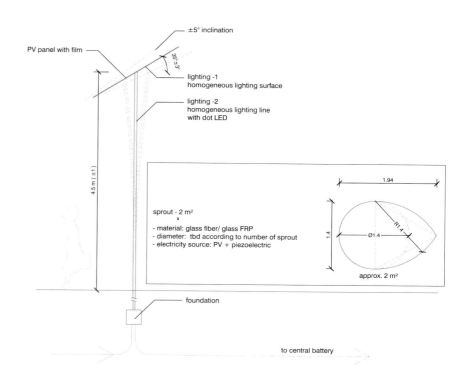

±5° inclination

PV panel with film

35°±3°

lighting -1
homogeneous lighting surface

lighting -2
homogeneous lighting line
with dot LED

4.5 m (±1)

sprout - 2 m²

- material: glass fiber/ glass FRP
- diameter: tbd according to number of sprout
- electricity source: PV + piezoelectric

1.94

R1.4

Ø1.4

1.4

approx. 2 m²

foundation

to central battery

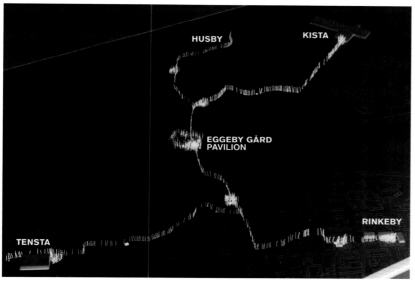

HUSBY   KISTA

EGGEBY GÅRD
PAVILION

TENSTA   RINKEBY

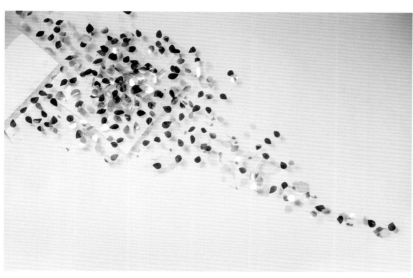

A battery-powered electric car, the **Tesla Roadster** can travel 394 km (254 miles) on a single charge.

Tesla Motors
—
Palo Alto, CA
USA
—
2003-present

Advancements in performance (opposite) and styling (this page) have resulted in the electric car's ability to come closer to matching those of conventional cars – and, sometimes, surpassing them.

The story of Tesla Motors, a Palo Alto, California company founded in 2003, begins with performance anxiety – battery performance.

'The battery has always been the bane of electric cars', says Franz von Holzhausen, Tesla's chief engineer. While such vehicles have certain advantages – their motors achieve full torque (the ability to pull or accelerate) instantaneously, and require virtually no maintenance – the challenge lies in creating a power source that balances efficiency and range. 'The power pack on a typical electric car is specifically designed for the vehicle, and has very big battery cells', Holzhausen explains. 'With a bigger battery, it's much more challenging to manage the stability of the power output – you can get better performance or better range but it's hard to get both.' Consequently, the hundred-miles-per-charge characteristic of most electric cars produces 'range anxiety' – the fear that, given the absence of charging options as ubiquitous (and as fast) as gas stations, one may end up stranded by a drained battery.

Tesla's founders hit upon the idea of stringing together much smaller off-the-shelf laptop batteries – standard form-factor lithium-ion cells, produced en masse by Sony, Panasonic, and others – to create a battery pack that optimized both power and reach. Apart from being more robust – 'if one cell goes down, it doesn't affect the rest of the pack', Holzhausen observes – a power source based on an open-market commodity would also be less susceptible to economic or availability fluctuations: 'If there's an issue in transporting or a rate hike, we simply go to another manufacturer.' Accordingly, the company developed a removable battery pack

incorporating 6,831 cells and enjoying a projected life of 160,000 km (100,000 miles). The charger can flexibly connect to 220- and 110-volt outlets – full recharge can be achieved in under four hours – which means the battery can be 'filled up' under almost any circumstances. 'I treat it like my cellphone', Holzhausen says. 'When I come home, I plug it in, and it's ready to go the next morning.' And 'ready to go', in the case of Tesla's Roadster, is transformative: it can travel some 394 km (245 miles) on a single charge – roughly two and a half times the present industry norm. More to the point, Tesla put that into a beautifully styled, high-performance sport model 'to show that an electric vehicle can be fun and go the distance', Holzhausen points out. 'No longer is it a glorified golf cart.'

Zero emissions is paramount among the virtues of electric cars, which are also considerably more efficient than those powered by internal combustion engines. Moreover, while gasoline is produced via expensive processes involving offshore drilling, refining, and the transportation of the finished product over long distances in fuel-burning trucks, electricity can – under the right circumstances – be generated immediately, sustainably, and virtually for free. 'Twenty to twenty-five per cent of Roaster owners in the Los Angeles area charge their cars using solar panels – completely off the grid', says Holzhausen. Tesla cars don't come cheap. 'But it's emerging technology – anyone who invests in a Roadster invests in the future of electric cars, and helps propel the idea that they aren't a compromise', Holzhausen affirms. 'They're better, more fun, and' – a reference to the Roadster's suave profile in comparison to first-generation green design – 'not "Crunchy Granola".' *Marc Kristal*

Infused with a photoluminescent powder pigment, the **Trap Light** stores energy while it is turned on and glows for up to eight hours after it has been shut off.

Gionata Gatto and Mike Thompson

—

Eindhoven, Netherlands

—

2011

Each Trap Light is hand-blown (this page); the photoluminescent powder within the glass absorbs light and glows at night (opposite).

The Trap Light, designed by Eindhoven-based designers Gionata Gatto of Studio Atuppertu and Mike Thompson, uses photoluminescent technology to create a light that continues to glow after the power goes out. The design, which was introduced to the market at the 2011 Milan Design Week, pushes the potential of electric lighting by converting electric light into ambient light; light is converted back into light. Each lamp is hand-crafted using the Murano blown glass technique. An LED bulb sits in the centre of the symmetrical glass form which is housed within a wood cast metal cage. The finished Trap Light can either be displayed as a free-standing object or suspended from a cord. When switched on, the LED bulb illuminates the lamp. Thirty minutes of LED charge powers the photoluminescent powder pigment for eight hours of glowing glass.

The jar-shaped lamps are given their glow-in-the-dark power through the photoluminescent powder pigment that is embedded between the layers of glass. Photoluminescence, also known as glow-in-the dark, is a process in which a substance absorbs energy and gradually releases that energy in the form of light.

This self-emitting light technology is enabled by the phosphors present in the photoluminescent powder pigment. These phosphors, a non-radioactive, naturally occurring rare earth mineral crystal, have a unique make-up which allows them to collect and store energy from surrounding light and slowly release it when the direct light source disappears. Interestingly, this process is a shift in energy within the atoms of the phosphors, not a chemical reaction. When energized by the light of the LED bulb, the electrons of the phosphors move to a higher orbit. When the light energy disappears, the electrons fall from the elevated energy level. The drop to a more stable energy level causes the electrons to emit energy in the form of ambient light. The particular powder pigment used in the Trap Light was provided by GloTech International, a New Zealand-based company that specializes in the manufacturing of photoluminescent powder pigments.

By keeping the light cycling within the object, the Trap Light engages contemporary issues of energy needs through a playful exploration of new technological capabilities. *Bareket Kezwer*

Gionata Gatto and Mike Thompson

Carefully positioned in order to save the living trees in its forest location, the **Traverwood Branch Library** also makes use of 60 beetle-damaged ash trees that were removed from the site.

inFORM Studio

Ann Arbor, MI USA

2008

Automatic blinds regulate the amount of sunlight entering the floor-to-ceiling glazing (opposite). Sections of fallen trees form structural columns on the building's interior, sitting just behind the glass (left); timber from the trees was also used to clad walls and ceilings on the main entry floor (right).

Located on forested land on the outskirts of Ann Arbor, a small city in Michigan, USA, the Traverwood Branch Library uses materials from the site on which it sits and, in return, gives something back to its surroundings.

Ann Arbor's existing library, which was well-used but too small, was located in a commercial strip mall. When the library purchased 1.6 hectares (4 acres) of land in 2005, mindful of parking difficulties at other branches, it envisaged a new library sitting squarely in the middle, with a large car park surrounding it. However, on their first visit to the site, the architects of inFORM Studio found it to be heavily wooded and filled with wildlife: woodpeckers, garter snakes, green turtles and deer.

The architects realized that clearing the trees from the site would decimate its established eco-system. So instead, they positioned the building at the southwest corner of the site, in the area least populated by trees. Addressing the need for ample parking, inFORM Studio placed one third of the on-site spaces under the building, and negotiated with the city's roads department to enable visitors to park on the adjacent roads.

An ecological study revealed that there were a number of dead American Ash trees on the site, killed by a destructive beetle called the Emerald Ash Borer. But the architects turned this negative aspect of the site into a positive element by reusing the dead timber in the library. The trees were removed from the woodland with as little disturbance as possible, by specialists who felled the trees individually by hand and dragged them out using horses, negating the use of heavy machinery and lessening root damage in the woodland.

The building is L-shaped in plan. In optimal conditions, primarily in the spring and autumn, sunlight and natural ventilation can be used to heat and cool the building. Natural light floods the entire ground floor through walls glazed from floor to ceiling, which offer views out into the woodland and reduce the requirement for artificial lighting. If the sun is shining too brightly, automatic blinds respond via daylight sensors and close to shade individual wings. Similarly, the internal temperature control system links with mechanically operable windows, which allow in cool air through low windows, and expel warm stale air through high windows.

Timber from 60 felled ash trees has been used throughout the library, creating a wonderful warm glow in the interior. The ash covers the floors, walls and ceiling from the main entry floor, and along the eastern interior edge of the building, culminating in ash-wrapped reading rooms, whose primary views are focused westward, where the wood originated. Additionally, sections of logs have been used as structural columns inside the glazed southwest facade. The bark has been stripped from these log columns, exposing the grooves and carvings that were created by the Emerald Ash Borer.

Cost constraints prevented the implementation of a designed green roof. Whereas a green roof would have retained much of the moisture that fell onto the structure, the use of a traditional one does not hold this precipitation. Instead, inFORM Studio worked out a rainwater dispersal strategy, where impervious material around the building minimizes pollutants being washed into natural water courses when heavy rain occurs; native shrubs, grass and stone are used instead. A subsurface stormwater filtration system, consisting of a series of buried stepped chambers, slows heavy water flow and helps contaminants to settle into the chamber bottoms, rather than flow into the local water course. *Will Jones*

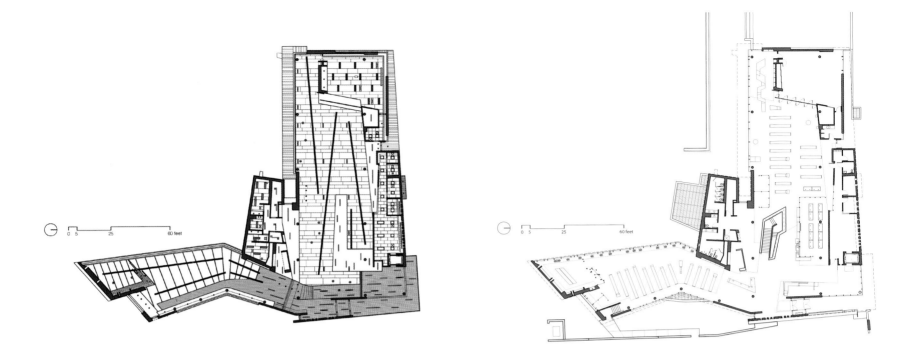

During construction the library's concrete foundation was poured to fit into the sensitive existing site, which borders the Stapp Nature Preserve (opposite). The reflected ceiling plan (top left) indicates the layout of the harvested wood panels lining the ceiling. The reading room at the south-facing end of the library overlooks the adult collection room (bottom right). The library's two main collection spaces also contain music, books for children, and a young adult collection (top right).

The construction of the **Truffle** literally took nature as a mould: it was formed from concrete, soil and bales of hay, with some help from a calf named Paulina.

Ensamble Studio
—
Costa de Morte, Spain
—
2010

Bales of hay served as formwork for the Truffle. They were first set into the earth and then covered in concrete. For one year Paulina the calf ate away at the hay to reveal the cave-like interior.

A calf called Paulina and 50 m³ (1,766 ft³) of hay played crucial roles when Madrid-based architecture practice Ensamble Studio attempted to build a guesthouse with a minimal impact on the environment on Spain's Galician coast. The exterior looks like a black truffle plucked from the earth, and the cave-like interior has a panorama window overlooking the Atlantic Ocean. 'We got the inspiration for the size and the interior from Le Corbusier's *Cabanon*', says Anton Garcia-Abril, founder of Ensamble Studio.

The *Cabanon* is Le Corbusier's cabin in Cap Martin on the Cote d'Azur, France. It was designed and built for Le Corbusier's wife in 1952 and, at 14 m² (150 sq ft), it houses only the bare necessities. 'The Truffle is the *Cabanon of Beton* (the concrete cottage)', says Garcia-Abril. Truffle is the size of an average hotel room and holds a bed, a fireplace, a shower and a stowaway toilet. There is no kitchen. It looks as though it has been eroded over time, to assume a rock-like shape in the rough landscape. To achieve this symbiosis, the exterior walls were cast in concrete and the surrounding earth was used as a mould. First, a sort of cauldron was created by digging away the topsoil of the site and hay bales were piled inside the cauldron to create the cabin's negative space. Concrete was poured in the space between the hay and the wall of soil without any extra reinforcement or form-work. Once the concrete had cured, the soil surrounding it was removed, revealing a round, irregular shape. It had taken the brownish colour of the earth and now resembled its namesake, the truffle. At this point it was more like a lump than any recognizable piece of architecture and there was no way of accessing the interior of the structure, but a few cuts were made using quarry machinery to explore the hay-filled middle, which formed an irregular rectangular space at the core of the lumpish form.

At this point, Paulina the calf enters the story. Truffle became her shelter for a year, as she fed on the hay bales. Once the calf had finished feeding – and by this point had grown into a 300 kg (600 lb) cow – the space had been hollowed out, revealing a cavernous room made of unreinforced concrete. The space was made fit for living without losing any of its rustic appeal – the square imprints of the hay bales can still be seen on the walls. One side of the cabin, which had been cut open, was re-sealed with a panoramic window overlooking the sea. The other two gaps became the chimney and the doorway.

Garcia-Abril says he created Truffle out of a 'desire to build with our own hands, a piece of nature, a contemplative space, a little poem'. Even small ideas tend to scale up, however, if they are interesting and since 2008, Ensamble Studio has been working on designs for a church in Valencia, Spain, to be built in the same manner. The church will also resemble a concrete rock, but on a scale approximately five times larger than Truffle, meaning that unreinforced concrete can't be used in the same way. Instead post-tensioning techniques, to make the structure more rigid and safe, need to be employed. Once the volume is completed, the church will, like Truffle, have large incisions made into the facade to create the entrance and light wells of the church room. Garcia-Abril sees both projects as part of Ensamble Studio's experiments. 'It's like scientific research – you do it with a rat, then you do it with a pig, and if it still works, you can try it out on humans.' *Johanna Agerman Ross*

Europe's largest inner-city redevelopment, the **Unilever Headquarters** consumes less than 100kWh of energy per m² (9.3 kWh per sq ft).

Behnisch
Architekten
—
Hamburg,
Germany
—
2009

The complex two-layer facade of the building is very robust. It's outermost layer is made of Ethylene Trafluoroethylene, a strong plastic that can withstand temperature fluctuation and high winds (opposite). The second layer of the building's facade is made of high-performance glass that works in tandem with the plastic layer (this page).

Unilever has spent the last decade building its green credentials. The global corporation began by targeting those products that it processes in the largest quantities, such as tea and palm oil. Unilever has pledged that by 2015 it will grow all its tea in Rainforest Alliance Certified farms and obtain palm oil only from farms that practice sustainable farming techniques. So it was important to Unilever that its headquarters embody its attitude to environmental concerns.

Resting on the banks of the River Elbe, Unilever's headquarters forms a major part of the Hafencity (Harbour City) currently under development in Hamburg. The 38,000 m² (409,000 sq ft) facility appears almost as a stationary cloud, thanks to the white structural elements that bind together an otherwise transparent shell. Designed by Behnisch Architekten, the building's irregular floor-plate system comprises seven storeys and creates a complex geometric pattern of glass facades that catch the sunlight and the reflections from the harbour. Traditionally, transparent buildings require double-layer glass facades, which are heavy, costly and energy-inefficient. Behnisch Architekten derived a simple yet original solution of two separate systems working together: an inner layer composed of high-performance glass and an outer membrane formed of Ethylene Tetrafluoroethylene (ETFE), a plastic that retains its strength over a range of different temperatures.

Across the south, east and west facades, venetian blinds are automatically controlled by a computer system on the roof, which tracks the sun's movements and protects the occupants from solar gain. Employees can override this system to maintain their comfort; similarly, operable windows ensure access to airflow. The outer 'membrane' is lifted 1 to 2 m (3 to 6 ft) away from the inner layer and is supported by an aluminium and steel frame. Compression bars within this framework adjust the ETFE layer, spreading tension across the entire surface to create a strong facade, which can withstand winds of up to 96 km (60 miles) per hour. Air can circulate through this two-layer system, naturally cooling the interior. Lightness and airiness also characterize the interior of the building, where visitors encounter a large atrium that defines the core of the structure. Offices are open in plan and all areas are illuminated by natural light from the atrium and the fully glazed exterior.

Although public spaces and natural lighting are the key aspects to the success of the Unilever Headquarters, other schemes reinforce the ethos of sustainability. The building uses less than 100 kWh per m² (9.3 km per sq ft) – four times less energy than a typical office building. LED lights, 70 per cent more efficient than traditional lamps, are used throughout the building. Water usage is optimized by a grey water system and an advanced sanitary solution that reduces the need for water in the urinals. Air pollution, the result of redeveloping an industrial site, is mitigated by ventilation spaces fitted into the floor. These compressed air floors contain filters that prevent pollution from entering the workspaces while simultaneously blocking out sound between levels. *Rob Fiehn*

Behnisch Architekten

The interior atrium space
of the building complex allows
natural light into the building's
interior, and facilitates the
ventilation of the building
complex (this page) as well as
interconnecting the vast amount
of office space (opposite).

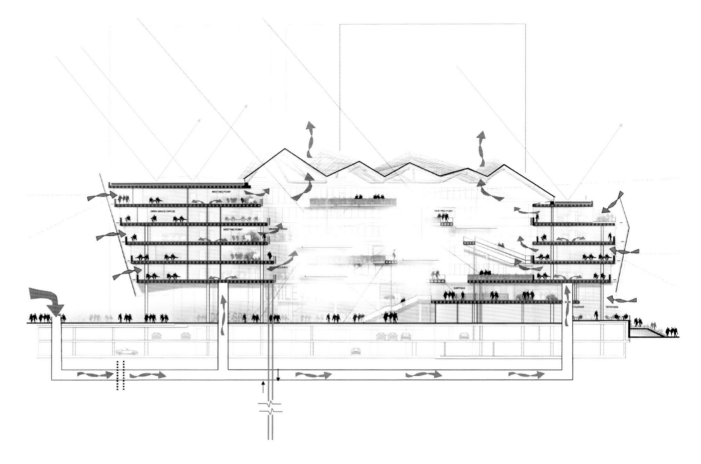

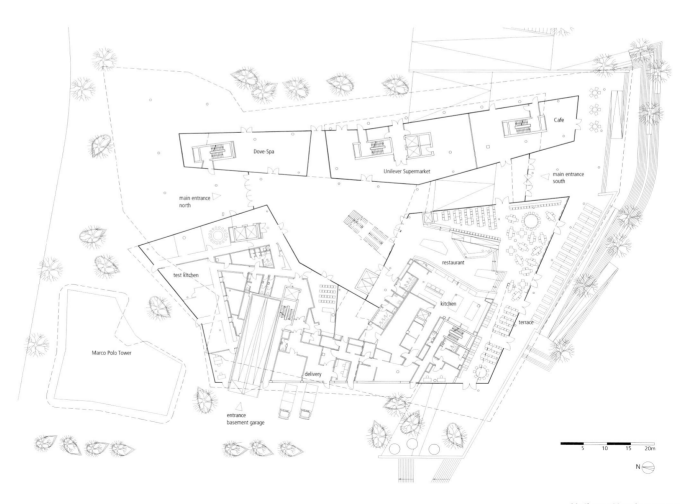

Victor Civita Plaza is an eco-park and open museum for sustainability that floats above a brownfield site as it is being remediated.

DBB Aedas and Levisky Arquitetos Associados

São Paulo, Brazil

2008

The wooden deck of the plaza (opposite) floats 1 m (3 ft) above the contaminated ground below, allowing for reuse of the previously abandoned site. Amphitheatres sit on top of the deck (this page).

Victor Civita Plaza, a 12,075 m² (130,000 sq ft) eco-park, built on a deactivated municipal incinerator, brings new life to a former brownfield site in São Paulo's Tietê river watershed. The plaza, which opened in 2008, includes lounging areas, gardens, an amphitheatre and bleachers seating 240 people, a centre for the elderly, a playground, a cobblestone plaza and a museum. The project was designed by Anna Dietzsch, managing director of the São Paulo office of the New York architectural design firm Davis Brody Bond Aedas, and Adriana Levisky, director of the Brazilian architectural firm Levisky Arquitetos Associados. The polluted site was originally intended to be covered with 0.5 m (1.6 feet) of soil but when this method of soil decontamination proved cost prohibitive, the team designed a deck that hovers 1 m (3 ft) above the toxic ground on a steel framework. Rather than hiding the contaminated area, the floating deck, which is constructed of reclaimed Brazilian hardwood, forms a diagonal pathway through the site.

This pathway leads visitors on an educational tour of the park's diverse plant life, which includes a mature grove of rubber, eucalyptus, ficus and fruit trees as well as plants that help purify the contaminated soil. Elsewhere, new plants grow in raised planters designed by landscape architect Benedito Abbud. Under these 'Tec-Gardens', the contaminated soil was levelled out with a layer of stone and gravel. Above this, a rubber base supports columns topped by an impermeable slate platform and geotextile blanket onto which clean soil was laid. Waterproof masonry walls enclose the gap between the rubber base and the elevated Tec-Garden

platform, creating a reserve in which rainwater is harvested and stored. Tubes lined with coconut fibres, a local material, run through the platform connecting the water reserve to the clean soil. Through capillary action, the tubes draw water up to the roots of the plants: a self-irrigating system that works without electricity. Rainwater is collected in a reservoir under the wooden deck and also helps to irrigate the gardens. Grey water from the facility's bathrooms runs through a two-stage water filtration system – first, through swamp vegetation and second, through an ornamental pond inhabited by water plants and micro-organisms – before it is reused for irrigation.

Victor Civita Plaza is a living demonstration of sustainable design strategies for urban renewal. Each plant species in the park was chosen for its ability to teach visitors about contemporary interventions that sustainably restore the ecological health of the site. Information panels along the deck explain the various features of the park and transform the plaza into an open museum for sustainability. The Tec-Gardens contain an organic vegetable garden for children's workshops and plants that can be harvested for alternative energy sources, such as biodiesel and ethanol. A museum for urban rehabilitation is located inside the former incinerator building, which was deactivated in 1990. By incorporating recreational and community facilities into the design of the plaza, the architects have created not only a centre for sustainable education, but also a site that promotes community involvement and development in a dense metropolis. *Bareket Kezwer*

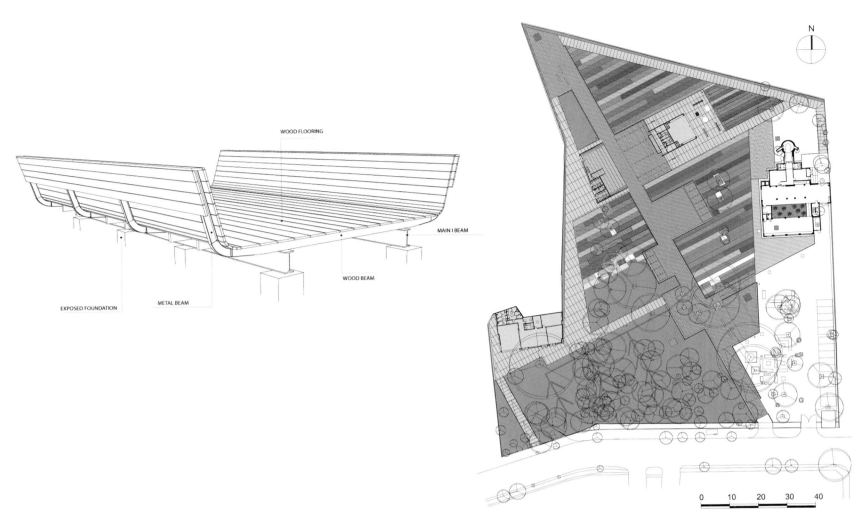

WOOD FLOORING

MAIN I BEAM

WOOD BEAM

METAL BEAM

EXPOSED FOUNDATION

N

0   10   20   30   40

Victor Civita Plaza

The construction of the floating deck (opposite, top left) created a pathway that connects gardens, an amphitheatre, a centre for the elderly, a playground (opposite, bottom) and museum space. The deck, which is made from reclaimed Brazilian hardwood (top), also contains multiple lounge areas (bottom). Eucalyptus, rubber, ficus and fruit trees populate the 'Tec-Gardens' that remediate the soil.

DBB Aedas and Levisky Arquitetos Associados

The **Viet Village Urban Farm** mitigates the disastrous effects of storm flooding in New Orleans while encouraging families to grow their own produce.

Spackman Mossop + Michaels with Tulane University

New Orleans, LA USA

2006–present

Community involvement is essential to the Viet Village Urban Farm. The inclusion of a market (opposite), playground and sports facility is intended to attract younger American-born members of the community to the farm, where they can learn skills and traditions from the older generation of Vietnamese immigrants. Additionally, construction of the whole project (this page) has been organized according to the necessary labour resources – professional contracting, skilled volunteer and unskilled volunteer – allowing the project's construction over a long period of time.

In 1975, Vietnamese immigrants established a community in New Orleans East. Upon arrival, the new community built gardens to grow the Vietnamese foods not available in local grocery stores. Gardens were set up in hundreds of vacant lots, and local growers sold their surplus food to earn extra income at an informal Saturday market. Almost all the gardens were destroyed when Hurricane Katrina hit in 2005. The Vietnamese community approached the destruction as an opportunity to re-establish its traditional gardening and market activities in a formalized setting. In 2006, Mary Queen of Viet Nam Community Development Corporation (MQVN CDC) was established and the Viet Village Urban Farm was begun. MQVN CDC rallied support for the project, which became the backbone of the rebuilding effort within the Vietnamese community.

An 11-hectare (28 acre) site in the heart of New Orleans East was secured to house the farm: 8 hectares (20 acres) were purchased from the city and 3 hectares (8 acres) are on long-term lease. A series of community meetings determined a design strategy, which included not only plans for the physical site and its systems, but also the coordination of funding and labour resources. The farm is a series of fully functional sub-projects that can be funded incrementally but which will eventually create a comprehensive system.

The fully realized Viet Village will include individual garden plots for personal consumption, commercial plots, a livestock area, a covered market area with stalls for restaurants, a playground and a sports field. The site will be bordered by a bamboo grove that will separate the farm from the neighbouring residential area and provide income through commercial harvesting. The playground is situated within individual plots, encouraging children to become involved in farming activities. When completed,

the site will be a community resource for the entire Gulf Coast Vietnamese community.

The main environmental issue on the site is the movement of water. The site is flat, has a high water table and lacks positive drainage, which makes it prone to storm flooding. Intuition and Logic, the project's engineering firm, needed to resolve a way to prevent waterlogged soil, bring water to crops and direct run-off from irrigation back into the system. Their solution is a system made up of a series of sub-watersheds, which can function independently in the event that a break occurs in the larger system. A main canal will run through the centre of the farm; it will be fed by side canals and connect to two major retention ponds. Water will be pumped from the ponds to the crops. Run-off water will be cleaned in an artificial wetland and then re-collected in the ponds and reused for irrigation. The canals and ponds are designed to accommodate storm water and to minimize flooding in the event of heavy rain.

Viet Village will adhere to international organic standards and will be enrolled in the Certified Naturally Grown program. To achieve the goal of energy and resource self-sufficiency, the site will include integrated pest management, crop rotation, cover-cropping and on-site composting of all green waste. In the future, the site will accept community green waste and generate income by selling its compost for gardening and farm use. The power needed to run the irrigation system will be generated from a windmill.

By focusing on reducing energy and resource consumption, and encouraging cultural and economic development through organic farming, the Viet Village Urban Farm offers a new model for community development that promotes both cultural and environmental sustainability.

Bareket Kezwer

The urban farm will be built in phases (bottom). A central bioswale will be constructed first and will serve as the backbone of the larger watershed system. This main bioswale will clean water as it is funnelled back to the main reservoir on the site (top). Later phases include a central boardwalk (opposite, top) and other circulation elements, the development of commercial plots, community gardens and a livestock area, and eventually the construction of markets and recreational facilities (opposite, bottom).

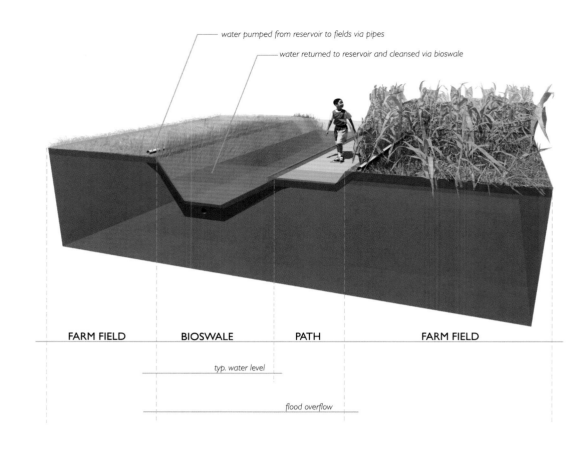

water pumped from reservoir to fields via pipes

water returned to reservoir and cleansed via bioswale

| FARM FIELD | BIOSWALE | PATH | FARM FIELD |

typ. water level

flood overflow

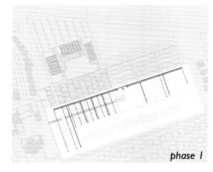

phase 1

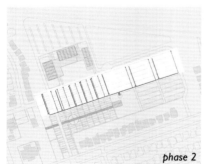

phase 2

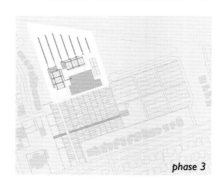

phase 3

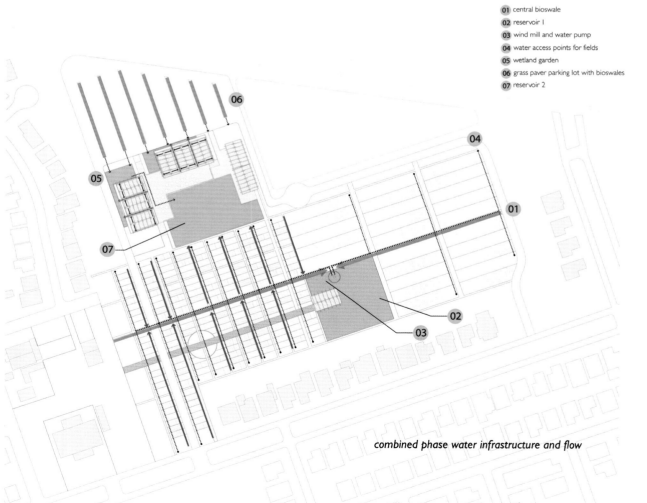

01 central bioswale
02 reservoir 1
03 wind mill and water pump
04 water access points for fields
05 wetland garden
06 grass paver parking lot with bioswales
07 reservoir 2

combined phase water infrastructure and flow

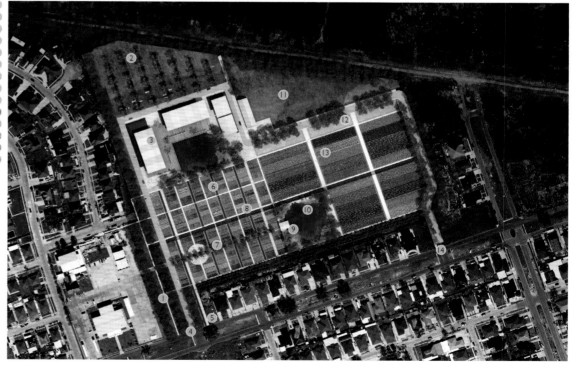

Sports Fields ①
Grass Paver Parking Lot ②
Market Buildings ③
Public Vehicular Entrance ④
Pedestrian Entrance ⑤
Community Farm Plots ⑥
Central Boardwalk ⑦
Central Bio-Filtration Canal ⑧
Community Pavilion ⑨
Central Reservoir ⑩
Livestock Farm Area ⑪
Compost ⑫
Commercial Plots ⑬
Service Entrance ⑭

Spackman Mossop + Michaels with Tulane University

The old concrete walls of **Villa Cirie** outside Turin now act like a sponge, letting in light and air while retaining 70 per cent of their original mass.

ecoLogicStudio

Turin, Italy

2009

On the outside, the redesigned exterior walls of the house are seamlessly integrated (opposite). The design of the wall and its variously shaped openings (right) filter incoming light and air.

If architectural form is essentially a means of separation, then the wall is perhaps the most fundamental architectural element. Villa Cirie, the conversion of a large 1970s villa in the just outside of Turin in northern Italy by London-based architects ecoLogicStudio, is an experiment in modernizing this primordial element. Beginning with the villa's existing, traditional Italian heavy masonry wall, ecoLogicStudio sought to exhaust the wall's potential to absorb, filter, refract and echo light, sound and air as they pass from outside to inside and back.

Thinking of the wall as a 'sponge', the architect used a set of formal parameters manipulated by an iterative, feedback-driven, computational design process to a create system of spiralling cavities. This allowed ecoLogicStudio to arrive at an optimized series of wall conditions that balance competing desires for openings and closures and differing levels of privacy with respect to the specific context of the site. The result is the replacement of many of the existing walls with porous walls that provide seemingly uninterrupted views over the surrounding landscape, while maintaining 70 per cent of their original mass. This application of new technology to an age-old architectural problem allowed ecoLogicStudio to create rich architectural variety by rethinking the form of the traditional wall.

As an experimental practice, ecoLogicStudio employs a design method that integrates the latest in digital computational design informed by ecological imperatives. In much the same way that the Villa Cirie was designed through an iterative process of feedback within a virtual formal system evolving within the computer, and its real material environment, so too is the practice itself feedback-driven.

Made of pre-cast, insulated custom concrete blocks, the experimental intelligence of Villa Cirie is, as the nickname for the project – 'Light Wall' – would suggest, largely in its walls. The compulsion to perforate, however, is ubiquitous. The large, rolling roof-scape, with pronounced eaves and ambitious dormer windows, is punctured with rectangular openings, drawing light from above to be diffused by the spiral-cavity interior walls. Even the many roof-top vents maintain the formal grammar of the principal intervention, as they are clothed in wire mesh sleeves that echo the contours of the spiralling cavities. Taken together, the perforations lighten the electrical load of heating and cooling as well as providing views to the exterior while retaining most of the mass of the wall, allowing it to insulate the house: evidence of the continuing dream of technological control over our environments to produce a better life.

Troy Conrad Therrien

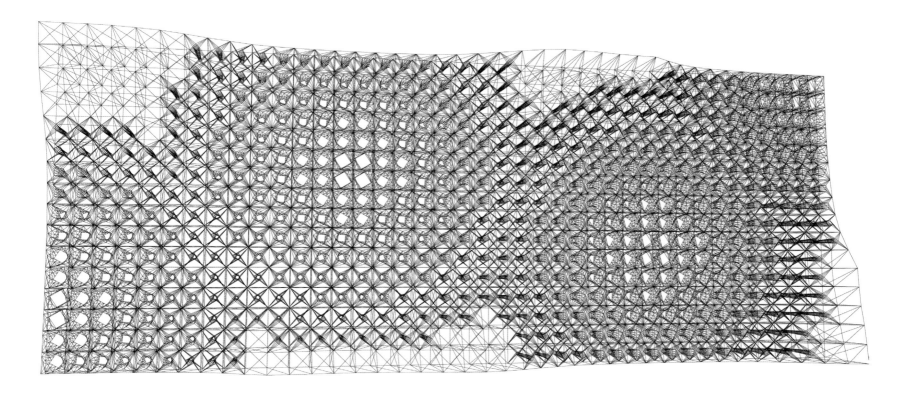

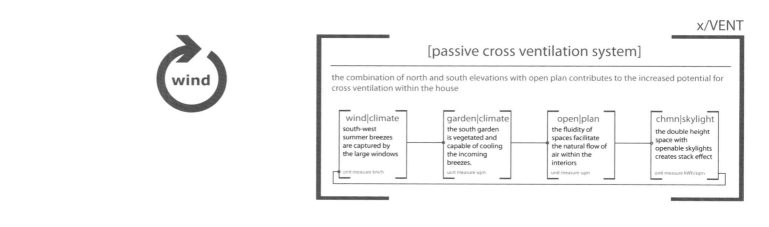

x/VENT

[passive cross ventilation system]

the combination of north and south elevations with open plan contributes to the increased potential for cross ventilation within the house

wind|climate	garden|climate	open|plan	chmn|skylight
south-west summer breezes are captured by the large windows	the south garden is vegetated and capable of cooling the incoming breezes.	the fluidity of spaces facilitate the natural flow of air within the interiors	the double height space with openable skylights creates stack effect
unit measure km/h	unit measure sqm	unit measure sqm	unit measure kWh/sqm

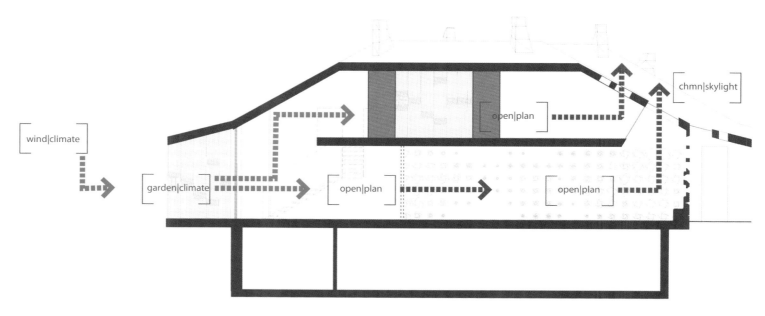

ecoLogicStudio used parametric
modelling tools to generate
the wall's shape (opposite top).
The wall's system of spiralling
cavities facilitates air flow
through the villa (opposite
bottom) and filters sunlight
entering the building (bottom).

light

[thermoregulation and light diffusion system]

north elevation , roof and sectional layout work as natural light diffusers.
internal spaces are flooded with light without direct glare and thermal loads
particularly in summer

sky/sect	light/wall	open/plan
luminosity from the sky is captured by north oriented window .	east and west elevation are contributing with diffuse light to the interior space.	the open plan layout allows light penetration throughout.
unit measure sqm	unit measure sqm	unit measure m

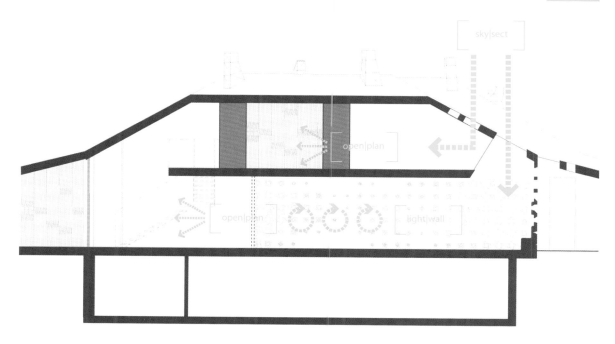

W+W reduces water consumption by 50 per cent through its innovative combined washbasin and water closet design.

Roca with Buratti + Battiston Architects

—

Barcelona, Spain

—

2009

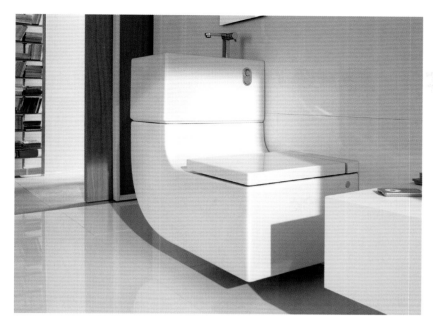

Spanish company Roca began making central-heating radiators in the early twentieth century. In 1925, the firm started to produce cast-iron baths; in 1936, Roca launched its first collection of porcelain bathroom fittings and in 1954, the company began to produce taps. The Victoria Water Closet, created by Roca's technical department in 1982, has become the world's best-selling water closet. An enviable success, the Victoria was executed by the company's internal staff.

Announced in 2009, Roca's W+W is actually two products in one: washbasin and water closet. This is not the first time that someone has tried to fuse these two pieces of bathroom furniture into a single item, to save water or just to economize on space. However, this design, which rolls the two items into one sinuous shape, is successful and elegant. In the arrangement of the elements and the overall shape of the piece, its function is clearly visible. Within the W+W is a water filtration and purification system that treats the water drained from the washbasin so that it is free of bacteria and odours by the time it reaches the water closet cistern.

The savings that the W+W achieves by reusing water are considerable. When used with the accompanying taps, the W+W can reach a 50 per cent saving in water consumption. The tap is called the Single Pro, and it was also developed by Roca. It is fitted with a progressive cartridge, called the Ecodisk, which limits flow-rate to 9 litres (2.4 gallons) per minute and stops the boiler from lighting unless hot water is needed, thus averting a release of carbon dioxide when cold water is drawn.

The W+W system and concept were developed by Roca's engineers with the designers Gabriele and Oscar Buratti, who form part of Buratti + Battiston Architects, a studio based in Milan. Collaboration between the internal team and independent professionals is a formula that has brought Roca good results: Ramón Benedito, Giugiaro Design, Schmidt-Lackner Design, Belén and Rafael Moneo, David Chipperfield and Giorgio Armani have all worked with Roca's design department. The Roca Design Centre, attached to its Innovation Lab, is an important part of the company, where unusual and innovative projects such as the W+W can be developed.

Like many other countries, Spain suffers from droughts and water shortages from time to time: global problems that are likely to become more frequent and more serious in the future. Without water, Roca would not exist. The company's decision to focus on sustainable design with the collaboration of external designers is an ethical one and not merely an aesthetic one: with the creation and promotion of projects such as the W+W washbasin, Roca is helping to raise awareness of the socio-political function of design today. *Ramón Úbeda*

Fitted with low-energy LEDs, the **W101 Paper Task Light** is made out of DuraPulp – a new, fully compostable material made of paper pulp and starch polymer.

Claesson Koivisto Rune

—

Helsingborg, Sweden

—

2010

Sheets of DuraPulp are pressed together to create the form of the lamp. The geometry of the folds gives rigidity to the lamp's structure, allowing it to stand on its own.

The desk lamp, in its many iterations, is one of the classic forms of modern design, but when made from disposable plastics and energy-intensive light sources, too often it is a nightmare for the environment. The W101 Paper Task Light, devised by Swedish architecture and design firm, Claesson Koivisto Rune, re-envisions the desk lamp by introducing a new perspective on this indispensable item.

The design team at Claesson Koivisto Rune produces the W101 Paper Task Light in collaboration with the Swedish lighting company Wästberg, which holds the mission to 'change society's basic view on lighting… [and] return light to human proximity'. To this end, the W101 Paper Task Light produces a directed LED illumination, reducing the amount of spill around the intended area. LEDs are the most efficient commercially available light source, producing far more light per watt than the standard incandescent light, but with little energy lost to heat. LEDs also last far longer than the traditional light bulb; where incandescent bulbs last for about 1,000 – 2,000 hours, manufacturers make the conservative estimation that LEDs last for around 35,000 – 50,000 hours. That means that less bulbs end up in the landfill and less energy is used per household.

And, of course, LEDs generate much less heat than conventional bulbs, making a noncombustible paper lamp possible.

To produce the W101 Paper Task Light, Claesson Koivisto Rune teamed up with Södra, a Swedish forestry cooperative. Södra is a leader in developing new ways of using wood pulp, a byproduct of its sustainably harvested softwood lumbar production. The W101 is crafted out of one of Södra's most innovative materials, DuraPulp. Made from a mix of paper pulp and starch polymer, DuraPulp is fully compostable and can be easily moulded using a minimal amount of materials to produce a lightweight, durable structure. Taking full advantage of this new medium, the W101 Paper Task Light is designed using precise angles and curves to promote strength and a sleek look. DuraPulp is pressed and cut into shape to produce the lamps. In the W101, four thin copper wires connect to a power supply base, giving the lamp stability and feeding power to the LEDs.

The shape of the W101 Task Lamp was designed to work with an absolute minimum of material, and most of that can eventually be returned to the earth: a bright idea indeed. *Maya Suess*

Made of three simple pieces,
the **Wabi Shoe** is easily
recycled and biodegrades
at the end of its life.

Wabi Shoe

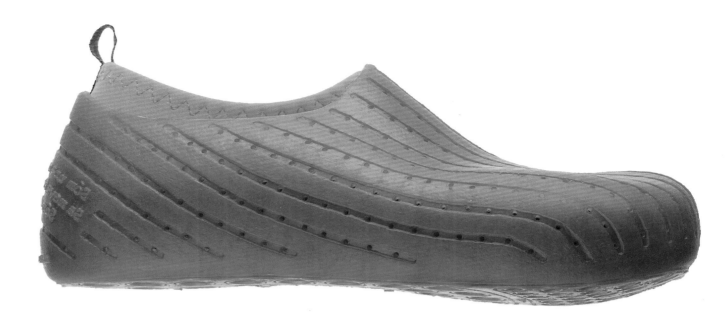

The shell of the Wabi shoe, which is made of TPE (thermoplastic elastomer), comes in many colours including red (opposite, left) and green (this page). The sock on the inside of the shell is made of cotton and can easily be removed and recycled separately. The sole (opposite, right) is made of natural fibres and called a Coco Footbed.

In 2000, the Camaleón shoe obtained the first Ecolabel issued by the European Union for a product in this sector. The same year, the Wabi shoe was born: it set out to be a manifesto of Camper's innovative spirit to create shoes that are functional and respect the environment. This shoe is just as healthy for people wearing it as it is for the planet. The Wabi shoe is ergonomic, and conceived to be worn indoors, as we spend many hours in the office or at home, wearing shoes that rarely respect the shape of our feet. Wabi (the name is a Japanese word that comes from the verb 'wabiru', which means 'ask for pardon') looks comfortable and its design is based on a simple concept. The components are pared down to a minimal structure, in order to reduce the level of industrial processes involved in the shoe's production to only four steps. It is made of three pieces that can be separated and recycled independently: a body composed of a thermoplastic elastomer (TPE), a natural fibre sole (Coco Footbed) and a cotton sock, which is 100 per cent organic and biodegradable.

Wabi is not just a specific product, though; it's a concept that evolves and is renewed every year with new designs based on the same scheme, for summer or winter. The original model, which has been on the market for 10 years, now has such a large family of variations that it has a shop of its own. Notable members of the family are the Sabi Wabi, intended for exterior use (distinguished by its openings and made with a double

injection system to give flexibility and protect the feet); the Campermeable boots and the Mon project. This latter, handicraft version involved substituting the TPE with natural fibres such as jute, sisal and banana or palm leaves, in a series of shoes to be made by hand by communities in Bangladesh, Ecuador and the Kola Peninsula.

'Camper' means 'peasant', and the first shoe was inspired by rural Spanish culture. Camper's origins go back to 1877, when Antonio Fluxà set up the first mechanized footwear factory on the island of Mallorca. In 1975, his grandson Lorenzo Fluxà reinvented the way in which Camper's shoes were designed, by combining the artisan tradition with new aesthetic ideas, creativity with quality and function, and a deep respect for Mediterranean history, culture and landscape. Similar to the traditional footwear used for working in the fields, the Camaleón, one of Camper's original shoes, was made of used tyres and recycled fabric.

At the outset, Camper started to put down the roots of its brand with an ecological shoe that respected the environment, as well as understanding the everyday needs of its wearers. All this goes to show that business and experimentation do not have to be at odds with each other, and that it's possible to evolve the process of research and development, while also valuing innovation (and imagination). *Ramón Úbeda*

Made from bamboo, reed pulp and bagasse, a byproduct of industrial waste, **WASARA** plates, bowls and cups biodegrade after they are used.

Shinichiro Ogata

—

Tokyo, Japan

—

2011

WASARA products include bowls, cups, and plates (opposite). The pulp-based tableware has four varieties of plates, three types of bowls, and three different cups for serving coffee, wine, and other refreshments (this page).

The notion of sustainable disposable tableware at first may seem an oxymoron. Paper plates and plastic cups – now ubiquitous throughout contemporary society – contribute to environmental damage at nearly every stage of their lifecycle: the production process often relies upon the destruction of virgin forests and the use of toxic chemicals; the consumption of single-use products encourages a culture of carelessness; and their disposal leads to increased pollution in already overstressed landfills. The Japanese company WASARA has developed a potential alternative to this destructive cycle by rethinking the fundamentals of how disposable goods are produced. The WASARA line of tableware is made from a mixture of renewable and recycled materials, and although the products are designed for single use, they are compostable and designed to biodegrade organically back into the earth. The hope is to provide a new model for manufacturing products that satisfy the market's appetite for disposable goods while maintaining a commitment to environmental responsibility.

Conventional paper plate manufacturers typically eschew recycled content in favor of virgin paper pulp; WASARA's approach instead combines three primary ingredients, all of which are sustainably sourced and rapidly renewable. Bamboo and reed pulp (both are plentiful and replenish much faster than timber) are mixed with bagasse, an industrial waste byproduct of refined sugar cane that is often otherwise discarded by sugar refineries. This innovative recipe yields a sustainable, robust, and entirely biodegradable paper material suitable for single-use applications and versatile enough to be molded into subtly curved geometries. The collection, designed by Shinichiro Ogata of the multifaceted Tokyo design practice Simplicity, includes dishes that vary in both size and shape. The curvature of each dish is crafted to serve a specific culinary purpose, such as a spout molded into a coffee cup, and a dipping basin integrated into a serving plate. The geometry is also informed by careful ergonomic considerations that reflect the Japanese custom of holding dishes while eating. A more complex formal logic begins to emerge once the plates are stacked and the intricate articulations of each dish combine into larger, dynamic compositions, loosely evocative of the repetitive patterns found in traditional Japanese shoji screens and textile designs. It is in this regard that the WASARA collection most transcends its original function as disposable tableware; by bringing a heightened design sensibility and a refined aesthetic to the typically mundane world of paper plates, WASARA has expanded the object's purpose beyond that of mere consumption and disposal.

The designers at WASARA prefer the term 'ephemeral' to 'disposable' when describing their product line; the nuanced distinction suggests an acute awareness and appreciation of the object's short-lived lifespan – a mindfulness not typically prompted by disposable goods. This notion of ephemerality, a kind of paradox of timelessness and single-use, dovetails with WASARA's innovative and ecologically informed manufacturing process to suggest a new future for the paper industry at large: that it is possible for products to be sustainably produced and responsibly disposed of. As manufacturers increasingly try to reconcile consumer demand for single-use goods with broader environmental concerns, WASARA's product line begins to point in the direction of a more balanced and healthy relationship between humans, the products they consume, and the world they inhabit. *Adam Marcus*

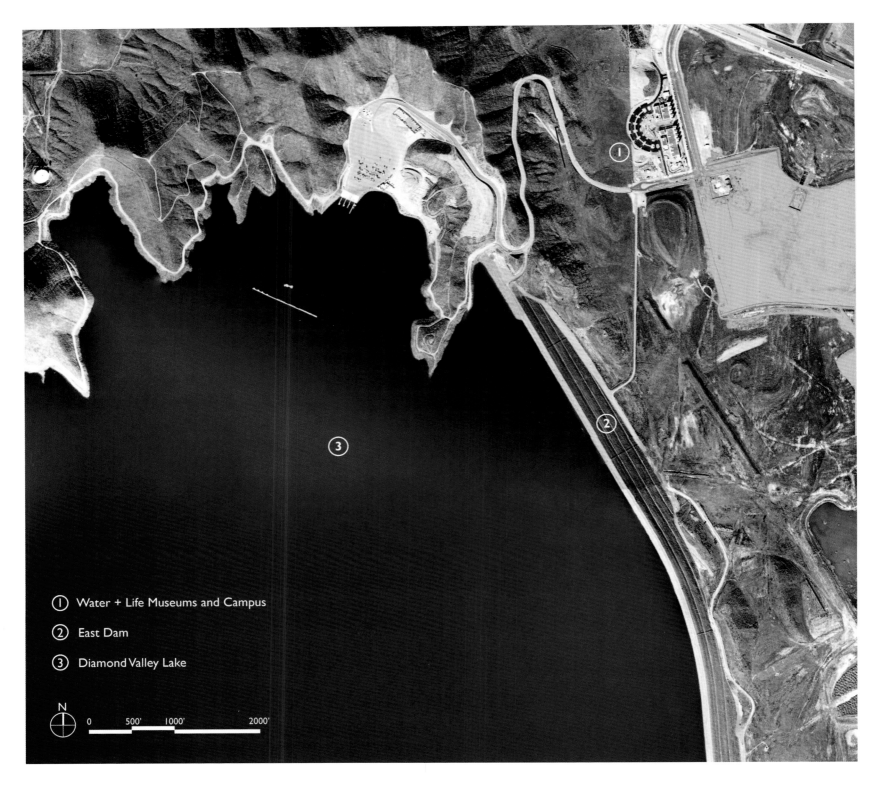

① Water + Life Museums and Campus

② East Dam

③ Diamond Valley Lake

N
0   500'   1000'   2000'

Sophisticated shading and cooling systems allow the **Water + Life Museums** to claim 68 per cent of the electricity they use from the sun.

Lehrer + Gangi Design + Build
—
Hemet, CA USA
—
2008

The Water + Life Museums and Campus are situated on Diamond Valley Lake, southern California's largest manmade reservoir (opposite). The 7 hectare (17 acre) campus (this page) is separated from the lake by the East Dam which is filled with earth-core rock obtained from the excavated site.

Completed at the end of 2006, the striking 6,500 m² (70,000 sq ft) complex of the Water + Life Museums was built to house the fossils and Native American artefacts discovered during the creation of Diamond Valley Lake in the 1990s. The lake construction turned a 1,820-hectare (4,500 acre) swathe of farmland into an enormous reservoir that holds 980 billion litres (260 billion gallons) of water. During the dig, evidence of a trading ground between desert and coastal tribes was discovered and the Centre for Water Education and the Western Centre for Archaeology and Paleontology were formed. The resulting Water + Life Museums sit in particularly hostile surroundings. In semi-arid Hemet, summer temperatures regularly exceed 37°C (100°F), violent downpours are not unknown and water can freeze in winter.

Inspired by the architecture of Gordon B. Kaufmann's Hoover Dam, the steel and glass building has an industrial, clean aesthetic. Ten metallic towers stand like wide columns, connected by shorter window walls, where glass stretches from floor to ceiling. The towers shade the glass from direct sun, while translucent solar panels shade the walkways between the museums. The firm Lehrer + Gangi Design + Build, formed especially for this project, is a collaboration between LA-based Lehrer Architects and Gangi Development, from Burbank, California. The design process was led by architects Michael Lehrer and Mark Gangi, who persuaded the clients to invest in a green approach by focusing on the amount of money the client could ultimately save and the positive message it would convey to the community.

The immense complex boasts a long list of sustainable features. A 540 kW, 3,000-strong array of solar panels takes care of 68 per cent of the buildings' energy needs.

Although the system cost £2.5 million ($4 million), grants from the California Energy Commission and Southern California Edison slashed the price in half. Savings on electricity bills are expected to recoup the remaining £1.25 million ($2 million) by 2014. Other features include a sophisticated mechanical system of radiant flooring and forced air units, which efficiently draw down cool air and force out hot air, reducing air conditioning needs and cutting costs. Heat-resistant windows maximize natural lighting while keeping the interior cool with a coating that makes the glass opaque to infrared wavelengths, keeping heat in on cold days and out on hot days. Rooftops are covered in a single-ply white membrane and shaded by solar panels to reduce the amount of heat absorbed from the sun's rays, and translucent banners hang in front of eastern walls to mitigate heat radiation.

There are interior and exterior lighting controls, outdoor light pollution controls, interior occupancy sensors, waterless urinals and dual-flush toilets. The terraced gardens feature drought-resistant native plants irrigated with grey water and red-braided artificial streams with permeable surfaces, which collect rainwater and allow it to percolate naturally back into the water table. Sculptural rocks reclaimed from the reservoir excavation add drama to the landscaping.

The Western Centre for Archaeology and Paleontology provides science education as well as displaying the finds unearthed during the reservoir dig, while the Centre for Water Education teaches visitors about the importance of water, on both a local and global scale. It is appropriate that museums about water and desert life should be living examples of water conservation and sensitive adaptation to the local environment. *Helen Babbs*

SUSTAINABILITY DIAGRAMS

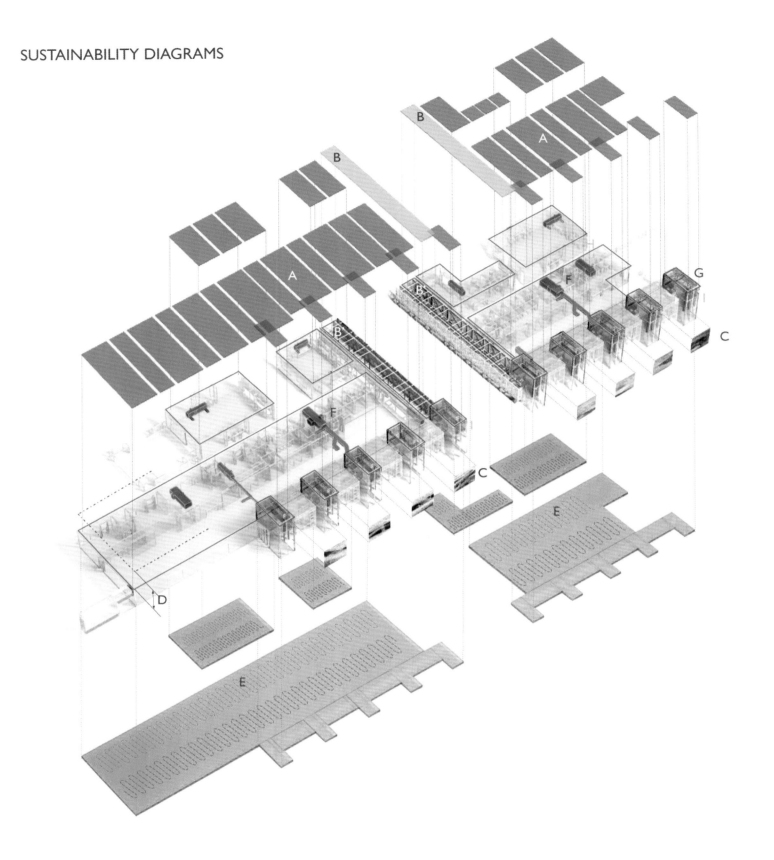

A **PHOTOVOLTAICS+INSULATION**

A ROOFTOP PHOTOVOLTAIC ARRAY OF 3,000 PANELS PRODUCES 540 KILO-WATTS. IT ALSO SHADES THE ROOF AND WILL PROLONG THE LIFE OF THE ROOF COVERING BY ABOUT 25%. THE SYSTEM WILL PROVIDE A PROJECTED SAVINGS OVER BUILDINGS LIFESPAN OF ABOUT $13 MILLION.

B **PHOTOVOLTAICS+SHADING DEVICE**

SPECIAL PHOTOVOLTAIC PANELS - SQUARE SILICON WAFERS IN CLEAR GLASS- PRODUCE SHADE AS DAPPLED LIGHT OVER FORMAL LOGGIA (B').

C **SHADING DEVICE**

TRANSLUCENT BANNERS SHADE THE EAST FACADE TO MITIGATE HEAT RA-DIATION.

D **DISTANCE BETWEEN PV AND ROOF**

THE DISTANCE BETWEEN THE ROOF AND THE PHOTOVOLTAIC PANELS WORKS AS A CLIMATE ZONE TO KEEP THE ROOF FROM OVERHEATING.

E **RADIANT HEATING + COOLING**

A RADIANT HEATING AND COOLING FLOOR SYSTEM IS FOUND THROUGH-OUT THE BUILDING.

F **MINIMAL FORCED AIR UNITS**

MINIMAL FORCED AIR UNITS WORK IN CONJUNCTION WITH RADIANT HEATING/COOLING.

G **INSULATION**

THICK WALL INSULATION MITIGATES COOLING LOSS TO EXTERIOR.

The 6,500 m² (70,000 sq ft) complex houses a collection of over one million fossils and 200,000 Native American artifacts found during the construction of the Diamond Valley Lake reservoir, which is 7.25 km (4.5 miles) wide.

The kite- and wind-turbine-powered **Wind Explorer** travelled over 5,000 km (3,100 miles) on less than £10 ($16) worth of electricity.

Dirk Gion and Stefan Simmerer

Essen, Germany

2011

By kite and turbine power alone, the tiny egg-shaped Wind Explorer car travelled thousands of kilometres across Australia at the beginning of 2011. For German co-pilots Stefan Simmerer and Dirk Gion, it was an epic journey – and something of a publicity stunt – which broke world records and highlighted the possibilities of effective, emission-free transport. They dubbed it the self-sufficient wind mobile and took a documentary team with them on their trip.

A lightweight body atop four bicycle wheels, the roadster-style invention is powered by an 8kW lithium-ion battery charged by a portable wind turbine. Fully charged, the Wind Explorer can travel 350 to 430 km (220 to 270 miles), achieving speeds of up to 80 km/h (50 mph). On windy days, battery power can be swapped for a large steerable kite, operated by the co-pilot. During Simmerer and Gion's 18-day trip, the battery was only plugged into the mains once, which meant their fuel bill for the entire 5,000 km (3,100 miles) was less than £10 ($16).

The Wind Explorer was a partnership project and Evonik Industries AG, from Essen in Germany, were particularly important to the designers. They provided the lightweight bodywork and the lithium-ion batteries. They also provided the wheel work. In terms of a sustainable legacy, Evonik is now preparing mass production of some of the Wind Explorer's key elements, including the battery cells and the lightweight construction, for the automotive industry.

The curved body is made from a polymethacrylimide foam called ROHACELL©, which is woven into a sandwich with carbon fibre. This cuts the weight of body parts by 60 to 70 per cent in comparison with a conventional steel body. The Wind Explorer body weighs in at just 90 kg (200 lb), plus 90 kg of batteries and the 20 kg (44 lb) wind turbine head, for a total of 200 kg (444 lb).

With an electric hub motor integrated into the rear wheel assembly, it's the lithium-ion battery cells that are at the heart of the car's power. They have a unique ceramic membrane that allows them to be fully re-charged in mere minutes, and they can be charged up to 3,000 times before their performance starts to decline. The batteries are also able to store energy from renewable sources. Gion and Simmerer would charge the batteries when resting. It took them half an hour to erect the portable turbine they carried, which had a 6 m (3.75 ft) tall telescopic mast made of bamboo.

Moved along by some deceptively humble looking bicycle wheels, the Wind Explorer in fact boasts two pairs of seriously fancy tyres. Tyres with technology from Evonik use silica as the active filler and organosilane Si 69 as the coupling agent between the silica and rubber. This system reduces the rolling resistance of tyres by up to 40 per cent. Lower resistance reduces fuel consumption and CO_2 emissions.

Perhaps more of a novelty than the vehicle of the future, the design does have value. The Wind Explorer uses a fraction of the energy that the most efficient of modern cars does. It shows how using lightweight construction material and lithium-ion rechargeable batteries can transform a vehicle into something economically efficient and environmentally sensitive. The journey also provided opportunities for industrial companies to test new technology under extreme conditions. *Helen Babbs*

In its smallest form, the **Windbelt** is a clean alternative to the AA battery; it harnesses wind-induced vibrations to produce cheap electricity.

Shawn Frayne

Honolulu, HI
USA
—
2004–present

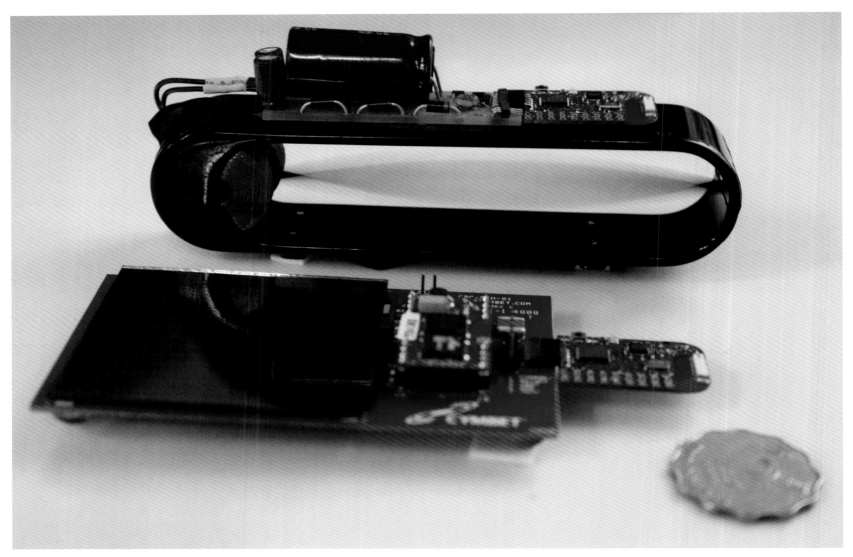

Windbelt

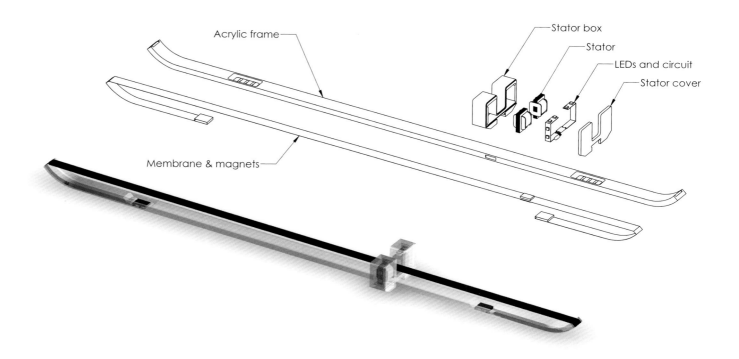

Acrylic frame

Stator box

Stator

LEDs and circuit

Stator cover

Membrane & magnets

The Windbelt turns wind into electricity, cheaply and without using a turbine. Shawn Frayne, who invented the Windbelt in 2004, co-founded Hawaii-based Humdinger Wind Energy in 2007 to explore and develop the idea. Frayne came up with the idea during a trip to Haiti. He was staying in a small town without mains electricity, where people relied on polluting and costly kerosene and diesel for generating power. Thinking that wind would be a great way to run domestic LED lighting, he tried and failed to design and build an affordable turbine. Instead he came up with the table-top sized Windbelt, which uses a flexible membrane rather than blades to catch the wind. His invention harnesses energy from the rapid wind-induced vibration of a flap of fabric. This motion is translated into electricity by magnets attached to the material. The vibrating fabric moves the magnets in and out of electromagnetic coils, creating a current in the coil's wire.

The aerodynamic phenomenon that the Windbelt relies on is known as 'aeroelastic flutter' – a self-feeding vibration that occurs when a structure is exposed to an airstream. While the phenomenon is known to be a destructive force – particularly on aircraft and bridges, most famously causing the wild collapse of the Tacoma Narrows Bridge – when controlled, flutter energy can be put to good use. The fluttering membrane is the Windbelt's key component and needs to be made from a material with very specific properties. It must be thin and light, so it acts like an airfoil when wind blows across it. It must be fairly rigid, with a high tensile strength, in order to cope with high wind speeds. It must also be able to maintain its shape over time. Frayne's belts are made from mylar-coated taffeta, which is a kite-making material.

Modular and available in three different sizes, Humdinger Wind Energy's plan is for the invention to power a range of devices, from the modest to the massive. The micro Windbelt is a clean alternative to the AA battery. It's especially suitable for use in the millions of small sensors in operation around the world to monitor things like temperature, air quality, humidity or geological activity. To work, the Windbelt needs airflow and so it could sit on the underside of a bridge to monitor stress, or by an air duct in a building with a climate control system. This smallest Windbelt has a 12 cm (4.75 in) long membrane, and can achieve a power output ranging from 0.2 mW in 3.5 m/s (11 ft/s) wind to 5mW in a 7.5 m/s (25 ft/s) wind.

The medium Windcell has a 1 m (3 ft) long membrane and can power larger devices, such as lights and WiFi repeaters. Designed to work alone or together, a few linked Windcells could fuel something like an ocean navigation buoy or a lighting array. Humdinger has been working on an individual light-up Windcell that directly powers a detachable set of LEDs. Weighing under 1 kg (2.2 lb) and only 3 cm (1.2 in) deep, it can operate in wind speeds of 2 m/s (6 ft/s) and more, and accepts airflow from multiple directions.

Arrays of Windcells could also be grouped together into panels with the hope of providing grid-based energy a much larger scale. Mounted vertically, each Windcell Panel will aim at energy costs of £0.3 ($0.5) per kWh in average wind speeds of 6 m/s (20 ft/s). First tested in Hong Kong in 2010, this 1 x 1 m (3 x 3 ft) square design is still a work in progress. The output of large installations varies on the size of the module, but could potentially produce power on a scale comparable to a wind turbine. *Helen Babbs*

The **Zollverein School** reuses the water that floods a local abandoned coal mine as a CO_2-free source of heating and insulation.

SANAA
—
Essen,
Germany
—
2006

The concrete walls of the school are actually filled with water pumped up from the mine below ground (this page). After this water is circulated through the building it makes its way into the neighbouring Emsch River (opposite).

The Zollverein School, designed by SANAA with climate engineers Transsolar, is built on the grounds of the former Zeche Zollverein mine, which was closed down in 1986. The school is a four-storey concrete cube measuring 35 x 35 x 34 m (115 x 115 x 110 ft). Square windows in many sizes are arranged so that each facade is different, and a roof garden on the fourth floor is open to the outside air and sun.

The most innovative feature of the building came from a close attention to the site. The climate in Essen is moderate, seldom reaching temperatures below freezing or hotter than 30°C (86°F). The shaft tunnels of the defunct mine, which reach a depth of 1,000 m (3,280 ft), are still maintained for possible future use. As a consequence, the owner of the mines has to permanently pump the ground water from these depths in order to keep them from flooding. This water, which is partially contaminated with heavy metals and minerals, maintains a temperature of 29°C (84°F). Transsolar, the climate engineers for the project, realized the water would be a remarkable CO_2 free energy source, which could be used to heat the building.

This free, local energy source led to the idea for an 'active insulation'. This consisted of building a monolithic concrete wall 0.3 m (1 ft) thick, containing plastic pipes through which the warm water from the mine could be pumped, giving the interior wall a surface temperature above 18°C (64°F) and guaranteeing comfort in the heated inside space. This type of innovative design requires an unusual degree of coordination between all the participants, and to ensure this it was vital to simulate the conditions in the interior of the building. This is really only possible with modern simulation programs, which allow precise calculations of the temperatures of the walls and interiors, integrating the influence of outside temperatures using weather data specific to Essen. A detailed analysis of the wall temperatures by the design team took a whole year. This was crucial in order to determine a pipe distance that could distribute heat equally and to enable the structural and climate engineers to integrate the piping system with the reinforcement of the wall construction, as the system can't be changed after construction. For a similar reason, to prevent freezing in the piping system in the walls, which could be caused if the system pumps failed, the system is designed to self-empty when a critically low temperature in the wall is reached.

The monolithic wall construction, even with the integrated piping system, was much cheaper than the original double-shell concrete wall design. This is a key reason why the mining-water system could be realized – a neighbouring building had wanted to use the mining water as well, but the idea was rejected, because no savings could cover the increased investment costs for the building, and therefore killed the economic balance of the approach. The system actually falls 75 per cent below the energy consumption regulations for heating, which saves operation costs for heating of about £6,000 ($10,000) per year and reduces the CO_2 load of the building by 31 tonnes per year. Also important is the example set by the building, which makes this unique energy source available for the design of other new buildings in the neighbourhood. *Matthias Schuler*

Warm water pipe

Temperature field for
ambient temperature ta=1.9°C

The active insulation is pumped
up into the building (top and
bottom). This insulation creates
a comfortable interior
temperature (opposite).

0.20 m

1.00 m

Outside

Inside

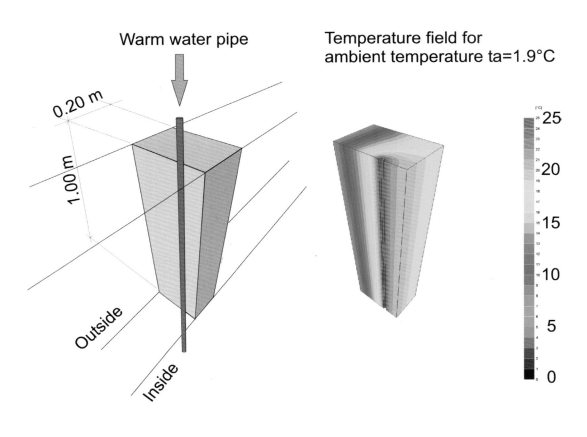

[°C]
25
24
23
22
21
20
19
18
17
16
15
14
13
12
11
10
9
8
7
6
5
4
3
2
1
0

External wall with
an active insulation

Tamb -10 °C

Troom 22 °C

Pump station with
heat exchanger (water /water)

mine Zollverein

filling of mine shaft

seeling

water level

geothermal well

tunnel filled with water

1200 m deep
mine shaft

hot water (~35 °C)
in disused mining shafts

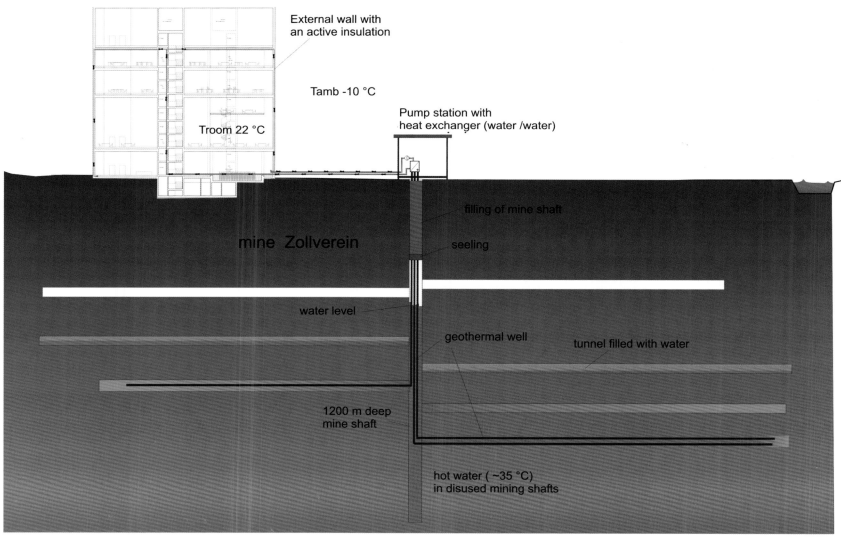

Biographies

Flavia Amadeu
Designer, Plymouth, UK
www.flaviaamadeu.com
Education M.Phil/PhD Researcher, Sustainable Design, Transtechnology Research Group, University of Plymouth, UK; [2006] M.A, Arts, University of Brasília.
Affiliations Chemistry Laboratory, University of Brasília.
Recent Works The Organic Jewellery Collection; Tecbor Project, Amazon rainforest.
Awards [2011] Nomination, Brit Insurance Design Awards, Design Museum, London; [2010] Nomination, Brazilian Biennial of Design.

Arup Associates
Architects, London, UK
www.arupassociates.com
Recent Works [2009] Citigroup Data Centre, Frankfurt; [2007] Kensington Oval, Barbados; [2002] City of Manchester Stadium; [2001-04] Druk White Lotus School, Ladakh, India; [2000] Imperial War Museum redevelopment, London; [1998] BP Solar Showcase, Birmingham.
Selected Publications [2008] *Arup Associates: Unified Design*, Wiley; [2005] *Plantation Lane, Time and Tide*, Wiley.
Awards [2008] Financial Services Technology Awards, Green energy efficiency award; Power of Aluminium Awards; Structural Steel Design Awards; [2007] Datacentre Awards, Green Data Centre Award; The LEAF Awards, Structural Design of the Year; [2005] Lighting Design Awards.

Aukett Fitzroy Robinson
Architects, London, UK
www.aukettfitzroyrobinson.com
Education Nitesh Magdani, [2002] Leeds Metropolitan University RIBA Part III; [2000] Dip.Arch, Leeds Metropolitan University; [1996] B.A (Hons) Architecture, Leeds Metropolitan University.
Recent Works [2011] Marks & Spencer Concept Sustainable Stores; [2009] Goodman International, Parque Empressarial de San Fernando de Henares, Madrid; [2006] Adnams Distribution Centre, Suffolk; [2003] The Grove Mansion Hotel restoration.
Selected Publications 'Green Gurus', *Building Magazine*, March 2007.
Awards [2010] Best Refurbished/Recycled Workplace in London, BCO Award; Regional Award for Best Corporate Workplace, BCO Award; [2000] The Ibstock Brick Award, Best Performance; The Allison Memorial Award, Best use of construction in design; The Philip Webb Award, SPAB.

Yves Béhar
Designer, San Francisco, USA
www.fuseproject.com
Education B.S, Industrial Design, Art Center College of Design, California.
Recent Works [2010] See Better to Learn Better program, Mexico; Leaf Light for Herman Miller; [2008] One Laptop Per Child project; [2006] ICON Bluetooth Headset for Jawbone;
Selected Publications *Time Magazine* (one of 25 global Visionaries); *Fast Company* (Masters of Design).
Awards [2010] IDSA Design of the Decade Award; Mobile Choice Awards; Spark Award; Communication Arts Design Annual; IDEA Award; [2009] Green GOOD Award; GOOD Design

Award; Red Dot Design Award; [2008] Design of the Year, Brit Insurance Design Award, London Design Museum; Good Design Award, Chicago Anthenaeum; iF Product Design Award; '50 Best Innovations of the Year', *TIME Magazine* [2007] INDEX, Design to Improve Life; Red Dot; ID Magazine; D&AD; iF Hannover.

Behnisch Architekten
Stuttgart, Germany
www.behnisch.com
Education Stefan Behnisch BDA, RIBA, FAIA / Diploma, Architecture, Technical University, Karlsruhe; B.A, Philosophy and Economics, Munich.
Affiliations Behnisch Architekten – Stefan Behnisch, David Cook, Martin Haas; Eero Saarinen Chair Visiting Professor, Yale School of Architecture; Miller Visiting Professor, University of Pennsylvania; Harry W. Porter Sr. Visiting Professor, University of Virginia School of Architecture.
Recent Works [2011] Max Aicher Arena ice skating rink, Inzell; [2010] Marco Polo Tower, Hamburg, Germany; National Centre for Tumour Diseases, Heidelberg; Genzyme Centre Headquarters, Cambridge, MA; Hysolar, Stuttgart; [2009] Unilever HQ, Hamburg; German Oceanographic Museum; [2008] Oceanographic museum OZEANEUM, Stralsund; [2004] Hilde-Domin-Schule, Herrenberg, Germany.
Selected Publications [2008] *Behnisch Architekten*, Jovis-Verlag, Berlin; [2004] *Genzyme Centre: Behnisch, Behnisch & Partner*, FMO Publishers, Stuttgart; [2003] *Behnisch, Behnisch & Partner: Buildings and Designs*, Birkhäuser-Verlag, Berlin; [2002] *NORD/LB Hannover*, Hatje-Cant-Verlagz, Stuttgart; [1998] *Natuur onder Architectuur*, Schuyt & Co, Haarlem, Netherlands.
Awards [2010] MIPIM Award Category Residential Development; RIBA International Award; International Architecture Award; Deutscher Stahlbaupreis Auszeichnung (German Steel Construction Award); European Museum of the Year Award; [2009] Umweltzertifikat der HafenCity Hamburg in Gold; Barcelona World Architecture Festival Award; BEX Award, Outstanding Contribution to the Built Environment of Hamburg, Ozeaneum, Stralsund, Germany; Nomination, Mies van der Rohe Award; Good Design Award; Beispielhaftes Bauen im Landkreis Böblingen Unileverhaus, Hamburg, Germany; [2008] Trendmarke; [2007] Global Award for Sustainable Architecture.

BioLite
Designers, Berkeley, USA
www.biolitestove.com
Education Jonathan Cedar, B.A, Engineering and Environmental Science, Dartmouth College. Alexander Drummond, B.F.A., Environmental & Product Design (under Viktor Papanek), Kansas City Art Institute.
Recent Works BioLite CampStove; BioLite HomeStove.
Selected Publications [2010] '2011 Tech Guide', *Men's Health*, 15 December 2010; 'The Innovator', *Guardian*, 12 September 2010; 'Microgrid Energy Rules the Sustainable Brands Innovation Open', *Fast Company*, 11 June 2010; [2009] 'Hearth Surgery', *New Yorker*, 22 December 2009.

Awards [2011] Winner, St. Andrews Prize for the Environment; Finalist, Index Awards [2010] Fellowship, Dasra Social Impact Program; Winner, Sustainable Business Innovation Open; Finalist, PopTech Social Innovation Fellowship; 1st place, Vodafone Wireless Innovation Prize.

Patrick Blanc
Botanist, Paris, France
www.verticalgardenpatrickblanc.com
Education [1978] Thèse de Doctorat, Pierre et Marie Curie, Paris VI University.
Affiliations French Academy of Sciences; Royal College of Art, London.
Selected Publications [2010] *Jardinons à la Verticale!*, Rustica Editions; [2009] *Vertikale Garten, die Natur in der Stadt*, Ulmer Editions; 'The 50 Best Inventions of the Year', Time Magazine, vol.174, no.20, 23 November 2009; [2008] *The Vertical Garden, from Nature to the City*, Norton.

Joshua Bolchover and John Lin
Architects, Hong Kong
www.newbetter.co.uk
Education Joshua Bolchover, M.A, Cambridge University; Dip.Arch, Bartlett School of Architecture, UCL. John Lin, The Cooper Union, New York.
Affiliations John Lin, Lecturer, London Metropolitan University and Cambridge University; Newbetter; Shrinking Cities international research and exhibition project; University of Hong Kong community project workshop (CPW); CCPW; Kadoorie Farm and Garden Corporation; Luke Him Sau Charitable Trust; Hope Education Foundation; Green Hope Foundation.
Recent Works [2009] Maison du Champagne, Wan Chai, Hong Kong; [2004] 'Re-Imagining the City' by Shrinking Cities; 'Remembering Tomorrow: Hulme as urban myth' installation by Newbetter.
Selected Publications [2004] 'Shrinking Cities presents convincing local views of a global problem', *Icon*, 17 November 2004; [2002] *Blur: The Making of Nothing*, Harry Abrams.
Awards [2011] Nomination, Award for Emerging Architecture, ar+d; [2010] Shortlist, Making Space Competition; Honorable Mention, Urbaninform Design Competition; [2009] AR Awards for Emerging Architecture, International Competition.

Brooks + Scarpa (formerly Pugh + Scarpa)
Architects, Los Angeles, USA
www.pugh-scarpa.com
Education Lawrence Scarpa FAIA [1987] M.Arch, University of Florida; [1981] B.Des, University of Florida. Angela Brooks AIA, LEED AP [1991] M.Arch, Southern California Institute of Architecture; [1987] B.Des, Architecture, University of Florida.
Affiliations Liveable Places, Inc.; Affordable Housing Design Leadership Institute; Solar Santa Monica.
Recent Works [2010] Cherokee Lofts; Vasquez Rocks Interpretive Centre; [2009] Step Up on Fifth, Santa Monica; Reactor Films, Santa Monica; [2005] Solar Umbrella House; Redelco Residence; Mill Centre for the Arts; [2004] Orange Grove Lofts, West Hollywood.
Selected Publications [2009] 'Better Living', *The Architect's Newspaper*, 22 May 2009;

Building Refurbishment, Instituto Monsa de Ediciones, Barcelona; *Sustainable Homes*, Links International, Barcelona; [2008] *The American House*, Phaidon Press, London; *The Phaidon Atlas of Contemporary World* Architecture, Phaidon Press, London; *The Sustainable Home*, Merrell Publishers, London; [2007] *Women in Green: Voices of Sustainable Design*, Ecotone Publishing.
Awards [2010] AIA Los Angeles NEXT Merit Award; AIA Los Angeles Design Honor Award; AIA California Council Merit Award for Architecture; Los Angeles Business Council Architectural Award; Slow Home Award, Best Apartment/Loft Design, Los Angeles; AIA National and State Architecture Firm Award; AIA Institute Honor Award for Housing; [2009] AIA Committee on Architecture for Education Merit Award; National AIA Young Architect Award; [2008] Stars of Design Award, Interior Design Magazine; [2007] National AIA Honor Award; Westside Prize for Urban Design.

Hugh Broughton Architects
Architects, London, UK
www.hbarchitects.co.uk
Recent Works [2005-2012] Halley VI Antarctic Research Station; [2007-2011] Juan Carlos 1 Spanish Antarctic Base.
Awards Two Civic Trust Commendations; International Property Federation; 2nd place, Building Awards Young Architectural Practice of the Year; two RIBA Awards for Architecture.

Bucholz Mcevoy Architects
Architects, Dublin, Ireland
www.bmcea.com
Education Karen McEvoy RIAI, NCARB, AIA, B.Arch (Hons), University College Dublin. Merritt Buchloz, M.Arch, Princeton University; B.Arch, Cornell University.
Affiliations Merritt Buchloz, Professor of Architecture, University of Limerick.
Recent Works [2009] Westmeath County Buildings and Library; [2008] Elmpark Green Urban Quarter; Siopa Pavilions, Dublin; [2005] Environmental Research Institute UC Cork; [2002] Fingal County Hall.
Awards [2010] 2nd place, Bismarckhöhe Werder/Havel; [2009] Shortlisted, Public Building of the Year, Emirates Glass LEAF Awards; Long List, WAN Civic Buildings Award; Europe & Africa Property Award, Best Architecture, Ireland; Award for Excellence: Europe, Middle East and Africa, Urban Land Institute Sustainable Galvanizing Award; Special Mention, Fassa Bortolo International Prize for Sustainable Architecture; Finalist, Green Buildings, MIPIM Award; Nomination, Mies van der Rohe Award; [2008] The Chicago Athenaeum, International Architecture Award; Finalist, The Green Awards; Opus Award Projects over €20 Million; RIAI Award Best Office Development /Commercial; [2007] Irish Concrete Society, Sustainability Award; RIBA European Award; RIAI.

Camper
Shoe designers, Barcelona, Spain
www.camper.com
Recent Works Camaleón Shoe; Pelotas Shoe; TWS Shoe; Brothers Shoe; Industrial Shoe; [1999-2002] Edible Gardens project, Madrid, London & Rome.

Eric Chan
Designer, Hong Kong
www.eccoid.com
Education Masters, Design, Cranbrook Academy of Art.
Affiliations ECCO Design.

Recent Works 9797 Bamboo Chair; Colgate Electric Toothbrushes; Virgin Pulse Entertainment Electronics; Lexus/Toyota I'Finesse Personal Pond; Herman Miller Spider Fast-Prep Work Station.
Awards [2004] Annual Design Review Awards, I.D.Magazine; PopSci Design Challenge Honorable Mention, Popular Science Magazine; Red Dot Design Award, Design Zentrum; Good Design Award, The Chicago Anthenaeum; [2003] Award for Design Excellence, Design Journal; [2002] IDEA Award, IDSA.

Chetwoods Architects
Architects, London, UK
www.chetwoods.com
Education Laurie Chetwood RIBA, ARB, Dip.Arch; B.A (Hons).
Affiliations Victoria & Albert Museum; Royal Academy, London.
Recent Works G. Park Blue Planet Business Park; Brighton New England Quarter; Butterfly House; Millennium Sainsburys, Greenwich, London; MAC Arts Centre; Oasis and Perfume Show Gardens.
Awards [2010] RIBA London Bridge Design Competition; [2008] Shortlisted, RTPI; [2007] Shortlisted, LEAF Awards; RHS Gold Medal Winner; [2006] Large House Winner, Housing Design Awards; Best Retail Park, Property Awards; Sustainability Award, Building Magazine; Runner-up, Major Housing Project of the Year; [2005] Architect of the Year, Award for Industrial/R&D, Building Design; Shortlisted, Architectural Practice of the Year.

Christensen & Co.
Architects, Copenhagen, Denmark
www.christensenco.dk
Education Michael Christensen, Aarhus School of Architecture.
Affiliations Danish University and Property Agency; Copenhagen University; Velux and Velfac; Henning Larsens Architects; Danish Association of Architectural Firms; Deutsches Architektenkammer.
Recent Works Green Lighthouse, Copenhagen; Climate friendly nursey, Solrød, Denmark; Panum Institute, Copenhagen; Rosendal Tennis Club, Sweden; New Campus, Roskilde Technical School.
Awards [2010] Shortlisted, World Architecture Festival Award; [2009] 'Building Material – Innovation Price', Danish Industry; Award for good and beautiful buildings, Copenhagen Municipality.

Civil Twilight Collective
Design Collective, San Francisco, USA
www.civiltwilightcollective.com
Education Kate Lyndon, [2007] M.Arch, UC Berkeley; B.A, Urban Studies & Planning, UC San Diego. Christina Seely, [2003] MFA, Photography, Rhode Island School of Design; [1998] B.A, Visual Arts, Carleton College. Anton Wills, [2006] M.Arch, UC Berkeley; [1999] B.A, Architectural Studies, Brown University.
Affiliations Christina Seely, Faculty, California College of Art; Walker Art Centre; American Institute of Graphic Arts; The Bronx Museum; The Centre for Contemporary Art and the Natural World, Haldon Forest, UK; Saturate Design.
Recent Works [2010] Origami Kayak; [2007] Lunar-resonant Streetlights; Biophilic Booth.
Selected Publications *Design and Designing: A Critical Introduction*, Berg Publishers, Oxford.
Awards [2010] Design Distinction, I.D. Magazine Annual Review; [2009] Finalist, INDEX: Design to Improve Life Awards; Finalist, California

Cleantech Open; [2007] 1st place, Metropolis Next Generation Award.

Claesson Koivisto Rune
Designers and Architects, Stockholm, Sweden
www.ckr.se
Education Mårten Claesson, Konstfack University of Arts, Crafts and Design, Stockholm; Parsons The New School for Design, New York. Eero Koivisto, Konstfack University College of Arts, Crafts and Design, Stockholm; Aalto University School of Art and Design, Helsinki; Parsons The New School for Design, New York.
Ola Rune, Konstfack University College of Arts, Crafts and Design, Stockholm; The Royal Danish Academy of Fine Arts, Copenhagen; Southwark College of Art and Design, London.
Recent Works Örsta Gallery, Kumla, Sweden; [2008] Folded Roof House, Muskö, Sweden; [2003] Sfera Building, Kyoto; [1994] Wabi, Stockholm.
Selected Publications [2010] *Smaller Objects: Claesson Koivisto Rune*, Fälth & Hässler; *Örsta Galleri – Claesson Koivisto Rune*, Galleri Örsta; [2009] *Parupu – Paper Pulp Chair*, Södra Book Publishing; *The Models: Claesson Koivisto Rune*, Gabor Palotai Publisher; [2007] *Claesson Koivisto Rune*, Birkhäuser Verlag; [2003] *Nine Houses: Claesson Koivisto Rune*, Sfera Publishing.

Michael Clausen and Robert Shaw
Photographer and Filmmaker, Berlin, Germany
http://prinzessinnengarten.net
Education Michael Clausen, History, Humboldt University, Berlin.
Robert Shaw, Documentary filmmaking, University of Fine Arts, Hamburg.
Affiliations Prinzessinnengärten; Nomadisch Grün; Association for the Advancement of semi-public space; Gob Squad performance collective; Floor + nonprofit organization, Hamburg; ActionAid.
Recent Works Advo-casting, with ActionAid, London.
Selected Publications 'Berlin's Mobile Garden Grows', New York Times, 28 February 2011.

Cloud 9
Architects, Barcelona, Spain
www.e-cloud9.com
Education Enric Ruiz Geli, Architecture, Escola Tècnica Superior d'Arquitectura de Barcelona.
Recent Works [2005] Villa Bio, Figueres; Blub.blob.lab, Cricursa Stand.
Selected Publications [2000] *Barcelona +*, Actar, Barcelona; Metápolis, Actar, Barcelona; *10x10*, Phaidon Press, London; *Less Esthetics More Ethics*, Actar, Barcelona.
Awards [2003] Premio de la Asociación de Críticos de Arte de Cataluña; [2000] Premio Concurso Internacional Aviario.

DBA
Designers, New York, USA
www.dba-co.com
Recent Works DBA 98 Pen; Endless Notebook; Heater; DBA Humidifier; PVC free Extension Cord.

DBB Aedas and Levisky Arquitetos Associados
São Paulo, Brazil
www.aedas.com
www.leviskyarquitetos.com.br
Education Anna Dietzsch, [1998] Masters Degree (Hons), Urban Design, Harvard University. Adriana Levisky, [2001] São Paulo University.
Affiliations Anna Dietzsch / Lecturer, City College of New York, New Jersey Institute of Technology, Escola da Cidade, São Paulo;

Adriana Levisky, Lecturer, Bandeirantes University; Braz Cubas University.
Recent Works [2008] Victor Civita Plaza, Open Museum for Sustainability, São Paulo; Vanderbilt University Medical Centre, Jacobson Research Building, Tennessee; [2007] Valeo Security Systems, São Paulo.
Awards [2010] Urban Land Institute Award; Mid-Atlantic Construction Best of 2010; AIA DC Award; The 2010 Community Advancement Awards; NOMA's Architect of the Year.

Design 99
Detroit, USA
www.visitdesign99.com
Education Gina Reichert, M.Arch, Cranbrook Academy of Art and Tulane University. Mitch Cope, MFA in Painting, Washington State University and BFA in Painting, College for Creative Studies, Detroit, MI.
Affiliations Museum of Contemporary Art Detroit; Detroit Tree of Heaven Workshop; Susanne Hilberry Gallery; KW Institute for Contemporary Art, Berlin; Subspace Gallery, Berlin; Kunsthaus Dresden; World Wokers Museum, Steyr, Austria; Tangent Gallery, Detroit.
Recent Works Power House Project; Talking Fence; The Neighborhood Project; Heartland Machine.
Selected Publications A People's Guide to Detroit, Design 99, 2008; 'Art as Security System', Rob Walker, New York Times, 5 July 2010; 'A Storefront for Creativity', Fabrizio Gallanti, Arbitare, 2 February 2009; 'Critics' Pick – Laith Karmo', Lynn Crawford, Art Forum, April 2008.

DIFFUS
Designers, Copenhagen, Denmark
www.diffus.dk
Affiliations Michel Guglielmi, Professor Danish School of Design in Copenhagen, Assistant Professor, Ålborg University, Institute for Media Technology and Engineering. Hanne Louise Johannesen, Mag. Art, Art History; Assistant Professor in Visual Culture at the Department of Cultural Studies and the Arts at University of Copenhagen; Current research is in the field of New Media.
Recent Works [2011] Solar handbag; [2009] Climate dress; Interactive garden; [2008] Karen Blixen Museum: En fantastisk fortælling; Interactive billboard; [2006-08] Responsive textiles.
Selected Publications [2010] Metamorfosis, Elisabetta Cianfanelli and Stoffel Kuenen, Edizioni Polistampa.

Diller Scofidio + Renfro
Architects, New York, USA
www.dsrny.com
Education Elizabeth Diller, B.Arch, Cooper Union School of Architecture. Richard Scofidio AIA, B.Arch, Cooper Union School of Architecture; B.Arch, Columbia Univesity. Charles Renfro AIA, B.Arch, Rice University; M.Arch, Columbia University.
Affiliations Elizabeth Diller, Professor of Architecture, Princeton University; Richard Scofidio, Professor Emeritus of Architecture, Cooper Union School of Architecture; AIA; American Academy of Arts and Sciences; Royal Institute of British Architects.
Recent Works [2011] Hypar Pavilion & Restaurant; [2010] Lincoln Center Public Spaces, New York; [2009] Alice Tully Hall renovation; The Juilliard School expansion; Governors Island Park, New York; [2008] Taekwando Park, Muju, South Korea; [2007] School of American

Ballet expansion, New York; [2006] Institute of Contemporary Art, Boston.
Awards [2011] Progressive Architecture Award; [2010] Architecture Honor Award, Society for College and University Planning; AIA New York Honor Award for Urban Design; Life Enhancer of the Year Award, Wallpaper* Magazine; [2009] AIA New York Medal of Honor, AIA New York Presidents Award.

Rolf Disch Solar Architecture
Freiburg, Germany
www.rolfdisch.de
Education Structural Engineering, Structural Engineering College, Freiburg; Architecture, University of Applied Sciences, Konstanz.
Affiliations State Design University, Karlsruhe; Chamber of Architects, Baden-Württemberg; German Werkbund, Baden-Württemberg; Eurosolar; German Society for Solar Energy; German Society for Sustainable Building.
Recent Works Since 2011 Weberhaus Övolution; Rabenkopfstraße Housing Community; 1994 Heliotrope; Munzingen Solar Garden; Lindenwälde Housing Community.
Selected Publications [2008] Jay Ingram, The Daily Planet Book of Cool Ideas: Global Warming and What People Are Doing About It, Penguin, Toronto; 200 Outstanding House Ideas, Firefly Books, New York; [2007] Sustainable Environments, Rockport Publishers, Massachusetts 2007; Small Eco-Houses, Taschen, Köln.
Awards [2009] Utopia Award; [2008] Innovation Award, Association of Entrepreneurs in the Social Democratic Party; German Local Sustainability Prize; Focus Green, International Design Prize, Baden-Württemberg; [2007] Creativity Award, Japanese PEN-Magazine; [2006] Germany's Most Beautiful Residential Community; [2005] Wuppertal Energy and Environment Prize; [2003] Global Energy Award; [2002] European Solar Prize; Dr. Rudolf Eberle Prize; House of the Year, Häuser Magazine.

Doshi Levien
Designers, London, UK
www.doshilevien.com
Education Nipa Doshi, [1997] M.A, Furniture Design, Royal College of Art, London; [1994] Furniture Design, National Institute of Design, Ahmedabad. Jonathan Levien, [1997] M.A, Furniture Design, Royal College of Art, London; B.A, Design, Bucks College, High Wycombe.
Affiliations Authentics; Tefal; Habitat; Moroso; Cappellini; Glass Idromassagio; Royal College of Art, London; Electrolux Design Lab; Richard Lampert.
Recent Works Kali Cabinet; Paper Planes seating collection for Moroso; Impossible Wood chair for Moroso; Capo chair for Cappellini; Rocker for Richard Lampert; Tefal Mosaic Range; Ananda Spa; Smart Tools; Swallow for Habitat; Melba for Habitat; Wellcome Trust Windows; Myth and Material installation at Moroso, New York.
Awards [2011] Best Steam Team, Wallpaper Design Awards; Best of Best Award, IMM Cologne; [2009] Best Domestic Design, Wallpaper Design Awards; [2007] Future Legend Award, Movado; Best Breakthrough Designer, Wallpaper Design Awards.

ecoLogic Studio
Designers, London, UK
www.ecologicstudio.com
Education Marco Poletto, Master, Environment and Energy, Architectural Association, London; [1999] Architecture/Engineering (Hons.), Turin Polytechnic. Claudia Pasquero, Master, Environment

and Energy, Architectural Association, London; [2000] Architecture/Engineering, Turin Polytechnic.
Affiliations Marco Poletto, London, Unit Tutor of Diploma8, London Metropolitan University; Marco Poletto and Claudi Pasquero, Unit Master of Inter10, Architectural Association School of Architecture; IAAC, Barcelona; Garanti Gallery, Istanbul; BIACS, Seville; Smart Geometry, London/NY; CITA, Copenhagen; TWDC, Turin; Nous Gallery, London; NABA, Milan; FMG gallery Milan; Caracas Case, Caracas; MSNT, Trento; UCB, Bolivia; Bio-inspired-forum, Sweden.
Recent Works [2010] Urban Algae Farm, Trento; Ro-Tanti wind field, Trento; [2009] Lightwall Installation, Cirie, Italy; Carugate ROOFscape, Milan; [2008] Fibrous Room, Istanbul; [2007] Acqva Garden, Milan.
Selected Publications Space Craft: Developments in Architectural Computing, RIBA Publishing; Environmental Tectonics, AA Publishing; 'Regimes of Slowness – Operational Landscapes', in Informal City – the Caracas Case, Prestel, New York; Systemic Architecture: Operating Manual for the Self-Organizng City, Routledge.

Ecosistema Urbano
Urban development consultants, Madrid, Spain
www.ecosistemaurbano.com
Education Belinda Tato Serrano, [1999] M.Arch, Escuela Téchnica Superior de Arquitectura, Madrid; [1997] Bartlett School of Architecture, University College London. Jose Luis Vallejo Mateo, [1999] M.Arch, Escuela Téchnica Superior de Arquitectura, Madrid; [1997] Bartlett School of Architecture, University College London.
Affiliations International Urban Development Association.
Recent Works [2010] Ecopolis Plaza, Madrid; [2009 Rain Water Park, Meco; Urban Voids, Madrid; [2007] Air Tree, Madrid; [2003] House of Steel + Wood, Ránon.
Awards [2009] Silver Award, Holcim Foundation for Sustainable Construction; [2008] Next Generation Award, Arquia Próxima Foundation; [2007] Nomination, European Union Prize for Contemporary Architecture Mies van der Rohe Award; AR Award for emerging architecture, London; [2006] Architectural Association and the Environments, Ecology and Sustainability Research Cluster Award, London; [2005] European Acknowledgement Award, Holcim Foundation for Sustainable Construction, Geneva.

Embrace
Social enterprise, Bangalore, India
www.embraceglobal.org
Education Jane Chen, MBA, Stanford University; Masters, Public Administration, Harvard University. Rahul Panicker, B.Tech, IIT Madas, India; PhD, Electrical Engineering, Stanford University. Naganand Murty, M.S, Management Science & Engineering, Stanford University; Masters, Aerospace Engineering, IIT, Bombay. Linus Liang, B.A, Computer Science, UC Berkeley; M.S, Computer Science, Stanford University.
Affiliations Stanford University School of Medicine; d.School, Stanford; Fenwich & West LLP; IDEO; Nishith Desai Associates; 3Strand; Kikiyo; D2M; Maternal Instinct; Gokaldas Images; Lemelson Foundation; Neumatic; Molten; The Packard Foundation; ASTIA.
Recent Works Embrace Infant Warmer.

Emeco
Designers, USA
www.emeco.net

Education Gregg Buchbinder, B.A, Business.
Affiliations Coca Cola; Frank Gehry;
Philippe Starck; Norman Foster;
Adrian Van Hooydonk; Sottsass Associati;
Andrée Putman.
Recent Works 111 Navy Chair; Superlight Chair;
Hudson Chair; Heritage Chair; Icon Chair;
1951 Chair; 20-06 Chair; Kong Chair;
Lancaster Chair; Nine-0 Chair.
Awards [2010] REBRAND 100 Global Awards.

Ensamble Studio
Architects, Madrid, Spain
www.ensamble.info
Education Antón García-Abril, PhD,
Architecture, Polytechnic University of Madrid.
Javier Cuesta, [1997] School of Technical
Architecture, Madrid.
Débora Mesa, Architecture, Polytechnic
University of Madrid.
Affiliations Antón García-Abril, Associate
Professor, Polytechnic University of Madrid;
Positive City Foundation; Materia Inorgánica,
Madrid; Massachusetts Institute of Technology.
Recent Works [2011] Balancing Act Installation,
Venice Bienale; [2010] The Truffle,
Costa da Morte, Spain; Reader's House, Madrid;
[2007] Berklee Tower of Music, Valencia;
Museum of America, Salamanca;
[2005] Hemeroscopium House, Madrid;
[2004] SGAE Central Office, Santiago
de Compostela.
Selected Publications *Archithese Magazine*,
May 2011; *Icon Magazine*, May 2011;
Casabella Magazine, April 2011; *a+u Magazine*,
March 2011; *Igloo Magazine*, March 2011.
Awards [2011] Mies Van der Rohe Award
Candidate; [2009] Rice Design Alliance prize
to emerging architects; [2005] Architectural
Record Design Vanguard Prize.

Environmental Quality International
Consultants, Cairo, Egypt
www.eqi.com.eg
Affiliations United States Agency for
International Development; Moqattam Garbage
Collector's Association; International Finance
Corporation; Private Enterprise Partnership
for the Middle East and North Africa.
Recent Works Adrere Amellal Desert Eco Lodge,
Siwa Women's Artisanship Development Initiative;
Organic Agriculture & Agro-Culinary Production;
The Zabbaleen Environment & Development
Project; The Small & Micro Enterprise
Development Project.
Selected Publications 'Andrere Amellal Siwa
Oasis', in *Inside Africa North and East*, Taschen,
2006; 'Hip Hotels: Herbert Ypma exclusively
reveals his top 20', *The Sunday Times Travel*,
29 May 2005; 'Building eco-tourism with mud,
salt and lost skills', *The Financial Times*,
10 May 2000.
Awards [2006] World Business Award for best
practice in alleviating poverty; [2005] Well-Being
award, Talents du Luxe Award.

Flansburgh Architects
Boston, USA
www.faiarchitects.com
Affiliations Boston Society of Architects;
US Green Building Council; National Business
Officers Association; Advancement of
International Education.
Recent Works [2010] Zero Plus Energy Lab,
Hawaii Preparatory Academy; Morey Elementary
School, Lowell, Massachusetts;
[2006] Auburn High School Performing Arts
Facility, Massachusetts.
Awards [2011] Merit Award, Wood Design &
Building Magazine; [2010] Walter Taylor Award;
Merit Award for Integrated Design, Excellence

in Sustainable Design and Development;
AIA New Design Award; [2007] Award for Design
Excellence, Boston Society of Architects;
Architectural Jury Citation, American Association
of School Administrators.

Foster + Partners
Architects, London, UK
www.fosterandpartners.com
Education
Norman Foster, Masters, Architecture, Yale
University; [1961] Manchester University School
of Architecture and City Planning.
Reent Works [2011] The Index, United Arab
Emirates; [2010] PricewaterhouseCoopers,
London; [2009] Lousail Stadium, Qatar; [2008]
Beijing Airport; [2007] Smithsonian Institution,
Washington DC; [2006] Dresden Station Redevelop-
ment; Living Wall, Amman, Jordan; [2002] City
Hall, London.
Selected Publications [2010] *Norman Foster
Drawings 1958-2008*, Ivorypress; [2009]
Norman Foster Works 5, Prestel; [2008] *Foster
Catalogue*, Prestel; [2007] *Wembley Stadium:
Venue of Legends*, Prestel; *Foster 40*, Prestel;
[2006] *30 St Mary Axe: A Tower for London*,
Merrell Publishers Ltd.
Awards [2011] RIBA Awards; [2010] SECC
Champion Award; Wallpaper* Design Awards,
Best Building Sites; AIA New York Architecture
Merit Award; DIFFA Excellence in Design Award;
RIBA International Award; London Planning
Awards; Tucker Design Award, Building Stone
Institute.

Shawn Frayne
Designer, Hong Kong
www.humdingerwind.com
Education B.Sc, Physics, Massachusetts
Institute of Technology.
Affiliations Humdinger Wind Energy;
Haddock Invention; Fuel from the Fields;
Friends of Petite-Anse; MIT.
Recent Works [2011] MicroBelt; Windcell
Panels; [2006 –present] Agriwaste Charcoal;
Sodis Bag; Water Purification Temperature
Indicator; Self-Inflating Packaging; Squeeze
Vacuum-Packaging.
Selected Publications The Energy Harvesting
Journal, 30 March 2010.
Awards [2010] Finalist, Rolex Awards for
Enterprise Young Laureates Programme;
[2009] '30 Under 30', Inc Magazine;
[2008] '20 Best Brains Under 40', Alternative
Energy category, Discover Magazine; Finalist,
CurryStone Design Prize; [2007] Popular
Mechanics Breakthrough Award.

FREITAG
Designers, Zurich, Switzerland
www.freitag.ch
Education Markus Freitag, [1991-93] Education
Program, Visual design, School of Art and Design,
Zurich; [1987-91] Exhibit and decoration
design apprenticeship.
Daniel Freitag, [1988-92] Commercial artist
apprenticeship; [1987-88] Preliminary course,
School of Art and Design, Zurich.
Recent Works V30 FREITAG SKID rack system
for POS; F-Cut design your own bag.
Awards [2009] Design Prize Switzerland,
newcomer category; Design Prize of the Federal
Republic of Germany, Gold, Product Design
category; [2008] Best of Swiss web,
Gold in Business Efficiency, Silver in Creation;
1. Award for Marketing and Architecture;
[2007] Yellow pencil, D&AD Awards, London;
[2006] contractworld.award, Gold;
ADC-Schweiz, Bronze, Photography/
Illustration category.

Education Sylvia Smith FAIA, LEED AP, B.A,
Studio Art and Art History, Dickinson College;
M.Arch, University of Virginia.
Affiliations Metzger Fellow, Dickinson College;
Design Trust for Public Space in New York City
Recent Works [2009] Redesign of the
Lincoln Center public spaces; The Juilliard
School Expansion; Alice Tully Hall renovation;
[2008] LEED Gold Certified Center for
Global Conservation and LEED Gold Certified
reconstruction of the historic Lion House,
The Bronx, NY.
Awards [2011] National Award, American
Institute of Steel Construction / IDEAS
Awards; Honor Awards for Urban Design
and Architecture, AIA, New York Chapter;
[2010] Annual Design Review Citation,
Architect Magazine; Firm of the Year, New York
State AIA; Professional Design Award,
Society of American Registered Architects;
Best Institutional Building, Environmental Design
+ Construction; Architectural Review/ MIPIM
Future Project Award; [2009] Best Urban
Design Project, World Architecture News;
Design Award of Honor, Society of American
Registered Architects; Masterworks Award
for Best Restoration Project, The Municipal Art
Society of New York.

Benjamin Garcia Saxe
Architect, London, UK
www.benjamingarciasaxe.com
Education Benjamin Garcia Saxe AIA, CFIA
[2007] M.Arch, Rhode Island School of Design,
Rhode Island, USA; Teaching Certificate,
Brown University, Rhode Island, USA;
[2004] Licenciatura en Arquitectura,
Universidad Veritas, San Jose, Costa Rica;
[1999] Bachelors of Honor, Ministry of Public
Education, Costa Rica.
Affiliations Rogers Stirk Harbour + Partners,
London.
Recent Works [2011] Containers of Hope,
Costa Rica; [2010] A Forest for a Moon Dazzler,
Costa Rica; [2007] Smith House, Cosa Rica.
Awards [2007] Bronze Medal Prize, Leadership
in the field of Architecture, USA; [2006] Award
of Excellence, Rhode Island School of Design;
[2004] Rhode Island School Graduate Fellowship;
Award for Best Graduating Academic Average,
Universidad Veritas, Costa Rica.

Gionata Gatto and Mike Thompson
Designers, Eindhoven, The Netherlands
www.atuppertu.com
www.miket.co.uk
Education Gionata Gatto, Industrial Design,
I.U.A.V., Venice; Masters, Man & Humanity,
Design Academy Eindhoven.
Mike Thompson, Masters, IM, Design
Academy Eindhoven.
Affiliations Studio Atùppertù;
Mike Thompson Studio; Spazio Rossana Orlandi.
Recent Works [2011] Trap Light;
Wifi Dowsing Rod; [2010] Unplugged; Latro;
[2009] UrbanBuds; Svitato; Blood Lamp.
Selected Publications [2011] *My Green City*,
Gestalten, Berlin; [2010] *Objets Urbains*,
Ici Consultants, Paris.

Dirk Gion and Stefan Simmerer
Wind Explorer Pilots
www.wind-explorer.com
Education Dirk Gion, Law, Ruhr-University Bochum.
Stefan Simmerer, Friedrich-Alexander University,
Erlangen-Nuerenberg.
Affiliations Evonik Industries; Velomobiel,
The Netherlands; Onyx Composites; Buckle-Up

Productions; Rohacell; Spleene; Conbam.
Recent Works Project Earthflyer; Projekt Chang Tang; Wind Race Car.
Awards [2011] Nomination, Clean Tech Media Award.

Simone Giostra & Partners
Architects, New York, USA
www.sgp-architects.com
Education Simone Giostra, M.Arch, Polytechnic School of Architecture, Milan; Erasmus Program, School of Architecture, University of Porto.
Affiliations Associate Professor, Pratt Institute, School of Architecture, New York; NABA Academy, Milan.
Recent Works [2010] Installation for the 2010 Design Triennial, Cooper Hewitt Design Museum, New York; [2005] Jingya Ocean Entertainment Centre, Beijing, China.
Awards [2010] Finalist, Zumtobel Award for Humanity and Sustainability in Architecture and the Built Environment; [2009] Medaglia d'Oro all'Architettura Italiana, Italy; Sustainable Design Award, Boston Society of Architects/AIA; SEGD Honour Award, Society for Environmental Graphic Design, USA; Award of Merit, Illuminating Engineering Society of North America, USA; [2008] ARCHI-TECH Award, ARCHI-TECH Magazine, USA; [2005] Silver Award, Horizon Interactive Awards, USA; Art Directors Medal, ADC, Italy.

Sean Godsell Architects
Architects, Melbourne, Australia
www.seangodsell.com
Education University of Melbourne; M.Arch, RMIT University.
Affiliations Smithsonian Institute's Cooper Hewitt Design Museum, New York.
Recent Works [2011] RMIT University design Hub, Melbourne, Australia; [2006] St Andrew's Beach House; [2003] Peninsula House, Victoria, Australia; [2001] Future Shack prototype.
Selected Publications [2010] Traite d'Architecture Sauvage, Editions du Sextant, Paris; Modos 2010: Crescendo and Renewal, The University of Auckland, New Zealand; 1:1 Architects Build Small Spaces, V&A Publishing, London; [2009] Living in the New Millenium, Phaidon Press, London.
Awards [2009] Award for Green Good Design and International Architecture Award, The Chicago Athenaeum Museum of Architecture and Design, USA; House of the Year, World Architecture Awards, UK; Innovation Steel Prize, Detail Magazine Awards, Germany; [2008] Finalist, Wallpaper International Design Awards; Record Houses Award for Excellence, American Institute of Architects; Nomination, Inaugural BSI Swiss Architecture Award for Architects under the age of 50; Nomination, Zumtobel Award, Germany; [2007] Barbara Capochin Residential Architecture Award, Italy; Chicago Athenaeum Award, USA; Detail Magazine Awards, Germany.

Green Toys™
Mill Valley, California
www.greentoys.com
Education Robert von Goeben, MBA, University of Southern California; B.A, Mathematics, State University of New York. Laurie Hyman, MBA, University of Southern California; B.A, Business Indiana University.
Affiliations Propellerhead Studios; Starter Fluid.
Recent Works Lunar Design; Sandwich Shop; Twist Teether; Green Toys Blocks; Green Toys Stacker; Fire Truck; Dump Truck; Recycling Truck; Tea Set; Jump Rope; EcoSaucer™ Flying Disc;

Cookware and Dining Set; Indoor Gardening.
Awards [2011] Dr. Toy Best Green Product; Babble.com Pick for 2011 Toy Fair; Cool Mom Picks Editors Best; Parents Magazine, Best Toys for 2010; Oppenheim Toy Portfolio 2010 Gold Award; [2010] Dr. Toy 10 Best Socially Responsible Products, 100 Best Children's Products, Best Green Product; Ebeanstalk Best Learning Toys; Canadian Toy Testing Council (CTTC) Best Bet Award; [2009] Oppenheim Gold Award; Teachers' Pick Award by Scholastic's Instructor Magazine; Green Parents' List Award; Goddard Schools and Eco-Child's Play: Top 10 Eco-Toys; ASTRA Best Toys For Kids; Fat Brain Toy Award; Iparenting Media Award; Dr. Toy Best Classic Toy, Best 100 Children's Products, Best Vacation Toy.

Martí Guixé and Antto Melasniemi
Designer and Restauranteur, Barcelona, Spain and Helsinki, Finland
www.guixe.com
Education Martí Guixé, [1986-87] Industrial Design, Scuola Politecnica Design, Milan; [1983-5] Interior design, Elisava, Barcelona.
Affiliations Ateljé Finne Restaurant, Helsinki; Kuurna Restaurant, Helsinki; Lapin Kulta beer.
Selected Publications [2004] New Shops & Boutiques, Harper Design & Loft Publications, New York; [2003] Bright Minds, Beautiful Ideas, Bis Publishers, Amsterdam; L'ABCdaire du Design, Flammarion, Paris.

Habiter Autrement
Architects, Paris, France
www.habiterautrement.net
Education [1992-1995] Mia Hägg, M.Arch, Chalmers University of Technology, Gothenburg, Sweden; [1995-1996] Erasmus program, Ecole d'Architecture de Paris-Belleville, Paris, France.
Affiliations [2007-present] Founder, Habiter Autrement, Paris and Locarno; [2002-2005] Herzog & de Meuron, Associate and Collaborator, Basel; [1998-2001] Ateliers Jean Nouvel, Collaborator, Paris, France.
Recent Works Armagnac, Cenon, Lormont: 3 housing projects in Bordeaux; Entrepôt MacDonalds Housing, Paris; Masterplan Toledo, Colina de Desportes Sports Centre, Toledo; Energy Systems, Järva, Stockholm, 100 Ordos Villa, Inner Mongolia.

Fritz Haeg
Artist/Gardener/Designer, Los Angeles, USA
www.fritzhaeg.com
Education Istituto Universitario di Architettura di Venezia; B.Arch, Carnegie Mellon University.
Affiliations California Institute of the Arts; Art Centre College of Design; Parsons School of Design; University of Southern California; Tate Modern, London; Whitney Museum of American Art; SFMOMA, San Francisco; Casco Office Of Art, Design and Theory, Utrecht; Mass MoCA; Institute of Contemporary Art, Philadelphia; Wattis Institute, San Francisco; Netherlands Architecture Institute, Maastricht; Indianapolis Museum of Art; MAK Center, Los Angeles; Center for Advanced Visual Studies, MIT, MacDowell Colony Fellow.
Recent Works [2005-12] Edible Estates; [2006] Sundown Schoolhouse; [2005-08] Animal Estates.
Selected Publications [2011] Roma Mangia Roma, Nero Publications, Rome; [2010] Edible Estates: Attack on the Front Lawn, Metropolis Books, New York; [2009] The Sundown Salon Unfolding Archive, Evil Twin Publications, New York.

[2008] Animal Estates Field Guides 4.0, 5.0, 6.0, Casco Office for Art, Design and Theory, San Francisco Museum of Modern Art, Cooley Gallery at Reed College.
Awards [2010-11] Rome Prize Fellow, American Academy in Rome; [2009-10] Nomination, National Design Awards.

John and Cynthia Hardy
Designers/Entrepreneurs, Bali, Indonesia
www.greenschool.org
Selected Publications 'How they grew a green school', The Financial Times, 13 September 2010.

Anna Heringer
Architect, Salzburg, Austria
www.anna-heringer.com
Education [2006] Doctorate studies, Technischen Universität, Munich; [2004] Diploma, Architecture, University of Arts, Linz.
Affiliations Project Manager, BASEhabitat; Visiting Professor, University of Art and Design, Linz; Gertrud Luis Goldschmidt Professorship, Institute for Public Buildings and Design, Stuttgart University; BRAC University Dhaka.
Recent Works [2010] Training Centre for Sustainability, Marrakech; [2009] The Infinite Vision of Summer, for V&A; [2008] Living Fabrics – green garment factory, Bangladesh; [2007-08] DESI–Vocational school for electrical training, Bangladesh; HOMEmade – pilot project for rural housing, Bangladesh.
Selected Publications [2010] Small Scale, Big Change: New Architectures of Social Engagement, MoMA, New York; Learning From Vernacular – towards a new vernacular architecture, Actes Sud, Paris; What architects desire, Springer Verlag; Earth Architecture, Princeton Architectural Press; Construire ailleurs: Tyin + Anna Heringer, Archibooks; Green Architecture for the Future, Louisiana Museum of Modern Art.
Awards [2010] 1st place, UIA Competition; [2009] Finalist, Curry Stone Design Prize; The European Colour Design Award; Swiss Solar Award; [2008] World Architecture Community Award; Emerging Architecture Award, Architectural Review, London; World Architecture Community Award; Nomination, DAM Award for Architecture, Germany; [2007] Aga Khan Award for Architecture; Hunter Douglas Award, World Best Graduate Projects, Archiprix International; International Bamboo Building Design Competition; Hans Schäfer Preis; Nomination, Zumtobel Group Award for Sustainability; Kenneth F. Brown Asia Pasific Culture And Architecture Design Award.

HHS Archiketen
Kassel, Germany
www.hhs-architekten.de
Education Manfred Hegger BDA, [1976] Planning Studies, University of London / London School of Economics and Political Science; [1973] Architecture, University of Stuttgart/Ulm Design School; [1970] Systems Engineering, Technical University Berlin. Doris Hegger-Luhnen BDA, [1978] Architecture, University of Kassel; [1974] Interior Architecture, Stuttgart Academy of Fine Arts; [1970] Interior Architecture, Krefeld Art School. Günter Schleiff BDA, [1980] Architecture, University of Kassel; 1975 Social Sciences, University of Göttingen. Gerhard Greiner BDA, Civil Engineering, Technical University of Braunschweig; Architecture, FH Darmstadt; Construction Management, Bauhaus University, Weimar. Andreas Wiege, Architecture, TH Darmstadt.
Affiliations Manfred Hegger, Professor, Technical University, Darmstadt (Energy Efficient

Building Design Unit); Union Internatioanle des Architectes Work Programme "Sustainable Architecture of the Future"; United National Environmental Programs; University of Hannover; Centre for Infrastructure Planning, University of Stuttgart; University of Darmstadt.
Recent Works [2010] SMA Solar Academy, Niestetal; [2009] Max-Planck Institute, Bad Nauheim; Service Centre, Eschborn; [2007] SMA Central Office Buildling, Niestetal; [2000] Concert Hall Nikolaisaal, Potsdam.
Selected Publications *Academy Mont-Cenis: Living Architecture*, Manfred Hegger & Françoise-Hélène Jourda, Meuller + Busmann.
Awards [2011] E2 Timber Development Competition, Finland; [2010] Energy Efficiency Award; [2009] BDA Architecture Prize; [2006] Deutscher Solarpreis; [2004] Building Award; [2003] Renault Traffic Design Award; BDA Good Building Award; Badenia Innovation Award.

Steven Holl Architects
New York, USA
www.stevenholl.com
Education Steven Holl, University of Washington; Architectural Association, London.
Affiliations Columbia University, School of Architecture, Professor ; American National Council of Architectural Registration Boards; AIA; American Association of Museums; Honorary Whitney Circle.
Recent Works [2011] Beirut Marina and Town Quay, Lebanon; Cité de l'Océan et du Surf, Biarritz, France; [2009] Linked Hybrid complex, Beijing, China; Knut Hamsun Centre, Hamarøy, Norway; Herning Centre of the Arts, Herning, Denmark; [2007] Nelson-Atkins Museum of Art; [1998] Kiasma Museum of Contemporary Art, Helsinki, Finland; [1997] Chapel of St. Ignatius, Seattle, Washington.
Selected Publications [2008] *Urbanisms: Working With Doubt*, Princeton Architectural Press; [2007] *House: Black Swan Theory*; *Architecture Spoken*; [2006] *Luminosity / Porosity*; [2002] *Idea and Phenomena*; [2000] *Parallax*; [1989] *Anchoring*.
Awards [2010] RIBA International Award; [2009] Best Tall Building Overall, Council on Tall Buildings and Urban Habitat (CTBUH); AIA Institute Honor Award; Green Good Design Award; Herning Building of the Year, Denmark.

Hopkins Architects
London, UK
www.hopkins.co.uk
Education Michael Hopkins CBE, RA, RIBA, Diploma, Architectural Association, London. Patty Hopkins FAIA, FRIAS, Diploma, Architectural Association, London.
Recent Works [2011] Olympic VeloPark, London; Energy from Waste, Jersey; [2009-10] Rice University, North and South College Redevelopment; [2009] Norwich Cathedral Hostry; [2007] Butterfield Park Innovation Centre; Kroon Hall, Yale University; Northern Arizona University, Applied Research and Development Building; [2006] Alnwick Garden Pavilion; [2005] Evelina Children's Hospital; Lawn Tennis Association's National Tennis Centre; [2001] The Forum, Norwich.
Selected Publications *50 Years of London Architecture, 1960-2010*, Wordsearch/ The Architecture Club; *Hopkins 1: The Work of Michael Hopkins and Partners*, Phaidon Press, London; *Hopkins 2: The Work of Michael Hopkins and Partners*, Phaidon Press, London; *Glyndebourne – Building a Vision*, Thames & Hudson, London.
Awards [2011] Contribution to the Profession Award, AJ100 Awards; RIBA Awards; Civic Trust

Award; [2010] AJ100 Building of the Year Award; Gold, BCSC Awards; New Build Modern Style Stone Cladding Award; APEX Award; [2009] BCO Regional Award Winner; RIBA International Award; [2008] AIA Southern Arizona Honor Award; [1994] RIBA Gold Medal for Architecture.

inForm Studio
Designers, Detroit, USA
www.in-formstudio.com
Education Gina Van Tine AIA, LEED AP, [1994] B.Arch, Lawrence Technological University; B.Sc, Architecture, Lawrence Technological University.
Kenneth Van Tine AIA, LEED AP, [1985] B.Arch, Lawrence Technological University; B.Sc, Architecture, Lawrence Technological University.
Michael Guthrie AIA, LEED AP, M.Arch, University of Michigan; B.Sc, Architecture, Lawrence Technological University.
Cory Lavigne AIA, LEED AP, [1996] B.Arch, Lawrence Technological University; [1994] B.Sc, Architecture, Ryerson University, Toronto.
Affiliations PDA Architects; Van Tine/Guthrie Studio; Southeast Michigan Resource & Development Council; Museum of Contemporary Art, Detroit.
Recent Works [2010] Bagley Street Pedestrian Bridge, Detroit; Withers Swash District Plan, Myrtle Beach; [2009] Farmington Hills City Hall; [2004] Detroit Public Schools Children's Museum; [2002-03] Grand Egyptian Museum design, Giza.
Selected Publications [2003] *The Grand Museum of Egypt International Architectural Competition*, Vol.1, The Egyptian Ministry of Culture.
Awards [2010] AIA Detroit Honor Award; AIA Detroit Young Architect of the Year; Roads & Bridges Magazine, Top 10 Bridges of the Year; [2009] AIA Michigan Honor Award; AIA Detroit Un-built Honor Award; [2006] AIA Michigan Honor Award; [2004] Canadian Museum of Human Rights Competition; [2003] Grand Egyptian Museum Competition Symposium, Cairo, Egypt.

James & Mau Architecture
Madrid, Spain
www.jamesandmau.com
Education Jaime Gaztelu González-Camino, Architecture, Universidad de Navarra. Mauricio Galeano Escobar, Architecture, Universidad de los Andes, Bogotá, Colombia.
Affiliations Infiniski sustainable architecture and construction.
Recent Works [2007] El Encofrador, Toledo, Spain; Aguas Manantial, Concepión, Chile; [2004] Elizondo, Navarra, Spain; [2000] Otazu winery, Navarra, Spain.
Selected Publications [2007] *The Big Book of Lofts*, Harper & Collins, London; [2006] New Dining Room Design, Editrial Daab, Germany; [2004] Wineries Bodegas, Editorial HK, Spain.

KARO* architekten
Leipzig, Germany
www.karo-architekten.de
Education Antje Heuer, Architecture, TU Dresden.
Stefan Rettich, Architecture, TH Karlsruhe.
Bert Hafermalz, Interior Design, Art and Design School Halle.
Affiliations BDA; SAK Saxony Acadaemy of the Arts; DASL German Academy of Town and Country Planning.
Recent Works [2007] Cotton Mill Hall, Leipzig; [2006] Engine House Industrial Museum, Leipzig.
Selected Publications [2010] 'Open Air Library',

in *In Favour of Public Space*, Centre de Cultura Contemporania de Barcelona, Actar, Barcelona.
Awards [2011] Brit Insurance Design Award; Shortlisted, Mies van der Rohe Award; Shortlisted, Deutscher Fassadenpreis VHS; [2010] European Price for Urban Public Space; German Town Planning Prize; Nomination, Urban Intervention Award Berlin; Nomination, DAM Award for Architecture in Germany; Nomination, Architecture Award of Saxony-Anhalt.

Kennedy & Violich Architecture, Ltd.
Boston, USA
www.kvarch.net
Education Sheila Kennedy AIA, B.A, History, Philosophy and Literature, College of Letters, Wesleyan University; Ecole National Supérieure des Beaux Arts; M.Arch, Graduate School of Design, Harvard University.
J. Frano Violich FAIA, B. Arch, University of California, Berkeley; M.Arch, Graduate School of Design, Harvard University.
Affiliations Sheila Kennedy, Associate professor, Harvard University, Graduate School of Design; Professor of the Practice of Architecture, MIT; MATx materials research unit.
Recent Works [2010] Riverfirst Minneapolis; [2009] Birmingham Amphitheatre; [2009] Soft Cities, Porto, Portugal; [2007] Clemson University Center for Architecture; MDR TB Home Treatment Kit; [2005] Solar Powered Luminous Bollard; [2004] MATx Portable Light Project, Renewable Energy Platform; [2002] Pressure Responsive Body Mat.
Selected Publications [2010] *Nomads and Nanomaterials: KVA/MATx*, University of Michigan.
Awards [2009] US Congressional Award; Energy Globe Award; [2008] Tech Museum Laureate Award.

Cordula Kerher
Designers, Karlsruhe, Germany
www.cordulakehrer.de
Affiliations Kilian Schindler; Silvia Knüppel.
Recent Works Zipac Messestand units; Bow Bins; Oona storage; Whee lamp; Movement Paper Models; Girls' Toilet; Translator Shirt.

Key Architects
Kanagawa, Japan
www.key-architects.com
Education Miwa Mori, [2002] Diploma Degree, Faculty of Architecture and Urban Planning, University of Stuttgart, Germany; [1999] B.Eng, Faculty of Architecture, Yokohoma National University, Japan.
Joerg Heil RIAI, [2002] Dip.Ing, Faculty of Architecture and Urban Planning, University of Stuttgart, Germany.
Affiliations Chamber of Architects, Baden- Württemberg, Germany.
Recent Works Yamagata Eco House.
Awards [2010] 2nd Place, German Passive House Architecture Award.

KieranTimberlake
Architect, Philadelphia, USA
kierantimberlake.com
Education Stephen Kieran FAIA, B.A, Yale University; M.Arch (Hons), University of Pennsylvania.
James Timberlake FAIA, Bachelor of Environmental Science (Hons), University of Detroit; M.Arch (Hons), University of Pennsylvania.
Affiliations DuPont; Permasteelisa; James Timberlake and Stephen Kieran, Adjunct Professors, University of Pennsylvania; Endowed Professors in Sustainability, University of Washington College of Architecture and Urban

Planning; Eero Saarinen Distinguished Professors of Design, Yale University; Max Fisher Chairs, University of Michigan.
Recent Works [2011] Brockman Hall for Physics, Rice University, Houston, TX; [2009] LivingHomes KTLH 1.5 House, Newport Beach, CA; [2008] Special NO 9 House for the Make It Right Foundation, New Orleans, LA; [2007] Yale University Sculpture Building and School of Art Gallery, New Haven, CT; Loblolly House, Taylors Island, MD; [2006] Sidwell Friends Middle School, Washington, D.C.; [2002] Melvin J. and Claire Levine Hall, University of Pennsylvania, Philadelphia, PA.
Selected Publications [2011] *KieranTimberlake: Inquiry*, Rizzoli, USA; [2008] *Loblolly House: Elements of a New Architecture*, Princeton Architectural Press, USA; [2004] *Refabricating Architecture*, McGraw-Hill, USA; [2002] *Manual: The Architecture of Kieran Timberlake*, Princeton Architectural Press, USA.
Awards [2010] Cooper-Hewitt National Design Award for Architecture; COTE Top Ten Green Projects; [2008] Architecture Firm Award, AIA; [2001] Benjamin Latrobe Fellowship, AIA College of Fellows.

Kilburn Nightingale Architects (formerly Callum and Nightingale Architects)
London, UK
www.kilburnnightingale.com
Education Ben Kilburn RIBA, 1979 M.A, Cambridge University.
Richard Nightingale RIBA, FRSA, 1990 M.A, Cambridge University.
Affiliations Colin St. John Wilson and Partners; Architectural Association.
Recent Works [2010] Parker Library, Corpus Christi College Cambridge; [2006] British High Commission, Kampala, Uganda; [2004] Studio for an Artist, Dulwich, London; [2002] New Embassy Theatre, Central School of Speech and Drama, London.
Selected Publications [2008] *The Eco-Travel Guide*, Thames & Hudson, London; *The Phaidon Atlas of 21ˢᵗ Century World Architecture*, Phaidon Press, London; [2007] *1001 Buildings you Must See Before you Die*, Cassell Illustrated, London.
Awards [2008] British International Expertise, Consultancy Project of the Year Award; RIBA International Award; Runner-up, Lubetkin Prize; BCCB British International Expertise Award; [2002] Civic Trust Commendation; City of Culture Architectural Conservation Award.

KPMB Architects
Toronto, Canada
www.kpmbarchitects.com
Education Bruce Kuwabara OAA, FRAIC, AIA, RIBA, [1972] B.Arch, University of Toronto. Thomas Payne OAA, FRAIC, AIA, [1974] M.Arch, Yale University; 1972 Ecole des Beaux Arts, Paris, France, UP2, Atelier Menard; 1971 B.Arch, Princeton University.
Marianne McKenna OAA, OAQ, FRAIC, [1976] M.Arch, Yale University; [1972] B.A, Economics and Art History, Swarthmore College, Philadelphia. Shirley Blumberg OAA, FRAIC, AIA, [1976] B.Arch (Hons), University of Toronto; 1972 University of Cape Town, South Africa.
Affiliations Bruce Kuwabara, Honorary Co-Chair for Fundraising, Frank Gehry International Design Chair, University of Toronto; First Chair of the Waterfront Design Review Panel for Waterfront Toronto; Board of Directors, Canadian Centre for Architecture.
Marianne McKenna, Board of Directors, Institute of Contemporary Culture, Royal Ontario Museum; Board of Directors, Toronto Arts Foundation; Board of Directors, Ontario College of Art and Design.

Shirley Blumberg, Regent Park Design Review Panel; Presidential Advisory Council, Ontario College of Art and Design.
Recent Works [2011] Vaughan City Hall; Rotman School of Management Expansion Project; The Power Plant Gallery; [2010] Canadian Museum of Nature; TIFF Bell Lightbox; [2009] Concordia University, John Molson School of Business; Royal Conservatory, Koerner Concert Hall; [2008] Luminato 2008; SugarCube.
Selected Publications [2008] *Integrated Design in Contemporary Architecture*, Princeton Architectural Press; [2007] *Architectural Inspiration: Styles, Details & Sources*, The Boston Mills Press; [2004] *The Architecture of Kuwabara Payne McKenna Blumberg Architects*, Birkhauser, Germany.
Awards [2011] Ontario Association of Architects Award of Excellence; RAIC Innovation in Architecture; [2010] United States Institute for Theatre Technology (USITT) Architecture Honor Award; American Institute of Architects, Institute Honor Award for Regional & Urban Design; AIA/ COTE Top Ten Green Projects Award; Sustainable Architecture & Building Magazine Award, Project; Royal Architectural Institute of Canada, National Urban Design Award; [2009] CTBUH Best Tall Building Award; Chicago Athenaeum International Architecture Award.

Latz + Partner
Landscape Architects, Munich, Germany
www.latzundpartner.de
Education Prof Peter Latz, [1969] Postgraduate studies, Town Planning, Institute of Urban Development and Regional Planning, RWTH Aachen; [1964] Diploma (M.A), Landscape Architecture, Technical University of Munich. Anneliese Latz, [1963] Diploma (M.A), Technical University of Munich.
Tilman Latz, [1997] Diploma (M.A), Architecture, University of Kassel; [1995-96] Architectural Association, London; [1993] Diploma (M.A), Landscape Architecture, University of Kassel.
Affiliations Peter Latz, Professorship for landscape architecture and planning, Technical University, Munich; Guest Professor, Harvard University; Peter Latz and Tilman Latz / Adjunct Professor and Lecturer, University of Pennsylvania; Deutsche Landentwicklung München.
Recent Works [2009] Place Flagey, Brussels; Lea River Park, East London; Havenwelten Old / New Harbour, Bremerhaven; [2008] Park Ariel Sharon and Hiriya Landfill Rehabilitation, Tel Aviv; [2003] Administration Building of SOKA-BAU, Wiesbaden.
Selected Publications [2010] 'Towards a Park for the Twenty-First Century', in From *Garbage to Garden*, Clusius Foundation, Leiden; [2009] *Learning from Duisburg-Nord*, Technische Universität München; [2008] 'Design is experimental invention', in *Creating Knoweledge,* Jovis Verlag, Berlin; 'Landscape Planning', 'Centre', 'Open Space Concept', in *SolarCity – Linz-Pichling: Sustainable Urban Development*, Springer, Vienna; [2007] *Syntax of Landscape – The Landscape Architecture of Peter Latz and Partners*, Birkhäuser, Basel.
Awards [2010] Concours Construction Acier, Special Steel Constructions; Green Good Design Award, Urban Planning/Landscape Architecture; IULA International Urban Landscape Award Silver; IULA International Urban Landscape Award Special Commendation; [2009] Green Good Design Award; National Award for Integrated Urban Development and Urban Culture 'Stadt bauen – Stadt leben'.

Mathieu Lehanneur
Designer, Paris, France
www.mathieulehanneur.fr

Education [2001] ENSCI-Les Ateliers.
Affiliations David Edwards; Ecole supérieure d'art et design, Saint-Etienne; MoMA, New York; SFMOMA, San Francisco; FRAC, Paris; Musée des Arts décoratifs, Paris.
Recent Works [2009] Age of the World, Demographic Jars; Flat Surgery, Anatomy Rug; Smoke Lamp; Show Window and Façades for Cartier Centenary; [2008] LaboBrain, David Edwards' private office, Paris; LaboShop, Paris.
Selected Publications [2009] *Whiff*, Fine Arts in Paris Editions; [2008] Artscience: *Creativity in the Post-Google Generation*, Harvard University Press,USA; [2007] *Niche*, Fine Arts in Paris Editions.
Awards [2008] Grand Prize of the City of Paris; Talent of Luxury; [2006] Carte Blanche VIA.

Lehrer + Gangi Design + Build
Los Angeles and Burbank, USA
www.lehrerarchitects.com
gangiarchitects.com
Education Michael B. Lehrer FAIA, [1978] M.Arch, Harvard University Graduate School of Design; [1975] AB Major, Architecture with Highest Honors, University of California Berkeley.
Mark Gangi AIA, [1990] B.A, School of Architecture, University of Southern California.
Affiliations WRL Design LLP, Los Angeles; Hollywood Planning and Design Review; Gangi Development; Michael Lehrer, Homeless Health Care of Los Angeles; Harvard Alumni Association; Faculty Member, University of Southern California; Mark Gangi, Architectural Evaluation Board, County of Los Angeles; Citizen Architect Committee; Californian Director of Water Resources for AIA.
Recent Works [2007] Shalom Institute, Malibu; [2006] Registrar-Recorder County Clerk Office, Los Angeles; [2000] Eureka Waste Transfer System, CA.
Selected Publications [2011] *Architects Sketchbooks*, Metropolis Books.
Awards [2009] Green Good Design Award; Honor Award, AIA California Council; [2008] 'Design 100, Best Designs in the World for 2008', Metropolis Home Magazine; Honor Award, AIA Los Angeles; American Architecture Award, The Chicago Athenaeum; [2007] Beyond Green High Performance Building Award, Sustainable Building Industry Council; Gold Nugget Award, Best Sustainable Commercial Buildings, Pacific Coast Builder's Conference.

Ross Lovegrove
Industrial Designer, London, UK
www.rosslovegrove.com
Education B.A (Hons), Industrial Design, Manchester Polytechnic; Master of Design, Royal College of Art, London.
Affiliations FCSD; RDI.
Recent Works [2009] Biomega Bamboo Bike; PRIMORDIAL, Galerist, Istanbul; [2008] LIQUID SPACE table and chandelier installation, Swarovski Crystal Palace, Design Miami; CELLULAR AUTOMATION – ORIGIN OF SPECIES 2, 21_21 Design Sight, Tokyo; [2007] SOLAR TREE urban lighting and Swarovski Crystal Aerospace, MAK, Vienna; Endurance, Phillips de Pury & Company, NYC; [2005] SUPERLIQUIDITY, Le Bain Gallery, Tokyo; [2004] DESIGNOSAURS, Segheria, Milan; [2003] DELIGHTED by Corian, Milan Salone; [2002] Expanding the Gap, Rendel&Spitz Gallery, Koln; [2001] Material Transition, Rheinauen Space, Koln; [2000] 'Sensual Organic Design', Yamagiwa Corporation, Tokyo.
Selected Publications *Supernatural, The work of Ross Lovegrove*, Phaidon Press, London.
Awards [2007] Condé Nast Vogue Traveller Ecology Prize; [2005] World Technology Prize,

Time Magazine and CNN; [2004] Royal Designer for Industry, Royal Society of Arts; D&AD Silver Medalist JANUS, Paris; 'G' Mark Federal Design Prize, Japan; Final Nomination, Prince Philip Design Prize; [2001] Designer of the Year, A&W, Germany; Nomination, Designer of the Year, Architektur & Wohnen, Hamburg.

Marcy Wong Donn Logan Architects
Berkeley, USA
www.wonglogan.com
Education Marcy Wong LEED AP, B.A, Art History, Barnard College; M.Arch, Columbia University; M.S., Structural Engineering, Stanford University.
Donn Logan FAIA, B.Arch, Arizona State University; M.Arch, Harvard University.
Recent Works [2011] Public Policy Institute of CA Bechtel Conference Center, San Francisco; [2009] Freight & Salvage Coffeehouse, Berkeley; [2008] Orange Memorial Park Recreation Center, South San Francisco; [2007] House For Two Artists, Sonoma County; [2005] Eastern Sierra Visitor Center, Lone Pine.
Awards [2011] Institute Honor Award, AIA; Best of Green Design and Architecture Award, TreeHugger.com; [2010] Honor Award, AIA California Council; Merit Award, AIA San Francisco Chapter; [2009] Preservation Design Award for Sustainability, California Preservation Foundation; Citation Award, AIA East Bay Chapter; Green Building Award, Sustainable San Mateo County; Good Design Award, Chicago Athenaeum; [2008] Design Award, Berkeley Design Advocates; Honor Award, National Trust for Historic Preservation.

Mass Studies
Seoul, Korea
www.massstudies.com
Education Minsuk Cho, Architectural Engineering, Yonsei University, Seoul; Graduate School of Architecture, Columbia University, New York.
Recent Works [2009] World Expo 2010 Shanghai: Korea Pavilion; [2008] Boutique Monaco; [2005] Nature Poem; [2004] Dalki Theme Park; [2003] Pixel House.
Awards [2010] Presidential Citation, Korea; Silver Medal, Architectural Design, World Expo Shanghai (BIE); [2008] Finalist, The International Highrise Award 2008 (DAM); [2003] U.S. Progressive Architecture Award (Citation); Finalist, PS1/MoMA Young Architects Program; [2000] Architectural Record Design Vanguard; Young Architects Award, Architectural League of New York.

Sean Meenan
Restaurateur, New York, USA
www.seanmeenan.com
Recent Works [2011] Habana Outpost, Brooklyn, New York, Owner; Café Habana, New York, Owner; Habana Works, New York, President, [2006] ETSY.com, Investor.
Selected Publications Time Out NY Kids; Edible Brooklyn; New York Magazine; Gothamist.com; Treehugger.com; NY Times.

Luyanda Mpahlwa
Architect, Cape Town, South Africa
www.mmaarch.co.za
Education [1997] M.Sc, Architecture, Technical University of Berlin; [1978-80] Diploma, Architecture, Natal Technikon.
Affiliations MMA Architects; Council of the University of Cape Town; Technical Advisory Committee on Stadium Construction, FIFA.
Recent Works [2010] O.R Tambo School of Leadership, Uganda; [2009] Freedom Park Museum, Pretoria; [2006] Maropeng at Cradle

of Humankind; [2004] Freedom Park Phase 1, Isivivane; [2003] South African Embassy, Berlin.
Selected Publications 'Cape of New Hope', The Financial Times, 13 November 2009.
Awards [2008] Curry Stone Design Prize; [2006] Loerie Award; World Architecture Award; [2003] Award of Excellence, South African Institute of Architects.

MYOO (formerly Adventure Ecology)
Environmental change organisation
www.myoo.com
Plastiki Team David de Rothschild, Matthew Grey, Andy Fox, Ashley Biggin, Andrew Dovell (Dovell Naval Architects), Michael Pawlyn (Exploration Architecture), Nathaniel Corum (Architecture for Humanity), Jason Iftakhar (Jamily), Greg Pronko (Smarter Plan LLC), Mike O'Reilly (Smarter Plan LLC).
Affiliations Smarter Plan LLC; Architecture for Humanity; Exploration Architecture; Jamily; seretex.com.
Recent Works [2007] Toxico; [2006] Top of the World; MYOOexplore; MYOOagency; MYOO connect.
Selected Publications 'The Plastic-Bottle Boat', TIME Magazine, 11 November 2010.
Awards [2010] Top 50 greatest inventions in 2010, TIME Magazine.

O-I
http://o-i.com
World's largest glass container manufacturer and preferred partner for many of the world's leading food and beverage brands, Perrysburg, USA.

Olson Kundig Architects
Seattle, USA
www.olsonkundigarchitects.com
Education James Olson, FAIA, B.Arch, University of Washington.
Tom Kundig, FAIA, B.A, Environmental Design, University of Washington; M.Arch, University of Washington, Masters of Architecture.
Recent Works [2010] The Pierre, San Juan Islands; Shadowboxx, San Juan Islands; [2009] The Lightcatcher at the Whatcom Museum, Belingham; Slaughterhouse Beach House, Hawaii; [2007] Glass Farmhouse, Northeast Oregon; Outpost, Central Idaho; [2005] Delta Shelter, Mazama, WA.
Selected Publications [2011] Architecture Now! Houses 2, Taschen; [2008] The Good Office: Green Design on the Cutting Edge, Collins; Phaidon Atlas of Contemporary World Architecture, Phaidon Press, London; [2006] Tom Kundig: Houses, Princeton Architectural Press; [2003] Architecture, Art and Craft: Olson Sundberg Kundig Allen Architects, The Monacelli Press.
Awards [2011] Washington Aggregates & Concrete Association, Excellence in Concrete Construction; National AIA Housing Award; Residential Architect Design Award, Project of the Year; [2010] Top 10 Most Innovative Companies in America, Fast Company; American Architecture Award, Chicago Anthenaeum; Stipendium of Finnish Association of Architects; Illumination Award, Illuminating Engineering Society of North America; [2009] Nomination, Forum AID Nordic Architecture Award; AIA Architecture Firm Award.

Pedro Pedrós and Elsa Zaldívar
Industrial Engineer and Social activist, Paraguay
www.ecoplax.com
www.basecta.org.py
Affiliations Ecoplax; Base ECTA; Inter-American Development Bank.
Awards [2008] Laureate, Rolex Awards; [2001] Ashoka Fellowship.

Practical Action Sudan
Rugby, UK
www.practicalaction.org
Affiliations Practical Action Consulting; Practical Action Publishing.
Recent Works Smoke Hoods; Renewable Energy Village, Gorhka, Nepal; Biogas.

R&Sie(n)
Architects, Paris, France
www.new-territories.com
Education François Roche, School of Architecture of Versailles; DPLG.
Stéphanie Lavaux, École des Beaux-Arts, Paris.
Toshikatsu Kiuchi, M.Arch, University of Tokyo.
Affiliations Advanced Studio – Professors, Graduate School of Architecture, Planning and Preservation, Columbia University, New York.
Recent Works and Exhibitions [2010] Louisiana, Denmark 2009; Le Laboratoire, Paris; [2009] Barbican, London; [2006] MIT's Media Lab, Cambridge; Tate Modern, London; [2005-6] Snake gallery, Paris; (Un)Plug, La Défense, Paris; Shearing, Sommières, France; Acqua Alta2.0; MAM / Musee d'Art Moderne,Paris
Selected Publications Bioreboot, Giovanni Corbellini, 22 Publishing, Milan; I've Heard About, Paris Musée, France; Spoiled Climate, Birkhäuser, Basel; Corrupted Biotopes, Document Design, Korea; Te(e)n Year After, Les Architectures Hérétiques, France.

Michael Ramage
Architect, Cambridge, UK
Education Architecture, Massachusetts Institute of Technology.
Affiliations John Ochsendorf, Massachusetts Institute of Technology; Peter Rich Architects, Johannesburg; Fellow in Architecture, University of Cambridge, UK.
Recent Works [2010] The Bowls Project, Yerba Buena Centre for the Arts, San Francisco; The Earth Pavilion, START Festival London.
Selected Publications [2010] 'Sustainable Shells: New African vaults built with soil-cement tiles', Journal of the International Association of Shell and Spatial Structures, December 2010; 'Design and Construction of the Mapungubwe National Park Interpretive Centre, South Africa', African Technology Development Forum Special Issue, October 2010.
Awards [2010] Silver Medal, International Sustainability Prize; Built Environment, The Earth Awards; [2009] World Building of the Year Award.

Renzo Piano Building Workshop
Architects, Genoa, Italy
www.rpbw.com
Education School of Architecture, Milan Polytechnic.
Recent Works [2010] Central St. Giles Mixed Use Development, London; [2007] New York Times Building; [2005] Zentrum Paul Klee, Bern; [2002] Parco De la Musica Auditoria, Rome; [2000] Potsdamer Platz, Berlin.
Selected Publications On Tour with Renzo Piano, Phaidon Press, London; Renzo Piano Building Workshop: Complete Works, Volumes 1-5, Phaidon Press, London; Renzo Piano Museums, Monacelli Press; Renzo Piano (Minimum Series), Motta Books.
Awards [2008] Gold Medal, AIA, American Institute of Architects; [2002] Medialle D'Or UIA, Berlin, Germany; [1998] The Prizker Architecture Prize, The White House, Washington D.C.; [1994] Goodwill Ambassador of Unesco for Architecture.

Roca
Barcelona, Spain
www.roca.com

Awards [2011] Gold IF Communication Design Award; [2010] WAN Awards; Environmental Innovation Product Award, KBB Industrial Award; Gold Lion, Cannes Lions; European Environmental Design Award; IALD Lighting Design Awards; Self Build Innovation Product Award; Wallpaper* Design Award; [2009] Red Dot Award for Informative Design/Public Space; Product of the Year, Best Eco Product, FX Award; Design Plus Award, ISH, Frankfurt.

Rudanko + Kankkunen
Architects, Espoo, Finland
www.rudanko-kankkunen.com
Education Hilla Rudanko, B.Sc (Hons), Architecture, Helsinki University of Technology; M.Sc, Architecture; Swiss Federal Institute of Technology; M.Sc, Architecture and Urban Planning, Aalto University.
Anssi Kankkunen, B.Sc, Economics, Turku University; B.Sc, Architecture, Helsinki University of Technology; M.Sc, Architecture and Urban Planning, Aalto University.
Awards [2010] Stipendium of Finnish Association of Architects; [2009] Nomination, Forum AID Nordic Architecture Award; [2008] Helsinki University of Technology 100th Anniversary Project Winner; [2007] Helsinki Architecture Guild Anniversary Pavilion Winner.

Rural Studio
Auburn University, Alabama, USA
www.cadc.auburn.edu/rural-studio
Education Outreach students, 2002: Floris Keverling Buisman, Ben Cannard, Philip Crosscup, Kerry Larkin, Marie Richard, James Michael Tate, Keith Zawistowski.
Recent Works 2010 Lion's Park Playscape; Safe House Museum; Thinnings II; $20K House V; Morrisette Kitchen.
Selected Publications [2005] *Proceed and Be Bold: Rural Studio After Samuel Mockbee*, Princeton Architectural Press, USA; *Samuel Mockbee and the Rural Studio: Community Architecture*, Birmingham Museum of Art, USA; [2002] *Rural Studio: Samuel Mockbee and an Architecture of Decency*, Princeton Architectural Press, USA.
Awards [2008] Finalist, Global Award for Sustainable Architecture, Cité de l'Architecture et du Patrimoine; Honorable Mention, World Architecture Foundation; [2002] Design Review Environmental Award, ID Magazine; Excellence Award, International Interior Trade Design Association; Community Supporter of the Year, Hale County Farm-City Committee; NCARB Prize for Creative Integration of Practice and Education in the Academy.

Samuel Wilkinson Design Studio
London, United Kingdom
www.samuelwilkinson.com
Education Sam Wilkinson, Furniture and Design, Ravensboure College of Design & Communication.
Recent Works [2011] Vessel Series; [2007] L'arbre de Flonville; Rock Lounge; Strap Chair; Recycle storage containers; Plychair '07.
Awards [2011] 'Design of the Year' Brit Insurance Design Awards, Design Museum, London; [2002] RSA Design Award.

SANAA
Architects, Tokyo, Japan
www.sanaa.co.jp
Education Kazuyo Sejima, Japan Women's University, 1981.
Ryue Nishizawa, Yokohama National University, 1990.
Recent Works [2009] The Rolex Learning Centre, EPFL (Ecole Polytechnique Federale de

Lausanne, Lausanne, Switzerland; Serpentine Pavilion, London, England; [2007] The New Museum of Contemporary Art, New York, USA; [2004] The 21st Century Museum of Contemporary Art, Kanazawa, Japan; [2003] Christian Dior Building in Omotesando, Tokyo, Japan.
Awards [2010] Pritzker Prize.

Sauerbruch Hutton
Architects, Berlin, Germany
www.sauerbruchhutton.com
Education Matthias Sauerbruch, Diploma, AA, London; Diploma, University of the Arts, Berlin. Louisa Hutton, First Class Honours Degree, Bristol University; Diploma, AA, London; RIBA Part III.
Affiliations Harvard University; Zurich Building Council; Bauhaus Dessau Foundation; Institute for Urban Design, New York; Academy of the Arts, Berlin; Erich-Schelling Architecture Foundation.
Recent Works [2010] Maciachini, Milan; Cologne Oval Offices, Cologne; [2009] KfW Westarkade, Frankfurt; Brandhorst Museum, Munich.
Selected Publications [2010] *KfW Westarkade Frankfurt am Main*, Sauerbruch Hutton, Berlin; [2009] *2G N 52 Sauerbruch Hutton*, Editorial Gustavo Gili, Barcelona; [2006] *Sauerbruch Hutton Archive*, Lars Müller Publishers, Baden; [2005] *Federal Environmental Agency Dessau*, Sauerbruch Hutton, Berlin.
Awards [2010] International Honour Award for Sustainable Architecture; Designs of the Year, Design Museum, London; [2009] DGNB-Certificate, Gold; National Award for Integrated Urban Design; Shortlist, Lubetkin Prize; [2007] Honorable Mention, Zumtobel Group Award; Selected Work, Mies van der Rohe Award; [2006] RIBA Award; [2003] Fritz Schumacher Prize; [1998] Erich Schelling Prize for Architecture.

Shidhulai Swanirvar Sangstha
Non-profit organization, Bangladesh
www.shidhulai.org
Affiliations Gonoshasthaya Kendra.
Selected Publications 'In Food-Prone Bangladesh, a Future that Floats', *The Washington Post*, 27 September 2007; 'Bangladesh Children Flock to School on Water', *Agence France-Presse*, 7 October 2007.
Awards [2007] Sasakawa Prize, United Nations Environment Programme; Ashden Awards for Sustainable Energy, UK; Heroes of Great Bengal of the Daily Prothom Alo and Grameen Phone, Bangladesh; [2006] Equator Prize, United Nations Development Programme (UNDP); Social Entrepreneur of the Global Philanthropy Forum; Global Social Benefit Incubator of Santa Clara University; [2005] Access to Learning Award, Bill & Melinda Gates Foundation; Recognition Award of the World Bank's Development Marketplace global competition; [2004] Global Junior Challenge Award of the Municipality of Rome; Intel Environment Award of the Tech Museum of Innovation; Second place, Stockholm Challenge Award.

Shim-Sutcliffe Architects
Toronto, Canada
www.shim-sutcliffe.com
Education Brigitte Shim FAIA, RCA, FRAIC, OAA, TSA, B.Arch, University of Waterloo; Bachelor of Environmental Studies, University of Waterloo; Reginald M. Brophy Memorial Scholarship.
Howard Sutcliffe FAIA, RCA, RAIC, OAA, TSA, B.Arch, University of Waterloo; Bachelor of Environmental Studies, University of Waterloo.
Recent Works [2011-1994] Harrison Island Cabin, Georgian Bay; Bet Ha'am Synagogue, Portland; The Corkin Gallery, Toronto;

[2006] Craven Road Studio, Toronto; Ravine Guest House, Toronto; Weathering Steel House, Toronto.
Selected Publications [2010] *Narrow Houses: New Directions in Efficient Design*, Princeton Architectural Press, USA; [2009] *10x10_3*, Phaidon Press, London; [2008] *The Phaidon Atlas of 21st Century World Architecture*, Phaidon Press, London; *Logotopia: The Library in Architecture, Art and the Immagination*, Cambridge Galleries, Toronto.
Awards [2010] Governor General's Medal for Architecture, Royal Architectural Institute of Canada; [2009] Architectural Woodwork Award; [2006] Award of Honour, Wood Design Award; [2005] Award of Merit, 31st Annual Heritage Toronto Awards; [2004] Governor General's Medal for Architecture, Royal Architectural Institute of Canada; Green Roof Award of Excellence; Designers of the Year, Interior Design Show.

SMIT
Designers, Brooklyn, USA
www.s-m-i-t.com
Education Samuel Cabot Cochran, Bachelor's Degree, Industrial Design, Pratt Institute. Teresita Brigitte Cochran, Masters, Interactive Technology, New York University; BFA, Rhode Island School of Design.
Benjamin Wheeler Howes, Bachelor's Degree, Architecture, Pratt Institute.
Affiliations National Collegiate Inventors and Innovators Alliance; Pratt Institute Design Incubator; Rosebud Seed Fund.
Recent Works [2011] Tensile Solar.
Selected Publications And Exhibitions [2009] *New York Times Magazine*, Year in Ideas; *Popular Science*;, New York, Design and the Elastic Mind, Museum of Modern Art, New York 2008.

Spackman Mossop + Michaels
Architects, New Orleans, USA
www.mossopmichaels.com
Education Wes Michaels RLA, LEED AP, Bachelors, Landscape Architecture, University of Georgia; Masters, Landscape Architecture, Harvard University.
Elizabeth Mossop, Bachelors, Landscape Architecture, University of New South Wales, Sydney; Masters, Urban Planning, Macquarie University, Sydney.
Affiliations Intuition and Logic, St Louis; Tulane City Center, New Orleans; Robert Reich School of Landscape Architecture, Louisiana State University.
Recent Works [2008] Couturie Forest and Scout Island Arboretum, New Orleans; Cook and Phillip Park, Sydney; Jones Hall Courtyard, Tulane University.
Awards [2010] Cooper Hewitt National Design Triennial; [2009] ASLA Award of Excellence for Scout Island Strategic Plan; [2008] ASLA Award of Excellence for Viet Village Urban Farm.

Studio Gang and SCAPE
Architects, Chicago and New York, USA
www.studiogang.net
www.scapestudio.com
Education Jeanne Gang FAIA, NCARB, LEED AP, B.Sc (Hons), Architecture, University of Illinois; Rotary Ambassadorial Scholar, Urban Design, Swiss Federal University of Technical Studies, Zurich; Certificate of Merit, AIA; M.Arch, Harvard University Graduate School of Design. Kate Orff (SCAPE STUDIO) CLARB, University of Virginia; Masters, Landscape Architecture, Harvard University.
Recent Works [2010] Aqua Tower, Chicago; Oculous, Taipei, Taiwan; [2008] SOS International

Children's Village Community Center, Chicago.
Selected Publications [2011] *Studio Gang Architects: Reveal*, Princeton Architectural Press; *Gateway: Visions for an Urban National Park*, Princeton Architectural Press; [2010] *The Power of Pro Bono*, Public Architecture; *10 x 10_3*, Phaidon Press, London; [2008] *A+T Density Projects*, A+T Architecture Publishers.
Awards [2010-11] Emerging Leaders, Chicago Council on Global Affairs; [2008] City of Chicago Committee on 21st Century; [2006] Academy Award in Architecture, American Academy of Arts & Letters.

StudioKahn
Designers, Jerusalem, Israel
www.studiokahn.com
Education Boaz Kahn, B.Sc, Physics and Astronomy, Tel Aviv University, Tel Aviv, Israel; B.Des, Industrial Design, Bezalel Academy of Art and Design, Jerusalem, Israel. Mey Kahn, B.Des, Industrial Design, Bezalel Academy of Art and Design, Jerusalem, Israel.
Recent Works [2009] Metamorphosis; [2008-2011] The FRAGILE Collection.
Awards [2011] Nomination, INDEX: Design to Improve Life Award; [2010] 3rd place, IIDA and Designboom Interntional Competition 'Green Heart'; [2009] Dr. Polonsky Award For Excellent Design Work; [2008] 1st place, Macef and Designboom International Competition 'Dining in 2015'.

Tesla Motors
Electric Vehicles, Palo Alto, USA
www.teslamotors.com
Education Elon Musk, Bachelors, Physics and Business, University of Pennsylvania. JB Straubel, Bachelors, Energy Systems Engineering, Stanford University; Masters, Energy Engineering, Stanford University.
Recent Works [2012] Model S.
Selected Publications 'Elon Musk: I'll Put a Man on Mars in 10 Years', *Wall Street Journal*, 22 April 2011; 'America's 20 Most Powerful CEOs 40 and Under', *Forbes*, 14 February 2011; 'Brave Thinkers – Elon Musk', The Atlantic, 14 October 2010; 'Supercharged: How Elon Musk Turned Tesla into the Car Company of the Year', *WIRED*, 1 October 2010.
Awards [2010] Automotive Executive of the Year Innovator Award; [2007] Index Award; [2006] Product/Industrial Design Award, Global Green Award.

Domingos Tótora
Designer, Maria da Fe, Brazil
www.domingostotora.com.br
Education [1987] Drawing, Fundação Armando Álvares Penteado, São Paulo – Brazil.
Awards [2008] Craft Design award; [2008] 2nd Place, Objeto Brasileiro Award; [2009] Top XXI Award, Sustainable design; [2009] Brazil Design Awards, Brasil Design Week; [2010] 24th Award of Design, Museu 9da Casa Brasileira, Furniture Category; [2010] BID Award, Bienal Iberoamericana de Design, Madrid, Spain; [2011] Nomination, Brit Insurance Design Award, Design Museum, London.

T.R.Hamzah & Yeang Sdn. Bdh.
Architects, Kuala Lumpur, Malaysia
www.trhamzahyeang.com
Education Tengku Robert Hamzah, School of Architecture, Architectural Association; Department of Tropical Architecture, AA School. Dr. Ken Yeang APAM, FSIA, RIBA, RAIA, FAIA, FRSA, Diploma, AA, London; PhD, Architecture, Cambridge University.
Recent Works [2004] National Library Board, Singapore; Mesiniaga Building, Malaysia;

[2000] Eco-Tower, Elephant & Castle, London; [1998] IBM Building, Malaysia.
Selected Publications *A Vertical Theory of Urban Design*, John Wiley & Sons; *The Green Skyscraper: The Basis for Designing Sustainable Intensive Buildings*, Prestel, Munich; *Hamzah & Yeang, Goundscrapers and Subscrapers*, John Wiley & Songs; *Hamzah & Yeang: The Ecology of the Sky*, Images, Australia; *Rethinking the Skyscraper: The Complete Architecture of Ken Yeang*, Thames & Hudson, London; *Ken Yeang: Bioclimate Skyscrapers*, Artemis, London.
Awards [2002] Excellence Industry Award for Export Services; [2001] Tokyo Fashion Association International Award; [2000] Sir Robert Mathew Award, Commonwealth Association of Architects; [1995] Aga Khan Award for Architecture.

Triptyque Architecture
São Paulo, Brazil & Paris, France
www.triptyque.com
Education Grégory Bousquet, École d'Architecture Paris-La-Seine. Carolina Bueno, École d'Architecture Paris-La-Seine. Olivier Raffaelli,École d'Architecture Paris-La-Seine. Guillaume Sibaud, École d'Architecture Paris-La-Seine.
Recent Works [2011] Colombia 325, São Paulo, Brazil; Media Library under construction, Osny, France; Fidalga 727, São Paulo, Brazil; Shop on the Oscar Freire Street, São Paulo, Brazil. [2010] *Contemplating the Void*, Guggenheim Museum, New York; Swarming Futures London Festival of Architecture, London; 1:1, V&A Museum, London. [2009] Creatures, Hong Kong/Shenzen's Biennale.
Awards [2010] Zumtobel Group Awards, Austria; Concurso Habitação para Todos, Brazil; [2009] 1st place, Architecture Biennale, Built Works, São Paulo; [2008] NAJA prize for young architects, French Ministry of Culture.

Urban-Think Tank
Designers, Caracas, Venezuela
www.u-tt.com
Education Alfredo Brillembourg, Architecture, Central University of Venezuela; M.Sc, Architectural Design, Columbia University; B.A, Architecture, Columbia University. Hubert Klumpner, M.Sc, Architecture and Urban Design, Columbia Univeristy; Masters, University of Applied Arts, Vienna.
Affiliations Guest professors, Graduate School of Architecture and Planning, Columbia University; Chairs for Architecture and Urban Design, Swiss Institute of Technology; Sustainable Living Urban Model Laboratory. Alredo Brillembourg, Guest professor, University José Maria Vergas; University Simon Bolivar; Central University of Venezuela; Venezuelan Architects and Engineers Association. Hubert Klumpner, German Chamber of Architects; Urbanism consultant, International Program for Social and Cultural Development in Latin America.
Recent Works [2010] Fava School for Individuals with Autism, Caracas [2010] El Carmen Social Housing, Guarenas, Venezuela [2009] Baruta Vertical Gymnasium, Caracas [2008] Catholic Cemetery Complex, Caracas [2005] City Lifter, Caracas [2003] Sustainable Choroni / Hacienda Service Module, Choroni, Venezuela.
Selected Publications 'On the Road Again: Alfredo Brillembourg and Hubert Klumpner in Conversation', in *New Towns for the 21st Century*; 'Rules of Engagement: Caracas and the

Informal City', in *Rethinking the Informal City*; *Beyond Modernist Masters: Contemporary Architecture in Latin America*; 2008 'Caracas MetroCable: Bridging the Formal/Informal City', in *Urban Transformation*; 'Metro Cable San Augustin', in *Architecture of Change: Sustainability & Humanity in the Built Environment*.
Awards [2010] Ralph Erskine Award, Swedish Association of Architects.

WASARA Co., Ltd.
Designers, Tokyo, Japan
www.wasara.jp
Shinichiro Ogata, Japan
Recent Works [2011] Yakumosaryo, WASARA Plate; Maru Bowl; Kaku Plate; Nagakaku Plate.
Awards [The 2010 GOOD DESIGN] Award from The Chicago Athenaeum: Museum of Architecture & Design for collaboration with 'WASARA [2009] 'Design for Asia (DFA) Award' Gold / Grand Award for collaboration with 'WASARA'.

Whitearchitecture
Brisbane, Astralia
www.whitearchitecture.com.au
Education Simon White, B.Arch (Hons) QUT; B. Built Environment (Arch), QUT. Jeff Brown, B.Arch (Hons), UQ; B.Design Studies, UQ.
Affiliations Australian Institute of Architects (AIA); Green Building Council of Australia (GBCA).
Recent Works [2011] Urban Edge apartments, Brisbane; [2010] The Hub maintenance compound, Gold Coast; Doomben Racecourse Redevelopment; [2008] Campus Alpha office building, Gold Coast; Water's Edge Sales Suite, Brisbane; [2007] Camp Hill house, Brisbane; Kingfisher Lane houses, Brisbane; [2006] Salisbury House, Brisbane; [2005] Jefferson Lane apartments, Gold Coast; [2004] Ascot house, Brisbane.
Awards [2011] AIA State Commendation; 2010 AIA State Commendation.

WORK ac
New York, USA
www.work.ac
Education Amale Andraos, B.Arch, McGill University; M.Arch, Harvard University Graduate School of Design. Dan Wood AIA, LEED AP, B.A, University of Pennsylvania; Masters degree, Columbia University.
Affiliations Princeton University School of Architecture, Professors; NYIT, Amale Andraos, Visiting Distinguished Professor.
Recent Works [2011] Shenzen Metro Tower; [2009] Shifting Sands, Brooklyn Navy Yard; Edible Schoolyard NY PS216, Brooklyn; [2008] Public Farm 1, PS1; Ordos Villa 99, China.
Selected Publications *Unfolded: Paper in Design, Art, Architecture and Industry*, Birkhäuser, Basel; *10 x 10_3*, Phaidon Press, London; *Atlas for Living*, Loft Publications, Spain.
Awards [2009] Finalist, National Design Award, Cooper Hewitt Design Museum; Merit Award for Architecture, AIA NY State Chapter; Engineering Excellence Diamond Award, Structural Systems, ACEC, New York; [2008] Best of the Best Awards, McGraw Hill Construction; Structural Engineering Merit Award, SEAoNY; 'Year in Architecture – Top Ten Designs', New York Magazine; 'Project of the Year: Park/Landscape', New York Construction/ENR; MASterwork Award, Best Adaptive Re-Use, Municipal Arts Society; Young Architects Program, MoMA / PS1 Contemporary Art Center.

Index